D0064634

THE TRANSFORMATION OF THREADNEEDLE STREET

The Deregulation and Reregulation of Britain's Financial Services

THE TRANSFORMATION OF THREADNEEDLE STREET

The Deregulation and Reregulation of Britain's Financial Services

James J. Fishman

CAROLINA
ACADEMIC
PRESS
700 KENT ST.
DURHAM, NC
27701

ISBN 0-89089-517-1
LCCN 92-73987
Printed in the United States of America

Carolina Academic Press
700 Kent Street
Durham, NC 27701
(919) 489-7486
FAX (919) 493-5668

To Liz, Lisi, Diana, and Rick

Contents

Preface

In January 1986 I became a visiting lecturer at the Law School at University College, London, as part of a joint program with that school and the Pace University School of Law. Shortly after my arrival I toured the London Stock Exchange. A film was shown for visitors in which the probity of the Exchange and its members, and its motto, "My Word is My Bond," were stressed throughout. On the day after my visit there appeared a front page headline in the *Times*: "Chancellor says fraud is not rampant in the City." I thought there must be more to this story, and of course, there was. I set out to learn the source of such diverging perspectives and stumbled upon an immense transformation, colloquially known as the "Big Bang," that was reconfiguring the financial services sector, forever changing the way its business is conducted. This book is an account of that transformation. It chronicles the deregulation and reregulation of Great Britain's financial services sector. This study examines the domestic and international forces that led in 1986 to a restructuring of the securities markets and the implementation of a new investor protection framework mandated by the Financial Services Act.

The underlying principle of the new framework of investor protection is self-regulation within a statutory framework. Private bodies backed by the authority of the law supervise investment businesses and individuals in the financial services sector. Described are the international economic developments and domestic political considerations that encouraged far-reaching structural, economic, and cultural change in the U.K.'s financial markets and eroded the boundaries between financial service businesses. Complementing these structural reforms was the establishment of a complex regime regulating business conduct in the name of investor protection. Change is always difficult to manage. The evolution of the U.K.'s financial services sector illuminates the inability of policy makers to foresee and guide the consequences of their programs.

Governmentally imposed regulation is a political response to the failure of markets and institutions to serve broader public interests. Regulation of the financial markets performs several inconsistent and competing purposes beyond the imposition of rules relating to business practice. It fosters investor belief in the integrity of the marketplace and provides legitimacy after a period of crisis or scandal. Regulation may protect the regulated industry from change in the marketplace. It may advance the commercial well-being of the industry. Financial regulation involves standard setting by which the industry is provided with guidelines to proper modes of conduct. This in turn increases predictibility, professionalizes business practices, and encourages shared norms of behavior.

Government imposed regulations also serve broad policy and societal purposes, forcing businesses to pursue goals they would not seek on their own. The U.K.'s investor protection system was supposed to produce for the financial services sector the broader political goals of Margaret Thatcher: efficiency, competition, and decreasing governmental intervention. Because of misjudgments in the implementation of the system and changes in the economic environment, these objectives were not achieved.

To be successful any system of regulation needs the acceptance and support of the regulated. It must attain a balance between proscription of conduct harmful to the public and protection and encouragement of industry profitability and competition. The U.K.'s financial services regulatory scheme fails on many accounts. This book studies that failure and offers prescriptions for change. Chapter One looks at the roots of the reform, the factors which led to market deregulation, and the introduction of the new system of investor protection. Chapter Two analyzes the evolution of thinking that led to the introduction of an industry-based self-regulatory system as opposed to governmental regulation. It discusses the Gower Report, which laid the groundwork for the new legislation, and the politics surrounding the enactment of the financial services legislation.

Chapter Three outlines the framework of investor protection. The next chapter, "Rule Making and Reaction," concentrates on the implementation of the investor protection system, its impact upon the financial services sector, and the reaction against what was perceived as an overly bureaucratic, complex, and expensive regime.

Chapter Five deals with enforcement of securities law violations and details the persistent enforcement problems such as conflicts of interest, insider dealing, and the increasing resort to the courts in takeover situations. Chapter Six analyzes the effect of the Big Bang on the marketplace, reviewing developments since the market break of October 1987 and the challenge of 1992, the single European market. The conclusory chapter evaluates the future of the self-regulatory concept, discusses the goals of regulatory reform that were accomplished and those that foundered, and offers proposals for reform.

I wish to thank the many people who took the time to explain to me what was happening and who patiently answered my questions. They included academics; solicitors; and officials of the Securities and Investments Board, the Stock Exchange, the Securities and Futures Authority, and the Department of Trade and Industry. Particular appreciation must be expressed to librarians at the University of London, the Institute for Advanced Legal Studies, and Brooklyn and Pace Law Schools who were unfailingly polite and helpful no matter how arcane the request. Thanks also to Pace University which provided support and a sabbatical for this project; to Coleen Barry, Jennifer Correale, Lori Caramanian, Scott Golden, James Lenihan, Ann Minihan, Sheila Murphy and Michelle Sensale who served as research assistants during a part of the project; to Madeleine Wilken who prepared the index; and also to Judith Caporale, Dorothy Fleury, and Rose Patti who typed the manuscript. Throughout this book I have used the masculine pronoun to represent both sexes.

James J. Fishman

Glossary of Acronyms

ADR   American Depository Receipts: Certificates issued by a depositary bank stating that a specified number of shares of a foreign corporation have been deposited with the bank.

AIBD   Association of International Bond Dealers: An overseas investment exchange that regulates the rules for trading in the secondary market for Eurobonds. AIBD changed its name in 1991 to the International Securities Market Association.

CNW   County NatWest: A securities subsidiary of NatWest bank.

COBRA   Capture of Bond Reports and Analysis: A computer system developed by the Securities and Futures Authority which tracks trading in the secondary Eurobond market and off-exchange trading in equities.

CSI   Council for the Securities Industry: A voluntary body that existed prior to 1986 responsible for nonstatutory aspects of supervision of the securities industry.

DPP   Director of Public Prosecutions: A public official and office responsible for instituting criminal prosecutions.

DTI   The Department of Trade and Industry: The government department responsible for implementation of the financial services legislation. It also overseas the enforcement of corporate law legislation, supervises insurance companies, and enforces the prohibitions against insider dealing.

ECMH   Efficient Capital Market Hypothesis: A theory which posits that prices of securities reflect all available information and capital markets are therefore efficient because prices rapidly adjust to new information.

ECU	European Currency Unit: A monetary unit composed of a basket of weighted European currencies issued by the European Monetary Cooperation Fund.
EEC	European Economic Community: The nations of the Common Market.
EMI	European Monetary Institute: A transitional form of what will become a European Central bank that will coordinate the economic policies of EEC states.
EMU	European Monetary Union: A stage of EEC integration whereby member states will cede control of their economic policy, a common currency will replace each state's own, and a European Central Bank will oversee monetary and fiscal policy.
FIG	Fraud Investigation Group: A task force established by the Metropolitan police to coordinate inquires in major fraud cases.
FIMBRA	Financial Intermediaries, Managers and Brokers Regulatory Association: A self-regulating organization whose members are independent intermediaries selling insurance, unit trusts, and other products of several companies.
FSA	Financial Services Act: The statute that authorized the investor protection system in the financial services sector.
FST	Financial Services Tribunal: An independent body that investigates matters dealing with authorization, enforcement, or disciplinary actions referred to it by the Securities and Investments Board.
FT/SE Index	Financial Times/Stock Exchange Index: An index of 100 leading U.K. equities similar to the Dow Jones Industrial Index in the United States.
GEMMs	Gilt-Edged Market Makers: Dealers registered with the Bank of England who make a market in U.K. government securities.
IDBs	Interdealer Brokers: Brokers who provide dealing services for market makers in government securities. IDBs allow GEMMs to unwind their positions anonymously.
IMRO	Investment Management Regulatory Organization: A self-regulating organization whose members manage pension funds or other large portfolios.

ISE
: International Stock Exchange: The International Stock Exchange of the United Kingdom and the Republic of Ireland, also called the London Stock Exchange.

ISMA
: International Securities Market Association: A designated investment exchange whose members deal in the international capital markets. Until 1991 the organization was known as the Association of International Bond Dealers.

ISRO
: International Securities Regulatory Organization: A trade association of 180 firms that participated in the Eurobond markets. Its members joined the ISE in 1986.

JMB
: Johnson Matthey Bankers: A merchant bank and major participant in the gold market who became overextended and was saved from bankruptcy by the Bank of England.

LAUTRO
: Life Assurance and Unit Trust Regulatory Organization: A self-regulating organization that regulates the marketing of life insurance and unit trusts and other collective investment schemes by firms who are creators of those products as opposed to intermediaries who merely market them.

LIFFE
: London International Financial Futures Exchange: A recognized investment exchange that trades financial futures and options.

LTOM
: London Traded Options Market: Options traded on the London Stock Exchange until 1992 when the LTOM merged with LIFFE.

MCA
: Maximum Commission Agreement: An agreement reached by insurance companies to limit the amount of commission paid to insurance salespeople.

MIBOC
: Marketing of Investments Board Organizing Committee: A counterpart to the Securities and Investments Board which dealt with the marketing of packaged insurance and mutual fund products. It merged with the Securities and Investments Board in early 1986.

MOU
: Memoranda of Understanding: Agreements between financial services regulators of two or more countries.

NASDAQ
: National Association of Securities Dealers Automated Quotation System: An electronic screen-based trading system for the U.S. over-the-counter market.

NatWest
: National Westminster Bank

NMS	Normal Market Size: A measure of an equity's liquidity.
NW	Norton Warburg: a defunct investment advisor and fund manager.
OFT	Office of Fair Trading: The U.K. governmental body concerned with competition matters.
PFI	Prevention of Fraud (Investments) Act: The principal statute regulating the secondary distribution of securities prior to the enactment of the Financial Services Act.
RCH	Recognized Clearinghouse: A body that provides services to settle or finalize transactions effected on an investment exchange and is recognized by the Securities and Investments Board as authorized to conduct such activity.
RIE	Recognized Investment Exchange: An organized market for trading in stocks, commodities, or other investments recognized by the Securities and Investments Board as authorized to conduct such activities.
ROLIC	Registry of Life Insurance Commissions: An insurance industry effort to regulate the size of commissions received by insurance salespeople.
RPBs	Recognized Professional Bodies: Organizations that regulate attorneys, accountants, or other professionals and recognized by the Securities and Investments Board as competent to regulate the investment activities of their members in conjunction with the practice of their profession.
SAEF	Stock Exchange Automatic Execution Facility: A computer system operated by the London Stock Exchange that allows automatic execution of transactions in the most liquid securities.
SEAQ	Stock Exchange Automated Quotations System: The electronic screen-based system that publishes price quotations of equities listed on the London Stock Exchange.
SEC	Securities and Exchange Commission: The independent administrative agency that regulates the primary and secondary securities markets in the United States among other responsibilities.
SEMBs	Stock Exchange Money Brokers: Brokers who operate a stock lending and financing service for market makers in the gilts market.

THE TRANSFORMATION OF
THREADNEEDLE STREET

THE ROOTS OF REFORM

London as a Financial Center

London is one of the world's greatest financial centers. It is a latter-day equivalent of a medieval market town for global money merchants.[1] The city's financial preeminence, dating from the end of the seventeenth century, has survived the decline of British economic and political power and the post-World War II loss of empire. While New York and Tokyo are larger financial markets, London's geographical location, its time zone, and its historic links with so much of the world have made it a hub of international finance. London became a financial crossroads because of its unregulated environment, geographical centrality, and history as a banking center.[2] The size and scope of London's financial center is astonishing. The "City" hosts stock, currency, futures, commodity, and shipping exchanges.[3] It has the largest foreign exchange market in the world.[4] More American banks are

---

1. Lohr, *A Resurgence in Finance*, N.Y. TIMES, Sept. 22, 1986, at D1, col. 2.
2. J. PLENDER & P. WALLACE, THE SQUARE MILE 30 (1985) [hereinafter PLENDER & WALLACE].
3. The "City," a term used to refer to London's financial district much the way "Wall Street" is used in the United States, includes members of the Stock Exchange, merchant and clearing banks, and insurance companies. These institutions are based around the Stock Exchange and the Bank of England on Threadneedle Street. Pimlott, *The Reform of Investor Protection in the U.K.—An Examination of the Proposals of the Gower Report and the U.K. Government's White Paper of January, 1985*, 7 J. COMP. BUS. & CAP. MKT. L. 141, n. 64 (1985) [hereinafter Pimlott].
4. The foreign exchange markets offering enormous liquidity, twenty-four-hour trading, and the opportunity to earn and lose immense sums, expanded in the late 1970s as currencies no longer had a fixed rate of exchange, but were permitted to float, and exchange control regulations were eased in several countries. The estimated *daily* volume of foreign currency trading in London in 1989 was $187 billion compared to $129 billion in New York

located in London than in New York City. Five hundred twenty foreign banks, including the one hundred largest in the world are found in London—more than in any other city.[5]

Crucial to the maintenance of London's financial preeminence has been its focus as the home of the Euromarkets, the array of financial activities based on the use of offshore dollars and other currencies.[6] London is the center of international trading in Eurobonds.[7] With a turnover in 1987 of nearly $467,000 billion, the Eurobond market is the world's most important source of debt capital.[8] A unique aspect of the Eurobond market, unlike bonds issued in the United States or in other domestic markets, was its lack of governmental regulation.[9] London manages the most internationally syndicated loans. More international insurance passes through London than anywhere else.[10] Lloyd's is the world's premier center for marine and aviation insurance and the largest international insurance and reinsurance market.[11]

---

and $115 billion dollars in Tokyo. *London as an International Financial Centre*, 29 BANK OF ENGLAND Q. 516, 520 (Nov. 1989) [hereinafter, *London as an International Financial Centre*].

5. It accounts for nearly one-fifth of the total international banking business. From 1975 to 1988 the international assets of banks in the U.K. increased from $184 billion to $1,124 billion. London's position was assisted by the absence of reserve requirements and the ease of establishment of franchises. H. McRae & F. Cairncross, Capital City: London as a Financial Centre 63 (1985) (citing *The Banker* as its source) [hereinafter McRae & Cairncross].

6. Eurodollars are American currency held outside of the United States by individuals, or more often, institutions. For instance, a dollar denominated bank deposit in Barclay's Bank in London is a Eurodollar deposit. The Euromarkets consist of $2,200 billion worth of capital, and two-thirds of that sum is traded in dollars. M. Levi, International Finance and the International Economy 189 (1983), Lascalles, *Euromarkets face uncertain fate*, Fin. Times, Mar. 1, 1989, at 25, col. 5.

7. Eurobonds are corporate bonds denominated in Eurocurrencies, purchased by investors, and sold outside of the domicile of the borrower. There is a secondary market in Eurobonds which is run by large international banks where previously issued Eurobonds are traded.

8. Pizzey, *AIBD Meeting Seen Focussing on Settlement Systems*, Reuters Nexis File, June 1, 1988. In the first half of 1989, $200 billion in new Eurobond issues were floated. *Strains in the Euromarkets*, Fin. Times, Aug. 22, 1989 at 14, col. 1. The weekly turnover in the primary and secondary Eurobond markets in 1988 was approximately $100 billion. Three-quarters of the secondary market turnover in Eurobonds occurs in London. *A Nation of Financiers*, Economist, Aug. 15, 1987 at 44.

9. In the 1970s, the Euromarkets exploded in size as petroleum exporting countries sought to find ways to recycle their dollar surpluses. New issues of Eurobonds increased from $26.7 billion in 1981 to $133.2 billion in 1985. *See The Euroequity Market*, Economist, Nov. 29, 1986, at 72.

10. McRae & Cairncross, *supra* note 5 at 1.

11. Reinsurance involves a contract under which one insurer agrees to indemnify an-

Though securities trading based upon the value of shares traded is less than in New York and Tokyo, it is almost as large as all other European securities markets combined.[12] London has the fourth largest domestic equity market by capitalization and only NASDAQ, the American over-the-counter market, has more companies listed. London is also the hub of the international medium-term lending market in Eurodollars, and one of two major centers for the swaps market. There are several exchanges trading futures and options. London is a major center of domestic and international fund management. In 1988, $16 billion in U.S. pension fund assets were managed there.

The importance of financial services to the U.K. economy cannot be overestimated. Financial services which include banking, the securities industry, insurance, business services, and leasing contributed £63.9 billion to the gross national product in 1987. Since the 1970s the financial sector has grown more rapidly than the rest of the U.K. economy. Its contribution to England's balance of payments has risen in real terms.[13] Since 1980 the cumulative surplus from Britain's financial services has exceeded that derived from oil, making it Britain's greatest earner of exchange.[14]

One of the City's principal attractions has been the minimally regulated banking and investment facilities available to multinational corporations, financial institutions, and governments wanting to borrow, lend, or invest in currencies or securities.[15]

Yet in the post-World War II era, there has been a dichotomy between the unregulated international financial markets and the closed, protected, un-

---

other for losses sustained under the latter's policy of insurance. Insurance companies that insure against losses arising out of fire or other casualties seek to minimize their exposure by sharing risks with other insurance companies. Thus, when the face amount of a policy is very large, the insurance company who has written the policy will turn to Lloyd's to get others to participate. MCRAE & CAIRNCROSS, *supra* note 5 at 163.

12. *Id.* at 127, 18. *London as an international financial centre, supra* note 4 at 519. *See infra* note 61.

13. Lambert, *Blue mood hangs over the City of London,* FIN. TIMES, June 1, 1989, at 10, col. 3.

14. The cumulative surplus of financial services was £38.5 billion ($61.6 billion) and for oil £33.5 billion ($53.6 billion) from 1980 to 1986. Earnings in 1987 are estimated at £900 million per month ($1.44 billion). In 1986 the City's profits rose to £9.4 billion ($15 billion), compared to £6.6 billion in 1985 ($10.56 billion). Insurance accounted for approximately 45% of the 1986 earnings. The financial sector's share (including banking, other financial institutions, and insurance) constitutes 7.5% of Britain's gross national product compared to the financial sector in America's share of 4.7%. *Is Greed Good,* ECONOMIST, February 21, 1987 at Britain Survey 12. *London's 'City' Gains Overseas,* N.Y. TIMES, July 31, 1987, at D12, col. 3, citing Central Statistical Office. *A nation of financiers,* ECONOMIST, Aug. 15, 1987 at 44.

15. PLENDER & WALLACE, *supra* note 2 at 13.

competitive domestic financial system. For example, the London Stock Exchange admitted no new firms to membership from 1945 to 1986 and prohibited foreign ownership of member firms. While most English stocks were traded on the Exchange, an increasing number of English companies' shares also were traded abroad by foreign institutions, and in addition, newer types of securities and financial instruments were traded outside of the Exchange.

Until 1986, financial services firms in the United Kingdom were restricted in the products they could sell and the scope of business they could conduct. The financial services sector was segregated by function. For instance, clearing banks, the British equivalent of commercial banks, took deposits and loaned money, but did little else. They did not engage in securities trading. Within a particular market, firms were channeled into specified functions. Thus, market makers, members of the London Stock Exchange who dealt in securities as principals, were prohibited from acting as brokers, who were agents for purchasers or sellers of shares. These requirements that Exchange members engage in only a single capacity or that banks limit their activities were not the consequence of legislation, but arose out of informally agreed upon guidelines—the rules of the Stock Exchange on the one hand and the desire of the Bank of England on the other.[16]

During the 1980s, international economic forces created new challenges for the London financial markets. Domestic policy considerations encouraged a far-reaching reorganization of the financial markets and led to a comprehensive system of regulation of financial services based upon statute rather than informal consent. The government also intended to lessen its participation in the economy and terminate state ownership of basic industries.

Undoing restrictive trade practices would permit the marketplace to determine prices based upon supply and demand. Privatizing previously nationalized industries and introducing the English middle classes to share ownership through changes in the tax laws would create new customers for the City.[17] Perhaps the greatest impetus for changing the regulatory framework was the cumulative effect of several scandals involving securities firms which threatened to undermine the integrity of the stock market, thereby discouraging new investors and driving business abroad. The government

---

16. S. L. HAYES & P. M. HUBBARD, INVESTMENT BANKING: A TALE OF THREE CITIES 195–96 (1990) [hereinafter HAYES & HUBBARD].

17. Great Britain has had fewer citizens owning shares than several other countries. At the end of 1985 only 6% of the population owned common stock compared to 16% in Japan, 17% in Germany, 19% in France, and 20% in Sweden. Fallon, *A Share in the Future*, THE SUNDAY TIMES (London), Mar. 23, 1986 at 25, col. 1.

reacted by comprehensively regulating the securities markets for the first time.[18]

That such fundamental change was initiated by a radical Tory government is ironic but not ideologically inconsistent. The Conservatives placed great faith in the benefits of free-market competition, but for such a marketplace to exist, there had to be a belief in its integrity, or in English jargon, a level playing field. The restructuring of the financial services sector is referred to colloquially as the "Big Bang" and officially occurred on October 27, 1986.[19]

The Institutions Behind the Big Bang

The Bank of England

Its Role as a Central Bank

At the figurative and literal heart of the City is the Bank of England. Physically standing astride Cornhill, Poultry, Lombard, and Threadneedle streets, the main crossroads of the square mile that encompasses the City, the Bank has formal supervisory control over the nation's banking system. Through its responsibilities in maintaining the liquidity of the financial system and setting capitalization requirements for trading in the money markets, it has an important indirect influence over the whole financial services sector. Almost all investment businesses are affected by Bank of England regulations and policies.[20]

While the Treasury Department formally owns the Bank and has ultimate control, the Bank retains more autonomy than other governmental agencies or nationalized industries. The Treasury has the power under the 1946 Bank of England Act to give directives to the Bank.[21] This power has never been exercised. Hugh Gaitskell, chancellor of the Exchequer in 1950–51,

---

18. M. CLARKE, REGULATING THE CITY 6 (1986) [hereinafter CLARKE].

19. The phrase "Big Bang," not used in its astronomical sense, suggests that the changes which occurred in the City from 1983 to 1986 were unique in their rapidity. Similar developments occurred in other financial centers but over a much longer period. The financial services legislation passed by Parliament in the autumn of 1986 was implemented in stages in 1987 and became fully operational in 1988. Gower, *'Big Bang' and City Regulation*, 51 MOD. L. REV. 1 (1988) [hereinafter *'Big Bang' and City Regulation*].

20. The Bank, founded in 1694 to raise funds for a war against France, was privately held until its nationalization in 1946. However, by the end of the nineteenth century it had assumed responsibility as the nation's central bank. PLENDER & WALLACE, *supra* note 2 at 9.

21. Bank of England Act, 1946, 9 & 10 Geo. 6, ch. 27, § 4(1).

complained that the Treasury displayed loyalty without expertise; the Bank of England expertise without loyalty.[22]

The Bank manages the government's raising of money through control of the gilts market. It provides advice to the government on monetary policy and implements such policy. It acts as a reserve bank, much like our Federal Reserve, for clearing and depositary banks. Since 1844 the Bank has had monopoly power in England to print and issue bank notes.[23] It manages the nation's gold and currency reserves and stores the gold reserves of several other nations. Unlike other central banks, the Bank does not fix the discount rate nor lend directly to commercial banks. The Bank operates on behalf of the government in the foreign exchange, bills, and gilts markets.[24] It controls the money supply. Only recently has the Bank obtained formal powers to regulate the banking system.[25]

The directors of the Bank are chosen by the prime minister on the advice of the Chancellor of the Exchequer. There are six full-time executive (inside) directors, including the governor and deputy governor. There are also twelve outside directors.[26] The board is formally named "The Court." The governor has been aptly called the "Prince of the City," for he is the single most important individual in the financial community.[27] His standing in the City can only be compared to the status Paul Volcker achieved when he was chairman of the Federal Reserve Board.

---

22. *Where the Treasury Rules*, ECONOMIST, Nov. 11, 1987 at 93. The Bank remains financially independent through the profitability of its operations. Its employees are not civil servants, allowing the Bank to offer salaries competitive with the private sector. PLENDER & WALLACE, *supra* note 2 at 90–91.

23. The Bank of Scotland has such power in Scotland. In the United States, this task is done by the Treasury.

24. *See* MCRAE & CAIRNCROSS, *supra* note 5 at 217–44.

25. The Bank has five departments. The Policy and Markets Department frames and carries out the government's monetary policy. Within this department is an economic division that collects data on the British economy and forms the basis of policy advice to the government and Whitehall. The Policy and Markets Department also sells government securities, controls the money markets, and is responsible for foreign exchange operations. The Bank's Operations Department handles its banking business, its responsibilities as registrar of quoted government securities, and its stocks of nationalized industry. Other departments oversee industrial and financial supervision, administration of the Bank, and banking supervision pursuant to the banking statutes. *Id.* at 217–21.

26. *Id.*

27. A. SAMPSON, THE CHANGING ANATOMY OF BRITAIN 268 (1982) [hereinafter SAMPSON, CHANGING]. Asked whether his position inspired fear, Gordon Richardson, then governor, replied: "I would not have thought the office of Governor still commands fear though I do think it commands a certain degree of respect and good will. It's true of Prime Ministers and Popes too, isn't it?" S. FAY, PORTRAIT OF AN OLD LADY: TURMOIL AT THE BANK OF ENGLAND 69 (1987).

The Informal Approach to Oversight
of the Banking System

Even prior to nationalization, the Bank of England's dominant position in the City and the banking system, and its historical role as the lender of last resort, made it responsible for ensuring that the banking industry conducted its affairs in a safe and stable way.[28] The Bank's regulatory style was somewhat unorthodox. It was based on informal communications with the components of the banking system: the acceptance houses, discount houses, and clearing banks, rather than statutory backing and rule-making authority.

Acceptance houses are the more exclusive merchant (investment) banks.[29] Discount houses borrow the surplus funds of banks and use them to purchase short-term government securities and commercial paper from corporations.[30] The clearing banks: Barclays, National Westminster, Midland, and Lloyd's are the leading personal and commercial banks. Today they provide a full range of banking services, but they historically concentrated on short-term loans to depositors. For many years British commercial banking was dominated by a price-fixing oligopoly consisting of the London clearing banks and their associates in Scotland and Northern Ireland. Together they had over 85 percent of deposits.[31]

In the 1930s the Bank of England, the discount houses, and the clearing banks created a cartel whereby the clearing banks agreed not to bid on treasury bills. The discount houses stipulated a common tender price, and the clearers received an agreed minimum interest rate for their funds. In return for this arrangement, the components of the banking system allowed the Bank of England to maintain a close watch on their activities and adhered to the Bank's wishes and policies.[32]

---

28. McRae & Cairncross, *supra* note 5 at 231.

29. They are members of the Accepting Houses Committee and "accept" bills of exchange; that is, they guarantee them. While any merchant bank can guarantee a bill, an acceptance by a member of the Accepting Houses Committee enables the holder of the bill to receive a better rate if he tries to sell it. *Id.* at 57–58.

30. As the discount houses purchase all government bills offered at weekly "tenders" they guarantee the government that it can sell all of its securities. For this service, they have a special relationship with the Bank of England and a protected market. As wholesale institutions that do not deal with the public, they are permitted to borrow a much higher multiple of their capital and reserves than retail banks. Clarke, *supra* note 18 at 13.

31. Fforde, *Competition, Innovation and Regulation in British Banking*, 23 Bank Eng. Q. Bull. 363 (1983) [hereinafter Fforde].

32. Deputy Governor of the Bank of England, *Supervision and Central Banking*, 22 Bank Eng. Q. Bull. 380–81 (1982).

The Bank would meet weekly with the discount houses to give its views of economic prospects. The representatives of the discount houses fixed their offering prices for treasury bills accordingly. This enabled the Bank to transmit its views to the banking community and to oversee economic policies. Such informality and trust were effective in regulating the banking sector because market entry was restricted, competition curtailed, and the penalties of exclusion severe.[33] The Bank's concerns were confined almost exclusively to traditional banking institutions and its responsibilities as the nation's central bank.

Indirection was the hallmark of supervision. Oversight was through "winks and nods." Banks would request the Bank of England's view on a proposed transaction or venture. The Bank's velvet glove of preferred opinion and comment concealed the mailed fist of command. The informal regulatory system's effectiveness was assisted by the banking community's social exclusiveness and cohesiveness, its shared outlook and common class background.[34] The traditional banking sector was conservative, hidebound, self-satisfied, and inward-looking.[35]

The Bank stood at the acme of this closed, stable, and autonomous banking sector. The informal regulatory system was possible because of the concentration of the banking industry, the Bank's position as the country's central bank, the overall stability and traditionalism of the banking community, and the willingness of the discount banks who accepted the Bank's supervision in exchange for their special market position. No explicit legislation was needed. Regional banks and deposit takers outside of the special relationship did not count and remained outside the Bank's umbrella.[36]

After the Bank's nationalization in 1946, its authority became quasi-legal, particularly with the increase of governmental intervention in the economy. The government charged the bank with the responsibility of inducing the banking system to go along with government policy.[37] However, the Bank's supervisory style remained flexible, informal, personal, discrete, and indirect. Only much later were the Bank's legal powers formalized.

---

33. M. MORAN, THE POLITICS OF BANKING 16 (1984) [hereinafter MORAN].

34. *See* CLARKE, *supra* note 18 at 13, and citing research on the social cohesiveness of British banking.

35. The attitude of the traditional banks has been described as being "like the British empire. There's nothing to gain and quite a lot to lose." A. SAMPSON, THE MONEYLENDERS 106 (1981).

36. Peeters, *Re-regulation of the Financial Services Industry in the United Kingdom*, 10 U. PA. J. INT'L BUS. L. 371, 377 (1988) [hereinafter Peeters].

37. McRAE & CAIRNCROSS, *supra* note 5 at 231.

The Secondary Banking Crisis

Banks had some legal requirements under the Companies Acts. Section 127 of the Companies Act of 1948[38] provided for a list of regular banks as agreed by the Treasury, the Bank of England, and the Department of Trade and Industry (DTI). Other deposit-taking institutions were covered by a different section.[39] These other or secondary deposit-taking institutions were exempt from the Money Lenders Act, but could not refer to themselves as banks in their advertising. Section 127 banks were subject to liquidity constraints and ongoing monitoring by the Bank of England. The only requirement of secondary banks was that they be in the banking business.[40]

The great difference for these secondary or "fringe banks" as they were known, was that they were unregulated.[41] Commencing in the 1950s, installment credit finance companies engaged in a rapidly growing market for consumer credit and bid competitively for wholesale deposits. Local municipal authorities borrowed from market sources which competitively bid and made needed funds readily available. Foreign and merchant banks also expanded their domestic sterling business in competition with the clearing banks. In the late 1950s and 1960s emerged a wholesale deposit market between banks. Wholesale lending of short-term loans to business and industry commenced at competitive rates.[42] In 1971 the clearing banks' interest rate cartel was ended.

New kinds of financial institutions emerged in the 1970s that combined previously segregated product lines. Their activities ranged across the financial services sector from life insurance, mortgaging, leasing, and real estate, to financial advice and mutual funds. These institutions were international in scope and engaged in ongoing growth. They were the opposite of the traditional banks: aggressive, risk-taking, and growth-oriented, and they won respectability through joint ventures with traditional banking institutions.[43]

The secondary banks were assisted in 1971 when the government relaxed the money supply to promote growth. They financed their own growth by investing heavily in property. By 1974, inflation ended the boom that oc-

---

38. Companies Act, 1948, 11 & 12 Geo. 6, ch. 38.
39. *Id.* at § 123.
40. CLARKE, *supra* note 18 at 25.
41. The Bank of England had no control over banks licensed under Section 123. These banks were licensed to take deposits but could not trade in foreign exchange. Only if a bank became involved in foreign exchange did it come under the Bank of England's net. McRAE & CAIRNCROSS, *supra* note 5 at 237.
42. Fforde, *supra* note 31 at 364.
43. CLARKE, *supra* note 18 at 26–27.

curred through the increased money supply. Credit was restricted and the property market collapsed. At the end of 1973, a fringe bank, London and County Securities, announced it was overextended. Thereafter a run began on its deposits and those of other secondary banks. When London and County failed, other fringe banks tottered.[44]

The Bank of England organized a rescue operation by mobilizing banks, pension funds, and its own resources to support the secondary banks.[45] The lifeboat operation was concerned with liquidity rather than solvency. The banks were thought to be, perhaps hoped to be, fundamentally sound. They were believed to be a victim of the financial climate rather than their own weaknesses. This was wishful thinking, for in many cases, such optimism was unfounded. Later the Bank of England allowed some of these banks to collapse. Still others were merged.[46] In the inevitable postmortem it was clear that the Bank of England had reacted too late on the basis of incomplete and inaccurate information. In its favor, under the Companies Acts, the Bank was not responsible for supervision of the secondary banking structure.

There had been banking collapses in the past, such as the famed South Sea Bubble in the eighteenth century and the collapse of Baring Brothers in the 1890s, and the Bank of England had come in as the savior of last resort of the banking system. The secondary banking crisis was different. It demonstrated that banking had changed; it had broadened its scope. The individuals who participated in these new financial institutions were not part of and wanted nothing to do with the old-boy system that had controlled English banking. This new breed were entrepreneurs, and they reflected recent developments in financial services that had been seen only in the Euromarkets.

The Bank and the Department of Trade and Industry had assumed that all financial institutions would act as did the traditional banks, prudently. Freedom from control, however, outside of the rigid social and cultural milieu of the traditional banks, led to innovation, growth, and risk. This economic and social transformation destroyed the environment that made it possible to rely solely on informal regulation and trust. A similar development would occur in the securities area. The banking community had increased in size and sophistication. New players and practices emerged. The new participants were not of the old order. Nor did they share its values.

---

44. *Id.* at 36–41.

45. Over £1 billion of funds were loaned to the secondary banks in 1974–75, nearly 40% of the total capital and reserves at the time. In addition, the Bank committed large sums of its own money. The rescue operation transferred the failing banks' deposits to clearing banks to stop the run by depositors. The clearing banks then replaced the depositors' funds with their own.

46. SAMPSON, CHANGING, *supra* note 27 at 268–70, CLARKE, *supra* note 18 at 36–41.

The Bank apparently never realized this and continued to supervise in the same old way as if the secondary banking crisis was an aberration like other bank collapses.[47]

A New Statutory Framework

The 1979 Banking Act was a response to the secondary banking crisis. It formalized the Bank's supervisory responsibilities over the banking sector by placing them on a statutory basis. The act was encouraged by an EEC banking directive, which required credit institutions to be authorized. Clearing banks were distinguished from licensed deposit takers. The Bank continued its traditional relationships with the clearing banks but increased control over licensed deposit takers. Traditional banks had to be authorized, and regional and secondary banks were classified as "licensed deposit takers" and were expected to report to the Bank of England.[48] The Bank was given supervisory control over all deposit-taking institutions except building societies.[49]

Despite the 1979 act, the Bank still operated as before, using informal techniques of control. The Bank wanted a statute that would allow it to retain its discretion and autonomy and use of the old methods, while enhancing its powers of supervision and control and fulfilling the requirements of the EEC directive and political expectations.[50] The Bank of England's concern remained with the soundness of the banking system, an appropriate role for a central bank. The Banking Act's focus was on protecting the individual depositor.

The weaknesses of the 1979 act became apparent in 1984 with the failure of Johnson Matthey Bankers (JMB), a major participant in the gold market. In 1981, after the bullion market slumped, JMB's merchant banking subsidiary expanded its commercial loan portfolio of Third World borrowers. In so doing, JMB did not increase the subsidiary's capital base to support this foray into high risk-investment banking. Johnson Matthey became overextended. In September 1984, financial houses in the Far East ceased dealing with British banks for fear of a general banking collapse.

---

47. MORAN, *supra* note 33 at 106.

48. Banking Act, 1979, ch. 37, §§ 3, 14.

49. Institutions were required to meet minimum managerial and financial requirements. Peeters, *supra* note 36 at 377. In this vein, the act created a Deposit Protection Board to guarantee deposits in institutions carrying on deposit-taking business through a deposit protection fund. It is a scheme analogous to the Federal Deposit Insurance Corporation. Banking Act, 1979, ch. 37, §§ 21–33. The Treasury, after consultation with the Bank, could issue regulations to control the form and content of advertisements inviting deposits. *Id.* at §§ 34–35.

50. CLARKE, *supra* note 18 at 43.

The Bank of England stepped in, foreseeing a threat to the whole banking system and a drastic reaction by the gold market if JMB collapsed. It developed a rescue plan. It forced JMB's parent to lend £50 million and requested leading London banks to make available £250 million in standby loans. JMB was nationalized and taken under the Bank of England's wing. The Bank lost £34 million in this operation. Despite the 1979 act, the Bank's supervision department had failed to notice the weakness in the bank's portfolio or to warn of the scale of JMB's problems. The rescue unleashed a storm of criticism of the Bank because it had not, in the normal course of its supervision, detected JMB's weaknesses. The clearing banks objected to bailing out a bullion dealer about whom they knew very little.[51] In the wake of Johnson Matthey the government established a committee to review the banking regulatory system.[52] This was followed by a White Paper,[53] which resulted in the Banking Act of 1987.

The Banking Act of 1987 gave the Bank of England two principal responsibilities: 1) to supervise the institutions authorized by it and 2) to review relevant developments to the exercise of its powers and the discharge of its duties.[54] It further formalized the Bank's powers and responsibilities in ways similar to other governmental agencies.[55] The act abolishes the two-tiered system of the 1979 act of recognized banks and licensed deposit takers. Anyone seeking to carry on a deposit-taking business must be authorized. Anyone who carries on a deposit-taking business without authorization has committed a criminal offense.[56] Authorization will be granted so long as the individual is a "fit and proper person to hold their respective positions."[57] The act requires the establishment of a board of banking su-

---

51. PLENDER & WALLACE, *supra* note 2 at 232–35, CLARKE, *supra* note 18 at 42–49.

52. Peeters, *supra* note 36 at 378–79.

53. HER MAJESTY'S TREASURY, BANKING SUPERVISION REPORT, 1985 (Cmd 9695).

54. Banking Act, 1987, ch. 22, § 1(2)(2).

55. The Bank must prepare a report to the chancellor of the Exchequer at the end of its fiscal year which will be presented to Parliament and published in a format the Bank feels appropriate. *Id*. at § 1(3).

56. *Id*. at § 3. A deposit-taking business is one which "in the course of the business money received by way of deposit is lent to others; or any other activity of the business is financed, wholly or to any material extent, out of the capital of or the interest on money received by way of deposit." The Treasury after consultation with the Bank may amend the definition of deposit or deposit-taking. *Id*. at § 7.

57. There must be at least two directors. The business must be conducted in a prudent manner, which means that it has adequate resources for the scope of its activities and minimum assets of £1 million. Adequate business records must be maintained. Sch. 3. A symbol of change from the 1979 act is the deletion of the requirement that an institution have high reputation and standing in the community. *See* Banking Act, 1979, ch. 37, sched. 2 § 1(1). A grandfather clause allows existing recognized banks and licensed institutions to

pervision consisting of three *ex officio* members of the Bank and six independent members to advise the *ex officio* members on the exercise of the Bank's functions.[58] The Bank may seek extensive information from authorized institutions and has greater opportunity for communication and contact with authorized institutions' auditors.[59] It must be notified when the authorized institution enters into transactions with a large risk of default.[60]

The Banking Act of 1987 greatly reinforces the Bank's formal supervisory powers over the banking system. The Bank continues to act, where possible, in its informal style in carrying out its central banking functions. It maintains an important, unseen, and growing role over the financial services industry. It was the impetus for the changes that led to the Big Bang.

The Stock Exchange

The value of the London Stock Exchange's common shares is third to the New York and Tokyo stock exchanges, but almost as great as all other European exchanges combined.[61] The London Exchange quotes over eight thousand separate securities, far more than any other exchange, but until the Big Bang, only two hundred were actively traded.[62]

---

be exempt from the authorizing process. Others are exempt. Banking Act, 1987, ch. 22, sched. 5, sched. 1.

58. The Bank must report regularly to the board on matters which it considers relevant to the independent members' discharge of their functions and provide them with other such information as they reasonably require. The board monitors the Bank's administration of the legislation and prepares an annual report. *Id.* at § 2.

59. Auditors do not breach their fiduciary duties to their banking institution by communicating information to the Bank of England pursuant to the Bank's responsibilities under the Act, Banking Act, 1987, ch. 22, § 47.

60. Banking Act, 1987, ch. 22, §§ 36–40.

61. The value of stocks traded on the various exchanges from January to September 1986, according to the New York Stock Exchange Nomura Research and the London Stock Exchange, was: New York, over $1 trillion plus $300 billion on other U.S. exchanges; Tokyo, $600 to $700 billion; London, $100 to $200 billion.

The 1985 bond market in the same countries, according to Salomon Brothers, was:

| | In billions of dollars | |
	Public Issues	*Private Issues*
United States	$ 3119.0	$ 269.5
Japan	1082.9	208.3
Britain	210.8	Not Available

N.Y. TIMES, Oct. 9, 1985 at C6, col. 1.

In 1991 the market capitalization (in billions of dollars) was New York 2,819.8, Tokyo 2,793.6, and London (domestic equities only) 861.9. Nickel, *Stock Trading without Borders*, FORTUNE, Dec. 2, 1991 at 157.

62. Bleakley, *The Yanks Muscle In On The City*, N.Y. TIMES, Sept. 28, 1986 at sec. 3,

The Origins of the London Stock Exchange

The rise of London as a financial center is linked to the importance of its port, which dominated England's foreign trade. London's traders needed ancillary financial services and at the same time generated the capital to finance them. According to McRae and Cairncross, in the early eighteenth century, the port of London dominated the country's foreign trade. London's traders offered a variety of financial services: commodity and ship auctions, insurance for ships and cargo, and most importantly, capital to finance their activities. This led to the founding of the money markets.

The bill of exchange was used to finance such activities.[63] The seller (shipper), who needed the money immediately, would swap the bill for cash, usually with a bank or institution called a discount house. The discount house would give the seller (shipper) less than the value of the bill, in effect charging interest for a loan for the period until the seller paid the face value of the bill.[64] The practice of discounting bills in the eighteenth century was an important development in London's rise as a financial center.

While the Stock Exchange was formally established and moved to its present location in 1802, organized trading in senior securities and common stock had existed for over one hundred years before.[65] Dealing in stocks and shares commenced in the early sixteenth century with the formation of joint stock companies engaged in foreign trade, such as the East India Company and various colonization companies. In this period, and throughout the seventeenth century, as the power of the central government increased, so did the cost of administering the country. Wars became larger and more expensive, and the Crown continually was forced into short-term borrowing.[66]

---

col. 3. Illiquidity of smaller companies remains a problem. *See infra* chap. 6. There are two kinds of securities issued and traded on the stock exchange. In terms of market value, roughly one-half are senior securities: debentures, loans, and preferred stock. Most of this long-term debt has been issued by the government and is called "gilts" because the securities are considered gilt-edged, i.e., backed by the credit of the state, and the certificates themselves have silver edges. In correct English terminology, government securities are called "stocks." "Shares" or "equities" or "ordinary shares" are equivalent to what Americans term common stock. INFORMATION AND PRESS DEPARTMENT, STOCK EXCHANGE, THE STOCK EXCHANGE 3 (n.d.). Gilts also can be bought or sold by the public on the Exchange after they have been issued. The other kind of securities, termed "shares," "equities," or "ordinary shares," is common stock.

63. A bill is similar to a postdated check. Instead of paying for goods immediately, the buyer of the bill, often a bank, gives the seller, a shipper or importer, a bill of exchange which says the buyer will pay at a certain time in the future.

64. MCRAE & CAIRNCROSS, *supra* note 5 at 2–3, 57–58.

65. E. MORGAN & W. A. THOMAS THE STOCK EXCHANGE 11, 68, 74 (2d ed. 1963) [hereinafter MORGAN & THOMAS].

66. *Id.* at 12–14, 17–18.

By the mid-1690s there was an informal but highly developed market in the trading of shares of joint stock companies and of bills with which the government financed the growing national debt. This trading occurred around the coffee shops in Exchange Alley. Throughout the eighteenth century, government debt, which greatly increased during an eight-year war with France that ended in 1763, dominated the organized securities markets.

In 1773 a group of brokers rented a building on Threadneedle Street, which later became the home of the Stock Exchange. At this time there was no attempt to limit membership. Trading merely moved from the coffee houses and from the rotunda of the Bank of England where, to the Bank's annoyance, brokers had congregated.[67] By 1800, stockbroking had become a specialized profession and present-day trading techniques were in use. A distinction between brokers and jobbers began to appear in the last thirty years of the seventeenth century.[68]

The Broker-Jobber Distinction

From the eighteenth century until October 1986 there was a separation of functions between brokers,[69] who executed trades (that is, purchased and sold shares on behalf of customers), and jobbers, who held shares as principals. This was termed the single-capacity system. Only jobbers could sell securities, and only brokers could deal with public customers.[70]

Jobbers carried books of shares, offering a price at which they would buy and another price at which they would sell particular securities. Because the jobber was a principal who dealt for his own account, he escaped much of the regulation required of brokers. The regulation of brokers by the City of London may have played a part in developing the broker-jobber distinction.[71] Under the English single capacity system there were several jobbers who might hold shares in the stock to be traded. At least two different firms would offer or "make" prices for each stock. The broker would contact jobbers who were offering prices in the particular stock to find the best price for the customer. When a jobber was short of stock, he would quote a price higher than other jobbers, attracting the sale of shares. If he had too many

---

67. *Id.* at 68.

68. *Id.* at 6. A. Jenkins, The Stock Exchange Story 19 (1973) [hereinafter Jenkins]. W. A. Thomas, The Big Bang 5 (1986) [hereinafter Thomas].

69. Unless otherwise specified, throughout this chapter we use the term "broker" in its more generalized meaning to encompass both brokers and jobbers.

70. A broker was forbidden to deal on his own account and was obliged to produce his dealing book and to disclose his principals on demand. However, anyone else could deal on his own account without restriction, thus the jobber did not have to take out a license.

71. Morgan & Thomas, *supra* note 65 at 66.

shares of a particular security, the jobber would lower the price to attract purchasers.

Brokers were not allowed to deal with one another.[72] The client's order was carried out through a jobber. The broker earned a fixed commission from each transaction, whereas the jobber earned his fee by setting a selling price for a share slightly above the buying rate, the difference being known as the "jobber's turn."[73]

The benefits of the single-capacity system were that it saved time for brokers commissioned to sell who would have had to seek other brokers with commissions to buy and vice versa; it broadened the market, stabilized prices, and facilitated the making of large deals; it increased the knowledge at the disposal of the market by enabling people to specialize in small groups of securities; and it worked well with heavily traded stocks.[74]

The Social Cohesiveness of the Exchange Community

The image of the Stock Exchange member as an individual with an Oxbridge background,[75] membership in a Pall Mall club, and service in an ex-

---

72. One exception to this was a situation where a broker could not find a sufficient number of jobbers or shares to complete a transaction. He would then contact another broker and complete the transaction by using the jobber in a formal sense to clear it on the Exchange. Another exception was where two institutional holders of stock wanted to trade a large block of shares. The broker would put together the buyer and seller and would then contact the jobber who would receive a commission. Such a transaction was called a "put through." MCRAE & CAIRNCROSS, *supra* note 5 at 138, 142. In the 1980s these transactions and others completely off the exchange floor demonstrated the superfluity of jobbers and the weakness of a system that was used increasingly by institutional investors when trading large blocks of shares. The "put through" merely increased transaction costs.

73. MCRAE & CAIRNCROSS, *supra* note 5 at 37.

74. MORGAN & THOMAS, *supra* note 65 at 145–46. The single-capacity system differed from the specialist system of the New York and American Stock Exchanges. The American system is an auction market system. Every stock listed on the New York and American Exchanges is assigned to a particular location or post on the floor of the exchange, and there is only one specialist or market maker for each listed stock. When a customer wishes to purchase or sell shares of stock, he/she calls a broker on the floor of the Exchange. The broker then goes to the "post" where the stock is traded and asks the specialist the prevailing bid and ask spread. The broker then offers to sell or purchase the stock either at the prevailing market price or at the price the seller/purchaser wants to sell or buy. If another broker is willing to engage in the transaction at an agreed upon price, the specialist maintains order by choosing which broker was first and determining how many shares are to be traded before he raises or lowers the price in order to execute more orders.

75. Oxbridge is a colloquialism for a graduate of Oxford or Cambridge University. It connotes someone from an establishment background. E. PARTRIDGE, A DICTIONARY OF SLANG AND UNCONVENTIONAL USAGE 1281 (6th ed. 1967) [hereinafter PARTRIDGE].

clusive guards regiment is relatively recent, dating from the last years of the nineteenth century. The Stock Exchange's cohesiveness and members' mutual trust has far less exalted origins: the low regard in which brokers and jobbers once were held and the lack of legal protection for certain securities transactions in the courts.[76] For instance, option contracts were prohibited by acts of Parliament because they were a common means of fraud by jobbers and brokers.[77] Effective self-regulation also was spurred by a persistent attempt in the eighteenth and nineteenth centuries to relax, and later to escape, supervision by the City of London.

The original image of the stockbroker was less than respectable. "Stockjobbing" implied speculative dealing in stocks and shares in general, usually with a sinister or dishonest overtone.[78] The derogatory image of the stock jobber continued for much of the eighteenth century. "Broker" did not have quite the same pejorative connotation, for the term referred to agents dealing in commodities and shipping as well as stocks and shares. During the nineteenth century and first years of the twentieth century, the

---

76. MORGAN & THOMAS, *supra* note 65 at 25.

77. An option contract is the right to buy or sell a share at a previously fixed price during a given period. Normally they are cheaper to buy than the underlying shares, but much more volatile, thereby increasing their risk. By manipulating the price of the underlying security, brokers and jobbers could make the option worthless or valuable at the expense of the customer.

78. X OXFORD ENGLISH DICTIONARY 999 (1933). An alternative seventeenth-century meaning was to trust to private gain or advantage. Dr. Johnson's dictionary defined the stock jobber as "a low wretch who makes money by buying and selling shares." 2 S. JOHNSON, A DICTIONARY OF THE ENGLISH LANGUAGE n.p. (2d ed. 1786). The term "jobber" suggested an individual engaged in sharp practices or rigging of the market. MORGAN & THOMAS, *supra* note 65 at 21. Daniel Defoe (1660?–1731), the author of ROBINSON CRUSOE, was a prolific pamphleteer and columnist. He wrote two pamphlets castigating stock jobbers, one pseudonymously as "By a Jobber," THE ANATOMY OF EXCHANGE-ALLEY: OR, A SYSTEM OF STOCKJOBBING. PROVING THAT SCANDALOUS TRADE, AS IT IS NOW CARRIED ON, TO BE KNAVISH IN ITS PRIVATE PRACTICE, AND TREASON IN ITS PUBLIC; BEING A CLEAR DETECTION I. OF THE PRIVATE CHEATS USED TO DECEIVE ONE ANOTHER. II. OF THEIR ARTS TO DRAW INNOCENT FAMILIES INTO THEIR SNARES, UNDERSTOOD BY THEIR NEW TERM OF ART (VIZ.) (BEING LED INTO THE SECRET.) III. OF THEIR RAISING AND SPREADING FALSE NEWS TO GROUND THE RISE OR FALL OF STOCKS UPON. IV. OF THEIR JOINING WITH TRAITORS IN RAISING AND PROPAGATING TREASONABLE RUMORS TO TERRIFY AND DISCOURAGE THE PEOPLE WITH APPREHENSIONS OF THE ENEMIES TO THE GOVERNMENT. V. OF THEIR IMPROVING THOSE RUMORS, TO MAKE A RUN UPON THE BANK AND RUIN PUBLIC CREDIT. VI. OF THE DANGEROUS CONSEQUENCES OF THEIR PRACTICES TO THE GOVERNMENT, AND THE NECESSITY THERE IS TO REGULATE OR SUPPRESS THEM. TO WHICH IS ADDED, SOME CHARACTERS OF THE MOST EMINENT PERSONS CONCERNED NOW, AND FOR SOME YEARS PAST, IN CARRYING ON THIS PERNICIOUS TRADE (1719). The other pamphlet was THE VILLAINY OF STOCK-JOBBERS DETECTED, AND THE CAUSES OF THE LATE RUN UPON THE BANK AND BANKERS DISCOVERED AND CONSIDERED (1710).

formal organization of the Exchange, followed by efforts to limit membership to exclude undesirables, improved the stockbroker's image. In 1802
the Exchange had 550 members and 100 clerks. During the nineteenth century, it grew slowly.[79]

In the nineteenth century, as it became known that the City provided an
opportunity to earn a substantial living without overexertion, the social
background and status of the membership rose. Exchange members began
to enter public life and to receive honors and titles.[80] Stockbroking was cul-
tivated by the Exchange as a gentleman's profession and was widely re-
garded as such both within and outside the City. Even as late as the mid-
1970s, Lord Poole, managing director of the merchant bank Lazard Brothers, could ascribe to his firm's success: "I never loaned to anyone who had
not gone to Eton."[81]

By the third quarter of the twentieth century, the circle had come round.
Individuals from diverse backgrounds entered the securities business and
investment banking.[82] Alongside—or more likely in competition with—
those from Oxbridge were "barrow boys," individuals from working-class
backgrounds who used skill, intelligence, and energy to compensate for deficiencies in bloodline or education.[83]

In addition, the increased internationalization of finance introduced a
large foreign element with differing ethical values and attitudes toward
business.[84] The growing American investment banking presence influenced
the way in which brokers worked and were paid. Salaries increased, loyalty

---

79. By the middle of the century membership had risen to 864, by 1870 to 1,471, by 1877
to over 2,000. The membership rose to 4,000 by 1900 and 5,567 by 1905. Thereafter,
membership decreased, mainly due to a stiffening of conditions for entry. Membership
dropped to 4,855 in 1914. At the end of 1986 there were 5,400 members. MORGAN &
THOMAS, *supra* note 65 at 68, 74, 140. *London Stock Exchange: Consenting Adults*, ECON-
OMIST, Nov. 15, 1986 at 94.

80. The 1900 members list contained three members of the House of Lords, nearly
thirty sons of peers, and ten members of the House of Commons. MORGAN & THOMAS,
supra note 65 at 170.

81. Lohr, *A Resurgence in Finance*, N.Y. TIMES, Sept. 22, 1986 at D1, D10, col. 2. According to WHO'S WHO IN THE CITY (2d ed. 1989), of its 8,000 entrants, only 25% at-
tended Oxford or Cambridge, 6% graduated from Eton, the exclusive public school. The
number of women entrants was fewer than 200, a 100% increase over the 1988 edition. *Ins
and outs of the City*, FIN. TIMES, May 31, 1989 at 18, col. 2.

82. Lohr, *London's Brokers Start Taking Off the Gloves*, N.Y. TIMES, Sept. 24, 1986 at
D1, D9, col. 1.

83. Barrow Boys is also a slang term for costermongers, hawkers of fruit, vegetables, or
fish. PARTRIDGE, *supra* note 75 at 35.

84. See Lohr, *London's Brokers Start Taking Off the Gloves*, N.Y. TIMES, Sept. 24, 1986
at D9, col. 1. See Lohr, *Job Losses Also Mounting In London Financial Center*, N.Y. TIMES,
Jan. 19, 1988 at D1, col. 1; *The Gilt market sweats it out*, ECONOMIST, Jan. 16, 1988 at 71.

to one's firm diminished, and executives switched jobs more readily. The comfortable lifestyle gave way to hard work, competition, and an unwavering focus upon financial results. However, since the market break of 1987, the bloom is off the financial services rose. Employment has declined and salaries have stabilized, but people still work very hard.

Yet the image of the stockbroker as an Oxbridge clubsman, more concerned with country weekends than earning money, has remained. It has become somewhat of a myth, yet an effective one, believed by the public, by members of Parliament, and by the City.[85] Until recently, the changes in social composition of the City did not affect the shared beliefs or the institutional code of behavior.

Resistance to Government Regulation

One of the continuities of the Stock Exchange's history has been the ongoing resistance of its members to government regulation. Regulation of brokers has been traced to a statute of Edward I in 1285, which authorized the Court of Alderman to license brokers in the City of London.[86] In the late seventeenth and the eighteenth centuries, parliamentary legislation regulated and restrained stockbroking. In November 1696, commissioners appointed to look after the trade of England reported abuses in the issuance of stock by "stock jobbers."[87]

In 1697 an act "To Restrain the Number and Ill Practice of Brokers and Stockjobbers" was passed.[88] No person could act as a broker unless licensed by the Lord Mayor of the City of London and the Court of Aldermen. The number of brokers was limited to one hundred. They were required to pay an admission fee and enter a bond of £500, which would be forfeited in case of misconduct.

For acting as a broker without a license, there was a £500 penalty for each offense, a staggering sum at the end of the seventeenth century. Brokers had to keep a record of their transactions, and their commissions were limited. Options extending more than three days were prohibited, and bro-

85. CLARKE, *supra* note 18 at 4.

86. I. L. LOSS, SECURITIES REGULATION 3 (2d ed., 1961) *citing* KILLIK, THE WORK OF THE STOCK EXCHANGE 12 (2d ed., 1934).

87. MORGAN & THOMAS, *supra* note 65 at 23. Attempts to regulate stock jobbing in Parliament had commenced in 1693. There were three main abuses complained of, all of which have a modern ring. Promoters of companies sold their interests in corporations to inexperienced business people, thereby causing the management of companies to suffer. Dealers conspired together and manipulated share prices to artificially raise and lower profits. Options trading was abused. Many transactions were fraudulent, which combined with manipulation of share prices, ensured investor losses. *Id.* at 25.

88. 8 & 9 Will. 3, ch. 32.

kers could not deal for their own account. The act of 1697 ran for three years and was extended for an additional seven years.[89] It then lapsed.

These statutes were neither effective nor rigorously enforced. However, they created legal consequences for brokers. The statutes imposed an additional risk on the broker who undertook speculative bargains, such as options for clients. If an unsuccessful speculator refused to pay the difference he owed, the broker was without a means of legal redress because Parliament had declared such transactions illegal.[90] The less the sanction of law in commercial dealings, the more important it became for Exchange members to rely upon their word. The difficult legal position of brokers helps to explain the later development of a strict code of honor.[91] Brokers were bound to follow the rules of the Exchange by reason of the contractual basis by which they became members. While Exchange rules could not be enforced in a court of law, expulsion from membership with no right of appeal was a severe sanction. Self-regulation became effective as brokers accepted the norms of business practice established by the Exchange.

Another source of the Exchange's self-regulatory tradition was the ongoing attempt throughout the nineteenth century to wrest regulatory power from the City of London. From the thirteenth century, the City retained general power over brokers of all commodities, including the right to admit brokers to practice in the City, to require an oath of good conduct, to confine admissions to freemen, and to require proof of good character and competence. The City also had the power to make regulations governing brokers' conduct. In actuality, the purpose of much of this regulation was to raise revenue. Brokers not only resisted regulation by the City, they ignored it by refusing to take out the necessary licenses.[92]

Friction continued between brokers and the City throughout the nineteenth century. In 1805, Francis Bailey, an eminent member of the Exchange who drafted the first rule book, unsuccessfully organized resistance against payment of the "brokers rent."[93] In the 1860s the City first tried to strictly enforce existing statutes, then repealed them, and finally transferred powers relating to brokers to the Committee of the Stock Exchange.[94] The Brokers Relief Act of 1870 abolished the oath, bonding, sureties, and all regulatory functions of the Lord Mayor and aldermen.[95] All that remained was that the City kept a register, and brokers were required to pay an annual

---

89. 11 & 12 Will. 3, ch. 13, § VII (1700).
90. MORGAN & THOMAS, *supra* note 65 at 64, 148.
91. *Id.* at 64.
92. *Id.*
93. *Id.* at 65–66.
94. *Id.* at 147.
95. 1870, 33 & 34 Vict., ch. 60.

rent of £5 per year. However, this too was abolished in 1886. For the following one hundred years, the Stock Exchange, unlike investment exchanges in most other countries, was unregulated by the government. Since its founding, the Exchange had disciplined members for violations of its rules, and as supervision by the City of London eased, the Exchange assumed powers of regulation over its members.

Because Barnard's Act and the Gaming Act of 1845 made many transactions legally unenforceable, the Committee of the Stock Exchange administered justice in dealings among members.[96] The Committee of the Stock Exchange did more than mediate disputes among its members. It was engaged in a mixture of self-regulatory activity. From its early years the Committee considered complaints from clients against their brokers and forced the same standards in dealing with nonmembers.[97] In some areas, such as the requirements for the issuance of securities for listing, the Stock Exchange's rules were stricter than statutory law. Self-regulation of transactions in shares among members was possible through the laws of contract and agency, but more importantly through a code of conduct exemplified in the exchange's motto, *Dictum meum pactum*, "My word is my bond." It is said that the Exchange's motto is derived from the agreement between a broker and a jobber which was noted in the dealing books of each party. There was neither formal agreement nor written record signed between the two.[98] From a legal perspective, the oral contracts were still valid as they were not barred by the Statute of Frauds.[99] A more likely origin of the motto, "My word is my bond," was the lack of enforceability of such contracts in the courts because of parliamentary hostility.

---

96. Barnard's Act invalidated contracts whereby a broker or jobber received a premium for the sale of a stock or an option to buy or sell securities. There were penalties up to £500. An act to prevent the infamous Practice of Stockjobbing 1734, 7 Geo. 2, ch. 8. Earlier in 1721, Commons had passed "An Act for the better establishing of Public Credit by preventing for the future of the infamous Practice of Stockjobbing" but the measure did not pass the House of Lords. MORGAN & THOMAS, *supra* note 65 at 62. The Gaming Act prohibited gambling. 8 & 9 Vict., ch. 109. The issue became whether the options were wagers within the meaning of the statute. Options are agreements to purchase or sell stock at some time in the future in the hope of making a profit on the difference between the price of the option contract and the price of the security on the day it was due. Initially, courts treated option contracts as coming within the statute, Grizewood v. Blane, 11 C.B. 538, 138 Eng. Rep. 578; *sub nom* Grizewood v. Blane, 19 L.T.O.S. 64 (1852), but in 1878 such contracts were excluded from the scope of the statute. Thacker v. Hardy, 4 Q.B.D. 685, 39 L.T. 595, 43 J.P. 221, 27 W.R. 158 (1878).

97. MORGAN & THOMAS, *supra* note 65 at 166.

98. PLENDER & WALLACE, *supra* note 2 at 81; MCRAE & CAIRNCROSS, *supra* note 5 at 138.

99. 1677, Stat. 29, Car. 2, ch. 3. The Statute of Frauds largely was repealed in 1954. Law Reform (Enforcement of Contracts) Act, 1954, 2 & 3 Eliz. 2, ch. 34.

Self-regulation became effective when standards of entry to membership grew more rigorous and the danger of expulsion became a severe professional and social sanction. As the membership of the Exchange grew, procedures of entry and discipline became more formal.[100] The Committee of the Stock Exchange developed into a quasi-public body with judicial functions. Parliament allowed the Exchange to regulate its members through the rule book. Such regulation was usually more stringent than that required under the Companies Act.[101] Social and welfare activities increased the sense of community and shared values. Members participated in sport and supported families of colleagues fallen on hard times through the ineptly named "Decayed Members' Fund."[102]

The Exchange's reputation for probity grew. The Stock Exchange's rules offered substantial protection to the public against fraud. The Committee on Quotation ensured that securities were both sufficient in number and sufficiently widely held to make a market, and it required companies to provide comprehensive information for the potential investor.[103] The Exchange's requirements for both listed companies and its members reassured the public of the integrity of the market. In March 1950 a compensation fund became available for members of the public who suffered loss because of a broker's negligence or misfeasance. This served to lower the likelihood of litigation and public scrutiny.[104]

The Institutional Structure

Until 1991 the Stock Exchange was a private association headed by a council of twenty-eight members who served three-year terms.[105] As a re-

---

100. In 1904 the exchange created a nomination system whereby new members had to purchase a nomination or membership from a retiring or deceased member. MORGAN & THOMAS, *supra* note 65 at 158.

101. For instance, the Stock Exchange could waive certain statutory requirements of the Companies Act of 1948, 11 & 12 Geo. 6, c. 38, so that its regulations superseded the statute! L.C.B. GOWER, REVIEW OF INVESTOR PROTECTION: REPORT PART I, 1984 Cmnd. No. 9215 at 132 [hereinafter cited as GOWER I].

102. MORGAN & THOMAS, *supra* note 65 at 166–68. In the 1880s the Decayed Members Fund became the more euphemistically called Benevolent Fund. JENKINS, *supra* note 68 at 99, 109–10. Other organizations included the Attenuated Sportsmen's Club, the Male Voice Choir, and the Stock Exchange Art Society. Self-regulation worked because transgressions from the norm led to severe professional and social sanctions. Rider, *Self Regulation: The British Approach to Policing the Conduct in the Securities Business, with Particular Reference to the Role of the City Panel on Takeovers and Mergers in the Regulation of Insider Trading*, 1 J. COMP. CORP. L. & SEC. REG. 319 (1978) [hereinafter Rider].

103. MORGAN & THOMAS, *supra* note 65 at 215.

104. Payments were made entirely at the discretion of the Exchange's council. From 1973 to 1978 £3.6 million were paid from the compensation fund. THOMAS, *supra* note 68 at 142.

105. *London Stock Exchange: Consenting Adults*, ECONOMIST, Nov. 15, 1986 at 94. At

The Roots of Reform 25

sult of the restructuring of the financial services industry wrought by the Big Bang, the Exchange's role has changed into a broad provider of market services.[106] In 1991 the Exchange incorporated and abolished its governing body and replaced it with a more modern corporate board of directors. The board will focus upon long-range strategy. As part of the change, the Exchange shrunk the size of the governing body and diversified its membership to include representatives of listed companies and fund managers as well as senior exchange officers. Previously, the council's members had been drawn from its member stockbrokers and market makers.[107]

Originally, only individuals could be members in the Exchange. However, at the end of 1986, in preparation for the new era after the Big Bang, the Stock Exchange voted to merge with the International Securities Regulatory Organization (ISRO), which consisted of 180 securities *firms* that participated in the Eurobond market. A major impact of ISRO corporate members' joining was that the membership voted to end unlimited liability between themselves.[108] The Exchange changed its legal name to the International Stock Exchange of the United Kingdom and the Republic of Ireland, Limited (ISE), though in 1991 it decided to again call itself the London Stock Exchange.

Until the late 1970s the Stock Exchange system of self-regulation worked well. Customers felt protected by the Exchange's compensation fund. Brokerage firms were stable in membership. By and large, members accepted and abided by the rules. Fraud and rules violations could be dealt with qui-

---

that time, forty-six members were brokers, five were outside, lay members, and one, an ex-officio member, the government broker who acted for the government in the gilts market. McRae & Cairncross, *supra* note 5 at 130–31. Exchange members, as a matter of contract, agree to abide by the rules of the Exchange, which are in the "Yellow Book." From 1976 until 1988 the chairman of the council was Sir Nicholas Goodison, the managing director of a member firm, who led the Exchange through the Big Bang. The current chairman is Andrew Hugh Smith. All important issues are determined by the council. Technically, the members of the Exchange only had the right to change their contract among themselves, called the settlement deed. Major policy issues were submitted to the membership, which before 1986 was dominated by the smaller firms. At a general meeting on November 11, 1986 the members changed the settlement deed to provide for two classes of stock. Member firms holding voting rights have Class B shares. Individual and external members have Class A shares which are redeemable for £10,000 upon the member's retirement. INTERNATIONAL STOCK EXCHANGE, ANNUAL REPORT 20 (1987) [hereinafter INTERNATIONAL STOCK EXCHANGE ANNUAL REPORT].

106. *See infra* Ch. 7.

107. The board shrunk to eighteen members representing institutional investors, listed companies, commercial banks, and other representatives of the securities industry. Mackay, *Stock Exchange shake-up marks end of Big Bang*, THE TIMES (London) Apr. 9, 1991 at 25; Waller, *SE council offers seats to companies and institutions*, FIN. TIMES, Apr. 9, 1991 at 1.

108. *London Stock Exchange: Consenting Adults*, ECONOMIST, Nov. 15, 1986 at 94.

etly, effectively, and swiftly. An Exchange employee in the enforcement division reminisced about the ease of enforcement prior to the Big Bang:

> If a firm was in violation of capital requirements, a telephone call would handle the matter. The firm would be in compliance in the next day or so and the matter would be forgotten. If a broker violated the rules, the matter would be handled internally and that would be the end of it. Now I've got to fill out forms, everything is a matter of public record. We've lost the flexibility we had.

Stock Exchange self-regulation worked because it operated in a closed community with a high degree of homogeneity, social exclusivity, common backgrounds, and, most importantly, shared values. Problems were handled internally. Private regulation served to boost the public's belief in the Exchange's integrity.

The Department of Trade and Industry

The Department of Trade and Industry (DTI) is a governmental agency with a patchwork of responsibilities. It oversees the enforcement of company law (corporate law) legislation, which includes the registration of companies and the filing of documents in relation to those companies. It conducts investigations into company affairs and monitors corporate behavior. The Department also supervises insurance companies, enforces the prohibitions against insider trading,[109] and until 1992, represented the government's international trade policy in the European Community and other international organizations. It directs and initiates government policy toward industry including nationalized enterprises, antitrust policy, fair trading, consumer protection, regional policy, and science policy and research. In 1987 the DTI had a staff of 12,843 and a budget of £1.272 million.[110] The department is headed by the Secretary of State for Trade and Industry.

Founded in 1796 as the Board of Trade, in the last one hundred years the department has presided over the decline of British manufacturing and industry. Its reputation is uniformly poor. Heading the department has not been a road to the top. In the Thatcher government's eleven years, there were twelve different secretaries. Given the problems of British industry in the post-World War II period, it is not surprising that successive governments have reorganized the department. In 1970 the Board of Trade became the Department of Trade and Industry. In 1974, DTI was split into several departments that were then reconstituted in 1983.

---

109. A. WHITTAKER & G. MORSE, THE FINANCIAL SERVICES ACT 1986: A GUIDE TO THE NEW LAW § 6.01 (1988) [hereinafter WHITTAKER & MORSE].

110. P. HENNESSY, WHITEHALL 431 (1988).

The Department was the governmental agency directly responsible for introducing the Financial Services Bill, which created the new framework for investor protection, shepherding it through Parliament and implementing the legislation after enactment. Powers under the act devolve directly on the Secretary of State for Trade and Industry. DTI selected the supervisory agency and can revoke such designation. Whereas the Bank of England's role in the Big Bang was informal, DTI was the locus of statutory and governmental authority.

Structural Change in the Marketplace: The Roots of the Financial Services Legislation

The Global Market

Several long-range domestic and international factors brought pressure upon the City for change and demonstrated the need for a more modern regulatory framework. A new economic environment, resource constraints, market changes, and new competitive forces placed British financial services at a disadvantage. Markets became supranational. Issuers looked beyond their domiciles to raise capital. Institutional investors began to diversify their portfolios internationally. Securitization, the raising of capital through the direct issuance of securities rather than through traditional intermediaries such as banks, became common for corporations. Other international developments affected London's future as a major financial center. A technological revolution electronically integrated the world's financial markets and created competition between them. Financial centers with lower information and transaction costs drew business from less efficient ones.

The Euromarkets portended the new international economic order. Innovative financial products and forms of securities such as floating rate notes and swaps set new boundaries between the supranational Euromarkets and national capital markets. These innovations significantly broadened product range and attracted business from national markets.[111] The Euromarkets' success was attributable to their lack of regulation compared to national capital markets.[112] In striking contrast to the highly restrictive national markets, the Euromarkets offered free competition unhindered by government; ease of entry and exit; access to huge pools of liquid capital that could be transferred anywhere, anytime, instantaneously; and low

---

111. HAYES & HUBBARD, *supra* note 16 at 49–56.
112. *Id.* at 63.

transaction and information costs. They were a threat and a competitor to the national markets.

The United Kingdom had been fortunate that the Euromarkets were situated in London, but they had become more important than domestic markets. British firms began to turn outward and develop an international focus even when it came to trading English securities or raising capital for English companies. London became attractive to foreign firms because of the Euromarkets, in spite of the difficulties of doing business in the restrictive U.K. markets. Eurobonds were a wholesale market, but it was not too difficult to foresee the possibilities of global retail markets as well. The Euromarkets were a catalyst in deregulating the domestic English capital markets and ending the separations between types of financial institutions.

The abolition of exchange controls in 1979 led to a flight of British capital abroad and an influx of foreign capital into the United Kingdom[113] The deregulation of restrictions against American pension funds placing funds in foreign investments brought about an invasion of American capital. As English institutional investors channeled their savings abroad, this created new demands for financial services. The restrictions on Stock Exchange membership, fixed commissions which supported the single capacity system, and other Stock Exchange restrictive rules resulted in the trading of increasing numbers of British securities off the floor of the Exchange. It became cheaper and more efficient to trade large blocks of shares in other capital markets such as New York.[114]

Global trading, the rise of other offshore financial centers, and the threat of competition by immense American and Japanese financial conglomerates threatened to make London a minor player in international financial markets.[115] Tokyo had emerged as an international financial center because of the strength of its economy. In contrast, the prosperity of Britain's financial services sector flourished despite an overall economic decline. If the City was unable to compete with other capital markets, the financial services sector, " 'Britain's fringe of prosperity,' might become just another declining industry."[116]

New investment vehicles and financial products emerged and bypassed the Stock Exchange. In 1982, in response to the success of the Chicago Mercantile Exchange's currency options, the London International Financial Futures Exchange (LIFFE) was formed to enable investors to hedge

---

113. McRae & Cairncross, *supra* note 5 at 124.

114. This was due not only to fixed commissions but to a stamp duty on transfers of securities. Thomas, *supra* note 68 at 34, 128–29.

115. Silk, *Global Finance: Tale of 3 Cities*, N.Y. Times, Oct. 31, 1986 at D2, col. 1.

116. Lohr, *Britain Braces for a Financial Free-for-All*, N.Y. Times, Dec. 22, 1985 at § F, 1, 27 at col. 2.

against interest rate and Exchange rate fluctuations and swings in stock portfolio values.[117] The international debt crisis made the banks more cautious and promoted the rise of an international securities market.[118]

The creation of substantially larger supranational financial organizations that combined the functions of commercial and investment banking and stockbroking meant that British firms could be shut out of the international financial markets because of a lack of capital. Changes in information technology made floor trading of securities obsolete and opened the possibility of twenty-four hour global trading.

Banks also traded in British and American equities off the floor of the Exchange. The Eurobond market was centered in London, but largely bypassed the Exchange and its regulations.[119] In 1983 the Association of International Bond Dealers listed 120 members dealing in Eurobonds and based in London. Only four were members of the Exchange.[120]

Domestically, the increasing influence of the institutional investor pressured the fixed commission system.[121] From the 1970s the Stock Exchange paralleled the experience of other countries in the growth of institutional investors, pension funds, investment trusts, and unit trusts.[122]

The Squeeze on Jobbers

The rise and increasing influence of institutional investors and unit and investment trusts placed pressures on the jobber, who required greater cap-

---

117. MCRAE & CAIRNCROSS, *supra* note 5 at 203–5. LIFFE was composed of bankers, commodity brokers, and stock brokers, but not jobbers.

118. PLENDER & WALLACE, *supra* note 2 at 41–46, 49–50. After the crash of October 1987, international share prices declined more on foreign markets than on their own domestic markets. *International shares go down—not out*, ECONOMIST, Dec. 26, 1987 at 75.

119. MCRAE & CAIRNCROSS, *supra* note 5 at 128, 144. Most Eurobond business is carried out between foreign and British banks. There is also a trading market in bonds already issued which is carried out by the underwriting Banks. *The Euroequity Market*, ECONOMIST, Nov. 29, 1986 at 72.

120. MCRAE & CAIRNCROSS, *supra* note 5 at 128.

121. MORGAN & THOMAS, *supra* note 65 at 175. It is sometimes assumed that institutional investment is an invention of the 1960s and 1970s. *See* MCRAE & CAIRNCROSS, *supra* note 5 at 89. In fact, institutions have always owned shares traded on the Stock Exchange. The growth of institutional investors as a percentage of all investors is what has grown in the United Kingdom and in other countries with stock exchanges.

122. Investment trusts were developed in the nineteenth century. A block of investments is vested in trustees under a trust deed dividing ownership into a number of shares or units which the public purchased. Generally, such trusts are incorporated. An investment trust is a kind of holding company or close-ended mutual fund with a fixed number of shares which purchases equities with a view to appreciation. L.C.B. GOWER, PRINCIPLES OF MODERN COMPANY LAW 266–67 (4th ed. 1979) [hereinafter GOWER'S PRINCIPLES].

ital to handle larger trades, and led institutions to engage in attempts to circumvent him. There were other strains upon the jobber. Most firms traded only in the leading equities, leaving only two firms to make markets in others. Until 1970, brokers and jobbers could not incorporate. This restriction hindered needed infusions of capital and prompted some Exchange member firms to merge. The Exchange rule that a single nonmember shareholder of an Exchange firm could own no more than 10 percent of the firm's shares constrained those firms that were incorporated.[123] Incorporated members still were personally liable for their debts, and directors of such corporations had to be members of the Exchange. In a financial environment where ever increasing capital was necessary for non-Exchange international broking activities, British firms could not compete outside the protected domestic market. Even the capital needs of Exchange members increased. The Exchange rules made membership nearly impossible for foreign companies.

Capital resources did not increase at the same pace as the volume of business. Inflation increased jobbing costs, which resulted in a lower return on capital. As a result of the lack of necessary capital and decreasing profits, the number of jobbing firms declined. By the time of the Big Bang, most members of the Stock Exchange were brokers.[124] The two largest jobbers dealt in over 90 percent of the government securities traded and in 60 percent of the equity or common stock trading. The institutional investor forced jobbers to cut their prices and to make a joint book, i.e., a fixed price on certain securities.[125]

Institutional investors have invested more of their funds in common stocks. Today they own nearly 50 percent of U.K. companies' shares compared to just 20 percent twenty-five years ago.[126] English institutions holding large blocks of securities, not only pressured the fixed commission rate, they also traded elsewhere. Increasing numbers of British investors purchased abroad the stocks of British companies, thereby evading the stamp duty imposed on securities transactions. This was accomplished through the use of American Depository Receipts (ADRs), which are certificates, actually receipts, issued by a depository bank stating that a specified num-

---

123. The Exchange increased the percentage of outside ownership to 29.9%, and in 1986 allowed full outside ownership.

124. In 1984 there were 3,600 brokers in 209 firms and 500 jobbers in 12 firms. By March 1987 there were 5,433 individual members and 357 firm memberships. CLARKE, *supra* note 18 at 92. INTERNATIONAL STOCK EXCHANGE, ANNUAL REPORT, *supra* note 105 at 19–20.

125. THOMAS, *supra* note 68 at 24–27.

126. MORGAN & THOMAS, *supra* note 65 at 177, 223, 234, 237. CLARKE, *supra* note 18 at 93.

ber of shares have been deposited. The certificates themselves are negotiable, and most leading British companies have an ADR facility.

The secondary Eurobond market also bypassed the Exchange. Between 1979 and 1983, life insurance companies, the largest institutional investors, raised the percentage of their assets held in non-English securities from 2.9 to 9.2 percent. Pension funds, the second largest institutional investor, increased their percentage of assets in foreign securities from 5.5 to 14.7 percent.[127] Although the Exchange had a near monopoly of trading in U.K. securities and gilts, trades on the floor of the Exchange accounted for only three-quarters of all securities traded in London.[128] International banks and large American brokerage firms merely bypassed the Exchange. They made markets in the stocks of international companies off the floor of the Exchange, traded offshore, or traded in other markets.[129]

The erosion of trading on the Stock Exchange reflected the internationalization of securities markets. As institutional investors became increasingly multinational in focus, this erosion from the inward-looking London Exchange grew and threatened both the Exchange and the British capital market. This was recognized by the Bank of England. Unlike the Bank, which had its pulse on the changing international economic picture, the Stock Exchange was hidebound. Though concerned about the erosion of trading abroad, it remained a self-satisfied cartel on the way to becoming a backwater. It seemed not to recognize the changes occurring about it.

The Domestic Origins of the Big Bang

The accession of Margaret Thatcher to the prime ministry in 1979 had a great impact on the financial services sector. Exchange controls were removed. Attempts were made to stem inflation and to reduce government deficits and taxes. The efforts stimulated the capital markets. Perhaps the most important step for deregulation of the financial markets was something the Tories didn't do—they declined to pressure the Office of Fair Trading (OFT) to abandon an investigation of the Stock Exchange.

Stock Exchange Restrictive Trade Practices

The domestic origins of the Big Bang can be traced to a restrictive trade practices service order issued in 1976 by Roy Hattersley, then the Labor

---

127. THOMAS, *supra* note 68 at 44.
128. W. KAY, THE BIG BANG, 66–67 (1986).
129. MCRAE & CAIRNCROSS, *supra* note 5 at 137. Similar factors ended the New York Stock Exchange's cartel that set minimum rates.

government's Secretary of State for Prices and Consumer Protection. The Restrictive Trade Practices Act is Britain's equivalent of the United States's antitrust laws.[130] The act assumes that agreements between competitors are likely to operate against the public interest. If so found, the agreement will be declared void. Such an agreement between Stock Exchange members was the basis of the Exchange's ability to set rules for and discipline its members.

A process of extension of coverage of the act began in 1974. At that time the Stock Exchange was informed by the OFT that it was under investigation both by the Monopolies Commission in regard to its advertising rules and by the Department of Trade, which was examining its supervision and conduct of the securities market. The Exchange claimed that its special position was recognized by several acts of Parliament, and its rules were consistent with its role as the primary regulatory body for the securities industry.[131]

The 1976 order extended the scope of the restrictive practices legislation to the services sector. Banks, building societies, and unit trusts were exempted, but the Stock Exchange was not.[132] The Exchange delivered its deed of settlement and rule book to the OFT to determine whether it should be included on a public register of restrictive trading agreements.[133] The alternative to delivery was to declare the rule book void. Sir Nicholas Goodison, the Exchange's chairman, wrote Hattersley and pleaded for an exemption.[134]

Under the Restrictive Trade Practices Act, the director general of fair trading had to refer the Stock Exchange rule book to the restrictive practices court for a ruling as to whether it operated against public interest.[135] Notice of reference was issued in February 1979.[136] The Exchange described the move as "a political decision taken in too much of a hurry."[137] Upon referral, the burden was placed upon the Exchange to demonstrate

---

130. 1976, ch. 34, §§ 11, 12.

131. THOMAS, *supra* note 68 at 35.

132. Lloyd & Randall, *Countdown to the 'Big Bang'*, FIN. WEEKLY, Oct. 31, 1985 at 16 [hereinafter Lloyd & Randall].

133. Restrictive Trade Practices Act, 1976, ch. 34, §§ 23–24.

134. Exemptions may be granted if in the national interest. *Id.* at § 29, if expressly exempted by statute. *Id.* at § 28, sched. 3(1) or for certain other reasons.

135. *Id.* at § 1(2)(c).

136. When the director general of fair trading determines an agreement is against the public interest, he refers it to the Restrictive Practices Court and may apply for an interim order to the court that the agreement is restrictive. The charged party has the right to defend such charge. The statute provides a number of exemptions in the public interest. *Id.* at § 19.

137. Lloyd & Randall, *supra* note 132 at 16.

that the rule book, though it had noncompetitive aspects, was in the public interest. Most observers speculated that the momentum behind this regulatory initiative would be lost when, in May 1979, the Conservatives were returned to power.

The Impact of Radical Toryism

The financial community expected that the Tories would drop the case because of their traditional sympathy toward business. Instead, as part of a broader ideological interest in free-market principles, the government scrutinized the practices of all professions for noncompetitive aspects. It instructed Gorden Borrie, director general of the Office of Fair Trading, to investigate the Stock Exchange with a view to ending its restrictive practices.[138] The OFT compiled a list of 173 restrictive practices in the Stock Exchange rule book but concentrated upon minimum commissions, single capacity, and restrictions on outside participation in the market.

Initially, the Exchange responded with a line-by-line defense. It argued that retention of single capacity offered the greatest investor protection, for it was potentially self-policing. Continuous dealing offered investors fair prices in a central marketplace. Investors were protected because jobbers competed only with each other for the broker's business and thereby ensured the lowest price for the security. Also, so the argument went, brokers had no direct incentive to overcharge the client for the price of the stock.[139]

The basic defense of the Exchange was that its rules were in the public interest and that it came under an exemption in the act for restrictive practices, the removal of which would deprive the public of substantial benefits.[140] The fixed commission, the Exchange maintained, enabled similar treatment of all clients guaranteeing the smallest investor the same price as an institutional purchaser. Another Stock Exchange defense was the linkage argument, which maintained that the abandonment of fixed commissions would put the system of single capacity at risk because the two were inextricably linked.[141]

---

138. CLARKE, *supra* note 18 at 94, 96.
139. PLENDER & WALLACE, *supra* note 2 at 82.
140. Restrictive Trade Practices Act, 1976, ch. 34, § 19(1)(b). THOMAS, *supra* note 83 at 39.
141. PLENDER & WALLACE, *supra* note 2 at 97. THOMAS, *supra* note 68 at 40–42. Once brokers' profits came under pressure as a result of lower negotiated commissions with large institutional investors, brokers would bypass jobbers and match buy and sell orders themselves. Jobbers would then insist on dealing with investors directly, thereby undercutting the investor's assurance of receiving the lowest price because the investor would not likely receive bids from competing jobbers.

The Bank of England had argued against the referral of the Stock Exchange's rule book to the Restrictive Practices Court. By 1982, however, the Bank had become concerned about the City's future as an international financial center. It conducted an internal study of British firms' competitiveness in international financial markets. The study was under the direction of an executive director of the Bank, David Walker. It showed that in the areas of banking, insurance, and commodities, British firms had held their own. In contrast, English brokerage firms had made little impact on the international scene. In fact, their share of international business had declined.[142]

Walker desired a greater Bank of England presence in the financial services area, particularly in light of securities firms' failure to assist the balance of payments. The Bank felt that some liberalization of Stock Exchange rules was necessary. A balance needed to be struck between the restrictive policies attacked by the restrictive practices litigation and the opening up of stockbroking to full-scale competition, which was widely thought would lead to an American takeover of the securities industry. The Bank then pushed for a compromise resolution, whereby the Stock Exchange would gradually change its commission structure while allowing new infusions of capital into brokerage firms to allow them to compete internationally. This would create jobs, assist the balance of payments, and preserve London's role as a multifaceted financial center. The Bank played an important behind-the-scenes role in resolving the restrictive practices litigation and in the shaping of the securities markets after the Big Bang. It also increased its influence over the whole of the financial services sector.

In July 1983 the new Secretary of State for Trade and Industry, Cecil Parkinson, intimated that if the Exchange could forward proposals for voluntary modifications of its rule book, the case before the restrictive practices tribunal might be withdrawn. Ten days later, in a private arrangement which drew substantial criticism, the Exchange agreed that minimum commissions would be phased out by the end of 1986. This was the only concession concerning its trading practices that the Exchange offered.

The agreement provided that lay persons were to be brought onto the Stock Exchange Council and it would serve as an appeals body on membership issues and the Bank of England would have a monitoring role along with the Department of Trade.[143] After the agreement, the government in-

---

142. PLENDER & WALLACE, *supra* note 2 at 91–94.

143. The official rationale for the settlement, which was objected to by the director general of fair trading, was that: (1) it was difficult to institute changes that would enable members of the exchange to compete internationally while litigation was pending; and (2) the danger that legal proceedings within the framework of the Restrictive Practices Act

troduced a bill to exempt the Stock Exchange from the Restrictive Practices Act, a step which was met with criticism in the press and in the House of Commons.[144] Neither the government nor the City foresaw the changes that the agreement would trigger. Initially, Exchange members and the government believed that single capacity would survive.[145] The government primarily was concerned with the anticompetitive practice evidenced by the Stock Exchange's power to fix commission levels.[146] Other than the Bank of England and the Stock Exchange's self-interest, there was little consideration of the impact of the settlement upon the securities industry's market structure.

The single capacity system crumbled swiftly. The linkage argument had a basis in fact. Negotiated commissions would cut into profits, particularly in the context of a marketplace where the size of each transaction and percentage of institutional trading was increasing. Brokers would do what other businesses attempt when profit margins shrink: cut out the middle-man jobber. Some of the major investment banks felt the agreement would lead to integrated, single capacity trading. They considered purchasing securities firms. A second, more important factor, was the position of the Bank of England, which desired to see international securities firms participate in the gilts market. The Bank pointedly gave no support to the jobbing system.[147] City firms bet that the Stock Exchange would vote to end the single capacity system, which would lead to the purchase and combination of brokerage and jobbing firms. Integrated financial services firms ensured foreign membership on the Stock Exchange would become a reality because firms needed greater capitalization, not all of which was available from English sources.

Then came one of the most significant developments impelling the Big Bang, the merger of several types of previously functionally separate finan-

---

might damage an effective operation which was necessary to the economy. 46 PARL. DEB. H.C. (6th ser.) 612–13 (1983). The agreement was seen by many as a craven surrender. *Big Bang and City Regulation, supra* note 19 at 3. Mr. Parkinson was unable to savor the agreement for long. He was forced out of office for impregnating his secretary and then refusing to marry her. Apparently this was not a particularly great scandal by Tory standards, for he reappeared in Mrs. Thatcher's 1987 cabinet as secretary of state for energy. *See* Hughes, *Parkinson is back: Tebbit Quits Cabinet,* THE TIMES (London), June 14, 1987 at 1, col. 5.

144. Even some Tories objected to the use of special legislation to halt pending litigation. The agreement left those whose commercial interests were at stake free to work out the settlement themselves, which is not the normal result of a government initiated-lawsuit. PLENDER & WALLACE, *supra* note 2 at 95–96.

145. *See* 46 PARL. DEB. H.C. (6th ser.) 612–13 (1983).

146. PLENDER & WALLACE, *supra* note 2 at 97.

147. *Id.* at 104–5. Two firms had accounted for over 75% of the gilts market and only eight participated. Waters, *Credit Lyonnais joins the retreat from London's main gilts market,* FIN. TIMES, Aug. 22, 1989 at 6, col. 4.

cial institutions: investment banks, merchant banks, insurance companies, and stock brokerage and jobbing firms.[148] In 1982 the Exchange had allowed foreign firms to acquire up to 29.9 percent of member firms. The Parkinson-Goodison agreement triggered a set of mergers between commercial and merchant banks that was followed by the purchase of brokerage and jobbing firms.[149]

What was clear was that events were moving so quickly that the single capacity system and protectionism were disintegrating. In 1984 the Exchange approved the establishment of international memberships for member companies dealing in foreign stocks. These members did not have to purchase shares through jobbers.[150]

The Public Consciousness of Scandal

Fraud and scandal have always existed in the City. Money and human weakness begat it. Because of the narrowness of the investing class, public and government concern about fraud usually was minimal. Until recently, the percentage of Britons who invested in securities was quite small.[151] The Thatcher government encouraged share ownership, and by February 1987, the number of British shareholders trebled to nearly 20 percent of the adult population compared to 27 percent of the adult population in the United States.[152] As the investing class expanded, financial fraud would come un-

---

148. For lists of the many mergers, *see* PLENDER & WALLACE, *supra* note 2 at 110–19, CLARKE, *supra* note 18 at 95.

149. The prices paid for the acquisitions and salary increments given to leading brokers and jobbers raised questions at the time about the economic viability of the mergers. Blackstone, *Brokers forced to take stock*, THE SUNDAY TIMES (London), Apr. 27, 1986 at 69, col. 1; Fleet, *Only 10 major players may survive Big Bang*, THE TIMES (London), May 3, 1986 at 21 col. 6. Ferguson, *New financial groups fare an overseas onslaught*, THE TIMES (London), June 30, 1986 at 22, col. 4; Lohr, *Cut throat Competition Expected in British Government Bonds*, N.Y. TIMES, Oct. 27, 1986 at D12, col. 1. The events of late 1987 confirmed that profits were often illusory. Joseph, *How Black Monday Took the Gloss from Glittering Prizes*, THE TIMES (London), Dec. 28, 1987 at 17, col. 1; Lohr, *Job Losses Also Mounting in London Financial Center*, N.Y. TIMES, Jan. 19, 1988 at D1, col. 1. Fallon, *Market-making made difficult*, THE SUNDAY TIMES (London), Dec. 13, 1987 at 52, col. 1.

150. The Exchange published a discussion document that proposed the end of single capacity, removal of the limit on outside stakes of member firms, limited liability, corporate membership, the sale of seats to new members, and a primary dealer system for gilts. The new dealing system was approved in July 1984. Lloyd & Randall, *supra* note 132 at 17.

151. Between 1958 and 1979, the proportion of individuals owning shares dropped from 7% of the population to 4.5%. The stock markets were depressed in the 1970s, and even by 1986, only 6% owned shares. Fallon, *A Share in the Future*, THE SUNDAY TIMES (London), March 23, 1986 at 25, col. 1.

152. The increase was a result of the government's privatization programs which ena-

der wider scrutiny. In the past, enormous misdealings such as the South Sea Bubble in the eighteenth century and the collapse of the Overend Gurney Bank in the nineteenth rocked the financial system. In such cases, the Bank of England intervened to restore confidence, and the crisis passed. The non-investing public was relatively unaffected.

More typically, misdeeds have been handled quietly by the City itself or within the particular institution or firm affected. When, in a rare instance, a client of an Exchange member was harmed by the member's malfeasance, the Council of the Stock Exchange could make use of its client's compensation fund to restore the injured client to his proper position. This was privately done, without public or parliamentary interest in such matters. The perception of the City as a bastion of integrity where one's word was one's bond was accepted by successive governments and enabled the Exchange and other financial institutions to retain complete freedom of operation.

By and large, the self-regulatory system worked. The social and professional sanctions of the Exchange community served as a workable deterrent to widespread fraud.[153] The self-regulatory system was flexible, and less admirably, closed from parliamentary view or public scrutiny. The basis of the system was trust—a belief that others in the institution operated under the same code of conduct.[154] Trust was reinforced by the shared values, belief in professional expertise, common social origins and experiences, and the exclusiveness of the City's participants.

Times change. The informal method of regulation that worked so well in the homogenous, village-like atmosphere of the City was destined to come under stress with the development, at home and abroad, of unregulated markets and new types of financial instruments. The lack of state regulation assisted the growth of the European money markets, new investment exchanges, and London's post-World War II resurgence as an international financial center. Postwar relations between the British government and the financial sector exhibited a tension between two conflicting demands: one,

---

bled investors to purchase shares in formerly nationalized companies at below the price immediately after the shares' issuance. Research has indicated that many such shareholders quickly sold their securities to lock in profits. *Share ownership in Britain more broad than deep*, ECONOMIST, Sept. 12, 1987 at 85–86. *See* VG, *Nearly a fifth with Abbey certificates sell holdings*, THE TIMES, (London), Aug. 19, 1989 at 21, col. 5. (700,000 shareholders of a building society that changed its structure to a corporation sold their shares shortly after the conversion, 17.5% of the 4,000,000 shareholders.) The October 1987 market break was a rude jolt for many new investors who learned for the first time that investing in securities could be risky, and that share prices went down as well as increased. Lohr, *Long Honeymoon Ends for Investors in Britain*, N.Y. TIMES, Oct. 22, 1987 at D17, col. 1.

153. Rider, *supra* note 102 at 319.
154. *Supra* pp. 23–24. CLARK, *supra* note 18 at 3–5.

the need to avoid excessive control that would strangle innovation and drive away the international financial presence; and the other, the need to protect individual investors and preserve confidence in the integrity of the market.[155]

New markets and opportunities brought with them different kinds of risk and methods of conducting business. They also attracted new participants to the City who did not share the traditional values. New ethics and norms of corporate responsibility clashed with the old. The merger of financial institutions into financial supermarkets offering all kinds of financial services to every type of customer raised questions about whether, in the absence of any regulatory body, there could possibly be a separation of functions that avoided conflicts of interest.

The response of the City was to proclaim that conflicts would be avoided through the establishment of "Chinese walls" separating such functions and clients, and that the firms themselves would resolve any conflicts so that their clients would not be harmed.[156] Professor L.C.B. Gower was more realistic when he commented that he had never seen a Chinese wall without a grapevine trailing over it.[157]

Later came a series of scandals affecting the banking system, Lloyd's, and the Exchange. In February 1981, Norton Warburg (NW), investment advisors and financial fund managers, collapsed. NW had been founded in 1973, but nevertheless had attracted attention as a manager of the finances of rock stars and other celebrities. Establishment institutions including the Bank of England looked with favor on their success.[158] A hindsight investigation showed early warning signals of improper accounting procedures that an established regulatory system would have uncovered. Funds were shifted from bank to bank to cover overdrafts.[159] Other accounting irregu-

---

155. PLENDER & WALLACE, *supra* note 2 at 151.

156. *Id.* at 152; Pimlott, *supra* note 3 at 159; GOWER I, *supra* note 101 at 62.

157. L.C.B. GOWER, REVIEW OF INVESTOR PROTECTION: REPORT PART II, 1985, Cmd. No. 9125 at 28 [hereinafter GOWER II].

158. Bourke, *Bank England offer to persons who lost money*, THE TIMES (London), Oct. 27, 1981 at 15, col. 4. CLARKE, *supra* note 18 at 103. The firm managed £16 million in funds including the portfolio of the rock group, Pink Floyd. After the firm went bankrupt, Pink Floyd alleged a loss of £2.5 million. *Pop group to sue investment co.*, THE TIMES (London), Mar. 11, 1981 at 17, col. 1; Robinson, *Liquidation Move at Norton Warburg*, THE TIMES (London), Feb. 23, 1981 at 15, col. 3. CLARKE, *supra* note 18 at 102–05 covers the Norton Warburg scandal and others during this period in relishing detail. The Bank, as part of an early retirement program, had allowed NW access to affected employees to discuss their investments with them. Approximately 20 had invested and lost heavily. In October 1981 the Bank indemnified its former employees who had invested in NW up to 90% of what they lost. Other institutions, which allowed NW to advise retired and current employees, were BBC, British Airways, and Unilever.

159. CLARKE, *supra* note 18 at 102–05.

larities occurred on an ongoing basis. And, in a pattern that occurred in other scandals, the exposed perpetrators fled to jurisdictions that lacked an extradition treaty with Great Britain. In this period, misdealing by other licensed dealers in securities and commodities caused bankruptcies. A major brokerage firm collapsed hours before a merger was to be implemented with the chairman of the Exchange's own firm, Quilter-Goodison.[160]

Challenges to successful self-regulation occurred with the Panel on Takeovers and Mergers (The Panel). The Panel was a nonstatutory self-regulating group that supervised the City code, a set of rules designed to establish fair play in takeover situations. It was a very successful example of how self-regulation based upon moral suasion and shared beliefs could work. The Exchange seemed unwilling or unable to prevent undisclosed creeping acquisition by a foreign concealed bidder of an English company. This skirted the spirit of the Companies Act and the letter of the Stock Exchange regulations. The case generated inquiries from Parliament and a report from the Department of Trade, both of which generated substantial publicity, but little else, and did great damage to the notion of effective self-regulation.[161]

Perhaps the most notorious if not the longest running scandal to affect the Stock Exchange was the Halliday Simpson affair, which involved a Manchester-based brokerage firm and a respected merchant bank. The scandal originated in 1978 and ended in 1983. It included two suicides, the ban of six partners of the Halliday Simpson brokerage firm from the Exchange for life, and suspension of others for a term. The misdeeds involved various kinds of self-dealing.[162]

The Exchange's scandals, as well as others in insurance, commodities, and banking, occurred in a societal, cultural, and regulatory climate quite different from the past. Now there was widespread publicity. The public, at least indirectly, was involved. Broad institutional ownership of securities by

---

160. The circumstances of the collapse indicated a lack of financial disclosure and fraudulent conveyances and raised questions about the Exchange's ability to regulate itself, not to speak of the judgment of the Exchange's chairman. The firm Hedderwich Stirling Gumbar failed to meet its debts on time and was expelled from the Stock Exchange. The firm recently had been the subject of an inquiry by the fraud squad and of two Stock Exchange internal investigations. Quilter Goodison did snap up many of the failed firm's clients. *See Nick Goodison's narrow squeak on Bad Friday*, ECONOMIST, Apr. 18, 1981 at 77.

161. *See* Prest, *The Strange Affair of St. Piran*, THE TIMES (London), Apr. 29, 1981 at 23, col. 4. CLARKE, *supra* note 18 at 112–14.

162. *See* CLARKE, *supra* note 8 at 114–18; Gilber & Sullivan, *The Rise and Fall of Halliday Simpson*, THE SUNDAY TIMES (London), July 31, 1981 at 55, col. 1; *Halliday, Simpson Behind the Bar*. ECONOMIST, July 18, 1981 at 76–7; Robinson, *Stockbrokers suspended for inquiry*, THE TIMES (London), July 11, 1981 at 17, col. 2; Robinson, *Arbuthnot suspends two top financiers*, THE TIMES (London), July 18, 1981 at 19, col. 2.

pension funds and investment and unit trusts, represented the savings of millions of people. Their managers had a fiduciary duty to the beneficiaries of these funds and trusts—the public—to ensure that their savings were invested properly. The implications of fraud and scandal were that should the market prove corrupt, the funds would be invested elsewhere.

The government feared that if the City was perceived to be ridden with misdeed and scandal, institutional business would move abroad, probably to the United States. Predictably, the response of the various City institutions was instinctive. They desired to deal with the matters privately and informally, hoping to preserve public confidence, a method that had worked so well in the past. Self-regulation, under criticism, became self-protection.

In July 1981 the Government responded to the scandals embarrassing the City. John Biffen, then secretary of state for trade and industry, commissioned professor L.C.B. Gower to undertake a review of the existing statutory protection for investors and of the need for new regulation.[163]

Gower's appointment was not welcomed in the City,[164] and he initially believed that his efforts would not be fruitful.[165] However, his report on investor protection was to lay the groundwork for the new structure of securities regulation created by the Financial Services Act.[166]

---

163. Gower, though unknown to the public, was Britain's preeminent company (corporate) law expert. From 1948 to 1962 he had been Sir Ernest Cassel Professor of Commercial Law at the University of London and then vice-chancellor of Southampton University. The vice-chancellor is the equivalent of a college or university president. Frequently, the chancellor, an honorary title, will be a member of the Royal family. Gower was a member of the Jenkins Committee on Company Law Amendments from 1959 to 1962, a law commissioner from 1965 to 1971, and had authored a leading treatise on English company law, GOWER'S PRINCIPLES, *supra* note 122. At the time of his appointment, Gower was a part-time advisor to the DTI for company law matters. Perhaps most important for this task, he was familiar with American securities regulation. Gower had been a visiting professor at Harvard Law School during the 1954–55 year, was a friend of the doyen of American securities law scholars, Louis Loss, and was a consultant to the American Law Institute's Federal Securities Code. While at Harvard, he had published *Some Contrasts Between British and American Corporation Law*, 69 HARV. L. REV. 1369 (1956) which is still cited.

164. PLENDER & WALLACE, *supra* note 2 at 153.

165. L.C.B. GOWER, REVIEW OF INVESTOR PROTECTION: A DISCUSSION DOCUMENT 87 (1982) at n. 50 [hereinafter DISCUSSION DOCUMENT].

166. In January 1982, after informal consultation with representative bodies, firms, and individuals, Gower published a DISCUSSION DOCUMENT which summarized the existing system of regulation and concluded that investor dissatisfaction was widespread throughout the financial services sector. After publication of the DISCUSSION DOCUMENT, he met with industry groups, professional bodies, and individuals and received formal written comments from many. In addition, Gower conferred with regulatory bodies and professionals in Australia, Canada, New Zealand, and the United States. Part I of the *Review of Investor Protection* appeared in January 1984, GOWER I, *supra* note 101. The government's

The Existing System of Securities Regulation

The framework of securities regulation that existed in the United Kingdom before 1987 was a patchwork of statutes and practices enacted piecemeal over time to deal with specific problems or abuses.[167] Statutes prohibited some of the more egregious abuses, such as the door-to-door sale of securities, but they were generally ineffective.[168] While Parliament has attempted to regulate brokers and dealers since the seventeenth century, the regulation of the sale of securities dates only to the mid-nineteenth century.

The Companies Acts

Since the landmark Joint Stock Companies Act of 1844, disclosure has been the fundamental philosophy of English securities regulation, as it became in the United States.[169] In 1867, for the first time, prospectuses had to disclose certain information. The Companies Act was amended to require the registration of the names and dates of contracts made prior to the issuance of the prospectus and the existence of such contracts had to be disclosed in written solicitations to subscribers.[170]

White Paper was published in January 1985, FINANCIAL SERVICES IN THE UNITED KINGDOM: A NEW FRAMEWORK FOR INVESTOR PROTECTION. 1985, Cmnd. 9432 [hereinafter WHITE PAPER]. Part II of Gower's report, *supra* note 157, which described the proposals in the government's *White Paper* and indicated where they differed from the proposals in Part I, appeared in 1985.

167. Pimlott, *supra* note 3 at 141.

168. *See* Companies Act 1928 and 1929, 18 & 19 Geo. V, ch. 45 and 19 & 20 Geo. V, ch. 23. The statutes prohibited sale of shares by door-to-door salesmen. They also provided that written offers of unlisted securities be accompanied by a statement giving information roughly similar to those required of companies listed on the Stock Exchange. The legislation was ineffective.

169. 7 & 8 Vict., ch. 110. GOWER'S PRINCIPLES, *supra* note 122 at 4041. The statute did not define prospectus but required that a copy of it "or circular, handbill, or advertisement or other such document . . . addressed to the public . . ." be submitted to the Registrar of Joint Stock Companies. The name, location, and purpose of the company, and names of officers and subscribers also would be filed. Joint Stock Companies Act of 1844, 7 & 8 Vict., ch. 10, § 4. Other provisions required shareholder access to company books, requirements of balance sheets, and selection of auditors. *Id.* at §§ 35, 38, 41. For a fuller description of the 1984 act and nineteenth-century English securities regulation, *see* Kilbride, *The British Heritage of Securities Legislation in the United States*, 17 S.W. L.J. 258 (1963) [hereinafter Kilbride] and GOWER'S PRINCIPLES, *supra* note 122 at 39, 52. Regulation of securities waxed and waned throughout the nineteenth century. In 1847, the registration requirements of prospectuses were deleted because of the burdens to promoters Joint Stock Companies Act, 1847, 10 & 11 Vict., ch. 78, § 4.

170. Companies Act, 1867, 30 & 32 Vict., ch. 38. This statute was ineffective, for pro-

In 1889 the House of Lords ruled that a director's firm belief in a statement contained in the prospectus, even in the absence of reasonable grounds for such belief, was not actionable, for the action of deceit would lie only where a misrepresentation was made with knowledge of its falsity or recklessness, not caring whether it was true or false.[171] The decision was reversed the following year by the Directors' Liability Act.[172] The statute, which had a decided modern ring that later appeared in the Securities Act of 1933,[173] provided that directors and promoters could be held liable for materially false or misleading statements even if they were made without knowledge.

Not until the Companies Act of 1900 were prospectuses required to contain specific disclosure of corporate information, including the subscription price, promoters' fees, and the interests of directors in any property to be acquired.[174] Thus, the Companies Act of 1900 firmly established the English philosophy of securities regulation as that of disclosure rather than supervision. The Stock Exchange and other City institutions were responsible for regulating the issuance of securities and ensuring the veracity of the contents of prospectuses. Subsequent companies acts strengthened the requirements for the issuance of securities.[175]

Until the enactment of the Financial Services Act, the primary statute dealing with the initial public issuance of securities was the Companies Act of 1948. It applied to companies not listed on the Stock Exchange or the Unlisted Securities Market.[176] Insider trading was covered by the Companies Act of 1980.[177] Secondary distributions and takeovers were governed by the Prevention of Frauds (Investments) Act.[178]

---

moters inserted waiver provisions in contracts and made oral solicitations rather than written ones. Also, the statute omitted to set out a time or place whereby the contracts could be examined! Kilbride, *supra* note 169 at 265. Until the passage of the Financial Services Act, regulation of securities was incorporated within the general corporate statutes.

171. Derry v. Peek, 14 A.C. 337 (1889).

172. 53 & 54 Vict., ch. 64.

173. 15 U.S.C. § 77a-aa (1987).

174. "Prospectus" was defined to include any written solicitation to the public, whether handled by the company or by promoters, and it had to be filed prior to issuance to the public with the Registrar of Joint Stock Companies. All directors had to sign the prospectus, and waivers of liability were prohibited. Companies Act of 1900, 63 & 64 Vict., ch. 48, §§ 30, 9, 10.

175. GOWER'S PRINCIPLES, *supra* note 122 at 362–63. 1 L. LOSS & J. SELIGMAN, SECURITIES REGULATION 6–7 (1989 Supp.).

176. 11 & 12 Geo. 6, ch. 38, §§ 37–51, 55.

177. Ch. 22, part 5, §§ 68–73.

178. 1939, 2 & 3 Geo. 6, ch. 16, replaced in 1958 by a new statute with the same name, 6 & 7 Eliz. 2, ch. 45.

Greater protection was afforded the potential investor in companies listed on the Stock Exchange or the Unlisted Securities Market. Since 1919 the Stock Exchange had listing requirements for the issuance of securities and had developed an effective and stringent process for the review of new issues listed on the Exchange.[179] However, the issuance of securities of more speculative unlisted companies occurred outside of the Exchange, subject only to the more lax provisions of the Companies Act.[180]

If an English company, unlisted on the Exchange or the Unlisted Securities Market, wished to issue shares for cash to the public, it had to comply with sections 37 to 55 of the Companies Act of 1948, which essentially required the company to publish a prospectus and send it to a companies registration office.[181] No official body would review the prospectus.[182] The theory of compliance was that promoters would fear criminal and civil liability if they breached the provisions of the Companies Act, or if the prospectus contained material misstatements.[183] However, the prospectus filing requirements only applied to public issues for cash. They had no application to the most common method of takeovers of one corporation by another, an exchange of shares.[184]

The Prevention of Fraud (Investments) Act

Early British securities legislation did not regulate the dealing in secondary trading, that is, the sale and distribution of securities previously issued.

---

179. MORGAN & THOMAS, *supra* note 65 at 208. If the issue was made without a prospectus, the advertisement giving information similar to that required in a prospectus had to be published in at least two London papers. Issuers had to comply with the Stock Exchange's Requirements for Admission to Listing set out in its Yellow Book, which included the publication and advertisement of a full prospectus. The Exchange's Quotation Department closely reviewed these prospectuses for accuracy.

180. *Id.* at 208. So long as a substantial number of companies issued shares outside of the Exchange, the Committee of the Stock Exchange's ability to check abuses was very limited.

181. GOWER I, *supra* note 101 at 130. If the issue was to be sold to the public generally as opposed to an existing group of shareholders, then the company would have to give additional information in Schedule 4 of the act. A foreign company issuing securities in the United Kingdom would be bound by Sections 417 to 423 of the Companies Act.

182. The Financial Services Act (FSA) has affirmed the authority of the Stock Exchange and now is a "Recognized Investment Exchange," in the listing of its securities. FSA §§ 142–157. The FSA also regulates investment securities and securities issued in the context of the takeover. These are regulated by the secretary of state and must be delegated. A recognized investment exchange would handle securities that seek to be listed. FSA §§ 158–171.

183. GOWER I, *supra* note 101 at 131.

184. Govt. Stocks & Other Securities Investment Co. v. Christopher, 1 W.L.R. 237 (1956), GOWER I, *supra* note 101 at 134.

The regulation of secondary distributions developed much more haphazardly, usually in response to a specific problem. For example, insider trading did not become a criminal offense in Great Britain until 1980 and enforcement thereafter was minimal.[185]

The principal statute regulating secondary distributions of securities was the Prevention of Fraud (Investments) Act (PFI) first enacted in 1939.[186] The PFI required any person conducting the business of dealing in securities to hold an annually renewable "principal's license" which was granted, refused, or revoked by the DTI. The DTI also promulgated rules for the conduct of investment business.[187] Exempted from the licensing regulations were, among other things, members of a recognized stock exchange, a recognized association of securities dealers, or individuals who dealt only incidentally in securities.[188] This exemption became a status symbol and was the norm for more-established investment businesses.[189] Also exempted from the PFI were "investment advisors" and "professional investors;" the latter term was construed broadly. One current source of resistance to the investor protection framework remains the view that the financial services world is divided between elite firms and those on the fringe, and the application of burdensome requirements of the Financial Services Act should apply only to the latter.

Section 13 of the statute made it a criminal offense to induce someone to enter into various types of investment contracts by making a dishonest statement, concealing material facts, or recklessly making any statement, promise, or forecast that was misleading, false, or deceptive.[190] Unlike the comparable situation in the United States, investors misled by such statements had no private right of action. The definition of what the term "investment contracts" covered was unclear.[191] Section 14 of the PFI made it a criminal offense to distribute or possess for the purposes of distribution unauthorized circulars (prospectuses) concerning the purchase or sale of securities.[192] However, the act did not define "circular."

---

185. Companies Act, 1980, ch. 22. Prosecutions were few and of low-level offenders. They were held in provincial courts. *See infra*, chapter 5, pp. 206–07.

186. The PFI was updated in 1958, 6 & 7 Eliz. 2, ch. 45. The 1939 act, 2 & 3 Geo. 6, ch. 18, was enacted to prohibit a number of frauds involving the sale of shares in worthless companies and the offering of facilities for specious margin transactions. Pimlott, *supra* note 3 at 143.

187. PFI Act, 1958, 6 & 7 Eliz. 2, ch. 45, §§ 1, 5, 7.

188. *Id.* at § 2. *See* GOWER I, *supra* note 101 at 34–38. Also exempted was a trustee in an authorized unit trust scheme.

189. Pimlott, *supra* note 3 at 145.

190. PFI Act, 1958, 6 & 7 Eliz. 2, ch. 45, § 13.

191. GOWER I, *supra* note 101 at 158–59.

192. PFI Act, 1958, 6 & 7 Eliz. 2, ch. 45, § 14.

The PFI largely was ineffective. While the DTI could revoke licenses, it could not suspend them for violations of the act. Revocation, in most cases, was too powerful a response to use. Moreover, because of a lack of effective enforcement, the criminal sanctions proved equally ineffective. There was little collaboration between law enforcement and regulatory authorities. No one person or office assumed responsibility for enforcement and focused upon such breaches.[193] A primary weakness of the existing regulatory system was its failure to treat alike those who conducted the same types of businesses. Enforcement was difficult and its perception capricious.[194]

The Control of Borrowing

Raising capital through the issuance of debt securities has long been controlled by the Treasury and more recently by the Bank of England through the Control of Borrowing Order of 1958.[195] Under this order, the Bank of England approved the timing of all sterling denominated financings over £3 million. In regulating access to British capital markets, the Bank considered the capacity of the market and the need to maintain orderly introduction of new issues. The Bank mediated capacity conflicts between private and foreign financings and the funding needs of the government.[196]

There existed, however, a more effective net of self-regulatory bodies that complemented the statutory framework. The Stock Exchange's "rule book" regulated disclosure requirements and the contents of prospectuses of issues listed on the Exchange.[197] The Panel on Takeovers and Mergers supervised the City Code on Takeovers and Mergers,[198] and the Council for the Securities Industry promulgated standards of conduct for investment firms.[199]

Professor Gower devastatingly identified the failings of the then existing regulatory system:

---

193. GOWER I, *supra* note 101, at 164–66, 174.

194. GOWER II, *supra* note 157 at 8.

195. S.R. & O. No. 1208. From 1946 until 1958, raising of capital required Treasury consent. Specific authorization was not required for issues by companies resident in the United Kingdom after 1958. *See* GOWER'S PRINCIPLES, *supra* note 122 at 345.

196. HAYES & HUBBARD, *supra* note 16 at 195–96.

197. COUNCIL OF THE STOCK EXCHANGE, ADMISSION OF SECURITIES TO LISTING (1984 and 1989 Supp.).

198. *See infra* ch. 5.

199. The Council for the Securities Industry had published a CODE OF CONDUCT FOR DEALERS IN SECURITIES (1980), GUIDELINES FOR PERSONAL DEALINGS BY FUND MANAGERS (1981), and RULES GOVERNING ACQUISITIONS OF SHARES (1981). Pimlott, *supra* note 3 at n. 30.

... complication, uncertainty, irrationality, failure to treat like alike, inflexibility, excessive control in some areas and too little or none in others, creation of an elite and a fringe, lax enforcement, delays, over-concentration on honesty rather than confidence, undue diversity of regulations and regulators, and failure overall to achieve a proper balance between Governmental-regulation and self-regulation.[200]

He concluded that there was no overall system of regulation of investments, but a series of piecemeal attempts. Nor was there logic to the method of regulation in a particular area. This lead to a blurring of the distinction between governmental regulation and self-regulation and between statutory and nonstatutory.[201] There was little disagreement with Gower's description of the problem. The solution was another question.

200. DISCUSSION DOCUMENT, *supra* note 165 at 137.
201. *Id.* at 53.

TWO

THE CREATION OF THE NEW REGULATORY FRAMEWORK

In all countries with financial markets some regulatory framework is necessary to assure investors and the public of the market's integrity, to proscribe improper behavior, and to create expectations of certain norms of conduct. Three approaches have been utilized in regulating financial services: the private ordering of markets by participants, termed self-regulation; a statutory system imposing direct state control; and a mixed system of regulation combining direct and self-regulation.

Financial markets tend to commence informally. Thereafter, participants develop their own rules. As a market develops, private control yields to some sort of governmental supervision. An exception to this pattern until recently has been the United Kingdom, where the financial markets, except for banks, for over three hundred years were regulated by private associations.

Cooperative regulation, a mixed system of statutory and self-regulation, is the approach of the United States and the United Kingdom. In the United States, the tilt has been toward the statutory side of the continuum.[1] In contrast, the U.K.'s new comprehensive regulatory regime would be primarily practitioner based, albeit with statutory backing.

The Functions of Regulation

Any analysis of regulatory reform requires a theory of the purposes of regulation and a framework for evaluating the effectiveness of the ap-

---

1. Over the last sixty years the SEC has exerted increasing authority over self-regulatory organizations (SROs). *See* Lipton, *The SEC or the Exchanges: Who Should Do What and When? A Proposal to Allocate Regulatory Responsibility for Securities Markets* 16 U. CALIF.-DAVIS L. REV. 527, 529 (1983) [hereinafter Lipton]. Not until 1975 was the SEC granted power to abrogate, add to, or delete from the rules of SROs. Pub. L. 94–29 *codified in* 15 U.S.C.A. § 785(c) (1981 and 1991 Supp.).

proach. At its most fundamental level, securities regulation is a political response to the failure of markets and institutions to serve the broader public interest.[2] Financial services regulation performs a number of often inconsistent and competing functions beyond imposing rules of business behavior. One is to require regulated firms to disclose information to the public about the products they sell. Disclosure and publicity encourage investors' faith in the integrity of the market. Another function is to provide legitimacy to the financial services sector after a period of fraud and scandal. Governmental intervention portends a new era. The imposition of a new framework of regulation is supposed to curtail the abuses of the past, or at least warn regulators earlier. Regulation also has a promotional aspect in which regulators and regulated have a comity of interest in furthering the commercial health of the industry. One way to accomplish that objective is to provide the public investor with more effective protection.

A third purpose of regulation is to protect the financial services sector itself from changes in the economic environment so as to enable the industry to adapt to new conditions. In the United Kingdom, a restrictive securities market was in danger of being bypassed by other financial centers, and the functional segmentation of English financial services firms made them too small to compete against larger American and Japanese conglomerates in an increasingly global market. Deregulation and the breakdown of barriers between different types of financial businesses permitted larger combinations of capital.

Regulation also involves standard-setting by providing guidance as to proper modes of conduct. The investor protection system under study represents a rationalization of the rules and behavior of the financial services sector.[3] A rational regulatory system leads to an increase in the predictability of actions. Under the system of informal self-regulation, ethical norms were shared. Absent were the detailed rules, procedures, and requirements of due process.[4] Transgressions from the norm were handled quietly on a case-by-case basis. The closer a legal order resembles a collection of idiosyncratic judgments, each tailored to a particular case and incapable of being subsumed under a limited number of identifiable rules, the less rational it remains.

---

2. R. Veitor, *Regulation Defined Financial Markets: Fragmentation and Integration in Financial Services*, WALL STREET AND REGULATION, 7, 52 (S. Hayes III ed., 1987).

3. We use rationalization in Max Weber's sense to reflect a system governed by rules and principles. Rights and obligations are determined by principles having some degree of generality and identifiability. *See* A. KRONMAN, MAX WEBER 73 (1983).

4. The Stock Exchange had a detailed set of rules relating to listing of securities. These rules were somewhat short on matters of due process. Members were bound to follow the rules on the basis of private contract. COUNCIL OF THE STOCK EXCHANGE, ADMISSION OF SECURITIES TO LISTING (Looseleaf).

Standard-setting is a method by which the public is protected from unethical members of the regulated community. Enforcement of the rules has deterrent, efficiency, and hortatory effects. Regulatory bodies obtain compliance with expected norms of behavior through the threat of penalties for rules violations or by promises of rewards through their licensing powers. Regulatory systems typically provide machinery for the settlement of disputes.

A regulatory system existing outside of a governmental structure may still exercise legislative powers through rule making, adjudicative functions through tribunals, and investigative and disciplining duties, which impose sanctions through private enforcement. However, this authority may be separate from the constitutional, judicial, and legislative nets that limit official behavior. The extent of due process procedures and protections and whether smaller, less influential participants in the regulated industry are discriminated against in favor of the dominant members becomes a concern.

In an organizational context, governmentally supervised regulation represents a shift from an informal, flexible system based on custom and shared norms to a legalistic one grounded in detailed rules. Compliance under a completely self-regulated system meant merely following the customs and practices of the industry. Acceptance of custom and ethical norms of behavior provided the glue that kept a totally private self-regulatory framework together.[5] The legal rational regulatory system requires more than acceptance. It demands expertise, which is largely in the hands of lawyers, compliance officers, and others with specialized knowledge.

The effective enforcement of legal rules assists the financial services industry by promoting comparable standards, professionalizing business practices, and policing marginal elements within the industry.[6] The danger of the implementation of a legal rational system is that it can be dominated by lawyers with a narrow technical focus, who by training and bureaucratic influence think small. Regulation expands as does bureaucratic tyranny. Enforcement becomes difficult and more expensive.[7] In such situations the regulated may attempt to evade the strictures of the regulatory system by

---

5. Cf. R. Karmel, *Securities Industry Self-Regulation—Tested by the Crash?* 49 WASH. & LEE L. REV. 1297, 1305 (1988) [hereinafter Karmel].

6. Two early chairmen of the U.S. SEC, James M. Landis and William O. Douglas, considered securities regulation a higher form of business management, for it raised ethical precepts, provided technical assistance to improve the operations of the constituencies affected, and resolved disputes. M. PARRISH, SECURITIES REGULATION AND THE NEW DEAL 181 (1970).

7. B. Manning, *Too Much Law: Our National Disease* 33 BUS. LAW. 435, 438–40 (1977).

3

50 *The Transformation of Threadneedle Street*

focusing upon the letter of the law rather than its spirit, or they may retreat to a less regulated center. Regulation also serves broader policy and societal purposes. Under the command of legislative direction, business strives for goals that it would not pursue on its own.[8] Regulation of financial services produces new standards and increases reliability and certainty in market transactions.

Professor Gower considered various regulatory approaches and concluded that a self-regulatory system, rather than a governmental structure, fit best within English historical and cultural traditions and reflected the political realities of the Thatcher government.

Self-regulation in Theory and Practice

Self-regulation has been defined by the Bank of England as:

> ... the realization by a group of individuals or institutions that regulation of their activities is desirable in the common interest, and their acceptance that rules for the performance of functions and of duties should be established and enforced. . . . In some cases the enforcement of such standards is entrusted to a committee of a profession or of practitioners in a market. Frequently, however, the enforcement of the regulations may be entrusted to an authority outside the group, which is or becomes customarily recognized and obeyed and which may also become the initiator of new regulations. . . . In both cases the system can be described as self-regulation, the first intrinsically so, the second by common consent.[9]

The English approach traditionally has been to devise methods of regulation that operated along less formalized lines than in other countries, with less emphasis on statutes and more on nonstatutory forms of regulation, especially self-regulation.[10] In the background of self-regulatory systems has been the specter of direct governmental regulation. This threat of statutory regulation has made some self-regulating bodies successful, such as the Takeover Panel. The Big Bang and the investor protection framework arose because of concerns that the Stock Exchange no longer adequately protected the public. Direct regulation is the usual response to inadequacies of private regulation.

---

8. Berk, *The "New" Social Regulation in Historical and Comparative Perspective*, REGULATION IN PERSPECTIVE 187, 196 (T. McGraw ed., 1981).

9. REPORT OF THE COMMITTEE TO REVIEW THE FUNCTIONING OF FINANCIAL INSTITUTIONS, THE WILSON REPORT SECOND STATE EVIDENCE, 1977, Cmnd. 7937, 89 para. 5.

10. *Id.* at para. 1072.

Advantages of Self-regulation

One argument in favor of practitioner-based self-regulation is that members of the affected industry can bring to bear their expertise, and in many cases expedition, not to be trusted of more-remote civil servants.[11] Informed practitioners are closer to regulatory problems and may be better able to solve them.[12] They know the texture of the regulated area as well as the limits, costs, and potential of regulation.[13]

Practitioner-based regulation is more likely to receive the support of the regulated because the regulators are assumed to know and sympathize with industry problems. Industry experts surely are more responsive to industry needs than governmental regulation which has several goals, of which the economic health of the industry is but one. The government's primary regulatory responsibility is investor protection through rule making and prosecution.[14] However, the supposed responsiveness of self-regulatory organizations (SROs) to change in the marketplace is not borne out by the Stock Exchange, which ignored the economic currents and preferred to turn inward rather than open itself to new competition.

Self-regulation by industry practitioners can be more inclusive and reach into more minute areas of conduct because industry experts can be deployed more efficiently. Expertise, however, can be used to thwart regulation if the SRO becomes a mere trade group. Industry experts can more easily resist effective regulation from government overview. Insulating an industry from government may lessen needed external supervision and control. To the contrary, self-regulation allows the government to deny responsibility for control it may or may not in fact exercise.[15] Self-regulation may remove some of the tensions between government agencies and industry.[16]

One of the more attractive arguments in favor of a self-regulatory system is that it is less costly than direct regulation. Moreover, the costs are borne

---

11. SEC, REPORT OF SPECIAL STUDY OF SECURITIES MARKETS, H.R. Doc. 95, 88th Cong., 1st Sess. pt. 4 at 722 [hereinafter SPECIAL STUDY].

12. Karmel, *supra* note 5 at 1306.

13. A special study of the securities markets by the SEC in 1963 addressed the advantages of industry expertise:

> The expertness and immediacy of self-regulation often provide the most expedient and practical means for regulation. By making those regulated actual participants in the regulatory process they become more aware of the goals of regulation and their own stake in it.

SPECIAL STUDY, *supra* note 11, pt. 5 at 197–98.

14. Karmel, *supra* note 5 at 1305.

15. Page, *Self-Regulation: The Constitutional Dimension*, 49 MOD. L. REV. 141 (1986).

16. Miller, *Self-Regulation of the Securities Markets: A Critical Examination*, 42 WASH. & LEE L. REV. 853, 858 (1985) [hereinafter Miller].

by the regulated and, ultimately, by industry users and customers. Because a self-regulatory system is practitioner-based, it is assumed regulators' expertise can be used to a cost-efficient advantage. There is a common belief that direct regulation will require a bloated bureaucracy to do the work of a leaner SRO. Undoubtedly, with self-regulation the government's cost is less. However, the duplication of agencies may actually increase the total expense of the regulatory system. The costs of regulation may produce a misallocation of resources within the financial system.

Even more important than the direct costs are the indirect costs of compliance. Because practitioner-based systems may be more intrusive than direct regulation, they may increase the total cost of compliance. Cost savings of self-regulatory systems are uncertain. Even SROs need professional bureaucracies. Because they are private organizations, their members are likely to be paid at the industry going rate, which is probably higher than the comparable civil service salary.[17]

What is probably true is that lower direct governmental expenditure of regulating an industry arouses less controversy from the public or political interests. On the other hand, industry sources of funding, which may not be able to pass all costs on to the public, may object to increases in expenditure even if the need is there. Practitioner-based budget raising is affected by the health of the industry. This became a problem with the U.K.'s investor protection framework in the post-October 1987 era of excess capacity and elusive profitability.

Other advantages of a self-regulatory system are its flexibility and informality. Because it is based upon freely entered into contracts with its membership, a self-regulatory system can amend its rules more easily without the necessities of public notice and other procedural steps. Flexibility permits self-regulators to react more quickly to changes in the economic environment than government regulation. Once a regulatory bureaucracy is in place, inflexibility develops. It is difficult to introduce change.[18] Direct regulation seems unable to react to changes in the markets quickly enough and seems less able to respond and provide solutions to industry problems such as overcapacity.[19]

Informality allows punishment to be meted out more quickly and quietly, and sometimes more efficiently. Government, because of its due process strictures, requires time, hearings, and appeals. There develops a resistance

---

17. Jennings, *Self-Regulation in the Securities Industry: The Role of the Securities and Exchange Commission*, 29 LAW & CONTEMP. PROB. 663, 677 (1964) [hereinafter Jennings].

18. S. HAYES, WALL STREET AND REGULATION 187 (1987).

19. Karmel, *supra* note 5 at 1305.

to changes in a regulatory pattern because of vested economic interests in its preservation. A self-regulatory system can better address the ethical practices of an industry than governmental regulation, which by nature proceeds through law and rule making to determine legal conduct. It may be impossible for government to regulate industry morals. Legal rules by definition determine the minimum parameters of conduct. Regulation of the ethics of an industry means a substantial degree of self-regulation.[20]

Self-regulation provides industry members with the incentive to cooperate, to develop shared norms for the common good of the industry, and to aspire to higher ethical behavior. Norms and rules developed by practitioners may be more psychologically acceptable to industry. The responsibility of participating in a system of self-regulation produces greater professional integrity and discipline.[21] Practitioners will operate from a higher standard and attempt to live up to the spirit rather than the letter of the law.

Direct government regulation is more often confrontational, whereas self-regulation is cooperative because regulators, industry, and the government share common goals of investor protection and industry prosperity.[22] SROs can mediate between the concerns of government, other interests that desire greater regulation, and the needs of the industry to be free from excessive fetters. Practitioner-based regulation can bring together disparate interests and constituencies to solve common problems and attain common goals.[23]

---

20. L. Loss, Fundamentals of Securities Regulation 615 (2d ed. 1988).

21. The Special Study of Securities Markets addressed some of the benefits of self-regulation:

> ... because participation by the regulated in the regulatory process tends not only to make regulation more palatable but also, by making the participants more aware of the goals of regulation and of their own stake in it, to make them individually more likely to discipline themselves and to render "voluntary" obedience.

Special Study, *supra* note 11, pt. 4 at 694; Financial Services in the United Kingdom: A New Framework for Investor Protection, 1985, Cmnd. No. 9432, 6, 13 [hereinafter White Paper].

22. Miller, *supra* note 16 at 859, n. 24.

23. Karmel, *supra* note 5 at 1299. William O. Douglas, when chairman of the SEC, said "Self-discipline is always more welcome than discipline imposed from above." He added:

> From the broad public viewpoint, such regulation can be far more effective [than direct regulation]. . . . Self-regulation . . . can be pervasive and subtle in its conditioning influence over business practices and business morality. By and large, government can operate satisfactorily only by proscription. That leaves untouched large areas of conduct and activity; some of it susceptible of government regulation but in fact too minute for satisfactory control; some of it lying beyond the periphery of the law in the realm of ethics and morality. Into these large areas self-government, and self-government alone, can effectively reach. For these reasons

Self-regulation can also be viewed as a reaction to the threat of government involvement. The fear of direct regulation often has served to energize self-regulatory bodies. If self-regulatory efforts prove unsatisfactory, statutory regulation follows. The Takeover Panel was successful because of clear intimations that if industry couldn't regulate changes in corporate control, government legislation would follow.

Problems with Self-regulation

SROs have a number of conflicting roles. They are expected to set standards and discipline their members so that investors will be protected. Because of the significance of the financial markets, private SROs serve public purposes and, in fact, assume public and governmental responsibilities. Their power to set standards and to mandate how business is conducted, to discipline, restrict entry, and expel, is in practice a delegation of state power to private bodies. This can lead to abuses of authority outside of the realm of due process.[24] Penalties for rule violators may be draconian or inadequate. SROs have a governmental aura without governmental accountability.[25] They have been analogized to quasi-public utilities in regard to their relation to the general public and thus require public oversight for many of the same reasons that railroads, power companies, and telephone companies do.[26]

Yet a totally private regulatory framework has little accountability to the public. Pressure for accountability to the public is a factor that led to an increased governmental role in the regulatory process. In addition, SROs have divided loyalties. As membership organizations, they have promotional responsibilities and function as mere trade associations. Inevitably, the pull of membership will overshadow loyalty and responsibility to the public or the investor.

It may be difficult for an SRO to discipline its membership, particularly if the member is part of the industry establishment as opposed to a fringe operator. In sheltered, smaller industries where regulators and members are known to one another, the fear of sanctions for violating ethical norms is

---

such self-regulation is by far the preferable course from all viewpoints.
Address before the Bond Club of Hartford, Connecticut, *quoted by* Jennings, *supra* note 17 at 678.

24. *See* Lowenfels, *A Lack of Fair Procedures in the Administrative Process: Disciplinary Proceedings at the Stock Exchange and the NASD*, 64 CORNELL L. REV. 375 (1979) and Poser, *Reply to Lowenfels*, 64 CORNELL L. REV. 402 (1979).

25. Karmel, *supra* note 5 at 1307.

26. SPECIAL STUDY, *supra* note 11, pt. 4 at 502.

an effective deterrent, but in large anonymous markets, such as in financial services, the industry regulators are as distant as government civil servants. The ethical and aspirational advantages of self-regulatory systems may not hold if the community is too diverse. In the financial markets of today the self-regulators who promulgate the standards tend to be less likely to violate them, while those on the fringe will treat such rules as they would government regulation. This creates an "us" versus "them" mentality that undermines the self-regulatory concept.

Almost all self-regulatory systems eventually require increasing governmental oversight. The correct balance between self and direct regulation is difficult to achieve. Left to themselves many SROs will tilt toward their trade association functions. There is a limit to the deregulatory vision, in that it does not respond to the way that SRO members act. It may assume a marketplace that does not exist.[27] At the other extreme, SROs may overregulate.

Restrictions on Competition, Interest Group Conflict, and Competition Between SROs

Self-regulatory organizations have strong anticompetitive tendencies because, at bottom, they are trade associations. SROs' regulation of their members' activities are essentially economic decisions.[28] Throughout their histories both the London and New York Stock Exchanges were cartels. The short-term interests of the Exchanges' dominant interest groups often sacrificed the greater health of the securities industry.[29] Absent government pressure, self-regulatory systems' reaction to changes in the economic climate are almost invariably to reduce competition.

Within SROs there often develops interest group conflicts in which the dominant elements promote their policies to the detriment of the membership and the public. Competition among interest groups within an SRO is complemented by competition against other SROs.[30] This competition in-

---

27. Rubin, *Deregulation, Reregulation and the Myth of the Market*, 45 WASH. & LEE L. REV. 1249, 1264 (1988).

28. Miller, *supra* note 16 at 867. The government's WHITE PAPER, which introduced the investor protection framework, admitted: "It is a risk of regulation by practitioner-based organizations that they may degenerate into rosy clubs or cartels," *supra* note 21 at 15, 23–24.

29. This has continued after the Big Bang. The Office of Fair Trading found that the International Stock Exchange had altered its rules in a way that had the effect of lessening competition. Searjeant, *Borrie condemns rule on reports of big share deals*, THE TIMES (London), May 1, 1990 at 25, col. 2.

30. Miller, *supra* note 16 at 878.

cludes developing innovative processes, trading new financial products, and seeking customers, and employees. SROs also seek to expand their regulatory turf by increasing authority and responsibility. This is an age in which new financial products regularly are developed, exchanges compete to offer them, and SROs strive to regulate those who trade in such instruments.[31]

Overregulation

A frequent criticism of self-regulatory structures is that they create complex, overlapping, duplicative nets that catch in their swath dissimilar firms and regulatory problems. Overregulation is not an inevitability, but all regulation tends to expand its scope as new problems arise and as self-regulators are pushed to improve the effectiveness of their efforts.

Self-regulating systems may be particularly intrusive because of ad hoc informal enforcement decisions that lack due process protections. This was the norm of private organizations such as the Stock Exchange. Modern securities regulation attempts to accomplish through detailed rules that which previously was done verbally or informally. The result is a web of legislation that cumulatively becomes much more comprehensive. Overregulation counteracts a purported advantage of self-regulation, its flexibility. SROs may overregulate because of the broad scope of authority granted to them. A prominent administrative law scholar has noted: "[t]he nostrum most approved by an administrator for the ills of a regulated industry is more regulation; to him it seems as obvious as to the doctors of another era that the remedy for unsuccessful bleeding is more bleeding."[32] This is less a problem of self-regulation versus a statutory system as it is one of organization and responsibility. Regulation seems to expand because once there are rules which pretend to completeness, new situations inevitably arise creating the need for additional regulations. It is extremely difficult to simplify rules, as it requires a retooling of knowledge, which leads to an increase in costs.

Lack of Regulatory Zeal and Resistance by Members

By the very nature of organization upon industry lines, SROs are industry dominated and have the attributes of trade associations. It is difficult

---

31. For example, in both the United States and the United Kingdom a primary battlefield has been over the trading of financial futures and equities. In the United Kingdom, the London International Financial Future Exchange has absorbed the ISE's options trading.

32. Jaffe, *James Landis and the Administrative Process*, 78 HARV. L. REV. 319, 322 (1964).

for them to avoid conflicts of interest in dealing with their members. The first criticism of self-regulatory enforcement is insufficient zeal.[33]

Almost by definition, SROs are captured by the industry they regulate. When issues arise the instinctive responses are less regulation rather than more, and allow the industry to work out the problem. The cheapest alternative often turns out to be the most favored despite the impact upon the public. Accompanying the general disinclination to regulate is resistance by firms to regulations promulgated by their SRO.

Because of self-interested behavior and the inability to enforce rules violations, self-regulatory systems give way to direct or mixed systems. The theory of self-regulation posits that the direct agency asserts its reserve power only if the SROs' initial exercise of authority is inadequate. This view, however, is inaccurate. The American experience has been that the Securities and Exchange Commission (SEC) not only has had to play more than this residual role, but has continually needed to expand its authority over American SROs.[34] Because the drift to self-interest is so strong, even in a mixed direct/self-regulatory scheme, the government agency must play an assertive initiatory role.

The Evolution of the U.K.'s Self-regulatory System: From the Gower Report to the Enactment of the Financial Services Bill

Gower considered the benefits and disabilities of direct governmental regulation and self-regulation as well as approaches to implementation. In suggesting possible lines of reform in a *Discussion Document*,[35] Gower offered five possible alternatives and proposed a system involving both governmental regulation and self-regulation. Enforcement could be improved by giving self-regulatory agencies the backing of statutory powers and

---

33. Miller, *supra* note 16 at 861. The SPECIAL STUDY noted:

> No business is eager for regulation . . . and it is only natural to expect less zeal for almost any aspect of the job on the part of a self-regulator than may be true of an outsider whose own business is not involved. To the extent that there are matters of degree the self-regulator, absent governmental oversight, is generally and understandably by self-interest to lean toward the lesser degree.

SPECIAL STUDY, *supra* note 11, pt. 4 at 695.

34. Lipton, *supra* note 1 at 528–29.

35. L.C.B. GOWER, REVIEW OF INVESTOR PROTECTION: A DISCUSSION DOCUMENT (1982).[hereinafter, DISCUSSION DOCUMENT].

keeping self-interest at bay, and by making such agencies subject to overall statutory control. The day-to-day supervisory function should be taken away from the DTI. The *Discussion Document* met with a mixed reception. In the City, Gower's proposals were thought to be interesting, but were dismissed as "academic."[36]

Throughout his efforts, Gower focused on a moving target. Developments arose that made some of his recommendations obsolete and increased the need for a comprehensive approach to securities regulation. By mid-1984 the focus of the regulatory debate concerned how to control conflicts of interest across the financial services sector in light of mergers of banks, brokerage houses, jobbers, and discount houses which had created huge financial conglomerates.[37] In addition, Parliament had enacted legislation to implement European Economic Community (EEC) Directives.[38]

Review of Investor Protection Report: Part I—The Gower Report

The *Review of Investor Protection*, the Gower Report, provided a foundation for the regulatory system that resulted. Its fundamental proposition was to recommend a system of self-regulation within a statutory framework subject to overall surveillance by the government. The Gower Report and the resulting legislation attempted to systematize and rationalize the legal regulation of an investment industry that had previously regulated itself on the basis of personal morality and trust.[39] Gower's approach rested

---

36. *Editorial*, J. Bus. L. 1 (Jan. 1986).

37. *See* Pimlott, *The Reform of Investor Protection in the U.K.—An Examination of the Proposals of the Gower Report and the U.K. Government's White Paper of January, 1985* 7 J. Comp. Bus. & Cap. Mkt. L. 141, 159–60 (1985). In April 1983 the DTI had published new, more stringent licensing regulations which tightened procedures for licensing and monitoring dealers under the Protection of Fraud (Investments) Act. The "Licensed Dealers Conduct of Business Rules" theoretically could have provided investors with greater protection, B. Rider, D. Chaikin, C. Abrams, Guide to the Financial Services Act 1986 15–16 (1987) [hereinafter Rider, Chaikin], but the PFI's limited scope made implementation of the new regulations difficult. L.C.B. Gower, Review of Investor Protection: Report Part I, 1984, Cmnd. No. 9215 at 1 [hereinafter Gower I].

38. The European Economic Community (EEC) issued three directives relating to corporate law which member states, including Great Britain, had to implement. These were part of a broader process of the harmonization of corporate law in the European community. *See* J.H. Farrar, Company Law, 598–608 (1985). They were (1) the directive on listing particulars to be published for the admission of securities to official stock exchange listing, 80/390 EEC; (2) the directive on the admission of securities to official stock exchange listing, 79/279/EEC; and (3) the directive on continuing disclosure of information relating to securities previously issued, 82/121/EEC.

39. White, *The Review Of Investor Protection—The Gower Report*, 47 Mod. L. Rev. 553 (1984).

upon finding the proper balance between self-regulation by independent self-regulatory associations, which would assume governmental functions, and governmental surveillance of such functions.

There are inherent tensions in every self-regulatory system. Self-regulation too severely restricted by the government would stultify its effectiveness, yet a professional body established to protect the interests of its members might not readily protect the public.[40] To achieve the necessary balance between governmental and self-regulation, Gower proposed that a governmental agency should be responsible for overall surveillance and residual regulation of the investment business, with day-to-day regulation left to self-regulatory associations (SRAs).[41] The government would directly regulate only those firms that were not regulated by one of the self-regulatory agencies. Every firm engaged in an investment business would have to register either with an SRA or with the government, or otherwise be guilty of a criminal offense.[42]

What type of governmental institution should oversee the SROs? The United States's system of an independent governmental agency, the SEC, which oversees self-regulatory agencies such as stock exchanges and the National Association of Securities Dealers, would seem a useful model, and in fact, was Gower's real choice.[43] Perhaps atypically for an academic, Gower exhibited substantial political realism, for he tempered his preference for a securities commission. For one reason, the Thatcher government desired to reduce the civil service and lower governmental expenditures.[44] Secondly, because of the City's hostility to the pre-Thatcher labor governments, there existed an almost irrational fear of governmental bureaucracy. There was a widespread and mistaken belief that the SEC was a mammoth, lawyer-dominated, overregulating bureaucracy, resistant to change.[45]

The advantages of a self-standing commission, thought Gower, would be that it would have more expertise, attract better people from the financial services sector, ensure a more flexible and businesslike approach, and be closer to the self-regulating agencies and the City. Also, it would be apolitical.[46] However, a commission would be cost-effective only if it had a sub-

---

40. GOWER I, *supra* note 37 at 5.

41. *Id.* at 11.

42. Gower was always vague as to the number of SROs and their relationship to the government. At one point he felt the DTI should be the government agency though it had been an inefficient and intermittent regulator under the previous regulatory system. At other times he suggested the Council for the Securities Industry, a trade association in the worst sense of the term. GOWER I, *supra* note 37 at 16.

43. *Id.* at 15.

44. *Id.* at 17, 20.

45. Pimlott, *supra* note 37, at 150.

46. GOWER I, *supra* note 37, at 17.

stantial amount of ongoing day-to-day work, which Gower did not foresee. Therefore, he recommended that the government role should be left to the DTI.

The SRO's rules relating to the conduct of business would be as stringent as those of firms that registered directly with the DTI. The SRO would have procedures and resources enabling it to effectively monitor and enforce observance of its rules and to investigate complaints against itself or members. The rules would not restrict competition unnecessarily.[47] The SRO's rules should provide for an appeal to an independent tribunal following a suspension, expulsion, or refusal to admit to membership, and recognized SROs should be empowered to apply to the courts for the issuance of subpoenas to compel attendance of witnesses and production of documents required in connection with disciplinary hearings.[48] If the principle of self-regulation was to survive, governmental oversight and review of SRO rules had to be sufficiently strong to ensure that they would be observed by investment businesses.

The number and structure of the envisaged supervisory agency changed substantially from Gower's report to the introduction of the Financial Services Bill. In 1978, at the urging of the Bank of England, a professional association for the financial services industry, the Council for the Securities Industry (CSI), was formed. The CSI was a voluntary body with general responsibility for nonstatutory aspects of supervision of the securities markets. Its function was to represent the securities industry in discussions with the government involving such matters as amendments to the Companies Acts.[49] The CSI's members included the Stock Exchange, City representative institutions such as the banking bodies, the Takeover Panel, and organizations representing institutional investors. The Takeover Panel became the executive arm of the CSI, and from 1983 the panel and CSI shared a joint executive. However, as Gower described it, the CSI was a fifth wheel on a carriage.[50]

---

47. *Id.*

48. *Id.* at 54–57.

49. Pimlott, *supra* note 37 at 157–59.

50. DISCUSSION DOCUMENT, *supra* note 35 at 137. Its weaknesses were its lack of administrative staff (only two full-time staff employees); infrequent meetings; a breadth of membership which made consensus difficult; and a lack of respect from its own constituency. In the new environment these would be terminal maladies. The DISCUSSION DOCUMENT seemed inconclusive on the government's role in the regulatory system. GOWER I argued the pros and cons of a self-standing commission versus a government agency such as the Department of Trade and Industry (DTI) assuming the role of government regulator. GOWER I, *supra* note 37 at 17–25, L.C.B. GOWER, REVIEW OF INVESTOR PROTECTION: REPORT PART II, 1985, Cmnd. No. 9125 at 5 [hereinafter GOWER II]. Gower thought the government's role could be left to the DTI. Subsequent to the publication of the DISCUSSION

As sound as Gower's recommendations might have been, they were the insights of an outsider and an academic. When it came time for legislation that would become an important part of the government's program, industry groups rather than the law professor took charge. Members of the City establishment reached consensus on the institutional structure, one that met the government's needs and the City's concern.

On May 23, 1984, both in reaction to the Gower Report and because of the need to move quickly in light of financial scandals, the governor of the Bank of England constituted a group of ten establishment figures from the City under the chairmanship of Martin Jacomb, deputy chairman of Kleinwort, Benson, Ltd., a leading merchant bank, to advise on the structure and operations of a self-regulatory system.[51]

In June 1984, Alex Fletcher, the Parliamentary Undersecretary for Corporate and Consumer Affairs, invited interested insurance professional associations to forward ideas for a self-regulatory structure that would cover the insurance industry. Thereafter, a second industry group, composed of insurance executives under the leadership of Marshall Field, chairman of the Life Offices Association, and general manager of the Phoenix Assurance Company, Britain's tenth largest insurance company, was formed to advise on the structure of self-regulation for the marketing of life insurance and unit trusts.

An astounding change had taken place in the reception to Gower's proposals. In January 1984 some had decried them as revolutionary. By the time of their discussion in the House of Commons on July 16, 1984, a minimalist solution unanimously had been rejected. The financial services industry was rapidly changing through a series of mergers and also in expectation of the Big Bang. The weaknesses of the existing regulatory scheme were so striking that both sides of the aisle agreed that the time was ripe for a major overhaul of the whole investor protection system. Events had surpassed Gower's one-time radical prescriptions.

The Governor's Advisory Group and the Association of Insurance Organizations reported before the end of August. Both focused upon the hierarchical structure of the new framework rather than on the nature and number of the SROs. Two nongovernmental boards were suggested. One

---

DOCUMENT, Gower discovered that political sentiment had shifted in favor of a self-standing commission and that "the role of Governmental regulator could [not 'should'] not be left to the Department." GOWER II at 5.

51. The individuals were called the Governor's Advisory Group with the wretched acronym (GAG) and were to advise within three months on the kinds of self-regulatory groupings that would cover securities activities, investment management, commodities, and financial futures, and which could garner sufficient industry support. GOWER II, *supra* note 50 at 6.

would cover dealings in investments, investment management, and investment advice. The other would cover the marketing of investment products such as life insurance and mutual funds.[52]

The Government's White Paper

As its title, *Financial Services in the United Kingdom: A New Framework for Investor Protection*, indicated, the *White Paper* presented with disarming clarity and simplicity an outline of the bill the government would introduce a few months hence. The government adopted Professor Gower's fundamental proposition that financial services should be regulated under the principle of "self-regulation within a statutory framework."[53] The stated objectives of the new framework for the protection of investors were efficiency, domestic and international competitiveness which would encourage innovation but not protectionism, confidence in the financial services marketplace by issuers and investors, and flexibility of the regulatory framework to react quickly to events and changes in the industry.[54]

The White Paper was also a political document, for underlying the new system was the Tory belief that market forces provided the best, most cost-efficient means of ensuring that the financial services industry would meet the needs of its customers. The marketplace would be efficient if there was full disclosure and encouragement of competition. Other goals underlying the reform were to provide a clearly understood set of general principles and rules; to focus the regulatory framework on the prevention of fraud; to enforce vigorously a simplified, albeit clear, investment law as a deterrence to fraud and malpractice; to promote as much as possible equivalence of

---

52. This proposed structure was revealed on October 17, 1984, when it was announced that a government WHITE PAPER would be published, as it was on January 17, 1985, shortly to be followed by legislation. This preempted Gower's original idea of preparing a draft bill. The second part of his report critiqued the WHITE PAPER.

53. WHITE PAPER, *supra* note 21 at 13. The objectives of the Financial Services Bill were in the words of the then Secretary of State for Trade and Industry, Norman Tebbit:

> ... The Government's task—in this sector as in others—is to create an environment in which [industry can respond effectively.] This is best done by allowing market forces to operate responsibly but without unnecessary constraints, in a way which promotes efficient and competitive business. A prerequisite for an internationally competitive industry is a clear regulatory framework within which practitioners and customers can deal with confidence.... This regulatory framework must be capable...of accommodating rather than stifling innovation. 72 Parl. Deb. H.C. (6th ser.) 89 (1984/1985).

54. WHITE PAPER, *supra* note 21 at 6.

treatment between products and services competing in the same market; and to encourage the concept that self-regulation offered a continuing and crucial contribution.[55] In short, the new framework provided minimum state interference with free enterprise. The system was practitioner-based, statute-backed, self-regulation.

Only duly authorized persons could carry on an investment business. All investment businesses would be covered except Lloyd's, the insurance association. Authorization could be obtained by membership in a recognized SRO. Presumably, only "fit and proper" persons would be authorized. Instead of a multitude of self-regulatory bodies reporting to the DTI as recommended by Gower, the White Paper adopted the City establishment's solution that the regulatory power should be transferred to two industry bodies: a Securities and Investments Board (SIB), which would cover the regulation of dealing in investments, investment management, and investment advice, and a Marketing of Investments Board, which would deal with the marketing of packaged insurance and mutual fund products. These supervisory organizations would be recognized by the secretary of state if they met certain criteria and would have statutory powers of authorization and regulation and would recognize the SROs.[56] The designated agencies would issue rigorous conduct of business rules, and the SROs would have equivalent rules for their members.[57]

The *White Paper* also dealt with the insurance industry. Life insurance policies would be treated as investments, and their marketing would be treated on the same footing as other prepackaged investments.[58] The government also promised to update and to bring under one statutory roof regulation of public issuance of securities, tender offers, and insider dealing. There would also be cooling-off periods, whereby an investor would have the right to rescind a transaction.[59] In contrast to the brevity and clarity of

---

55. *Id.*

56. *Id.* at 15.

57. The Secretary of State could require the revocation or amendment of rules of the boards of SROs if they were contrary to U.K. international obligations or unduly anticompetitive. If the boards did not live up to the statutorily prescribed criteria, the secretary of state could revoke and resume the delegated powers. The boards would report annually to the Secretary of State who would transmit the reports to Parliament. Finally, decisions of the board relating to authorization or discipline would be appealable to a newly constituted tribunal whose members would be appointed by the Secretary of State. *Id.* at 14–15. Because the board would exercise statutory and governmental powers even though a private body, its actions would be subject to judicial review. R. v. Panel on Takeovers and Mergers *ex parte* Datafin & Prudential Bache Securities 2 W.L.R. 699 (1987).

58. WHITE PAPER, *supra* note 21, at 9–10.

59. *Cf.* F.T.C Rules, Cooling-Off Period for Door-to-Door Sales, 16 C.F.R. § 429.1 (1988).

the *White Paper*, the Financial Services Bill was a dense, detailed document containing 166 clauses and 13 schedules and appendices. It would become even longer, if not more complex, before receiving the Queen's assent in November 1986.

In March 1985, a few weeks after the publication of the *White Paper*, the government invited Sir Kenneth Berrill to chair the Securities and Investments Board, the new organization that would be a designated agency under the new regime. Later, Sir Mark Weinberg was appointed chairman of the Marketing of Investments Board Organizing Committee (MIBOC). That October, the Council for the Securities Industry, an idea whose time had come and gone, dissolved.[60]

The SIB and MIBOC concluded that the consistency and effectiveness of the new regulatory system would be enhanced if responsibility for its operation were placed in the hands of a single authority rather than divided between the two.[61] In early 1986 the two boards merged. In retrospect the boards should have remained separate. The demand for equivalence of the SRO's rules resulted in one of Gower's criticisms of the old system being turned on its head: unlike investment businesses were now treated alike. One of the greatest difficulties was to make a distinction between wholesale and retail markets. The marketing of insurance or mutual funds is almost completely to retail markets. The sale of certain investments such as futures or Eurobonds are usually to sophisticated investors. Although the SIB has attempted to deal with different levels of investor experience, its rules are burdensome to professional investors. The separation of boards, as initially suggested in the White Paper, might have lessened the demands for exact equivalence of SRO rules, thereby enabling such rules to better meet the needs of differing financial services sectors.

---

60. Gower objected to the two board structure because their roles would be overlapping and conflicting. He felt that the role of the MIBOC would be relatively narrow in comparison with the SIB, i.e., regulating and marketing "pre-packaged" collective investments. Many firms and SROs would be subject to both boards. This is a problem that exists for many of the financial supermarkets who carry out investment businesses covered by more than one SRO. In that situation, one SRO becomes the lead regulator with sole responsibility for financial matters for a multiauthorized firm. *See* RIDER, CHAIKIN, *supra* note 37 at 36. The same procedure could have been adopted if there were two boards, thereby reducing overlap. Striking a responsive chord with the government, Gower added that dual boards would be wasteful and duplicative of human resources. GOWER II, *supra* note 50 at 9–10.

61. SECURITIES AND INVESTMENTS BOARD, REGULATION OF INVESTMENT BUSINESS: THE NEW FRAMEWORK 1 (1985).

The Politics of the Financial Services Bill

The City, more than most other sectors of the economy, represents the natural preserve of the Conservative Party. Few Labor votes are to be garnered there.[62] Most persons employed in managerial positions in the City are from the middle or upper-middle classes, or at least have such pretentions. The success of the City and the astronomical salaries and profits earned by some of those working there—many of whom are unseemingly young—contrast sharply with the problems of unemployment and economic decline in the north of England and the Midlands, the traditional sources of Labor votes. Conservatives, traditionally, have been solicitous of the City's problems.

Much of the City's resistance against a self-standing commission was a reaction against the arthritic, bureaucratic socialism of the Labor governments of the 1970s. However, the Tory victory of 1979 was not a return to power of the Conservative Party of landed gentry and old business. Rather, like its American counterpart, the Republican Party of the 1980s, it was the dawn of a new conservative age that attempted to unravel the sociopolitical framework of the postwar period.[63]

During the 1970s the Labor Party moved to the left, toward its trade union base and away from its intellectual center in the great universities. To Labor, the scandals in the City, the attempt to protect one's own, and the frequent inability to prosecute the perpetrators demonstrated the unacceptable face of capitalism. Class infuses British politics in ways unfamiliar to Americans. Parliamentary debate and committee discussions in the United Kingdom are much more vitriolic, partisan, and class-biased than their American counterparts. The problems of the City and the need to protect the small investor enabled Labor to score potent political points. Labor favored the Financial Services Act, but wanted a more traditional statutory means of regulation. Basically, it had three criticisms of the bill: (1) the SIB should be a self-standing statutory commission like the SEC, (2) several provisions impacting upon investor protection needed to be strengthened, and (3) additional private bodies, Lloyd's (the huge insurance market), and the Takeover Panel should be included under the jurisdiction of the SIB.

---

62. *See* Kynaston, *The Love Labour Lost*, FIN. TIMES, Oct. 19, 1991 at II, 1 (" 'Guilty Until Proved Innocent' is a typical City view of Labour; 'offensive parasites' has been Labour's retort.").

63. *See generally*, P. JENKINS, MRS. THATCHER'S REVOLUTION (1987).

The Powers of the Securities and Investments Board

Throughout the consideration of the bill, an ongoing question was how powerful would be the designated agency? How much would the balance tip towards the "statutorily backed" as opposed to the "private practitioner-based" body? The initial bill envisaged that the designated agency would be primarily an oversight body responsible for authorization of SROs and of investment businesses that sought direct authorization. Its investigative functions would be limited to individuals directly authorized by it. It would develop conduct of business rules for the SROs, but the SIB would have no authority to force an SRO to change its rules. It could revoke recognition or apply to a court for a rule change. In the government's view, the basic role of the SIB was not to enforce the enforcers; that is, ensure that the SROs were fulfilling their responsibilities. Prosecuting functions would remain with the DTI. The private practitioner-based SROs would be the day-to-day regulators.[64]

The Labor Party, on the other hand, wanted the SIB to "serve the new role as a powerful and comprehensive public watchdog." The government was forced to yield on several points that strengthened the designated agency. It had resisted the mention of the SIB in the bill on the grounds it would tip the scales toward the statutorily based side and lessen the ideological argument that the agency was a private body.[65] There was a certain *Alice in Wonderland* quality to this, for at this same time the SIB was working closely with the DTI and issuing proposed rules that would apply after it was designated.

Initially, the only investigatory powers given the SIB extended to investigate those who had been directly authorized by it to conduct an investment business. Individuals who were not authorized, but who were conducting an investment business, would be investigated by the DTI or the applicable SRO. Also, the agency was to have no prosecutorial powers, the government having yielded on the scope of investigatory and prosecutorial powers. Still, it was expected the SIB would refer serious offenses to a newly created Serious Frauds Office. The SIB would not become involved in investigating insider trading.

---

64. In the words of Sir Kenneth Berrill, the chairman of the SIB: "We set the standards in the rulebook then designate or recognize. Our main job is to be happy that they [the SROs] are doing their job...." Crable, *Enforcing the Enforcers*, EUROMONEY, Apr. 1987 on NEXIS.

65. However, when sued in an American court for damages arising from an SIB investigation, the SIB argued it was entitled to sovereign immunity because it is an agency or instrumentality of a foreign government. European American Corporation v. SIB Civ., no. 89–2333, 1990 Fed. Sec. L. Rep. (CCH), para. 84, 521.

Investor Protection

An ongoing debate ensued over the extent of protection to be provided to the individual investor. The government felt investors should take the responsibility for their own misjudgments and foolish investments, but recognized that *caveat emptor* was insufficient. For investors to have confidence in the market, measures were needed to reduce fraud and to encourage high standards in the conduct of investment business.[66] The scope of investor protection touched many areas. Issues were often resolved by the SIB's publication of rules. The disputes during the consideration of the enabling legislation set a tone for the new system. A major area of disagreement concerned the immunity of SROs from suit.[67]

More than any other issue, whether SROs should have immunity from suit, evidenced the influence of the City establishment in shaping this legislation. The bill as introduced said nothing about SROs' immunity.[68] If the ideological function of self-regulation by private bodies was to be maintained, why should there be immunity of an SRO from suit by a member or by an investor? The government suggested that the SROs and their boards

---

66. WHITE PAPER, *supra* note 21 at 7. Other disputes were in the insurance area concerning cold calling; the door-to-door sale of income and unit trusts, which at one time was prohibited; but through loopholes the door-to-door hawking of investments existed. Gower recommended that cold calling be banned except for life insurance, unit trusts for professional investors, and on existing clients.

67. Investor protection issues also included whether employee share shops should be covered under the legislation and in the insurance area whether the door-to-door selling of insurance and mutual funds should be permitted. A common method of encouraging worker share ownership was through the employee share shop where employees and their families could purchase and sell shares in the company for which the employee worked. The statute excluded such places from the legislation. The share shop is a place where companies' employees differed greatly in their sophistication and in inside knowledge of the company's prospects. Employees purchasing in share shops trade in a situation where they were most vulnerable, because of the familiar context of workmates and perhaps supervisors. Because there was the great possibility that some traders would possess inside information, employees needed someone to provide objective advice, for most would be the least experienced of investors. However, independent advice, argued the government, was more expensive for the corporation. Share shops were not covered by the legislation.

68. The Securities and Investments Board was given immunity so long as an action was not taken in bad faith, a phrase which presents a rather difficult burden of proof. Originally the SIB's immunity was located in schedule 7, paragraph 3 of the bill which dealt with qualifications of the designated agency. It is now Financial Services Act (FSA) § 187(3). Since the SIB was statutorily backed and exercised public functions, a fact even the government had to admit, immunity made sense. However, the SROs were different. They were private bodies that had no statutory backing, similar to the Stock Exchange, which had always been subject to suit from its members or investors.

could achieve voluntary immunity from suit by members through the contractual basis of the membership agreement.

However, the SROs and the City were ever mindful of the flood of securities litigation in the United States. They did not seem to notice that almost none of it was against the stock exchanges, the SROs in the American system of securities regulation. The International Securities Regulatory Organization (ISRO), a trade association and potential SRO formed in early 1986 which was composed of international traders of stocks and bonds, many of whom were American, vociferously favored immunity. Yet most of their business was with professional investors who could protect themselves rather than with members of the public. Potential members of SRO boards threatened refusal to join an SRO board without immunity, and several leaders of the newer SROs threatened to dissolve them if they were not given immunity.[69]

In the face of this intensive interest group lobbying, the DTI completely backed down. The government lamely explained that it was a "pragmatic decision to get the system of SROs off the ground and to get its members to serve."[70] It argued that SROs would be more willing to take disciplinary actions against their members if they did not have the threat of massive lawsuits in the background.[71]

The legislation provides that an SRO, its staff, and governing body are not liable to members or investors in damages for anything done or omitted in the discharge of their functions, except if they can be shown to have acted in bad faith.[72] Even the *Times*, hardly a critic of the City, felt that granting such broad immunity did not bode well for the future:[73] The government

---

69. Fleet, *U-turn on immunity is a worrying omen*, THE TIMES (London), May 9, 1986 at 32, col. 6.

70. *Id.*

71. SROs, the government claimed, would be held hostage and harassed by unscrupulous members who would tie up investigations in litigation. An award of damages against an SRO would be disruptive to the whole system. The fear of litigation would lead SROs down the road to the most minimal regulation. Standing Committee E. Parl. Deb., 173–5 (Feb. 11, 1986). Nothing of the sort had occurred with the Stock Exchange, but the government maintained that the experience of the Stock Exchange was not relevant, because of the internationalization of the securities markets and the coming of the litigious Americans. Even acknowledging the validity of these arguments, the government granted more civil immunity under the statute than necessary. Interestingly, Lord Denning, former Master of the Rolls, who extended the concepts of the negligence to previously immune institutions throughout the commercial world, supported the immunity provision on grounds of public policy, the same justification he used to extend negligence concepts. Fleet, *Let battle commence over SRO immunity*, THE TIMES (London), July 7, 1986 at 17, col. 6.

72. FSA § 187(1)(2).

73. Fleet, *U-turn on immunity is a worrying omen*, THE TIMES (London), May 9, 1986 at 21, col. 8. During its consideration in Congress in 1933 and 1934, the New York and

needed the SROs more than the City, which gave the latter strong bargaining power, and it was being bullied.

The Eurobond Markets and Stabilization

Throughout the drafting and consideration of the bill ran a debate over whether and how to include the international securities industry and the Eurobond market in the legislation. These groups were incorporated into the regulatory net, but the final act took into account the importance of the market and the ease with which such markets could move to another financial center.[74] The special rules for Eurobonds are regulated in principle through designation of the Association of International Bond Dealers (AIBD) as "an overseas exchange." Members of AIBD had to join The Securities Association, an SRO that supervises the conduct of business of international Eurobond firms. The fit of the Euromarkets has not been without strain.

On the unregulated Euromarkets, securities firms regularly stabilized the price of new issues they underwrote by purchasing the new bonds or shares themselves.[75] Underwriters made competing bids for new securities so as to hold up their prices for the first few weeks after issuance. This facilitated the orderly distribution of securities issued by preventing a decline in price.[76]

The bill initially provided that underwriters could stabilize the price in Eurobonds, but that any other attempt at stabilization would be a criminal offense. ISRO and the Stock Exchange lobbied to allow stabilization of all international equities; otherwise, they claimed, they could not manage to underwrite large international issues. ISRO claimed that without an exemption for international securities it would not be able to remain in London. The SIB supported the amendment so long as small investors were protected.

The government compromised in favor of the financial services industry. The statute allows stabilization for all issues if the SIB makes rules that ensure protection of small investors.[77] The SIB's rules provide for when and

---

other stock exchanges and their members were uncompromising in their opposition to the Securities Act of 1933 and the Securities Exchange Act of 1934.

74. S.L. Hayes & P.M. Hubbard, Investment Banking: A Tale of Three Cities 204 (1990).

75. Where illegal, stabilization is known by the less euphemistic terms, "price rigging" or "market manipulation." Stabilization was not permitted with secondary distributions of domestic securities.

76. Rider, Chaiken, *supra* note 37 at 96.

77. FSA §§ 48(2)(i), 48(7).

for how long stabilization must occur and mandate disclosure to investors that the price of a security might be stabilized. Still, investors, particularly unsophisticated ones who would be purchasing secondary distributions as opposed to new issues of Eurobonds, might be better protected if prices could fall to their market level.

The stabilization issue portended a problem after the act became effective: the need to distinguish between professional investors who did not need all of the safeguards that members of the investing public required. As financial services products became more sophisticated, many participants in highly specialized markets could protect themselves. The Financial Services Act and the rules promulgated by the SROs initially failed to keep this distinction in mind.

Lloyd's

Another controversy was whether Lloyd's, the insurance market, should come under the new regulatory framework. Lloyd's is the world's premier center for marine and aviation insurance and the largest reinsurance market.[78] It began in the late sixteenth century in a coffee shop operated by a man named Lloyd where ship insurers met to conduct business. Now it is an association of thousands of individuals.

Aside from staff, there are four categories of individuals connected with Lloyd's. First are the "names," individuals who put money up for the risks taken and are organized into nearly five hundred syndicates.[79] Second are the underwriting agents who manage the syndicates. Their task is to supply names, of which there are thousands, to syndicates to enable the latter to underwrite policies and the former to make money when the insured condition does not occur. Third, there are the underwriters who assess the risks, set the premium rates, and sign the policies. Finally, there are the brokers, who place the business with the syndicates.[80] Historically, these four

---

78. H. MCRAE & F. CAIRNCROSS, CITY CAPITAL 163 (1985) [hereinafter MCRAE & CAIRNCROSS]. Reinsurance involves a contract under which one insurer agrees to indemnify another for loss sustained under the latter's policy of insurance period. Insurance companies that insure against losses arising out of fire or other casualties seek to minimize their exposure by sharing risks with other insurance companies. Thus, when the face amount of a policy is very large, the insurance company who has written the policy will turn to Lloyd's to get others to participate.

79. Names must have a net worth of £100,000. In 1986 there were nearly 30,000 names. *Lloyd's of London: A name at risk*, ECONOMIST, Nov. 22, 1986 at 85. Most have no other connection with Lloyd's. They are like general parties in the syndicates who share in profits and are subject to unlimited liability for losses. The syndicates usually specialize in a particular area of insurance—aviation, for instance.

80. MCRAE & CAIRNCROSS, *supra* note 78 at 166–67. Underwriters may also be names. Some work only for a salary and commission from underwriting agents.

categories have overlapped. The same individuals served in several capacities, which led to conflicts of interest.

Underwriting agents are the link between the syndicate and the names. There are twelve large underwriting agencies. Most of the underwriting agencies were owned by the large brokering firms. Thus, the underwriter who wanted to insure a risk at the highest premium allowable was in conflict with his role as the broker who sought the lowest possible premium for his client. For twenty years the relationship between the underwriting agencies and their names had been criticized. Brokers might pass off the worst risks onto the syndicates they controlled.[81] Names received insufficient information about the risks they were taking. The underwriting agencies, which were owned by brokers who put together the syndicates, received up to 25 percent of a syndicate's profits in a good year and passed off all losses to the names in a bad one.[82]

Lloyd's was an SRO. While the insurance business was regulated by the DTI, until 1982 the governing body of Lloyd's, the Lloyd's Committee, governed the organization. Commencing in 1975, public scandals including Lloyd's names, greatly tarnished the reputation of the City and generated much of the momentum for the legislation that resulted in the Financial Services Act.[83]

Self-regulation was increasingly ineffective as a means of controlling Lloyd's huge membership. In reaction, Lloyd's appointed a committee of representative names headed by Sir Henry Fisher, a former judge. The Fisher Report concluded that the Lloyd's Committee should have outside members and greater powers over Lloyd's members. It also wanted the ties between brokers and underwriting agencies served.

The Bank of England intervened and required the appointment of a chief executive who would serve on the renamed governing body, the Lloyd's Council. The government concluded that parliamentary backing was needed. This resulted in the Lloyd's Act of 1982.[84] Even after the act be-

---

81. In 1970 the Cromer Report anticipated the relationship between the underwriting agencies and their names. Criticism of Lloyd's practices usually results in the appointment of a committee that publishes the inevitable report which leads to some reforms.

82. MCRAE & CAIRNCROSS, *supra* note 78 at 168.

83. The scandals are described in M. CLARKE, REGULATING THE CITY 53–89 (1986) [hereinafter CLARKE].

84. Insurance Companies Act, 1982, ch. 50. The main objects of the bill have been described as divestment, divorce, immunity, disclosure, and regulation. Divestment of ownership of brokers, underwriters, and managing agencies by the same organizations was required. Divorce referred to the requirement that managing agents who recruited names for syndicates could not themselves operate syndicates. Therefore, managing agents could provide objective advice. Immunity referred to freedom from suit from members of Lloyd's to sue the new governing body, the council. This would ensure the council's boldness, an ar-

came effective in 1983, new scandals strained the organization. When a leading brokerage firm was taken over by an American broker, £55 million was found to be missing from the accounts. In another scandal, one of the leading brokerage firms, Minet, which owned several underwriting agencies, arranged for reinsurance with offshore agencies who diverted £40 million abroad. One of the pillars of Lloyd's establishment, Minet's chairman, John Wallrock, was discovered to be part of the scheme.

Gower had pointed out that the underwriting agents of Lloyd's clearly undertake an investment business in seeking and advising names in the underwriting of syndicates. While some of the managing agents took out licenses from the PFI, most did not.[85] The *White Paper* treated underwriting agents as solicitors, accountants, or other professionals who should be regulated by the Lloyd's Council unless their investment business was a significant part of their activities.[86]

Lloyd's, however, was excluded from the bill. Gower disagreed with this result as did the Labor Party. Lloyd's and the government argued that it was an insurance business regulated by the DTI and, therefore, it should be excluded. Sir Kenneth Berrill stated that the SIB did not have the resources to supervise Lloyd's: "We need to keep the speed of responses of the Takeover Panel and with Lloyd's. The SIB would be taken into the realm of general insurance. It has to stop somewhere. The job would be too big."[87] The government also felt that because Lloyd's had set up a new regulatory structure in 1982, they should allow that structure to prove itself.

In January 1987 a committee of inquiry headed by Sir Patrick Neill concluded that while it knew of no professional or equivalent organization that accomplished such a major program of reform in such a short time, Lloyd's had still not achieved standards of investor protection for its members comparable to those mandated in the Financial Services Act. The balance of initiative still lay too much in the hands of market professionals. The Neill report offered a series of recommendations that would make Lloyd's more like an SRO except it was exempted from supervision of the SIB.[88]

To Labor, Lloyd's symbolized self-regulation that did not work: therefore, it was a particularly odd candidate for special treatment. Countering

---

gument that was to reappear with the SROs. Disclosure referred to requirements that members' interests and accounts of syndicates had to be disclosed. Regulation referred to the new administrative structure of Lloyd's. In addition to the sixteen members of the old Lloyd's Council, the act added eight external members and four nominated by the Bank of England, one of whom is the chief executive. CLARKE, *supra* note 82, at 86.

85. GOWER I, *supra* note 37, at 31; Gower II, *supra* note 50 at 17.

86. WHITE PAPER, *supra* note 21 at 10.

87. Crable, *Enforcing the Enforcers*, EUROMONEY, Apr. 1987 on NEXIS.

88. Bunker, *The Neill Report on Lloyd's*, FIN. TIMES, Jan. 23, 1987 at 10. Bunker & Riddel, *Lloyd's Ordered to Reform Rules or Face Legislation*, FIN. TIMES, Jan. 23, 1987 at 1.

the argument that Lloyd's was an insurance business and already regulated by DTI, Labor pointed out that almost every other institution covered by the Financial Services Act was regulated by some other agency. Labor interpreted the 1982 Lloyd's Act as an assertion of self-regulation which in and of itself was no longer enough, for it had proved inadequate to protect investors. The Financial Services Act exempts Lloyd's.[89]

The intervening years have not been good ones for Lloyd's. New alleged scandals, catastrophic losses estimated at more than three billion pounds in the three years to 1990, a shrinking membership base, a liquidity crisis, and successful litigation by members may bring fundamental change in the way Lloyd's operates.[90]

The Passage of the Financial Services Act

Ironically, despite constant attention by the press and minute analysis by affected interest groups, the impact of the new system on the City and the public was an unknown. By the time of its passage, the bill had expanded to 212 clauses and 17 schedules and appendices. It was subject to over one thousand parliamentary amendments, six hundred of them added in the waning minutes of consideration in the House of Lords. These were considered in three days at the beginning of October 1986.[91]

The reason for the rush at the end was that groups and organizations suddenly realized that they would be affected by the new framework. For instance, in July 1986, corporate treasurers discovered they conducted an investment business when they bought and sold securities for their company's account. When they mobilized a protest, the government at the last hour exempted them.[92] Many of the flaws in the bill were pointed out only at the last minute. Labor's spokesman for the bill, Brian Gould, stated the Labor view of the Financial Services Act:

> We continue to regard the Bill as a missed opportunity. . . . [The Bill] is defective, not only in the myriad small ways . . . but in major matters. It does not

---

89. FSA § 42.

90. The most significant proposed change would be the creation of a fund to mitigate the problems associated with unlimited liability of syndicate members for losses. In 1992 still yet another committee recommended that names have better access to syndicate information, the right to approve larger syndicate transactions, and greater rights of governance and access. Sir David Walker, outgoing SIB Chairman headed an inquiry to consider allegations that working names, those employed by Lloyd's agents and brokers, have benefitted at the expense of outside names who were placed in poorly performing syndicates. *See, Lloyd's: A Route Forward*, (1992) [the Rowland Committee Report]. Lapper, *Evolutionary change rather than radical overhaul*, FIN. TIMES, Jan. 16, 1992 at 8. *Financial Times Survey: Lloyd's of London in World Insurance*, FIN. TIMES, Mar. 30, 1992 at IV.

91. *After Big Bang, watch out for Guy Fawkes day*, ECONOMIST, Oct. 25, 1986 at 85.

92. FSA, sched. 1, para. 23.

cover the ground that it should cover. The exclusion of Lloyd's is a blot on the Bill and the government. Failure to put in place a proper independent statutory commission will be regretted by the government and already is being regretted by the City. Because we believe that those failings are important, we shall return to them when we return to power. . . . [93]

The passage of the Financial Services Act demonstrated that there was a consensus for change, but the implications of the Big Bang and the framework for investor protection were not fully understood. Only after the new system was in place and the costs of compliance with the SIB's massive rule book were realized did the resistance to regulatory efforts emerge.

---

93. 99 Parl. Deb. H.C. (6th ser.), 628, June 12, 1986.

THREE

THE SYSTEM OF
INVESTOR PROTECTION

The Regulatory Framework

The Financial Services Act (FSA) initially grants to the Secretary of State for trade and industry the authority to regulate investment businesses. This includes, the power to authorize, which allows investment businesses to open their doors; oversight of self-regulating organizations and investment markets; and broad powers of investigation and prosecution. Many of these powers have been transferred to a designated agency, the Securities and Investments Board (SIB).[1]

Compared to American securities legislation, where discrete statutes segment the regulation of the financial services industry, the swath of the Financial Services Act is quite broad. The statute regulates the sale of stocks and bonds, life insurance, mutual savings banks, collective investment schemes such as mutual funds, limited partnerships, and investment syndicates, and all other investment businesses. It covers the marketing of investments including advertisements in newspapers. It also restricts "cold calling," that is, unsolicited calls or visits to potential investors. All those involved in financial services must be authorized or face civil or criminal penalties.

There are extremely detailed conduct of business rules that cover broker-customer relationships, capitalization requirements, segregation of funds and the operation of clients' accounts, indemnity rules, and client compensation. Firms are required to maintain adequate financial resources, to implement sufficient compliance and recordkeeping systems, and to regularly

---

1. Financial Services Act, 1986, ch. 60, § 114 [hereinafter FSA].

notify regulatory bodies of changes in position. The act creates broad investigatory and enforcement powers and also provides due process protections to firms, employees, and investors. The statute provides the basis for international cooperation and reciprocity with foreign regulators.

Still, areas of financial regulation remain outside of the new regulatory framework or are only mentioned tangentially. Insider trading enforcement remains largely with the DTI. The Stock Exchange's rules still govern the official listing of securities, that is, the bringing of new issues to market and the prospectus requirements for those securities.[2] Transactions in the wholesale money market by institutions listed by the Bank of England and Lloyd's, the reinsurance association, remain outside of the new framework. A private body, the Takeover Panel, regulates mergers and tender offers through an industry code, the City Code on Takeovers and Mergers. Investigation and enforcement responsibilities are divided among several departments.

The Financial Services Act created three layers of authority over the financial services industry. At the top are the DTI and the Bank of England. At a second level is the SIB, a private agency to which has been transferred specified powers from the DTI. At the third tier are four SROs, nine professional bodies, six investment exchanges, and two clearinghouses. These organizations, private functionally organized industry bodies, directly monitor the activities of their members. The investor protection framework requires that all financial services firms must be authorized to engage in "investment business."

"Investments" and "Investment Businesses"

No firm can engage in an investment business unless it is authorized to do so by the SIB or by an SRO after a review of its background. "Investment business" means the business of engaging in one or more of the activities listed in Schedule 1 of the statute.[3] The definition of "investment business"

---

2. The DTI is responsible for the offering requirements of unlisted securities.

3. FSA § 1(2). The schedules and the notes accompanying the schedules have statutory force. A. WHITTAKER & G. MORSE, THE FINANCIAL SERVICES ACT 1986 A GUIDE TO THE NEW LAW § 2.03 (1988).

The definition of "investments" sets a boundary to the regulated area. Investments include shares in a company, debentures, certificates of deposit and other instruments creating or acknowledging indebtedness, government and public securities, warrants, options or other investments entitling the holders to shares, certificates representing securities (such as ADRs), units in a collective investment scheme such as a unit trust, financial and commodity futures if made for investment purposes, contracts for differences such as options or stock exchange futures, certain long-term insurance contracts, and rights and in-is broad. It ranges from full-service brokerage activities to the part-time postmaster in a candy store who sells national savings certificates.[4]

Authorization

Central to the new regulatory system is the requirement that no person can carry on an investment business unless authorized to do so or exempt from such authorization.[5] The justification for the system of authorization

---

terests in investments such as a beneficial interest in an investment trust. FSA § 1, schd. 1. The definition of "investments" is broad enough to include collective investment schemes in race horses, trees, and theater syndicates. Goldsmith, *Fun Things Caught in the Act*, THE TIMES (London), Feb. 20, 1988, at 29, col. 6. *Cf.* Reves v. Ernst and Young, 494 U.S. 56 (1990); Securities Act of 1933, § 2(1), 15 U.S.C.A. § 77b(1); T. HAZEN, THE LAW OF SECURITIES REGULATION, § 1.5 (2d ed. 1990).

Excluded from the definition of investments are trade debts in the normal course of business, checks, bills of exchange, bank notes, currency, letters of credit, and futures contracts of a commodity or property if made for commercial rather than investment purposes where one of the parties intends to take delivery for use in the party's business within seven days. FSA, § 1, para. 8. The definition does not include the outright purchase of tangible property such as land, antiques, and other "collectibles," although participating rights in such property might be an investment as a collective investment scheme. I. PALMER'S COMPANY LAW 434 (C.M. SCHMITTHOFF, ed., 1987).

4. A person carries on an investment business if, by way of business, he engages in: (1) dealing in investments, such as buying, selling, subscribing for, or underwriting investments or offering to do so either as a principal or agent; (2) arranging deals in investments, such as making, offering, or agreeing to make arrangements with a view to another person's buying, selling, subscribing for, or underwriting a particular investment; (3) managing investments, such as managing or offering or agreeing to manage assets belonging to another person, if those assets consist of or include investments or could be turned into investments at the discretion of the manager; (4) advising on investments, such as offering or agreeing to give advice as to the purchase, sale, subscription for or underwriting of investments or as to the exercise of rights conferred by investments; or (5) establishing, operating, or winding up collective investment schemes, including acting as a trustee of such investments. FSA, schd. 1, Part II, §§ 12–16.

Excluded from the definition of investment business are buying and selling investments for one's own portfolio; dealings between financial institutions in the same corporate group or sales of goods or services where that is the seller's main business and the investment activity takes place in connection with the sale of the goods or services; acting as a trustee; dealing in investments in connection with an employees' stock ownership or stock option plan; advice given in the course of professional practice of noninvestment business; advice given in a bona fide newspaper or periodical as opposed to an investment newsletter or tip sheet: dealings involving corporate treasury functions in noninvestment businesses; and the sale of shares in certain close corporations. This is an extremely complicated area which will probably develop a rich administrative and judicial common law. FSA, schd. 1, para. 17–25. B. RIDER, D. CHAIKEN, C. ABRAMS, GUIDE TO THE FINANCIAL SERVICES ACT 1986, 53–62 (1987).

5. FSA at § 13.

is that allowing only fit and proper persons to engage in investment businesses will be the most effective and cost-efficient way to prevent abuse of
investors. There are severe criminal and civil sanctions for operating an unauthorized investment business.[6] While authorization may be obtained in
seven different ways, the most important is through membership in an SRO
recognized by the SIB.[7]

Exempt from authorization requirements are the Bank of England and
recognized investment exchanges and clearing houses.[8] Partially exempt
with respect to insurance-related activities are members of Lloyd's. Certain
insurance salespeople, termed appointed representatives, are exempted
from the statute with respect to investment business carried on by them as
representatives of an insurance company.[9]

The Secretary of State required investment businesses to apply for authorization to an SRO or the SIB by February 27, 1988 ("P Day"). Because
of the expected deluge of applications, the secretary of state allowed firms
that had applied but were not yet processed by the SRO to receive interim
status. Those that did not apply by "P Day" would not receive interim status and had to cease doing business. April 29, 1988, was selected as "A
Day," when companies would be conducting business illegally if they had
not been authorized or received interim authorized status.

---

6. *See id.* §§ 4, 5. Criminal sanctions include up to two years in jail, civil sanctions include agreements being unenforceable and voidable at a court's discretion and the SIB seeking injunctive and restitution orders *Id.* § 6.

7. *See id.* at § 7(1). Another approach is direct authorization from the SIB, which has
been discouraged. Only 127 of the 35,000 authorized investment businesses chose this
route. SECURITIES AND INVESTMENT BOARD, ANNUAL REPORT 1987/88, 65 (1988) [herein-
after SIB ANNUAL RPT. 1987/88]. A third route to authorization is through membership in
a recognized professional body such as the Law Society, which regulates solicitors. Authorized status will be granted to a national of an European Economic Community country
who is authorized in that country provided the authorization standards are equivalent to
tɪe United Kingdom's and the person has no permanent place of business in Great Britain.
FSA § 31. Other methods of authorization include EEC open-ended investment companies
or other collective investment schemes. *Id.* at § 86. Insurance companies and friendly societies are automatically authorized pursuant to specific legislation applying to each type
of organization. *Id.* at §§ 22, 23.

8. FSA §§ 35–36, 38.

9. *See id.* at § 344. An appointed representative is a person who is employed by an authorized person ("his principal") under a contract for services. An example would be a
self-employed life insurance agent who sells insurance under contract for a particular life
insurance company. This means that an appointed representative is brought within the
scope of the principal's authorization and the principal assumes liability for the agent's
activities. The appointed representative's exemption is limited to the activities of the principal and the terms of the agent's contract. Also exempt from obtaining authorization are
several varieties of probate judges and similar officials who manage funds. FSA § 45.

At first, firms ignored the deadlines. Then came a huge rush to file for interim authorization. By "A Day" one-half of the investment businesses that had applied for authorization to an SRO had not had their applications fully processed. Yet, by June 30, 1988, 31,000 of the 35,000 investment businesses were fully authorized.[10]

To some extent the authorization process worked as a disinfectant on the financial services sector. Over six thousand firms commenced the authorization process only to disappear when further information was requested or firms were rejected.[11] Only a very few appealed their rejections. One must assume that at least some fringe operations were excluded from the industry.

Tiers of Authority

The ultimate responsibility for the new system of investor protection lies with the Secretary of State for trade and industry, the government minister who oversees the DTI. The Secretary of State has transferred many but not all of his powers under the Financial Services Act to the SIB. He can resume all or any functions transferred.[12] In consultation with the governor of the Bank of England, the Secretary of State appoints and may remove the chairman and other members of the SIB's governing board. In 1992 the Treasury assumed responsibility for overseeing EEC and other international obligations in the securities area and for coordinating cooperation with other countries in the areas of law enforcement and multilateral securities regulation.[13]

The DTI is primarily responsible for investigation and enforcement activities under the Financial Services Act. The Secretary of State appoints all members to the Financial Services Tribunal. Most importantly, the DTI sets the tone and texture of the SIB. When the first chairman of the SIB came under criticism for the complexity and rigidity of the SIB rules, Lord Young, then Secretary of State, chose not to reappoint him. The message, although

---

10. SIB ANNUAL RPT. 1987/88, *supra* note 7, at 65.

11. Riley, *A Birthday for Security Rules*, FIN. TIMES, May 2, 1989 at 19, col. 1.

12. FSA § 115. The check on the DTI, a partisan government agency, is that an order resuming transferred functions can be annulled by Parliament.

13. The DTI has retained the right to extend or restrict exemptions of investment businesses from authorization. It grants certificates of authorization to individuals authorized in other countries, if such foreign authorization provides equivalent protections that English investors would have from a U.K. authorized firm. The department can also grant exemption to certain advertisements from the restrictions on advertising. It has the ultimate authority to approve the SIB's rules and guidance communications. Guidance communications are similar to IRS letter rulings.

unspoken, was that the regulators had to be more flexible and sympathetic to industry members. The role and authority of the SIB then shifted direction.[14]

The Bank of England has an indirect yet central role at the apex of the regulatory system. It had a crucial, albeit behind the scenes role in the developments that led to the Big Bang. The Bank was reluctant to take a more formal role in the new regulatory framework for two reasons: one, the infrequent use of its influence, uttered informally, made its presence more powerful than an ongoing supervisor's, and two, its desire not to be perceived as the lender of last resort for failing securities firms.[15]

The Financial Services Act tries to keep the regulation of banks separate from other investment businesses.[16] It exempts from its authorization requirements institutions listed by the Bank of England as eligible to participate in the money markets in certain permitted transactions.[17] However, the growth of financial conglomerates, the development of nonbank banks, and the breakdown of the boundaries between investment and banking businesses has made this separation impossible.[18] The Bank and the SIB have reached a memorandum of understanding on regulating the securities activities of banks.[19]

The Bank of England's statutory powers over the financial services system are modest: it must approve the secretary of state's appointment of the chairman of the SIB, and in conjunction with him, it appoints the other members of the SIB board.[20] However, the Bank's role over the investor protection framework is pervasive though statutorily undefined.

In the months following the Big Bang, the Bank quietly moved to expand its authority. It established capital adequacy standards for the previously unregulated Eurobond market, issued rules for the wholesale money markets, and drafted a code of conduct for interest rate and currency swap dealers. It tightened regulation of the wholesale markets in sterling, foreign

---

14. *See infra* Ch. 4. For an analysis of DTI's enforcement duties, *see* Ch. 5.

15. *Bank of England: Right turn at Threadneedle Street*, ECONOMIST, June 11, 1988 at 20.

16. Under the Banking Act, it is illegal for a nonbanking institution to take deposits while conducting a deposit-taking business unless exempted from this prohibition. The Banking Act exempts the Stock Exchange and the London International Financial Futures Exchange from this prohibition.

17. FSA § 43.

18. RIDER, CHAIKEN, *supra* note 4 at 37.

19. Securities and Investments Board, FINANCIAL SERVICES RULES AND REGULATIONS, Ch. 4 (1988) [hereinafter SIB RULES].

20. FSA schd. 7(2). One explanation for this convoluted approach is that it would prevent a labor government from recovering the SIB's board to install their own.

exchange, and bullion. None of these actions came under the Financial Services Act.[21]

The Bank served as a regulatory interventionist counterpart to the Thatcherite policy of deregulation. It expanded its influence as the government preached retreat of governmental authority. This creeping regulatory stance has been supported by the Government. Though its rules have been promulgated informally, the Bank and government have threatened to follow up with legislation if the investor protection system faltered.

Given the breakdown between the functional divisions of investment businesses, the question remains whether the Bank should and ultimately will become the single regulator of the financial services industry. The division between brokerage and bank monitoring may make the early spotting of problems difficult. The Bank fills a complementary role in areas where the SIB lacks authority, such as the wholesale money markets. It has taken the lead in calling for an international agreement on securities regulation.[22] The Bank of England, like the Federal Reserve Bank in the United States, may be the regulator of last resort. In the meantime, it has had an important say in the evolution of the investor protection framework.[23]

The Securities and Investments Board

In May 1987, as expected, the Secretary of State transferred power to the SIB.[24] The transferred powers included recognition, refusal of recognition, and revocation of recognition of SROs, professional bodies, investment businesses that could apply directly to the DTI, investment exchanges, and clearing houses.[25] The SIB now had the authority to make a series of binding rules and regulations regarding the conduct of investment business. It

---

21. It has been suggested that the Guinness scandals led the Bank to take an increased role. Then it moved to force the resignations of two investment bankers involved. Cohen, *Bank of England Seen Boosting Regulatory Powers*, Reuters, Nexis Library, Apr. 23, 1987.

22. Fleet, *Bankers Take a Wary View of the Future*, THE TIMES (London) Feb. 6, 1986; Thomson, *Governor Calls for a Closer World Link on Supervision*, THE TIMES (London) May 8, 1986.

23. When the Secretary of State decided not to reappoint the first chairman of the SIB, his successor, David Walker, was a senior official at the Bank. This may signify the growing influence of the Bank over the whole securities regulatory system.

24. FSA 1986, (Delegation) Order 1987, S.I. 1987, No. 942. The future selection of the SIB as the designated agency was known by all throughout the bill's passage through Parliament. Even though the SIB was in existence and publishing a series of draft rules from 1985, the statute still contained detailed qualifications for an unnamed designated agency. Only after a substantial battle did the government permit a one-time mention of the SIB in the statute. FSA § 114.

25. FSA §§ 10, 11, 25–30, 36, 37.

could establish a compensation fund for defrauded investors, promulgate financial and liquidity requirements, and regulate advertising and unsolicited calls on investors.[26] The SIB also was given investigatory and disciplinary powers.[27] The importance of the SIB's rule-making authority was that SROs were required to have "equivalent" rules in order to receive authorization.[28] Despite a somewhat similar scope of authority, no one could mistake the SIB for the United States Securities and Exchange Commission. There is a consistent thread throughout the statute to limit the designated agency's scope, to combat excessive regulation and the perceived disease of "civil servantitis."[29]

Selected to chair the SIB Board was Sir Kenneth Berrill, who had a distinguished academic career as an economist at Cambridge from 1949 to 1969.[30] In the press conference announcing his appointment, Berrill conveyed the impression that he would not be a poacher turned gamekeeper, but an ambassador communicating the City's cause to the outside world.[31] However, Berrill was no diplomat; he was a regulator who came across as overly legalistic and inflexible. Roy Croft, a graduate of Cambridge with a degree in economics, and a civil servant from 1959 to 1985, was appointed chief executive of the SIB responsible for day-to-day management.[32]

All of the SIB's board members had full-time positions of substantial responsibility. The amount of time that they could devote was limited. The

---

26. *See id.* at § 48.

27. *See id.* at §§ 104–06.

28. This requirement has since been amended, but caused problems for the financial services industry and the SIB. *See* Companies Act, 1989, ch. 40, § 194.

29. FSA, schd. 7. The SIB lives under the threat, however unrealistic in practice, that if it does not fulfill its functions as envisioned, the Secretary of State will order a resumption of transferred functions. FSA § 115. When the Secretary of State orders a resumption of any or all of the functions transferred to the designated agency, the order is subject to annulment by the resolution of either House of Parliament. The SIB's public functions and quasi-statutory powers are subject to public law review by the courts. Regina v. Panel on Takeovers and Mergers, *ex parte* Datafin 1 All Eng. Rep. 564 (Ct. App. 1987).

30. He had worked in the Treasury between 1969 and 1973 as chief economic adviser. From 1974 to 1980 Berrill became head of the Central Policy Review Staff, a government think tank. In 1981, he worked in the City for the first time, as head of Vickers da Costa, a medium-sized brokerage firm in which Citicorp had purchased a 29.9% interest in 1983.

31. J. PLENDER & P. WALLACE, THE SQUARE MILE 57 (1985).

32. In the civil service he was involved with negotiations for Britain's entry into the EC, civil aviation policy, and the government's relations with British Airways. From 1976 to 1979 he was Finance Officer in DTI and from 1980, the Deputy Secretary in charge of a group of divisions concerned with telecommunications, information technology, aerospace, and related matters. Croft did not have direct responsibility for the financial sector while at DTI, but he came into close contact with the City through the privatization of Cable and Wireless and British Telecom. Croft resigned from the civil service to join the SIB. Riley, *U.K. Names Head of Financial Watchdog*, FIN. TIMES, June 7, 1985 at 16.

board met approximately every two weeks. Most but not all members were passive until a matter affected their area of the financial services industry. While the board was fully briefed on all rules and decisions, it hardly could be described as deliberative. For one thing, it was too big. Berrill knew what he wanted and pushed his agenda through.[33]

Underneath the chairman and executive director are four groups: legal, compliance and enforcement, retail markets, and capital markets. Beneath the groups are fourteen divisions, most of which are headed by a divisional director supported by one or more deputy directors. The size of the SIB's staff is surprisingly small. In February 1987 its total staff was seventy-two, thirty-six of whom were management. By July 1988 the staff had grown to 151, to 161 in March 1989, to 167 in 1990, and 181 by 1991.[34] By contrast, after its first year the staff of the SEC Commission numbered seven hundred.[35]

In 1985, long before the Financial Services Act had received the Queen's assent, the final step before a bill becomes law, the SIB had organized itself and begun to structure the new regulatory system. Of particular importance were negotiations with potential SROs so that the self-regulatory structure could be in place when the Financial Services Act became effective. This would mean that most investment businesses could be authorized by the SROs rather than overwhelming the SIB.

Chapter V of the Financial Services Act and the delegation orders provided that the designated agency make rules as necessary on such topics as the conduct of investment business,[36] financial resources,[37] cancellation of investment agreements,[38] notification by investment businesses of various circumstances to their SRO or the SIB, indemnity rules against claims of and liability against authorized investment businesses,[39] compensation ar-

---

33. The board would receive draft rules and other documents one day in advance—a huge pile of paper which could barely be read, let alone digested. Board meetings were held in the basement dining room of the SIB's headquarters. Staff were squeezed into a small kitchen. The ambience hardly engendered thoughtful discussion. Because the SIB had little time to set up the new framework and had to publish its own rules to give guidance to the SROs, this steamrolling approach was the only way to get the system on-line. The haste, however, would lead to unforeseen consequences.

34. REPORT OF THE SECURITIES AND INVESTMENTS BOARD 1990/91, 64 (1991) [hereinafter 1990/91 SIB REPORT]. REPORT OF THE SECURITIES AND INVESTMENTS BOARD 1989/90, 53 (1990) [hereinafter 1989/90 SIB REPORT]. SECURITIES AND INVESTMENTS BOARD, ANNUAL REPORT 61 (1987). SECURITIES AND INVESTMENTS BOARD, FEB. 1987 REPORT (1987). SIB ANNUAL RPT. 1987/88, *supra* note 7, at 44.

35. SECURITIES AND EXCHANGE COMMISSION, FIRST ANNUAL REPORT 38 (1935).

36. FSA § 54.

37. *See id.* at § 49.

38. *See id.* at § 51.

39. *See id.* at § 53.

rangements to reimburse investors owed money by authorized firms that became insolvent,[40] segregation of clients funds into escrow accounts,[41] and unsolicited calling on customers.[42] The statute also required the designated agency to make provisions to meet a wide range of investor protection objectives.[43]

The SIB's first years were spent publishing its rules, recognizing SROs, investment exchanges, and clearinghouses, and reviewing the SROs' own rule books. By April 29, 1988, the SROs had been recognized and investment businesses had received at least interim authorization to carry on their activities. The new system was in place. Thereafter, the SIB's supervisory responsibility involved two formal tasks and one informal one. The main tasks involved ensuring that each recognized body conducted its responsibilities appropriately and had in place what was expected, and that recognized bodies, rules, and practices worked satisfactorily. The informal task was to fight a widespread reaction to the complexity of the legislation.

This failed, and in the next few years, the SIB became involved in a massive endeavor to rewrite the rule books and create a new settlement with the financial services industry.[44] The new approach attempted to streamline the rules, make the division of responsibility between the SROs and the SIB more efficient, and lighten the regulatory yoke. This effort continues today. As even the chairman of the SIB admitted, there has been a widespread sense of regulatory fatigue and a desire by the financial services industry for a period of quiet consolidation rather than additional policy formulation and change.[45] Thus, more than five years after the Big Bang, the SIB is still seeking the appropriate balance between regulation and self-enforcement in a dynamic commercial environment and discerning its own role within the regulatory structure.

The Self-regulating Organizations

The fulcrum of the new system is the four self-regulating organizations.[46] An SRO is a body that regulates the conducting of investment busi-

---

40. *See id.* at § 54.

41. *See id.* at § 55.

42. *See id.* at § 56.

43. These included the promotion of high standards of integrity and fair dealing in the investment business, the subordination by authorized persons of their interests to those of their clients and to act fairly between clients, the disclosure of material interests and facts to the customer, and the disclosure of the capacity in which and the terms on which the firm acts, enabling investors to make informed decisions, and rules for the protection of investors' property. The act also requires the SIB's rules to take into account the differing needs for protection of public, sophisticated, and institutional investors. FSA, schd. 8.

44. This is discussed in Ch. 4.

45. 1990/91 SIB Report, *supra* note 34, at 4.

46. Originally there were five SROs. On April 1, 1991 the smallest self-regulating body,

ness of any kind by enforcing binding rules upon its members or others subject to its control.[47] The SRO is responsible for the day-to-day enforcement
of investment business under the system but is subject to the SIB's rules and
criteria for recognition. To safeguard investors, SROs must have rules governing the carrying-on of investment business by their members which, together with statements of principle and core rules promulgated by the SIB
pursuant to the Financial Services Act,[48] afford an adequate level of
protection.[49]

After the SIB recognized an SRO, the SRO's members were authorized to
conduct investment business.[50] Before recognizing the SRO, the SIB had to
be satisfied that criteria specified in the statute were met. First, the membership of the SRO's governing body had to be balanced between the interests of the SRO's different members and the public.[51]

A second criterion was that the SRO have an effective scope rule to preclude its members from carrying on an investment business of a kind with
which was SRO is not concerned.[52] The SRO had to demonstrate its commitment and competence to regulate the investment business it sought to
cover. An SRO's rules and practices had to be at least as effective as the SIB's
own and had to ensure that its members were fit and proper to carry on
investment business of the kind with which the SRO was concerned.

The SRO had to have firm and reasonable rules and an independent procedure for appeals relating to the admission, expulsion, and discipline of
members. It had to have conduct of business rules that afforded protection
to investors, adequate financial and personnel resources to carry out its

---

the Association of Futures Brokers and Dealers (AFBD), merged with the Securities Association to form the Securities and Futures Authority. The AFBD's member firms conducted
business in connection with dealing, arranging, and advising on deals of futures, options,
and contracts for differences and with investment management of futures instruments
portfolios. There had been substantial overlap in membership between the Securities Association and AFBD though the latter had a more diverse constituency and serviced several
different kinds of investors. The merger reflects the increasing links between conventional
securities markets and derivative markets and may presage a larger reorganization of the
self-regulating framework.

47. FSA § 8(1).

48. FSA Ch. V, Conduct of Investment Business, encompassing §§ 47–63B.

49. FSA, schd. 2, Safeguards for Investors.

50. *See id.* at § 7.

51. The governing body had to include a sufficient number of independent or nonindustry persons to ensure the public's interest. In practice, this meant that each SRO board had
a few tokens, often academics, to numerically balance practitioners. The SIB has suggested
that the minimum number of independent persons should be between one-quarter and one-
third of the governing board. FSA, schd. 2, para. 5; SIB RULES, *supra* note 19.

52. *Cf.* THE SECURITIES ASSOCIATION RULES [hereinafter TSA RULES] rules 10.01–10.04
(1988).

functions, resources for the effective monitoring and enforcement of compliance with its rules, and effective arrangements for the investigation of complaints. Furthermore, the SRO had to promote and maintain high standards of integrity and fair dealing in the marketplace and had to willingly cooperate and share information with the SIB.[53]

SROs are private bodies in which membership is voluntary. Their authority over members derives from contract. Sanctions over wayward members rest ultimately on their powers of expulsion. Recognition of an SRO does not entail delegation of powers by the SIB. Instead, the use of certain powers is waived or modified with respect to the members of the SRO for as long as the SRO remains recognized.[54] The SIB has the draconian authority to revoke an SRO's recognition.[55]

The Securities and Futures Authority

Gower had envisioned a multitude of SROs, and if they had been built upon existing professional associations, there would have been many indeed. However, the costs of staffing combined with the lack of personnel with regulatory experience meant that several professional groups inevitably would come together, if for no other reason than economies of scale.

Clearly one of the SROs would represent members of the Stock Exchange. The question then became whether international securities firms would still bypass the Exchange and the regulatory system and drive away still more trading from London. Initially, the international securities traders, those who purchased foreign equities and British stocks abroad through ADRs, hoped to avoid regulation under the Financial Services Act. When they found that they would be covered, they formed their own regulatory organization, the International Securities Regulatory Organization (ISRO). In 1986, its members represented 187 financial institutions from more than one dozen countries.

Almost all of the large securities firms and international banks had joined ISRO.[56] Thus, there were two potential SROs dealing with securities: one

---

53. SIB Rules, *supra* note 19, schd. II.

54. Securities and Investments Board, Regulation of Investment Business 7 (1987).

55. *See* FSA § 11. This decision may be overruled by the Secretary of State. The SIB can apply to a court for a compliance order, *id.* at § 12, or direct the SRO to amend its rules to make them equivalent to the SIB's. *Id.* at § 13. *Cf.* Exchange Act, § 19(c), 15 U.S.C.A. § 78s(c).

56. Its members included a number of participants in trading associations, including the members of the International Primary Markets Association, an organization concerned with the issuance of new bonds, and members of the Association of International Bond

domestic, the Stock Exchange, and one international, ISRO.[57] The Stock Exchange feared that firms would drift from it towards the international body because of lesser regulation, lower trading costs, and increasing internationalization of the securities markets. ISRO members could have moved out of London and taken new business elsewhere. The Stock Exchange needed a merger. In early 1986, negotiations commenced between the Stock Exchange and ISRO to consider a merger and the formation of one SRO.[58] In September 1986, the Stock Exchange and ISRO agreed to merge and formed The Securities Association, an SRO that would cover all trading in equities.[59]

The Stock Exchange changed its name to the International Stock Exchange of the United Kingdom and the Republic of Ireland (ISE) and became a recognized investment exchange. It became the primary U.K. marketplace for trading in domestic and foreign securities, gilts, traded options, and debentures. Although the Exchange sought to recapture some of its lost trading, its prominence was diminished, for it was just one of several recognized investment exchanges.

The Securities Association, now the Securities and Futures Authority (SFA) dominates the investor protection network. Its membership of approximately one thousand accounts for approximately one-half of the revenues of all U.K. investment firms covered by the act.[60] Member firms con-

---

Dealers (AIBD), a trade association of securities firms involved in the secondary distribution of bonds. This latter group of dealers, whose membership overlapped with the International Primary Markets Association, participated in a completely unregulated market based in Zurich. During 1985, $2,200 billion Eurobonds changed hands, 70% of which were traded in London. If it remained in London it would be subject to the new regulatory system, D. LOMAX, LONDON MARKETS AFTER THE FINANCIAL SERVICES ACT, 95 (1987) [hereinafter LOMAX]. However, overregulation would move bond trading out of London to Europe. The AIBD became a designated investment exchange.

57. *Id.* at 94.

58. For ISRO, the merger's attraction was the experienced staff and track record of self-regulation of the Exchange. The advantages of one SRO were economies of scale, simplification of reporting requirements—as many securities firms would join both, and the Stock Exchange's long experience in overseeing its members activities. Wolman, *Dominating Investor-Protection Framework*, FIN. TIMES, Apr. 28, 1987 at 7 [hereinafter Wolman].

59. The organizational structure of The Securities Association's governing body initially consisted of nine members appointed by the Stock Exchange Council, nine appointed by the ISRO steering committee, with each group appointing three independent or nonindustry members. At the end of 1986, ISRO transferred its assets to the new SRO. The cost savings to member firms were substantial: the budget of The Securities Association was estimated to be £ 7.5 million pounds compared with a cost of £ 10 million pounds if ISRO had remained a separate SRO.

60. At the end of March 1991, The Securities Association had 1,009 member firms and 29,806 registered persons, compared with 1,003 firms and 30,126 registered persons at the

duct business in such activities as dealing and arranging deals in shares, debentures, government and other public securities, rights and interests in securities, and futures and options in securities and their derivatives. If the securities business is the main activity of the firm, the SFA can authorize and regulate other activities which are not the major part of the firm's business, such as investment advice and management and advising on collective investment schemes.[61]

Many of the regulatory responsibilities once performed by the Stock Exchange have been undertaken by The Securities and Futures Authority. There continue to be close links between the two organizations. Essentially, the enforcement division of the Stock Exchange became The Securities Association, located in the Stock Exchange's building, and in the first few years there was a substantial overlap in staff.[62] Approximately one-third of SFA's members belong to the ISE, and the SFA's director of enforcement held the same title for the exchange. The SFA's regulatory responsibilities have extended to Euromarket activity. Its member firms are active in the Stock Exchange, the London International Financial Futures Exchange (LIFFE), the Association of International Bond Dealers, and other recognized investment exchanges and branch offices of foreign banks.[63]

Critics of the authority have argued that its scope is too broad and that it is too big, for its members range from huge investment banks to provincial stockbrokers. It is also said to lack the common interests or cultural bonds that made the Stock Exchange an effective regulator for so long.[64] The former members of ISRO, the large international firms, have had a disproportionate influence on the organization's development. Whereas former exchange members had experience as self-regulators, ISRO members

---

end of April 1990. SECURITIES AND FUTURES AUTHORITY, REPORT AND ACCOUNTS 10 (1991) [hereinafter 1991 SFA REPORT]. Interestingly, only 48% of member firms were owned by U.K. interests, 20% by continental European, 14% by American, and 9% by Japanese interests. *Id.* The largest category of member firms by type was security dealers and brokers (449); followed by investment advisory firms (216), overseas banks (110), U.K. banks (85), and overseas securities houses (63). *Id.* at 11. The AFBD had 394 members as of March 31, 1991. 1990/91 SIB REPORT, *supra* note 60 at 20. We use the terms The Securities Association (TSA) and Securities and Futures Authority (SFA) interchangeably in this section.

61. TSA RULES *supra* note 52, ch. I. *Guidance Notes on The Regulatory Scope of The Securities Association* 1.1–2.1.

62. In 1990, SFA staff who were employed under dual contracts with the SFA and the International Stock Exchange had their contracts terminated and are now employed under single contracts by one of the two organizations. 1991 SFA REPORT, *supra* note 60, at 22, 39.

63. THE SECURITIES ASSOCIATION, AN INTRODUCTION TO THE SECURITIES ASSOCIATION 3– 4 (1987).

64. Wolman, *supra* note 58, at 7.

had experience with complex regulation and influenced the SFA's initial legalistic and overly detailed rule book.

The SFA has been the most effective self-regulating organization. It has had at least four advantages over the other SROs. The first was self-regulatory experience which was available because the SFA was hived off from the enforcement arm of the Stock Exchange. Second, it had sufficient financial resources to undertake the responsibilities delegated to it. Third, it commenced its SRO responsibilities early on, long before it received formal recognition from the SIB. Finally, its membership was known, finite in size, and sophisticated.

Well before its recognition as an SRO, The Securities Association invited firms to apply for authorization.[65] Admission to membership involved more than an assessment of whether the applicant was able to meet the standards imposed by the Financial Services Act and would obey the association's rules. In addition to reviewing the firm itself, the association registered over thirty thousand directors, managers, partners, and employees who dealt with the public or traded on behalf of the firm. Registered persons had to meet the standards of a fit and proper test, which considered financial integrity, character, absence of prior convictions, reputation for efficiency and honesty, and proven competence.

Firms also had to pass a fit and proper test.[66] They must maintain adequate capital resources to meet investment business commitments and to withstand the risks to which their business is subject.[67] Firms also must have efficient monitoring systems so they know their capital position, keep suitable records, supervise their employees, and regularly notify the SFA of problems involving their capital situation or other developments. They must prepare and submit to the authority financial and auditing information.[68]

---

65. Almost all of its applications were received and reviewed by the date firms had to have at least applied to an SRO. A staff of 45 reviewed the applications, and 363 applicants were members of the Stock Exchange.

66. The firm had to be honest, reliable with money, efficient, and have suitable experience and qualifications. To show an ability to meet these tests, a firm had to submit a business plan. Fitness and properness are measured against the scale of business activities and the firm's ability to operate on the proposed scale. TSA RULES, *supra* note 52, ch. 2. *The Fit and Proper Test*, R. 1.1–1.17. In this section, we cite the original rule book which was in effect during the period discussed. The Securities Association rule book and those of the other SROs have been revised in response to changes in the SIB's regulatory approach. *See infra* ch. 4, pp. 144–45.

67. *See* TSA RULES, *supra* note 52, at ch. 3, Financial Regulations, sec. 4 rules, 40.01–63.14A.

68. The rules adopted by the SFA and other SROs are based upon the SIB's core rules. The core rules are discussed in ch. 4, pp. 139–144.

Enforcement and Due Process

The theory of self-regulation is grounded in the view that SROs will effectively enforce the business activities of their members.[69] The compliance system is backed by an effective enforcement mechanism. The SFA has over one hundred staff monitoring members' activities and investigating rule breaches. All member firms are subject to an unannounced inspection visit at least once per year from one of ten teams of five inspectors each.[70]

Routine monitoring of a surveillance database, which tracks all trades, is undertaken to identify problems such as repeated failure to obtain best execution for customers. All financial statements are reviewed by the enforcement division staff to ensure that firms are in compliance with financial regulations such as the capital adequacy requirements. A financial database contains all financial information submitted by each member firm and alerts the authority to potential problem areas. Complementing the inspection powers are notification requirements which mandate that a member firm inform the association upon the occurrence of various events ranging from a name change to bankruptcy.[71]

The authority also can intervene where there has been or is likely to be a breach of the rules, in which case it can issue a direction[72] requiring a member firm or registered person to take specific steps to avoid a breach or further breach of the rules. In situations requiring immediate action, it can issue a protective intervention order which places a prohibition on a firm or part of a firm from engaging in the securities business or from disposing of any assets.[73]

---

69. Enforcement and due process and adjudication of disputes in the investor protection system at large is the subject of Chapter 5. We discuss the procedures of one self-regulatory organization here.

70. During 1990–91, The Securities Association enforcement inspectors carried out full inspections of 760 firms and made an additional 425 nonroutine visits. 1991 SFA REPORT, *supra* note 60 at 19. Special visits can be made at any time to investigate a particular problem. Each team is assigned a group of member firms. Inspection staff includes lawyers, accountants, ex-stock exchange members, former police officers, and experienced stock exchange surveillance staff. The head of investigations coordinates sources of intelligence, leads special investigations into apparent breaches of conduct of business rules and other misconduct, and obtains evidence in support of disciplinary cases. There are additional specialist teams which focus upon violation of the conduct of business rules, financial regulation, futures and derivative investments, complaints and conciliation, international supervision, intelligence, and systems and controls.

71. Notification must be given of any change in the directors, managers, partners, or registered representatives and whether the change was a termination of employment. All convictions other than traffic violations, refusal of licenses, or imposition of disciplinary measures also must be reported. TSA RULES, *supra* note 52, ch. 2, Rule 150.

72. *Id.* at ch. 5, Rule 30.04.

73. *See id.* at Rule 5.60.

Violations of SFA rules by firms or individuals are not criminal offenses.[74] A rule violation makes a firm liable to discipline based upon the contract between the member and the firm.[75] Disciplinary tribunals are able to impose penalties ranging from reprimand to fines up to £100,000 to expulsion. Tribunal decisions are published.[76] The statute requires that an SRO have an appeals system, but says little more.[77] Attorneys are not permitted by right at the preliminary hearing, but are in fact always present. One of the criticisms of the appeals process is that the two levels are too legalistic.[78]

Investor Complaints

The statute requires an SRO to have sufficient management capabilities for the investigation of complaints against the organization or its members.[79] In the first instance, the investor must seek to resolve the problem with the firm. Member firms are required to have a process for dealing with customers' complaints promptly. If the complaint is not resolved by the firm, then the matter can be handled by the Complaints Bureau, which has

---

74. FSA § 62(4). The SIB may apply to a court for a restitution order. *Id* at § 61. There may be a cause of action for the customer, FSA § 62(1).

75. When a firm seeks authorization, it agrees to abide by TSA rules. Disciplinary action is appealable to the courts, which are not unsympathetic unless the SRO was arbitrary and in violation of natural justice. If, after a market inquiry or monitoring, it is concluded there is a need for a formal investigation in connection with an alleged disciplinary violation, the firm is given a formal Notice of Investigation. Regina v. Panel on Takeovers and Mergers, *ex parte* Datafin 1 All Eng. Rep. 564 (Ct. App. 1987).

76. In 1990–91, TSA investigated formal disciplinary proceedings against six firms and twelve individuals for acts of misconduct including churning clients accounts, breaching the suitability rule, failure to maintain adequate capital or systems and records, failure to segregate clients' funds, and failure to issue to clients appropriate risk warnings. Seven of the eighteen cases proceeded to the tribunals, and two additional cases from 1989–90 were heard. All but two resulted in conviction leading to censures, fines, and banishment from The Securities Association register. The other eleven cases were settled with fines or censures. 1991 SFA REPORT, *supra* note 60 at 19. There is an appeal from the decision of the disciplinary tribunal to an appeals tribunal consisting of a chairman, who has a legal background, a practitioner, and a lay person.

77. FSA, schd. 2, 2.

78. Confidential interview. From the Authority's perspective, the Appeals Tribunal has been too independent. Of six cases where the authority rejected an application for authorization and the authorizations tribunal affirmed, all six were reversed upon appeal to the Appellate Tribunal. This has been attributed to the legalism of the proceedings in contrast to the more informal approach desired by The Securities Association. Another explanation is that denial of a person's livelihood is such a drastic action that proof beyond any reasonable doubt should be required, and rigorous due process procedures should be followed.

79. FSA, schd. 2, 2.

been established by The Securities Association and the International Stock Exchange. The complaint cannot be the subject of pending litigation or arbitration, and there is a two-year statute of limitations. In 1990–91, 649 investors made formal complaints against Securities Association members to the Complaints Bureau. Approximately one-half were found to be partly or wholly justified, and of those, nearly all complainants received some form of redress.[80]

Upon receipt of a written complaint, the Complaints Bureau investigates the matter and renders a decision. It can either refer the matter back to the firm or attempt to conciliate the differences between the customer and the firm. If a satisfactory resolution is not achieved, the customer can avail himself of The Securities Association's arbitration schemes.

A complaints commissioner, an independent person appointed by the SFA, is available if a customer is not satisfied with the way in which the Complaints Bureau discharged its responsibilities. The complaints commissioner undertakes the role of ombudsman and makes observations and recommendations about the bureau's procedures in any case referred to him.[81] The commissioner can then remand the complaint back to the Complaints Bureau for further consideration.

The SFA also operates two arbitration schemes: a customer scheme for amounts below £25,000 and another for amounts above that limit. The more simplified consumer scheme may be used by a private customer or former private customer with a claim against a member firm involving £25,000 pounds or less. When a claimant chooses to use the consumer scheme, the member firm is obliged by the rules to have the dispute resolved by arbitration.[82] The full arbitration scheme is available for claims that do not qualify for the consumer scheme or for claims between member firms. In this second procedure, the parties are responsible for all expenses of arbitration, and the arbitrator has the power to make an award for costs.[83]

---

80. 1991 SFA REPORT, *supra* note 60 at 20. Of the complaints, the most common involved delay in payment (23.9%), administration within firms (18.3%), dealing problems (15.7%), and mismanagement of portfolio (10.2%). *Id.*

81. THE SECURITIES ASSOCIATION, THE SECURITIES ASSOCIATION REPORT AND ACCOUNTS 25 (1988).

82. The claimant pays a registration fee of £10, and the Authority pays the costs of the arbitrator and all expenses. The claimant is responsible for his legal fees but does not have to reimburse any costs of the member firm unless his case was frivolous and totally without merit. The maximum costs that may be ordered against a private customer or expert investor is £500. The arbitrator's award normally is made on the basis of submissions of written statements and documents, although an oral hearing can be convened if appropriate. The decision of the arbitrator is final. SECURITIES AND FUTURES AUTHORITY, CONSUMER ARBITRATION SCHEME 4 (n.d.).

83. In 1990–91, only eleven cases went to arbitration. 1991 SFA REPORT, *supra* note 60.

The Life Assurance and Unit Trust Regulatory Organization

The Life Assurance and Unit Trust Regulatory Organization (LAUTRO), formed in July 1986, regulates the marketing of life insurance and unit trusts and other collective investment schemes by firms who are creators of those products as opposed to intermediaries who merely market them. LAUTRO's members are insurance companies and friendly societies engaged in retail marketing of life insurance products or operators of collective investment schemes engaged in retail marketing of these units. LAUTRO's members sell their products through employees or appointed representatives, commonly called "company reps" or "tied agents."[84] For LAUTRO membership, the companies, not the employees, must be authorized. However, agents may be only nominally tied to a company, and some work for more than one.

The Secretary of State rather than LAUTRO authorizes insurance companies and Europersons, and the SIB authorizes unit trusts. As a result, LAUTRO does not have to establish financial criteria for its members, as they are determined under other authorizing legislation.

At the SIB's insistence, LAUTRO introduced conduct of business rules that have revolutionized the sale of life insurance. The rules are aimed at preventing product bias. This occurs when an insurance salesman is encouraged to sell an unsuitable contract because he receives a higher commission or other incentive for the particular policy. Many individuals who are sold insurance or unit trust contracts do not truly know what they are purchasing.

LAUTRO's regulations require investors to be given comprehensive details of the contract, including product disclosure, details of the underlying funds, descriptions of the investment objectives and risk of volatility, details of charges, particulars of the taxation basis, and the surrender or cash-in value of the policy. The rules also require all life insurance companies to provide standardized illustrations of costs and benefits.[85] Perhaps the most

---

84. This distinguishes LAUTRO from FIMBRA. The latter's members are independent financial advisors and insurance salespersons and must be authorized individually. LAUTRO also regulates the marketing of life insurance and unit trust products by Europersons i.e., organizations established in other member countries of the EEC and properly authorized in their own country. LOMAX, *supra* note 56 at 137–47.

85. Promotional materials provided by the companies about their products must conform to SIB and LAUTRO advertising rules. Media advertisements are subject to the rules which include providing product information. Short, *Tougher Rule to Give Investors Even More Security*, FIN. TIMES, July 2, 1988, VI col. 1. The issue of disclosure is discussed in Chapter 4.

significant benefit to the investor of the new framework is that for the first time, disclosure is required in the marketing of investment products of items that are disclosed as a matter of course in the United States.

The Financial Intermediaries, Managers and Brokers Regulatory Association

The largest and most troubled SRO is the Financial Intermediaries, Managers and Brokers Regulatory Association (FIMBRA). Its origins date to 1979 when a group of market makers, portfolio managers, and life insurance and unit trust intermediaries established the Association of Licensed Dealers in Securities to gain status as a recognized association of dealers in securities under the Prevention of Fraud (Investments) Act, thereby exempting themselves from the requirement of obtaining a license from the DTI.[86] On July 6, 1986, the successor of the association changed its name to the Financial Intermediaries, Managers and Brokers Regulatory Association and applied for recognition as an SRO.[87]

With over eight thousand members, FIMBRA is by far the largest SRO. Its membership has a diffuse focus and is involved in a gamut of activities, primarily advising on and selling life insurance, authorized unit trusts, and similar collective investment schemes, or providing investment advisory and management services to retail customers. FIMBRA members are a diverse lot of independent intermediaries who sell the products of several companies. Because of the small size of the typical FIMBRA firm, the diversity of the SRO's constituency, the breadth of products sold, and the members' overall lack of business sophistication, FIMBRA has had an uneasy relationship with its membership. Some have not accepted the need for elaborate regulation, while others did not think the new framework applied to them. Most did not understand it.[88] For many, the membership fees and compliance costs have been a real financial burden.

From its commencement, FIMBRA's administrative burdens were greater than the other SROs. The sheer size of the potential membership

---

86. The Association had a membership of slightly over one thousand. In December 1982 it changed its name to the National Association of Securities Dealers and Investment Managers. Three years later it merged with another recognized association, the Life and Unit Trust Intermediaries Regulatory Organization (LUTIRO), which had twenty thousand members who sold life insurance and unit trust products. LUTIRO's members ranged from large insurance brokerages to retired individuals who sold insurance or other financial products part-time.

87. LOMAX, *supra* note 56, at 49.

88. Short, *Finance and the Family; "Tax" Could Be Needed to Bail Out FIMBRA*, FIN. TIMES, August 6, 1988, at 5.

created enormous financial and supervisory burdens and an increased need for effective regulation. This led to cost overruns that created problems.[89] FIMBRA had to expand its staff to cope with the flood of applications for authorization. Then, in the summer of 1988 it conducted several investigations of independent intermediaries that had placed business with a bankrupt investment management firm, Barlow Clowes, in return for gratuities. Initially, FIMBRA, like all of the SROs, was kept solvent through overdraft privileges with the Bank of England. However, these loans had to be repaid over the next few years.

FIMBRA was bedeviled by a members revolt in 1989 over its expenses and a compulsory indemnity insurance scheme that collapsed just before it was to become effective. The plan was to provide investors a minimum of £ 100,000 recovery and would have met claims awarded by the investment referee, who handles disputes between investors and members. Some FIMBRA members had their own insurance plans and would have to join FIMBRA's plan with a selected broker. However, the plan was scrapped when the underwriter refused to take on the scope of potential liability. The members' revolt represented a serious attack on an already weakened SRO and forced the premature retirement of its chairman. The insurance scheme was the catalyst for the opposition to FIMBRA's leadership and reflected a perceived lack of members' input and the financial straits of the membership.[90]

In 1988 and 1989 FIMBRA received a cash infusion from insurance companies. In early 1991 it was faced with another financial crisis because of the compensation claims against its members. Once again it was bailed out by LAUTRO members and firms directly regulated by the SIB. The resources of the investors compensation scheme, which protects defrauded investors, have been insufficient to meet claims caused by errant FIMBRA members.[91] FIMBRA's immediate financial needs as well as the burdens on its members were eased when a group of life insurance companies contributed £ 1.5 million to provide support through April 1992.[92]

FIMBRA's financial problems are but part of a deeper crisis involving its membership. Since 1986 an estimated four thousand independent intermediaries have left the insurance industry or exchanged their independent

---

89. Bunker, Short, *Funding to Give FIMBRA an Assured Future*, FIN. TIMES, July 29, 1988 at 6.

90. Goldsmith, *Fimbra insurance scheme collapses*, THE TIMES (London), Nov. 1, 1989 at 25, col. 2; Barchand, *Members of FIMBRA launch revolt over running costs*, FIN. TIMES, Nov. 27, 1989, at 9, col. 7.

91. Under the investor compensation scheme, an SRO's members must make up shortfalls caused by members in the SRO. *See infra* p. 106.

92. Waters, *SIB will review investor protection*, FIN. TIMES, Mar. 19, 1991 at 8.

status by becoming employees of insurance companies.[93] A long-term solution to FIMBRA's financial problems and those of its members must be
developed. It has been difficult to pass the regulatory costs on to consumers
because of the disclosure requirements that apply to independent intermediaries.[94] FIMBRA may have to be merged with LAUTRO, creating an SRO
representing the whole insurance industry.

The Investment Management Regulatory Organization

Until the Financial Services Act, U.K. fund managers and investment advisors virtually were unregulated. They needed a license from the DTI for
dealing in securities. If they became involved in unit trust management, the
unit trust had to be authorized by the DTI. There was no separate regulation of investment managers. Unlike the other SROs, the Investment Management Regulatory Organization (IMRO) is a completely new organization formed after enactment of the Financial Services Act. IMRO covers
investment management firms where this is the sole or main activity of the
member or where the member firm holds itself out as offering discretionary
management services distinct from its other activities.

IMRO's 1,247 members are managers of large-scale corporate pension
funds or other large portfolios. They include merchant banks, investment
trusts, pension fund managers, unit trust managers, insurance companies,
and other such firms that manage savings and investments.[95] IMRO's members' activities include managing and operating collective investment
schemes, acting as a trustee of collective investment schemes, managing investment trusts, managing in-house pension funds, acting as a pension fund
trustee, and giving investment advice to institutional or corporate
customers.

The jurisdiction of IMRO impinges upon other SROs. On one side is
FIMBRA, whose members provide financial advice to individuals. On the
other is the SFA whose members manage funds on behalf of clients.[96] IMRO

93. *British Life Assurance Firms Not Waving but Drowning*, ECONOMIST, Nov. 5, 1988.

94. In other financial services sectors costs have been passed on to investors or consumers indirectly because they have been hidden in general charges or commissions. In the
insurance area, agents tied to one insurance company are more attractive to the average
policyholder because the company pays all regulatory fees and the costs to the consumer
are hidden in the premium and not disclosed. Short, *FIMBRA Puts Its House in Order*, FIN.
TIMES, Oct. 15, 1988, at 6.

95. LOMAX, *supra* note 56, at 125–34; 1990/91 SIB REPORT, *supra* note 34, at 20.

96. The SFA reached a memorandum of understanding with IMRO whereby it will mon-

has a close association with LAUTRO. Under the regulatory scheme for unit trusts, a manager and trustee must be independently authorized before the unit trust, as a whole, is given authorization by the SIB. The marketing and investment management aspects must be regulated on a continuing basis. Therefore, IMRO regulates the investment management aspects of unit trusts and LAUTRO regulates their marketing. IMRO is responsible for the financial monitoring of firms under joint jurisdiction with LAUTRO.

The vincibility of dividing pension and fund management among several regulators became apparent with the discovery that Robert Maxwell, through his control of two fund management companies, had looted Maxwell companies' pension funds of hundreds of millions of pounds. IMRO was severely chastised by a House of Commons Select Committee on Social Security for the authorization of Bishopsgate Investment Management (BIM) and London & Bishopsgate, despite questions about Maxwell's financial past, for the infrequency of visits to authorized fund managers, and for a lack of concern when administrative irregularities surfaced.[97]

Investment Exchanges, Clearinghouses, Overseas Investment Exchanges, and Designated Investment Exchanges

An investment exchange provides an organized market for trading in stocks, commodities, or other investments. The exchange's rules prescribe the framework for orderly buying and selling and settlement procedures.[98] Traditionally, investment exchanges authorized, regulated, and disciplined their membership. Under the new regime a "recognized investment exchange" (RIE) is not an SRO but a separately recognized body.[99]

---

itor investment management if this service is offered in conjunction with other services authorized by SFA, principally to private customers. A firm seeks authorization from IMRO for investment management business where such business is undertaken within and is the principle activity of a separately incorporated subsidiary or a separately identified division of a securities firm or where a firm markets investment management services for institutional customers. TSA RULES, *supra* note 52, ch. 1, Rule 2.3; LAUTRO RULES, pt. 5, Rule 5.13.

97. BIM was authorized as an occupational pension scheme member under section 191 of IMRO's rules, which subjected it to lighter regulation than most fund managers even though Maxwell and his son were trustees. The Commons report recommended a thorough reorganization of pension oversight. Maddox, *An inspector should call a lot more often,* FIN. TIMES, Mar. 5, 1992 at 8; *Revamping pensions law,* FIN. TIMES, Mar. 10, 1992; Maddox, *A spectacle to make even Pontius Pilate blush,* FIN. TIMES, Mar. 10, 1992 at 8.

98. RIDER, CHAIKEN, *supra* note 4, at 313.

99. FSA §§ 36–37.

The statute provides that the SIB will recognize investment exchanges that meet specific criteria relating to financial ability and enforcement of its rules, procedures for the investigation of complaints, regulations to ensure investor protection, arrangements for effective monitoring and compliance with its rules, promotion of high standards of fair dealing, and cooperation with the SIB.[100] While the procedure for recognition and some of the criteria are similar to the SRO recognition process, RIEs are not required to determine whether exchange members are "fit and proper" persons. The responsibility and granting of authorization to conduct investment business is the task of the appropriate SRO. This means that every member of a recognized investment exchange must also be a member of an SRO, most frequently, the SFA.[101] The SIB has recognized six exchanges.[102]

A clearinghouse assists an investment exchange by providing services to settle or finalize transactions effected on an exchange.[103] Clearinghouses match contracts to facilitate settling transactions. The SIB has the authority to recognize a clearinghouse (an RCH) if it is satisfied that the clearinghouse meets the requirements of Section 39(4) of the act with regard to such matters as the provision of clearing services, financial resources, monitoring, enforcement, the promotion of high standards of integrity and fair dealing, and cooperation with regulators. The SIB has recognized two

---

100. *Id.* at schd. 4.

101. Memberships of Recognized Investment Exchanges held by SFA member firms as of June 30, 1991, were International Stock Exchange, 379; London International Financial Futures Exchange, 171; London Futures and Options Exchange, 129; International Petroleum Exchange, 108; and London Metal Exchange 43.

102.   Recognized Investment Exchanges

Exchange	*Market*
International Stock Exchange of the United Kingdom and the Republic of Ireland	U.K. and foreign equities, gilt-edged and fixed interest stock,
London Futures and Options Exchange (FOX)	Futures and Options contracts in cocoa, coffee, sugar, and other commodities
London International Financial Futures Exchange (LIFFE) and LIFFE Options	Financial futures and options
London Metal Exchange	Futures and options contracts in various non-ferrous metals and silver
International Petroleum Exchange London	Futures contracts in gas, oil, gasoline, heavy fuel, crude oil, and options contracts in gas and oil
O. M. London	RMX Swedish equity index GEMX German Equity Market Index Swedish stock options.

103. FSA § 38(2).

clearinghouses: the International Commodities Clearinghouse, which provides clearing services to the RIEs, and GAFTA, which provides clearing services for grain contracts traded on the London Commodities Exchange.[104]

Some overseas exchanges might conduct substantial business and desire some kind of recognition in the United Kingdom, yet they do not wish to subject themselves to regulation by a foreign body. The secretary of state has retained powers under Section 40 to recognize overseas exchanges and clearinghouses if they have a U.K. address for service of process; are subject to supervision in their home country, which has rules and regulations that will provide U.K. investors with equivalent protection; and, if the home country will cooperate with U.K. regulators, and have adequate procedures for cooperation between U.K. and home country regulators.[105] The Secretary of state has recognized forty overseas investment exchanges.[106]

The internationalization of securities trading has led many English citizens to purchase and sell equities listed on foreign exchanges. The companies whose shares are purchased would not submit to English jurisdiction because of these transactions alone.[107] To avoid a potential jurisdictional conflict if not to save face, the SIB introduced the concept of "designated investment and clearinghouses exchange" for such exchanges. The New York and American Stock Exchanges are such designated exchanges. Designated exchanges and clearinghouses are expected to provide investors with protection equivalent to that provided by recognized exchanges.[108]

The International Securities Market Association

With a turnover in 1990 of $6.2 trillion, the international bond market is the world's most important source of debt capital.[109] The Association of

---

104. The Stock Exchange takes care of its own clearing.

105. FSA § 40.

106. 1990/91 SIB REPORT, *supra* note 34, at 50.

107. Nor are overseas exchanges and clearinghouses, which happen to conduct business with English citizens, required to seek recognition under Section 40. In fact, they would resist submission to English jurisdiction.

108. At the request of the SIB, the designated exchange is supposed to provide a copy of its rules or provisions for its clearing services and has indicated a willingness to investigate complaints by U.K. investors against its members and to advise the SIB of the results of any investigations. English authorized investment businesses that conduct business on designated exchanges do not have to report such foreign transactions at the close of each business day.

109. Keller, *Eurobond Profit Fears, Identity Crises Face AIBD*, REUTERS, Nexis File, May 13, 1991.

International Bond Dealers (AIBD) was founded in 1969 by traders who hoped to introduce greater stability and order to the secondary market in Eurobonds. It changed its name to the International Securities Market Association (ISMA) in 1991. The ISMA has nearly one thousand members in forty-seven countries, comprising all major European banks and financial institutions active in the international capital markets, as well as substantial numbers from around the world.[110] While only one-fifth of its members are based in the United Kingdom, this 20 percent accounts for 70 percent of total market turnover.[111] The British government desired to keep the Euromarkets in London, but needed to regulate them in some way. Because trading is by computer screen and telephone, there is no central trading floor. If U.K. regulation was too burdensome, the Euromarkets easily could move to a more pliant regulatory climate.

Despite the Euromarkets' success in the decades after world War II, profits of trading firms have narrowed, if not disappeared, and the size of the Eurobond market has peaked. The number of dealers, termed market makers, also has declined.[112] The Euromarkets needed a larger investor base and more liquidity, along with an effort to control common unscrupulous practices.[113] The problem was how could the market maintain its traditional independence yet remain in London's regulatory environment? The solution was to create a special category of "designated investment exchange" for ISMA with less onerous reporting requirements than those of a recognized investment exchange.

This compromise ensured that the Eurobond market would remain in London. While a London-based member faced greater regulation, all ISMA members would have a more efficient trading system. The ISMA issued new

---

110. Sedacca, *Information Technology in Finance; New Trade-Matching System Launched*, FIN. TIMES, Nov. 10, 1988, at 14. The AIBD's secretariat is based in Zurich with a technical services staff of thirty in London.

111. Jackson, *Regulator's Net Begins to Tighten Around Eurobonds, International Bonds*, FIN. TIMES, Nov. 10, 1988, 40 [hereinafter Jackson].

112. Market makers are individuals or firms who will buy, sell, or quote prices for trading previously issued Euromarket bonds. In 1987 there were 135 dealers. By May 1988, the number had fallen to 110. *How to Stop the Eurobonds Market from Committing Suicide*, EUROMONEY, May 1988 at 5 [hereinafter EUROBONDS]. Many corporate issuers have returned to the domestic market, which has lowered the volume in the markets. There always have been problems with the liquidity of Euromarket issues; that is, the ability to resell Eurobonds once issued. However, subsequent to the 1987 market crash, there has been a noticeable decline in liquidity.

113. Two complementary practices are "ramping" and "dumping." Ramping occurs when a firm corners the market for an illiquid issue to drive the price up. The result is that the issue is difficult to purchase except from the firm that has the issue. Dumping is the opposite, a device to lower the price.

rules that bound members to comply with just and equitable principles of business and trade, observe good market practices, and develop a more effective disciplinary system.[114] The rules were an attempt to boost investor confidence. The ISMA submitted to the SIB a copy of its rule book, a report on how the rules are enforced, arrangements for clearing, stabilization rules, and a mechanism for responding to complaints by U.K. citizens.[115] The ISMA members who complied with the association's rules would conform automatically to the Financial Services Act. Also, U.K.-based firms must join the SFA.

Most importantly for the new regulatory system, ISMA introduced the TRAX system at the urging of the SIB. This provides an audit trail for all trades by London-based members. TRAX is a screen-based system that allows the details of each trade to be reproduced within thirty minutes. Trades are officially confirmed by the ISMA's computer in London. Most Eurobonds had been traded over the telephone, which led to a surprising percentage of unmatched or failed trades, estimated at from 7 to 15 percent of the total volume. Also, there were too many clearinghouses: Euroclear in Brussels and CEDEL in Luxembourg.[116]

At first, Trax will be a risk management tool in that the trader will be informed within thirty minutes of any nonmatched trades. This will eliminate disputes between traders and provide an audit trail for all trades by London-based members.[117] All U.K.-based members report all transactions in international securities to ISMA.[118] The last price at which a security is traded is published daily. Previously, there was almost no way to determine the last trading price of a security; only bid/quote prices were available. Eventually, the true price information will be displayed on the screen, which could lead to a Eurobond futures market.

Many of the non-U.K. members objected to the new rules and the new system. ISMA has been hesitant to impose a penalty on firms who fail to use Trax. It has been caught between its desire to become a securities exchange and the dealer-driven nature of the Euromarketplace which has resisted any regulatory effort.[119] In the primary market, where new issues are

---

114. Prior, the only sanctions were expulsion or suspension, now there are fines, disciplinary committees, and appeals procedures.

115. EUROBONDS, *supra* note 112.

116. ISMA has been involved in ongoing unsuccessful negotiations with the clearing houses to improve settlement procedures. Under its rule 221, trades are supposed to be cleared in one day.

117. EUROBONDS, *supra* note 112.

118. JACKSON, *supra* note 111.

119. Thus, in 1990 AIBD sought to become the long-term securities market for the Euromarkets in the European Community by filing its rule book with the European Commis-

introduced, ISMA has been less aggressive, permitting relations between issuers to be governed by guidelines of a trade association, the International Primary Market Association. The lack of price transparency in the primary market has led to an inability to sell issues and the widespread use of stabilization and subsidies to borrowers.[120] The designated investment exchange approach maintains the Euromarkets' traditional independence yet provides a veneer of regulation that may curtail some of the abuses.

Recognized Professional Bodies

Lawyers, accountants, and other professionals often engage in an investment business as an incidental part of their practice. An attorney might be a guardian *ad litem* or an executor of an estate. Such professionals are regulated in the exercise of their powers and practices by a "professional body." The act provides that professional bodies, such as the Law Society which regulates solicitors, or the Institute of Chartered Accountants in England and Wales must apply to the SIB for recognition.[121] Such "recognized professional bodies" (RPBs) must meet certain criteria outlined in the statute and regulate the investment activities of their members in the course of or in conjunction with the practice of their profession and must have adequate and equivalent rules of investor protection.

Recognition of the professional body means that its members are authorized to carry on that limited investment function. However, an attorney who also managed pension funds would have to seek recognition from the appropriate SRO. The SIB has recognized nine professional bodies.[122]

Restrictions on Investment Advertisements

Fraudulent and misleading advertisements on television and in print media, that relate to investment products such as insurance, pensions, options, and unit trusts have been a continuing problem. Typically misleading

sion in Brussels. Freeman, *AIBD tries to become Euromarket securities exchange*, FIN. TIMES, May 21, 1990 at 19, col. 3.

120. *Strains in the Euromarkets*, FIN. TIMES, Aug. 22, 1989 at 14, col. l. Stabilization is a form of legalized price manipulation permitted under the FSA to stabilize the price of new issues for a short period after their introduction to the marketplace.

121. FSA § 16(1), schd. 3.

122. The recognized professional bodies are the Law Society of England and Wales, The Law Society of Scotland, the Law Society of Northern Ireland, the Institute of Chartered Accountants in England and Wales, the Institute of Chartered Accountants of Scotland, the Institute of Chartered Accountants in Ireland, the Chartered Association of Certified Accountants, the Institute of Actuaries, and the Insurance Brokers Registration Council.

advertisements omit adequate warnings about risk, do not fully describe the advertised product, or present a misleading impression of past performance. The Financial Services Act provides that the secretary of state [now the SIB] can make rules regulating " . . . the form and content of advertisements in respect of investment business."[123] Advertising rules apply to all advertisements except specifically exempted advertisements (ordinary corporate advertising or a tombstone ad); those published in relation to the issuance of securities or governed by the rules of a designated investment exchange, takeover advertisements, or an advertisement issued in circumstances that would be unlikely to be communicated to private customers.[124]

Section 57 provides that "no person other than an authorized person shall issue or cause to be issued an investment advertisement in the U.K. unless its contents have been approved by an authorized person. The violation of this provision is a criminal offense."[125] The investor can cancel any agreement to which the advertisement related or can recover restitutionary damages. The advertising regulations have a long-arm quality. If an advertisement is issued outside of the United Kingdom, it is treated as issued inside the country if directed to persons within the country.[126]

When a firm issues an advertisement, it must ensure that it is approved prior to its issuance by an individual within the firm appointed for this pur-

---

123. FSA § 48(e). In the U.S. no security that is an initial public offering can be sold without giving a prospectus to the purchaser which meets the requirements of the Securities Act of 1933. The definition of prospectus is broad including circulars and advertisements. There is an exception for "tombstone advertisements" which are merely records of public offerings and are regulated as to content by the Securities and Exchange Commission.

124. SECURITIES AND INVESTMENTS BOARD, THE FINANCIAL SERVICES (Conduct of Business) Rules 1990, Core Rule 40. [hereinafter SIB CONDUCT OF BUSINESS RULES]. Exempted from the advertising rules are those made in connection with listing of securities under FSA § 154, which are covered by another part of the statute, *id.* § 48(5), and reissue of approved advertisements.

125. An "advertisement" includes "every form of advertising, whether in a publication, by the display of notices, signs, labels, or show cards; by means of circulars, catalogs, price lists, or other documents; by an exhibition of pictures or photographs or cinematographic films; by way of sound broadcasting or television; or the distribution of records; or in any other manner." FSA § 207(2). An "investment advertisement" is any advertisement inviting persons to enter or offer to enter into an investment agreement or to exercise any rights conferred by an investment to acquire, dispose of, underwrite, or convert an investment or containing information calculated to lead directly or indirectly to persons doing so. *Id.* at § 57(2).

126. FSA § 207(3). There are a number of exceptions to the advertising restrictions, which relate to advertisements of public bodies or those bound by the rules of RIE's or clearinghouses, and by foreign nationals in the course of investment business lawfully carried on by him in another state, or advertisements subject to listing applications. FSA, § 58. The Secretary of State has not transferred his power to exempt from Section 57 certain kinds of investment advertisements, such as advertisements of a private character that deal with investments only incidentally, or advertisements issued to experts. *Id.*

pose and that individual must reasonably believe the advertisement is fair and not misleading.[127] The contents of advertisements must prominently display a number of required statements. A firm issuing or approving a specific investment advertisement, that is, one that identifies a particular investment or investment service, must identify both itself and its regulator. In dealing with a private customer, the advertisement must give information about the market or investment services, the terms of the offer, and the risks involved. An advertisement for a derivative product can only be sent to a customer for whom the firm believes the investment or investment service to be suitable.[128] Advertisements to U.K. investors by unregulated overseas persons or firms are regulated.[129]

The theory of the advertising restrictions is that the content of the advertisement and the form and manner of its presentation shall be such that it cannot be misunderstood by those to whom it is addressed, including persons who cannot be expected to have any special understanding of the matter in the advertisement. The level of sophistication required in advertisements can be laughably simple. For example, the SIB rules require "an advertisement which refers to taxation shall contain a warning that the levels and basis of taxation can change."[130]

The Investors' Compensation Fund

The statute provides that the Secretary of State may establish rules for a compensation fund to restore funds to investors from firms that have in-

---

127. SIB CONDUCT OF BUSINESS RULES, *supra* note 124, Core Rule 5. The firm can rely on a third party to provide the review.

128. A synopsis of an investment must give a fair view of the investment and the investment agreement. There are detailed rules on recommendations, comparisons with other investments, information about past performance, and risk warnings. SIB RULES, *supra* note 19, § 7.06; SECURITIES AND FUTURES AUTHORITY, BOARD NOTICE No. 2, PART 1 CONSULTATING DOCUMENT ON NEW CONDUCT OF BUSINESS RULES, 6–12 (1991). [hereinafter SFA CONDUCT OF BUSINESS RULES].

129. SIB Core Rule 6, SIB CONDUCT OF BUSINESS RULES, *supra* note 124, restricts firms from issuing or approving an investment advertisement to a private customer which might lead to an overseas person carrying on business which is not regulated with a U.K. private customer. An authorized firm issuing an advertisement on behalf of an unregulated overseas person to a client list must ensure that the ad contains prescribed disclosures and the firm has no reason to doubt the honesty and reliability of the overseas person in dealing with U.K. investors. The advertisement must disclose the nature of the protections lost by entering into the investment with an unregulated overseas person.

130. SIB RULES, *supra* note 19, Rule 7.18. *See also* SFA CONDUCT OF BUSINESS RULES, *supra* note 128, *Guidance on Advertising,* 13a.

curred civil liabilities but are unable to pay because of insolvency.[131] Investors, other than professional investors who place money with authorized firms in which the firm is acting as an intermediary, were given protection for up to £50,000 should an authorized firm become insolvent. The investor can collect his whole loss up to £30,000 and has the right to claim 90 percent of a further £20,000 loss. The compensation fund has a limit of £100 million in outlays per year. If that amount of claims is exceeded, payment to claimants may be scaled down. If the £100 million total is not reached, claims cannot be carried over to another year. The default must be incurred by the firm in connection with the regulated business done with the investor, and there is a six-month statute of limitations from the time the investor became aware or should have become aware of the default. Compensation totalling £5.1 million has been paid to 1,142 investors as of March 31, 1991.[132]

The scheme is not a fund, but a surcharge on all authorized firms. The total amount levied in any one year cannot exceed £100 million, which, given the size of recent scandals, is an inadequate sum. When a firm defaults, the compensation scheme manager assesses the claims against the firm and pays compensation to eligible investors. Professional investors have lesser rights to compensation.

The Investors Compensation Plan has been widely criticized. A major dispute between The Securities Association and the SIB was that the former wanted firm capital as opposed to revenue to be the criterion, because the minimum capital requirements were prescribed and monitored by regulators. The amount of capital reflected the riskiness of the firm's business, while gross revenue, the basis of assessment, does not. The SIB's position was that firms too easily could manipulate their capital. The Consumers

---

131. FSA § 54.

132. 1990/91 SIB REPORT, *supra* note, 34 at 34. The scheme does not cover interim authorized firms, insurance companies where the existing Policyholders Protection Act of 1975 remains in place, or business conducted through building societies which have their own scheme to cover deposits. Nor does the investors' compensation scheme apply to members of recognized professional bodies that have their own funds. Likewise, investors who suffer from losses in shares that are invested with unauthorized firms outside of U.K. jurisdiction or illegally operating in the United Kingdom are not covered under the scheme. SECURITIES AND INVESTMENTS BOARD, Annual Report 1988/89, 39 (1989) [hereinafter, 1988/ 89 SIB REPORT]. Goldsmith, *Customer pays for act of confusion*, THE TIMES (London), April 29, 1989 at 23, col. 1. The compensation fund is run by a private company, the Investors Compensation Scheme Limited, which is funded by authorized businesses but run independently. The act requires that any central compensation scheme be administered by a body representative of the members of any SRO involved. The interests of SROs, SIB authorized firms, and the public are represented on the board of the independent company. A. WHITTAKER, BUTTERWORTH'S INTERNATIONAL BANKING, 5, 6 (January 1989).

Association and the Labor Party felt that the scheme was too limited, too impracticable, and the sums available too small, and it would not increase public confidence in the financial services industry.[133]

A funded scheme could smooth out payments over several years and not disadvantage defrauded investors who discovered their losses at the end of the year. Not all sections of the financial services industry participate. Insurance companies and building societies, have their own compensation plans. There was a general criticism that member firms contributed according to revenue size as opposed to the riskiness of their investments. Lord Boardman, then chairman of National Westminster Bank, Britain's largest, commented: "I do not like the principle of the strong and good institutions bailing out the weak and less good."[134]

Initially, compensation is levied from other member firms of the SRO to which the firm in default belongs. The initial burden on SRO members is limited to a proportion of the £100 million levy equal to the proportion of the total of all authorized investment business conducted by the SRO.[135] The scheme, as enacted, reduces the cross-subsidization between different SROs. SFA members are less likely to go into default than members, of FIMBRA. This has led to severe problems for FIMBRA and its members who are unable to financially bear additional assessments.

FIMBRA's financial fragility was never more evident than in January 1991 when it requested a review of the compensation scheme. Because of the financial collapse of several authorized firms and the potential liability to FIMBRA members, the SRO faced insolvency. The SIB and the Investor's Compensation Scheme applied to the High Court for an interpretation of Section 54(1) of the Financial Services Act and to decide whether the com-

---

133. Goldsmith, *Banks Attack SIB Fund for Compensation*, THE TIMES (London), July 27, 1988 at 19, col. 2.

134. *Id.*

135. For example, if the SFA's members account for 65% percent of the total income of all investment businesses, SFA's liability would be a maximum £65 million. The remaining costs of up to £35 million would then be levied on all of the SROs, including SFA, in proportion to its declared income. Thus, SFA members' maximum liability for the compensation scheme would be £87.75 million, £65 million plus 65 percent of the £35 million remaining. The liabilities falling on any SRO are allocated between the member firms in proportion to their individual firm incomes. The same formula is used to levy administrative costs. Declared income is defined as total revenue excluding costs from commission, management, and other advisory fees. Profits from dealing in securities and other assets may be offset by losses, but losses cannot be offset against other types of revenue. SIB RULES, *supra* note 9, at ch. 9, pt. 4, Rule 4.02. To ease the burden on participating firms, the first levy was postponed until the 1989/90 fiscal year. Costs were funded through a line of credit from a syndicate of major international banks. 1988/89 SIB ANNUAL REPORT, *supra* note 132, at 55.

pensation plan had to reimburse investors who placed money with firms that collapsed in the period between the passage of the Financial Services Act in December 1986 and the official starting date of the compensation plan in August 1988.[136]

The SIB's position was that the compensation plan should reimburse anyone who lost money after August 1988 because of an authorized firm's collapse no matter when they invested funds. FIMBRA argued for a more restrictive approach. It claimed liability only for investments made with a collapsed firm after the scheme became effective in August 1988.

In June the court reached a compromise solution. It held that FIMBRA was liable for losses to investors caused by collapsed member firms from December 18, 1986, the date the Financial Services Act received the Queen's assent. However, compensation was available only for investments made after the statute's effectiveness. Prior investments, even if the collapse occurred after the implementation of the compensation plan, could be recovered, if at all, from the government.[137]

FIMBRA's liability was capped at £5 million. LAUTRO bailed out the struggling SRO assuming the next £14 million of liability by levying members who used FIMBRA members to distribute their products.[138] This called into question the viability of the plan and the future of FIMBRA.[139]

Other self-regulatory bodies have wanted to supplement the compensation plan. Prior to the Financial Services Act the Stock Exchange had a compensation scheme that indemnified an investor who lost money because of the misdeeds of a member firm. It was forced to join the general compensation plan. To the SIB's dismay, the Exchange announced that it would provide compensation to private investors who lose money through share frauds when it introduces a paperless trading system in 1992.[140]

All financial services compensation plans should come from one fund instead of separate schemes for insurance companies and building societies. The internationalization of financial services and 1992 raise questions of the scope of the scheme. Should English investors be covered for investments in a U.K. branch of an overeseas company? In turn, should overseas

---

136. Hughes, *Court considers investors' compensation*, FIN. TIMES, June 14, 1991 at 7. In February 1991 the Investor's Compensation Scheme froze all payments to investors pending resolution by the High Court.

137. SIB v. FIMBRA, 4 All E.R. 398 (Ch. 1991). The ruling meant that 160 investors would receive approximately £2 million in compensation.

138. Authers, *FIMBRA compensation plan announced*, FIN. TIMES, July 31, 1991 at 9.

139. Ellis, *Finance and the Family: Investor compensation can now be paid*, FIN. TIMES, Aug. 10, 1991 at IV.

140. Waters, *Compensation for share fraud losses to rise*, FIN. TIMES, Mar. 22, 1991 at 8 Waller, *SIB Rebukes Exchange*, FIN. TIMES, Mar. 22, 1991 at 13, col. 1.

investors be included if they invest in a U.K. authorized firm?[141] There is little doubt that the compensation plan will have to be altered.

The Prevention of Restrictive Practices

Throughout the new system is a concern that the SIB and SROs do not become mere trade associations for the financial services industry, reinstitutionalizing the anticompetitive practices that preceded the Big Bang.

Anticompetitive tendencies are a problem with any SROs, for there is an inherent conflict as to whom the organization primarily will be accountable, the statutory and supervisory authorities such as the SIB and the DTI, the public, or its membership.[142] Throughout the Financial Services Act is a requirement that the new regulatory organization's rule books be subject to review by the director general of fair trading to determine effects that are likely to reduce competition.

One payoff from the settlement of the dispute between the Stock Exchange and the Office of Fair Trading in 1983 was the Restrictive Trade Practices (Stock Exchange Act) of 1984 which provided the Exchange with an exemption from the Restrictive Trade Practices legislation.[143] That exemption has been continued, subject to a review by the secretary of state of trade and industry, even after delegation of regulatory functions to the SIB and the SROs. The review is to ensure that the rules, regulations, and guidance, " . . . do not have, and are not intended or likely to have, to any significant extent, the effect of restricting, distorting or preventing competition or, if they have or are likely to have that effect, that the effect is not greater than is necessary for the protection of investors."[144]

The development of the regulatory system described was a considerable achievement. A staggering amount was accomplished in a very short time. Whole industries were reorganized. Detailed rules were introduced that fundamentally changed the manner of conducting business. The complexity of the system, however, produced a reaction that forced a change in its direction and structure just as it got underway.

---

141. *See Compensation for Investors*, FIN. TIMES, Aug. 25, 1989 at 14, col. 1; RH, *SIB seeks to protect investors from default*, Aug. 26, 1989 at 21, col. 1.

142. *See* Page, *Self-Regulation: The Constitutional Dimension*, 49 MOD. L. REV. 141, 163–166 (1966).

143. Restrictive Trade Practices (Stock Exchange Act), 1984, *repealed by* FSA § 125(8) (1986).

144. FSA § 121(1). WHITTAKER & MORSE, *supra* note 3, at 12.01–12.14.

FOUR

RULE MAKING AND REACTION

Rules are at the heart of any regulatory system. They govern the conduct of business within the regulated area, determine access to the industry regulated, and establish norms of behavior. Monitoring compliance with administrative regulations and imposing sanctions for their violation are key responsibilities of regulators.

The setting of standards and the process of rule making often render the texture of a regulatory system and define the boundaries of its effectiveness and acceptance. In his classic book, *The Administrative Process*, James Landis spoke of the use of standards and presaged some of the implementation problems of the SIB:

> Standards, if adequately drafted, afford great protection to administration. By limiting the area of the exercise of discretion, they tend to routinize administration and to that degree relieve it from the play of political and economic pressures which otherwise might be harmful. The pressing problem today, however, is to get the administrative to assume the responsibilities that it properly should assume. Political and official life to too great an extent tends to favor routinization. The assumption of responsibility by an agency is always a gamble that may well make more enemies than friends. The easiest course is frequently that of inaction. A legalistic approach that reads a governing statute with the hope of finding limitations upon authority rather than grants of power with which to act decisively is thus common.[1]

The process of rule making, the reception of rules by the regulated, and the impact of regulation upon behavior can assist in the analysis of the effectiveness of the regulatory system. The SIB's rule making accentuated the Financial Services Act's weaknesses and the lack of support within the City for the regulatory system. In this chapter, we examine the problems in im-

---

1. J. LANDIS, THE ADMINISTRATIVE PROCESS 75 (1936).

plementation of the SIB's rules, the need for a retrenchment from the original approach, and a new settlement with the financial services industry.

Rule Making Authority Under the
Financial Services Act

The investor protection framework was conceived to ensure that principles of fair dealing permeated the financial services industry. This included
safeguards against abuses arising from conflicts of interests, obligations of
fair dealing, duties of disclosure, protection of clients' assets, maintenance
of proper records, adequate financial resources, and internal compliance
procedures in the conduct of investment business.[2]

The SROs were required to have rules governing the carrying-on of investment business by their members which, together with statements of
principle and rules, regulations, and codes drafted by the SIB pursuant to
the Financial Services Act, afforded an adequate level of investor protection.[3] In a self-regulatory system, the firm is the primary monitor of its employees. To achieve compliance from investment businesses, firms joining
an SRO agree to bind themselves to the rules of that body. The SIB's authority to promulgate binding rules on the SROs is based on principles in
the enabling statute.[4]

---

2. FINANCIAL SERVICES IN THE UNITED KINGDOM: A NEW FRAMEWORK FOR INVESTOR
PROTECTION, 1985, Cmnd. No. 9432, at 19–22.

3. Financial Services Act (FSA), 1986, ch. 60, sched. 2, "Safeguards for Investors."

4. In the first instance, the Secretary of State for Trade and Industry can promulgate
regulations prescribing anything which by the Financial Services Act is authorized or required to be prescribed. This rule-making authority is subject to annulment by resolution
of either house of Parliament. FSA pt. X, § 205. The Secretary of State for Trade and Industry's rules are exercisable by statutory instrument. There is a broad flexibility for rule
making in that different provisions can be made for individual cases. *Id.* at § 205(3). There
is a requirement that the rule-making authority publish information and advice about the
act. Private advice to firms and investors may also be given. A. WHITTAKER & G. MORSE,
THE FINANCIAL SERVICES ACT 1986: A GUIDE TO THE NEW LAW § 21.71 (1988). The statutory basis for the SIB's rule-making authority is Section 114(9), which provides that the
secretary of state shall not make a delegation order transferring any legislative functions
unless the agency has furnished a copy of the instruments it proposes to issue or make in
the exercise of those functions, and he is satisfied that those instruments will afford investors an adequate level of protection and comply with the principles of schedule 8. FSA
§ 114(9) *as amended by* Companies Act, 1989, ch. 40, sched. 23, 12 (1989). The recent
amendments to the Financial Services Act reflect the SIB's change in philosophy which add
statements of principle in addition to rules and regulations that were specified in the original version of the section.

The principles of schedule 8 require the designated agency to have high standards of in-

The statute and delegation orders provide for the SIB to make rules on a variety of topics, including the conduct of business, financial resources, cancellation of transactions, handling of client's money, and unsolicited or "cold" calls.[5]

Although most of the SIB's rules only apply to the hundred or so firms authorized directly by it, and to interim authorized firms while their applications are being reviewed by the appropriate SRO, they have a direct impact over the whole range of financial services because of the mandate of equivalence. Initially, this required SROs or recognized professional bodies to have rules that "afford investors protection at least equivalent to that afforded" by the SIB. More recently, equivalence has been replaced by a lesser standard that rules provide an "adequate" level of investor protection. The SIB's rule book set the standard for the SROs. Because of the scope of financial services, the SIB's rules had to be of more general application than those of an SRO.

The Process of Rule Making

Commencing in August 1985, the SIB published consultative documents and policy papers.[6] By the time of the SIB's application to the Secretary of State for designation, the SIB's rule book had grown to 430 pages in length and over four pounds in weight, covering all aspects of conducting business in stunning detail, at least to the City. The new framework had become an oxymoron. Deregulation of financial services had become regulation of the most detailed sort.[7]

---

tegrity and fair dealing in the conduct of investment business; provisions for requiring authorized persons to act with skill, due care, and diligence in providing any service; and requirements that firms subordinate their interests to those of clients, act fairly between clients, and have due regard for their circumstances. The agency must mandate disclosure of material facts such as commissions, interests, and the capacity in which the firm deals; have requirements that firms disclose sufficient information to ensure investors make an informed decision; make proper provisions for protection of customer's property; and keep records and provide for their inspection. The designated agency must recognize that rules which are appropriate for regulating the conduct of business for some classes of investors may not be appropriate for others. FSA, sched. 8.

5. *Id.* at §§ 48–49, 51, 54–56. The SIB's original rule book dealt with the above mentioned subject matter in excruciating detail. *See* SECURITIES AND INVESTMENTS BOARD, FINANCIAL SERVICES RULES AND REGULATIONS (1988) [hereinafter SIB RULES].

6. In February 1986 it began publishing draft sections of its rule book. The first and larger part of the rulebook, including those rules needed to judge the "equivalence" of the rules of potential SROs and Recognized Professional Bodies, was issued on October 7, 1987. Further rules, regulations, and amendments to the originally published rules have been published periodically.

7. The SIB has an internal rules committee. The public process of rule making com-

Fears of the civil service and of a runaway agency pervade the statute. The Financial Services Act directs how the SIB should discharge its rule-making responsibilities; in other words, decisions must be made at the appropriate level, rather than by the clerks or lawyers. The SIB's governing body, its board, as opposed to staff, must make any rules or regulations. Public members of the board should not be window dressing.[8] In fact, the statutory injunctions were worthless. Board members approved the draft rules when first published and again if there were major changes. The technical nature of the rules, their quantity, and the board's deliberative process, or lack thereof, made the rules the work of the drafters. Nor was the consultative process broad or responsive enough to demands for change. Only when the first draft rules were published did much of the City gain an inkling as to what the new statute had wrought.

Implementation of the Rules

To many in the financial services industry, the purpose of this new regulatory system was to reassure the public of the integrity of the financial markets and prevent fraudulent schemes against the unsophisticated investors by fringe operators. It was important to have sanctions against the marginal elements, but the new system was not expected to intrude upon the practices of the respectable. In the words of John Quinton, then chairman of Barclays: "It must not be forgotten that regulation is the servant of the financial system."[9]

Even the Prevention of Fraud (Investments) Act prohibited fraudulent and deceitful activities. It is one thing for a statute to say in effect: thou shall not steal. The vast majority of firms don't need that injunction. However, it is quite another to require the honest firm to submit documents verifying such probity. While many in the City yelped against any regulation,

---

mences with the publication of consultative documents or policy papers which invite comments from the public. Interested individuals or groups meet with the SIB. After publication of the consultative papers, the actual drafting of rules commences. A retired parliamentary draftsman, Henry DeWaal, in consultation with working parties of practitioners and the SIB staff, drafted the original rules which were then published, often followed by amendments. During this whole process, the SIB met with the DTI and groups within SROs affected by a particular rule. The statute mandates consultation with the public through publication in the manner best calculated to bring the proposals to the attention of the public together with representations as to cost and that the public can submit comments on the proposals. FSA, sched. 9(12) *as amended by* Companies Act, 1989, ch. 40, sched. 23(6) (1989).

8. FSA, sched. 7(2)(1),(2),(4).

9. *Global Equities Markets 8: Grave Doubts About the Rule Books*, FIN. TIMES, Oct. 21, 1987 at 1, col. 6.

there were legitimate issues and grievances. The scope and detail of the rule books were universally criticized. The rules were just not fit for the purposes envisaged. According to John Plender, the respected financial journalist:

> The scope of the rulebook [was] contentious. The original intention was to protect the private investor while leaving the professionals in the wholesale financial markets to carry on with minimum interference. But instead of protecting Aunt Agatha, many of the rules appear to be protecting National Westminster Bank and Citicorp.[10]

Though the government had used the comforting term "self-regulation," in fact, the SIB's staff of lawyers and former civil servants imposed excruciatingly detailed rules.[11] Why were the rule books so complex? At least four justifications have been offered. One, the public posture of the SIB, was that the act's mandate, particularly in the schedules relating to SROs and the SIB, gave the designated agency no choice but to draft an all-inclusive rule book.

Privately, the SIB offered a very different reason: the DTI had insisted on such detail.[12] DTI had forced the SIB to add items to its "detailed" rule books. Throughout much of this early period the SIB was undesignated and wanted to ensure that it satisfied the DTI. Two other justifications for the complexity of the rule books have been offered. One was the SIB's narrow interpretation of the concept of "equivalence." The second was the fear by the SROs that Section 62 of the act would lead to widespread frivolous and expensive litigation. The nub of the complexity, inflexibility, and comprehensiveness of the SIB's rules was the interpretation of the "equivalence" requirement. Originally, the City believed that the "equivalence" of an SRO's commitment to investor protection would involve an overall evaluation by the SIB of a range of factors concerning an SRO, such as the quality of its staff, its complaint and monitoring systems, and an evaluation of the SRO's rule book as a whole rather than a section-by-section critique. Instead, the SIB undertook a line-by-line analysis of the SROs' rule books and

---

10. Plender, *Cries of Foul: Regulating the City from the Maze,* FIN. TIMES, Sept. 25, 1987 at 18, col. 1 [hereinafter Plender].

11. Brierly, *City Revolts Against the Regulators,* THE SUNDAY TIMES (London), Feb. 21, 1988 at D3, col. 1.

12. The published rules were very different from their initial conception. Gower, who became the SIB's legal advisor, initially suggested a series of general principles that would be fleshed out as necessary by the SROs. The SIB's earliest internal drafts reflected this generalist approach. This was rejected by the DTI, which felt this would relieve the financial services industry from the mandate of the legislation. It directed a more detailed, legalistic approach that would ensure that the SROs offered an adequate level of protection.

engaged in acrimonious trench warfare to gain its version of equivalence.[13] Its justification was that the statute's mandate required as much. If the SIB's rule book was too general, then equivalence would be undefined and the investor would be harmed.[14]

The City became united in its view that the financial services business was misunderstood both in form and spirit by its regulators. The rules were not the guides the City expected, but rather mandates. The new system required the City not only to pursue criminals but also to rethink and reorganize the way it conducted its business.[15]

Turning the act's intentions into clear, consistent, and certain rules became a much greater task than expected. The rule book reflected a lack of balance between rules needed to protect the small investor—a small part of the financial markets except for sales of insurance and unit trusts—and the need of professionals to compete in the most cost-efficient way. The SIB's rules reflected a definitional difficulty in distinguishing between the wholesale and retail markets. Protecting the small private investor in the retail markets also affected the professional investor in the wholesale markets. There was no balance between the clarity of the rules and the desire for certainty. The SIB considered the criticism exaggerated, reacting to it with disdain and even a hectoring manner. "There is no such thing as a user friendly rulebook," said Sir Kenneth Berrill.[16]

There was general protest that the SIB's rules were drafted by lawyers, accountants, and civil servants rather than by practitioners. The City felt that the SIB's staff misunderstood the nature of the financial services business. Berrill, though he had worked for five years in the City, was considered a civil servant at heart. Sir Kenneth's manner toward the regulated was that of academic to student. He was authoritarian, aggressive, undiplomatic, and uncompromising in defense of the rule book.[17]

---

13. Plender, *supra* note 10.

14. *See* the comments of John Morgan, chief executive of IMRO; Wolman, *Detailed Investor Protection Rules Also Shield Firms*, FIN. TIMES, July 6, 1988 at 6.

15. Berrill's response was that the act didn't divide people into good and bad: "The rules state that if you are doing a certain kind of activity you must follow certain rules." Brewerton, *Berrill on the firing line as the City Revolution arrives*, THE TIMES (London), Feb. 5, 1988 at 24, col. 3.

16. *Id.*

17. At one point the SIB responded to criticism of the lack of practitioner input by suggesting that final judgment on the SROs' rule books would be made by the practitioner-dominated board. Without a line-by-line examination to determine equivalence, the SIB's staff could not provide the board with adequate information. Plender, *supra* note 10. We have discussed the quality of board deliberation, where Berrill's agenda was an express train whizzing through a local stop. In fact, there was practitioner input, but it was reactive rather than initiatory. Such advice was inadequate at the drafting stage. The practitioner

Throughout 1986 and the beginning of 1987 the SIB bulldozed ahead with its rules. Its position was reinforced by the Guinness scandal, which became public at the end of 1986. Guinness, which involved market manipulation in the context of a takeover bid, had predated the Financial Services Act. However, it signified something seriously awry in the City.

The SIB managed to clash with the City's most powerful vested interest groups: the clearing banks, the insurance companies, the unit trust industry, the professions, the large foreign banks, and the securities industry. The issues of dispute affected the degree of investor protection, the relationships between the SROs, the SIB, and other regulators, and the scope and cost of the new system. Rule making became a means of drastically reorganizing the financial services sector and mandating how business should be conducted. Though the SIB got its way on most of these issues, its credibility and support eroded with each victory. There were several difficult disagreements between the SIB and the SROs, particularly The Securities Association. The SIB's approach to equivalence forced the SROs to draft detailed rule books as well.[18]

Matters of Contention Between the SROs and the SIB

Section 62: Private Rights of Action

Section 62 provided for an action for damages for a person who suffered loss as a result of the contravention of an SRO rule by a member of an SRO or a person certified by a recognized professional body.[19] This section produced an onslaught of lobbying and outrage against the SIB and the act,

---

participation primarily occurred from the SROs after the SIB's rule book was drafted, so that such contributions were amendatory.

18. The SROs' rule books exceeded even the SIB's in their attempts at completeness. On the advice of counsel (the solicitors Allen & Overy). The Securities Association drafted a rule book that attempted to provide certainty for every situation. If a securities firm knew exactly what was expected of it in advance from The Securities Association rule book, it would be protected from suit for a minor breach of the rules under Section 62.

19. FSA § 62(2) provided: Subsection 1 [which grants a cause of action to a person who suffers loss because of a contravention of the conduct of business rules, a violation of conditions of conducting investment business under section 50, any requirements imposed by an order requiring the obtaining of insurance under section 50, or the employment of prohibited person] applies also to a contravention by a member of a recognized self-regulating organization or a person certified by a recognized professional body of any rules of the organization or body relating to a matter in respect of which rules or regulations have been or could be made under this Chapter in relation to an authorized person who is not such a member or so certified.

with the large international firms leading the fight. They feared Section 62 would become like the SEC's Rule 10b-5,[20] an expansive concept that would encourage litigation over minor breaches of the rules by professional investors who had lost money or wanted to delay payment. However, this was a misconception, for under U.S. securities law, there is no explicit statutory authorization for a private cause of action for violation of a rule of an SRO, and the majority rule is that none can be implied.[21] There also was concern that suits would be brought shortly after the rules became effective, giving an inadequate shakedown period.

The section was drafted ambiguously. The language was unclear as to who could sue.[22] Still, the fear of Section 62 was overblown, for at most, it codified a common law cause of action. In addition, its opponents failed to consider a very real difference between the English and American legal systems: in the English system the loser pays attorneys' fees, a substantial detriment to strike suits.

Despite the merits of such opposition, the length and complexity of the rule books were due to the fear of Section 62. There also was a fear of the judiciary. Obligations had to be defined precisely so that judges could not interpret the rules liberally and tilt toward plaintiffs. Section 62 was the single greatest cause of anger and frustration with the new framework.[23]

After vigorous lobbying by The Securities Association, on November 21, 1987, Lord Young delayed the implementation of Section 62(2) until October 3, 1988, so as to allow the act to settle in.[24] The delay in implementation did not benefit firms directly authorized by the SIB or those with interim authorization. At the end of 1988 the government introduced a new section, 62A, to the Financial Services Act which restricted actions for damages to those by private investors only.[25] This reduced potential liability to firms, as business customers and professional investors would be relegated to their common-law rights.

There were other major disputes over the rules between the SROs and the SIB, the result of which had a significant impact upon the shape of financial

20. 17 C.F.R. § 240.10b-5.
21. *See* Walck v. American Stock Exchange, Inc., 687 F.2d 778, 788 (3d Cir. 1982), *cert. denied*, 461 U.S. 942 ["no basis for an inference that the Exchanges in their quasi-legislative capacity intended to subject themselves to damages for non enforcement"].
22. Whittaker, *Development, Structure, and Principal Features of the Regulatory System*, in 1 FINANCIAL SERVICES LAW AND PRACTICE (A. Whittaker ed., 1991) [hereinafter FINANCIAL SERVICES LAW AND PRACTICE] at 28–30. It has been suggested that the provision creates strict liability with the result that unintentional contraventions could violate the section.
23. Plender, *supra* note 10.
24. FSA, 1986 (Commencement) (No. 6), Order 1987, S. I. 1997.
25. Companies Act, 1989. Ch. 40, § 193 (1989).

services practices. Among the most complex of the disputes was the amount of capital adequacy members of The Securities Association would be required to maintain, who would monitor compliance with financial regulations, and with whose rules would members of the Securities Association have to comply—the SIB's or the more rigorous Bank of England's.

Lead Regulators

The requirement that all investment businesses be authorized pointed up some of the system's complexity. Membership in an SRO does not permit a firm to engage in every kind of investment business.[26] Subsidiaries of large financial conglomerates must obtain authorization by joining several SROs. For example, the securities activities of the investment bank Kleinwort Benson required it to join The Securities Association. Its fund managing subsidiary joined IMRO. Sharps Pixley, its bullion trader, became part of the Association of Futures Brokers and Dealers. KG Insurance Brokers, its insurance subsidiary, is a member of FIMBRA. Kleinwort Barrington joined LAUTRO to enable it to sell unit trusts and joined IMRO so it could manage those trusts.[27]

Barclays de Zoete Wedd made twelve different applications to three SROs. As an investment bank and gilts dealer it also had to report to the Bank of England. Its parent, Barclays Bank, a clearing bank, is regulated by the Bank of England but made six applications to various SROs for authorization of other activities.[28]

To minimize the complexity and inconvenience of multiple authorizations and supervision, the SIB established the lead regulator concept, whereby the Bank of England, the SIB, or most commonly, one SRO whose focus related to the largest part of a firm's business, became primarily responsible for financial surveillance and for monitoring compliance with liquid capital requirements.[29] The lead regulator concept ensures that responsibilities of financial surveillance are allocated to a single authority.

SROs are required to share information with one another. The lead regulator receives and assesses all information relevant to the capital adequacy of the firm and notifies other SROs if there is a deficiency. When a firm has inadequate capital, the other SROs are expected to take steps to limit the firm's conduct of business. The lead regulator normally would not monitor compliance with conduct of business rules in areas not within the scope for

---

26. *See* THE SECURITIES ASSOCIATION, RULE BOOK, Ch. I, rules 10.01–10.04 (1989).

27. *Finance Brief—British Investors' bill of rights,* ECONOMIST, Apr. 30, 1988 at 80.

28. *From Berrill Lynch to Slater Walker,* ECONOMIST, Mar. 5, 1988 at 73.

29. *See* SECURITIES AND INVESTMENTS BOARD, BANKS AND SRO MEMBERSHIP, Guidance Release 1/87 (July 1987).

which it has authorized a firm. Nor would it judge the fitness and properness of the firm outside of its capital adequacy. This is the responsibility of
the SRO that is charged with monitoring the investment business of the particular subsidiary.[30]

Capital Adequacy Requirements

The capital adequacy requirements of all financial services firms are not
the same. Capital adequacy refers to the minimal financial resources necessary to conduct business. Some investment businesses, such as banks, are
supervised by other regulators, such as the Bank of England which has different standards and goals for capital adequacy than the SIB. This became
a source of early conflict between the two regulatory bodies. Who would
monitor the capital adequacy requirements of the securities subsidiaries of
banks?

The Bank of England's regulations for capital requirements of banks is
more rigorous than those of the SIB, although there is an overlap between
the two. A securities firm involved in the wholesale money markets must be
an institution listed by the Bank of England. If that firm engages in the
Eurobond markets, it is subject to regulation by both bodies. Where a securities trader is also a bank, there is the additional problem of overlapping
responsibility. This led to difficult negotiations between the SIB and the
Bank of England.

The Bank desired to create a greater convergence between U.K. and U.S.
regulatory practice such as it sought with the U.S. Federal Reserve Board in
banking regulation. It suggested that the SIB adopt the SEC's capital adequacy requirements.[31] However, the SIB rejected this because it felt that the
SEC's rules were neither broad nor flexible enough.[32] The SIB's rules represent a missed opportunity to harmonize regulation across international
boundaries.

In July 1987 an agreement was reached whereby the SIB, rather than the
Bank of England, would have primary responsibility for drafting regulations governing the securities activities of banks. The Bank would be responsible for monitoring compliance and capital adequacy.[33] What the

---

30. SECURITIES AND INVESTMENTS BOARD, REGULATION OF INVESTMENT BUSINESS: THE
NEW FRAMEWORK, 10–11 (1985).

31. 17 C.F.R. § 140.15c(3)(1).

32. A major difference between SIB and SEC capital adequacy requirements is that certain U.K. companies must maintain the equivalent of three months' expenditures in liquid
form. *See* SIB RULES, *supra* note 5 at Ch. II, rule 9.

33. The Bank of England is the central point of conduct for overseas banks in London.
One reason for this approach was a disagreement with the SIB over the Bank's approach to

agreement means in an age of financial conglomeration is that a bank that separates its securities business from its banking business by establishing a subsidiary to deal in securities will be regulated by the Bank of England. However, a bank whose business is almost exclusively in the securities area will have applied to it the relevant SRO's rules without modification. The Bank of England acts as lead regulator and will apply its own capital adequacy requirements to banks whose business is spread evenly between investment business and banking. The capital requirements for the securities business are guided by the rules of the relevant SRO, but the Bank monitors them. Bank of England rules will apply without modification to banks with a very small securities business.[34] Which approach is taken is decided on a case-by-case basis. There is an inevitable overlap.[35]

The agreement between the Bank of England and the SIB has not achieved regulatory parity. In February 1989, First Interstate Capital Markets, the U.K. investment banking subsidiary of First Interstate, a Los Angeles bank, created a separate subsidiary to handle its securities activities so that the SFA rather than the Bank of England would be the lead regulator. The reason for the switch was the belief that the Bank's capital requirements were more onerous than SFA's, which are formulated for securities firms with shorter-term assets than banks. Other banks have considered making such a switch, which could create a kind of regulatory arbitrage.[36] Such a confusing and ad hoc approach is the result of having two regulators in overlapping areas, one of which is operating under a statute, the other, largely informally.

The Regulation of Foreign Bank Branches

London has long been a magnet for financial institutions, particularly for banks chartered elsewhere. Domestic banking activities of foreign banks in

---

capital adequacy requirements. The SIB wanted capital adequacy judgment on a transaction-by-transaction basis, whereas the Bank is more inclined to look at the entity as a whole in determining capital requirements. Cohen, *UK Regulators Agree on Bank Securities Supervision*, REUTERS, July 2, 1987 (Nexis Fin. file).

34. O'Donohue, *Looking After Aunt Agatha et. al.*, EUROMONEY, Sept. 1987 at 459 (Nexis Fin. file).

35. In Berrill's words, "The banking supervisor and the investment supervisor are tied together by handcuffs. They've both got to agree all the time that the combined operation is still viable." Duffy, *New British Law is Step to Regulate Global Business*, AM. BANKER, July 20, 1987 at 1 (Nexis Fin. file) [hereinafter Duffy]. Most banks with securities subsidiaries would suggest they wore the handcuffs.

36. Campbell, *US bank to hive off securities business*, FIN. TIMES, Feb. 27, 1989 at 8, col. 5; Campbell, *Casting doubt on the parity of City rules*, FIN. TIMES, Feb. 28, 1989 at 9, col. 2.

the United Kingdom are supervised by the Bank of England. One of the most contentious issues in the implementation of the Financial Services Act was the extent of SIB regulation over foreign banks' securities subsidiaries that conducted business in the United Kingdom. Clearly, the Financial Services Act enabled the SIB or The Securities Association to monitor the conduct of business and marketing of investments. Could the SIB impose capital adequacy requirements? Most banks did not maintain separate capital reserves for their securities activities.

Justifiably, the SIB was concerned about investment firms chartered in a country that had a primitive or evolving scheme of securities regulation or had no capital requirements for conducting securities activities. This would place U.K. securities firms, required to maintain adequate reserves of capital, at a competitive disadvantage and leave British investors at risk if an undercapitalized foreign firm failed.

However, stringent regulation or demands for regulation of foreign corporations would be perceived as an infringement upon foreign sovereignty and contrary to the EEC's Second Banking Directive, which intended to lower transnational banking barriers to create a unified banking structure by 1992.[37] British banks feared that the EC countries would retaliate and make the opening of U.K. branches on the continent more difficult if the SIB regulated the foreign branches' securities activities too severely.

The Securities Association became involved in this controversy because many of the affected institutions were the broking subsidiaries of large American banks and had a prominent role in The Securities Association. These subsidiaries were barely capitalized and tended to be chartered in Delaware, a jurisdiction known for its sympathy to management. They threatened to move elsewhere if they could not gain authorization.

The original proposal was to develop a lead regulator arrangement whereby the SIB would enter into memoranda of understanding with home supervisors. The SIB would be the lead regulator, but would rely to varying degrees upon home-state supervisors to monitor financial stability. Banks with securities subsidiaries would be placed into one of three categories depending on the willingness of the home regulator to exchange information and the equivalence of the home regulatory system to the United Kingdom's. The greater the willingness to exchange information and the more equivalent the standards to the home supervisory regime, the more willing

---

37. Under the Second Banking Directive, banks from European Community countries would be treated like domestic banks no matter where they did business. Proposal for a second banking directive on the Coordination of Laws, Regulations, and Administrative Provisions Relating to the Taking-up and Pursuit of the Business of Credit Institutions and Amending Directive 77/780, Eur. Comm'n Doc. (COM No. 715 final) (1988) [hereinafter Second Banking Directive].

the SIB would be to apply the home country's financial standards. Where the home regulator was unwilling or unable to share information or home supervision was inadequate or nonexistent, the SIB would apply its financial regulations.

The SIB found it difficult to obtain memoranda of understanding. Only the United Kingdom and the United States insisted upon financial reserves to support securities activities. While most foreign banks are subject to a banking regulator in their home jurisdiction, their supervisors are not accustomed to sharing information with other *securities* regulators and resisted on that ground. In Europe, where banks regularly engage in the securities business, banking authorities had little desire to supply information to the SIB. France and Germany were particularly reluctant to participate, as the EEC was expected to produce its own regime.[38]

As this was played out, international banks were left with interim status on "A Day," which to "carriage trade" firms was an embarrassment and possibly off-putting to the public.[39] Interim status had to be disclosed on the firm's letterhead. That the interim status was a result of a dispute between the SIB, The Securities Association, and foreign regulators, of course, was absent from the stationery.

The Securities Association strongly desired to authorize these foreign branches as soon as possible, but obtain a third-party guarantee of their financial backing. However, the SIB instructed TSA to postpone final authorization. The Securities Association then suggested that the SIB allow the Bank of England to contact the home supervisor of banks with London securities operations to ascertain whether the capital was adequate.

In August 1988 the SIB retreated. It redefined the requirements of provision of information by home regulators. Now information would be expected from the home regulator only when there was a cause for concern. The process of full authorization of foreign firms began. The supervisory duties of foreign banks remain with the Bank of England, which receives the information from the foreign regulator. The home regulator, rather than the SIB, is the lead regulator. The SIB has access to the information if there is a reasonable cause for concern.[40] The SIB's retreat affected only the

---

38. *SIB Under Siege*, ECONOMIST, July 30, 1988 at 71.

39. *See* Chapter 3, *supra* at pp. 78–79. The most serious consequence to international firms of interim status was ineligibility to participate in the compensation scheme, which might have frightened retail customers. Nor would the postponement of the implementation of Section 62 apply, thereby opening them to potential liabilities.

40. Prestley, *U.K. Regulatory Body Makes More Overseas Pacts*, REUTERS RELEASE, Sept. 5, 1988 (Nexis Fin. file). If a firm is in difficulty or at risk, the foreign regulator provides a report to the SIB or appropriate SRO. The SIB will do the same for the foreign regulator. The Securities Association reserved the right to require branches to submit state-

capital adequacy requirements of foreign branches securities activities. Market conduct and investor protection requirements are enforced by the SIB under its rules or those of the appropriate SRO.[41]

The SIB's hard line seemed difficult to comprehend. The EC's Second Banking Directive scheduled to become effective in 1992 states that once a bank is licensed by its home state, it can trade securities or conduct other business in branches anywhere within the community.[42] Therefore, the efforts to obtain memoranda of understanding seemed a waste of effort. If the SIB was successful, U.K. regulation would be stricter than other EC states. Why would any bank want to do business in London or come under British supervision after 1992?[43]

Polarization

A fundamental goal of the Financial Services Act is protection of the small investor whose main contact with the financial services industry is through purchase of life insurance or collective investments such as unit trusts. The average Briton's primary assets are his house and pension entitlement, both of which may involve life insurance policies that are mortgage or pension related. The typical consumer is at a severe informational disadvantage. Available products are complex and highly differentiated, making it extremely difficult for the investor to know precisely what he is buying or how to comparison shop. The selling costs have been high, undisclosed, and front-ended, discouraging the investor from cashing out his investments.

The small investor needed competent advice. Even if he received it, often he would not know the capacity in which it was given: whether it was independent and unbiased, whether the advisor was tied to one insurance company, or whether the available market was surveyed before making the recommendation. Frequently, investment and insurance advisors were tied to a particular company though the investor was unaware of this fact. Even independent intermediaries had links to a few companies through hidden

---

ments showing their position risks and to notify it when taking large risks. Wolman, *Accord Reached on Authorization of Foreign Banks*, FIN. TIMES, Nov. 10, 1988 at 14.

41. At the same time, the SIB reached memoranda of understanding with foreign regulatory bodies to share information. With such recalcitrant regulators as the German Federal Supervisory Office, the SIB agreed to redefine the circumstances under which it would seek information. Where an agreement was reached with an overseas regulator, it was provided that information would be shared with the SIB and TSA, the latter being a signatory to the arrangement.

42. Second Banking Directive, *supra* note 37 at Art. 5.

43. *SIB Under Siege*, ECONOMIST, July 30, 1988 at 71.

support or volume overrides; that is, a salesman receives a higher commission by placing more volume with a particular company.[44]

The Gower Report discussed widespread abuses in the behavior of insurance agents such as inaccurate disclosure of commissions, harsh selling techniques, and often excessive inducements given to agents to sell a particular type of policy.[45] Life insurance, mutual funds, and similar investment products are sold on the basis of commission. Costs that reduce an investor's return are the commission taken by the broker or salesman and an expense charge by the company.[46] Gower disclosed that insurance salesmen were selling policies and investments that gave the salesmen the highest commission, but which were not necessarily the most suitable for the investor.

A major force in the sale of life insurance and unit trusts and in money management are the clearing banks which have branches throughout the country. Bank branches offered a wide range of services ranging from personal financial advice to travel services. All of the large banks owned insurance companies and managed unit trusts. The private investor often used his local bank branch officer as a financial advisor and purchased insurance or other investment products of bank subsidiaries without realizing that he was not receiving independent advice or that he was purchasing the "house brand" insurance or unit trust.

To remedy these problems the SIB developed the concept of polarization. Anyone giving advice or selling life insurance or unit trusts had to make a choice. He could be either a company representative, working for one company or group and selling the products of that group, or an independent intermediary, acting as an agent for the customer and scanning the whole market for the most suitable product for the investor, (known as "best advice"). If a bank or building society chose to be an independent intermediary, it could sell all products but its own. All of the clearing banks, save National Westminster, chose to sell their own products.

Polarization was not required in other areas of the financial services industry.[47] With one fell swoop Berrill took on the building societies, the

---

44. *See* SIB Briefing Note: *Polarisation*, Feb. 24, 1987. An estimated $13 billion in insurance premiums are paid each year, much of that figure comes from the poorest and least sophisticated of investors. *Death of a Salespitch*, ECONOMIST, Aug. 5, 1989 at 67.

45. L.C.B. GOWER, REVIEW OF INVESTOR PROTECTION: REPORT PART I, 1984 Cmnd. No. 9215, 87–93.

46. D. LOMAX, LONDON MARKETS AFTER THE FINANCIAL SERVICES ACT, 143–47 (1987) [hereinafter LOMAX].

47. The SIB concluded that investors would be confused as to the nature of the service available to them and disclosure of status alone would not provide sufficient protection. *See* SIB Briefing Note: *Polarisation*, Feb. 24, 1987. Financial products subject to the polar-

clearing banks, the unit trust industry, and the life insurance companies and radically changed the way they did business. He could have merely required disclosure of conflicts of interest, but he felt this was insufficient. He was probably right. However, the SIB had not a clue as to the impact of such a change on the life insurance industry's structure.

The SIB required the independent agent to disclose that he received a commission from the life insurance company whose policy was sold and, if requested, to disclose the amount of the commission.[48] Tied salesmen had to disclose that they were an employee of a particular company, but they did not have to disclose their fees, salaries, or commissions. Both tied agents and independents had to send policyholders follow-up letters with information about cost-to-premium ratios. Only the independent agent had to disclose the percentage of the policy premium that was paid to him each year as part of his commission. Another problem for the independent intermediary was that best advice to the client usually did not correlate with best commission for the salesman. A tied agent only had the duty to recommend the most suitable policy of his company.

There were two justifications for this disparate treatment. The independent intermediary was the agent of the customer, whereas the tied salesman was the agent of his employer, the insurance company. Second, the tied agent was compensated in many ways other than through commissions, so the impact of commission disclosure could be vitiated.[49]

Competition within the insurance industry had led to a gradual increase in commissions. Companies attempted to expand or tried to gain the favor

---

ization principle include life insurance, authorized unit trusts, personal equity plans with a built-in unit trust component, and recognized collective investment schemes. In 1992, polarization will apply to investment trust savings plans. All of these are called "packaged products."

48. Polarization is now derived from principle 6, *see infra* p. 138, which requires firms to avoid conflicts of interest, or where they arise, to ensure fair treatment to all customers through disclosure, internal rules of confidentiality, declining to act, or otherwise. Core rule 4 (polarization) mandates a firm advising a private customer on packaged products to do so as a product company or as an independent intermediary. A firm which is a product company cannot advise private customers as to packaged products which are not part of its group. The polarization principle is reinforced by core rules 16 (suitability) and 17 (standards of advice on packaged products). Under the suitability requirement all firms must recommend only products or services that are suitable for the customer in light of information provided by him and his investment objectives. The best advice obligation piggybacks on the suitability requisite. It requires firms to be knowledgeable about the products available, to assess the customer's needs, and prohibits independent intermediaries from recommending the product of another company in the same corporate group unless it is better than any other available product.

49. *See British life assurance: Spiking the independents*, ECONOMIST, Dec. 17, 1988 at 91.

of brokers by offering "overrider" commissions, which meant that the scale of commission would increase with the volume of policies sold. The broker, supposedly independent, would then steer the investor toward one company or policy or emphasize one company's products. The more of that product he sold, the greater his commission income.[50]

To correct these abuses, industry representatives contacted the DTI and attempted to reach an agreement on commission levels. Because of the anticompetitive aspects of a commission agreement, such a plan needed statutory backing. At the end of 1983, the insurance industry founded the Registry of Life Insurance Commissions (ROLIC), an industry attempt to rationalize, or in less euphemistic jargon, "fix" the commission system. A Maximum Commission Agreement (MCA) was reached by industry members, which limited the amount of commission payable to the salesperson.

The Financial Services Act undermined these efforts. Neither the statute nor SIB's rules required disclosure. The SIB contracted with Peat Marwick to investigate the subject—a way of buying time. At first, LAUTRO allowed members to choose whether or not to be bound by the ROLIC rules and the MCA. Those members who elected not to be bound were required to make detailed and specific disclosure to the client of commissions paid, and the amount if the broker's commission exceeded the industry's scheduled rates. However, the Office of Fair Trading, which reviewed the SROs' rule books for antitrust implications, refused to accept the LAUTRO rule book because of the anticompetitive aspects of the MCA.

The dislocation caused by polarization was substantial and unforeseen. It led many independents, including over seventy building societies, to become tied agents.[51] The SIB spent nearly three years attempting to find ways to assist the independent agent but preserve polarization. To right the balance, the SIB moved up the date when the LAUTRO MCA could be breached. Commencing May 1, 1989, companies had the option to pay independent intermediaries more than the agreement rate. Though commissions had been slowly rising, many insurance companies increased the commissions paid to independent brokers by 30 to 40 percent.[52] This may have helped the independent insurance sector, but it was paid for by the public. The SIB also loosened the best advice rules. Overall, that benefits the sales-

---

50. LOMAX, *supra* note 46 at 144.

51. For an overview of the impact of the Financial Services Act on the insurance industry, *see British life assurance: whose life is it anyway?* ECONOMIST, Feb. 18, 1989 at 84. The percentage of independent intermediaries declined from 60% before the Big Bang to 40% or less in 1991. Riley, *Finance & the Family: Financial Retailing to be Reviewed*, FIN. TIMES, Apr. 27, 1991 at IV.

52. *Capture of a Regulator*, FIN. TIMES, May 31, 1989 at 18, col. 1.

man more than the consumer because insurance companies tempt salespeople by offering higher commissions for certain policies.

A related issue was that of disclosure of premiums, charges, and commissions. Parliament desired disclosure of expenses and charges. The life insurance companies strongly opposed this on rather shaky grounds: disclosure could not be accomplished with precision, many figures would be totally misleading, and the public had no interest in disclosure so long as commissions or company expenses were not a fixed charge.[53]

The SIB could have required insurance companies to fully disclose the return of an insurance investment, the size of the commission in relation to the policy, and any other expenses in a single understandable form. However, after placing the independent intermediaries in jeopardy through polarization, the SIB overreacted to protect them. Instead of simple disclosure of decisions, the SIB created a kind of "Miranda Warning"[54] for purchasers of life insurance. Before a purchaser of an insurance policy listens to the agent's pitch, he must be given a two-page standardized buyer's guide by the agent. If business is conducted by telephone, the guide must be mailed immediately. The guide sets out considerations of which the client should be aware. In 1991 the SIB considered scrapping the guide, in part because many agents didn't distribute it.

After the sale, a policyholder receives a letter detailing the amount of the premium that is paid for expenses, commissions, and charges. Instead of the presentation of the monetary amount in pounds, or a percentage deduction from the premium, the company shows expenses as a percentage deduction from the investment return, a less readily understandable figure.[55] The impact of disclosure would be greater if the investor were provided with the information *before* he entered into the contract, rather than written fourteen days after purchasing a policy. Cancellation is a more complicated step than saying "no." In May 1990 the Office of Fair Trading found that the SIB's approach was inadequate because consumers would not understand the figures. It recommended that consumers be told when

---

53. Short, *Finance and the Family, Time for Decisions*, FIN. TIMES, May 21, 1988 at IV, col. 1.

54. This refers to Miranda v. Arizona, 384 U.S. 347 (1967), which requires police to inform those accused of a crime that they have a right to remain silent, to seek counsel, and that their statements may incriminate them.

55. SECURITIES AND INVESTMENTS BOARD, LIFE ASSURANCE AND UNIT TRUST DISCLOSURE: A NEW FRAMEWORK, Consultative Paper 27 (1989); Short, *Relief as expenses are spelled out*, FIN. TIMES, Aug. 4, 1989 at 7, col. 4. The Consumers' Association found that even the most basic mandated disclosure was lacking. Two-thirds of intermediaries surveyed did not disclose whether they were independent or tied. *Caveat Regulator*, ECONOMIST, Nov. 9, 1991 at 96.

they purchase the policy the pound amount of expenses and charges. In April 1991 the SIB commenced a review of the retail financial markets examining polarization, disclosure requirements, suitability and best advice, and the jurisdictional boundaries of regulators of the retail markets. In a discussion paper published in September 1991, the SIB decided to retain the polarization principle.[56] It concluded that the suitability rule was not working as it should and more attention should be paid to the definition of appropriate investment.[57] It also proposed reformulating the best advice obligations in simpler terms[58] and reconsidering the reach of polarization.

These issues have sharply divided relevant interest groups. The insurance companies always oppose greater disclosure because it may reduce earnings from products with the greatest commissions or charges. The Consumers' Association opposes anything other than full and timely disclosure.

In 1992 the SIB retreated in the face of pressure from insurance companies and withdrew plans to require life insurance agents to disclose companies' charges. Instead, sales agents only have to inform customers of the average cost of similar policies sold by all insurance companies and make projections of how much those charges will offset investment returns over the life of the policy. It also backed away from the requirement that companies express policy costs in pounds. Instead costs will be expressed in percentages of reduction in investment return or premiums paid.[59]

After several years of shifting its approach to disclosure and polarization, the SIB has yet to find the appropriate balance between the needs of the independents, the power of the insurance industry, the demands of the Office of Fair Trading, and fairness to the public. The SIB rules have changed the face of the insurance industry in ways not expected. Whether

---

56. SECURITIES AND INVESTMENTS BOARD, RETAIL REGULATION REVIEW, DISCUSSION PAPER 2—*Polarisation*, September 1991. The arguments for retaining the polarization principle were investor confusion if it was modified or abandoned; weakening of the independent intermediary sector; and disruption of commercial arrangements, including substantial investment costs of retraining.

57. It proposed to amend the definition of suitability: to be "suitable," an investment recommended must not be one which on any reasonable view the customer would be better off without; and suitability means not recommending one type of savings or investment vehicle when another type would plainly be more appropriate for the customer.

58. The SIB has suggested that the agent, having already established that a particular type of packaged product is suitable for a client, offer clients impartial advice on the basis of access to a reasonably wide selection of packaged products and companies, and take reasonable steps to recommend the packaged product from within his competence that will, in his professional judgment, best meet the customer's needs.

59. Cohen, *SIB Bows to life co's lobbying: Plan to require sales agents to disclose policy charges is dropped*, FIN. TIMES, Mar. 5, 1992 at 18.

the additional disclosure requirements and polarization have helped the public is questionable. Because polarization helped insurance companies with tied agents, it may be more difficult to find independent advice. There is an irreversible trend toward large insurance conglomerations. Commissions will rise as there are fewer salespeople, which will eventually make insurance more expensive for the public. What is clear is that policies that do not take into account their impact upon the marketplace are bound to cause more dislocation when corrective measures have to be taken.

Reform of Unit Trust Pricing

Unit trusts, the English equivalent of open-ended mutual funds, are a £50 billion industry with over three million investors. In a unit trust the underlying shares are held in trust for the unit holders, who by selling their units, obtain their share of the value of the underlying securities minus costs. Unit trusts are the primary investment vehicle for the small investor. The regulation of unit trusts had been a backwater in the DTI. Regulators were understaffed, untrained, and often captured by industry interests.[60] Unit trust managers had engaged in several questionable practices to increase profits. Such devices included the manipulation of the timing of the valuation of the underlying trust when an investor bought or sold units in it and the addition of undisclosed charges.

The maximum value of a single unit of a unit trust is determined by a formula established by the DTI. There are two unit trust prices: the offer price and the bid price. The offer price is the price at which trust managers sell units to the public.[61] The bid price is determined by taking the underlying values of the securities realized in the market if the fund were liquidated, plus a stockbroking fee for the sale of the securities, minus a rounding down of the price similar to the way the prices are rounded up. Some trusts place additional charges over and above those just mentioned, such as audit fees, registration fees, custodial fees, and even the cost of holding annual meetings.[62]

---

60. Wolman, *Unit Trusts 2: Hidden Charges Unmasked*, Fin. Times, Oct. 22, 1988 at VIII [hereinafter Wolman Unit Trusts].

61. The bid price is the price at which units are redeemed from the public. The DTI formula for determining the price at which trusts are offered to investors adds to the underlying value of the trust's portfolio (cash and stocks), stockbroking commissions, a stamp duty of 0.5%, a sales charge of 5% tacked onto the basic price, and a unit trust duty. The sum was then rounded up by a maximum of 1.25 pence or 1%. The total price is divided by the number of units in the fund to give the value of a single trust unit. *Unit Trusts Revolution in Financial Services*, Economist, Feb. 21, 1987 at 85.

62. Wolman Unit Trusts, *supra* note 60.

Though the offer price was determined by the DTI formula, fund managers had in practice opportunities to manipulate the actual price that was paid by investors. In the United Kingdom, unit trust prices had reflected historical prices; that is, the share price from the previous day. This meant that a unit trust manager could build in an extra profit when an order was received. If the price of the underlying portfolio had risen from the previous day, the unit trust would sell shares from its portfolio that had been purchased earlier. In a constantly rising market, which was the case in the United Kingdom from 1982 to 1987, a unit trust manager would ask the trustees to create new units at the previous day's market price and sell them to new investors at the current, higher price. The losers were the existing unit trust holders, whose interest in the fund was diluted on an ongoing basis by the issuance of new units at artificially low prices. If the value of the trust had fallen from the previous day, the unit trust manager would sell to investors units at the previous day's price and pocket the difference.[63]

The SIB assumed the regulation of the marketing of unit trusts. Initially, it intended to abolish historic pricing and introduce forward pricing. Not surprisingly, the Unit Trust Association contested this. They claimed that investors only wanted to know the market price at which they purchased the units, and it would be unfair to require disclosure for unit trust managers unless disclosure was simultaneously imposed on all other financial products.

Lobbying led the DTI to force an SIB retreat. The new regulations impose a two-hour limitation on the ability of managers to exploit timing differences when creating and canceling units. Units may be created or canceled only during the two-hour valuation period. Within this time period the unit trust manager must notify the trustee of the number and value of units created.[64] The choice of method of pricing has created confusion. The strict limit on the period within which the manager must make his valuation decision will eliminate some of the abuses. The future may bring real-time

---

63. In contrast, the United States has used forward pricing to determine mutual fund valuations. The price of the unit is determined by valuing the portfolio at a time following receipt of the order. This means investors do not know the price of the units which they are purchasing until their orders are placed. Fuller, *Unit Trusts 4, A Step Towards Real Time*, FIN. TIMES, Oct. 22, 1988 at X.

64. SECURITIES AND INVESTMENTS BOARD AUTHORIZED UNIT TRUST SCHEME REGULATIONS (Pricing of Units and Dealings by Trustee and Manager) 1988, S.I. No. 280 Part III (1988). Under the new system, unit trust managers are not forced to adopt forward pricing. However, many trusts have switched to the American system except when an investor otherwise requests. If the prices of the underlying securities in the trust change by more than two percent from the previously quoted price, the unit trust must use forward pricing. Unit trust managers do not have to accept historic prices for "large deals," defined as those greater than £15,000. S.I. 1988, No. 280 reg. 2, 18.

pricing, whereby unit trusts are valued minute by minute. Perhaps the most important advance in the unit trust area was the SIB's push for improved disclosure. The front-end charge must be separately identified. Provisions for rounding up and down are reduced, and as a result, pricing is thus more transparent. The responsibilities of unit trust trustees have been strengthened. Now they are required to report to unit holders confirming that the trust has been managed properly.

The pricing reforms and the 1987 market break have had a significant impact on the profitability of unit trust managers. There is a question as to how much the public will actually benefit from the new rules. Currently, unit trust prices are determined by differing criteria. The savings resulting from the Big Bang's ending of fixed commissions on sales and purchases of equities have not been passed on to the unit trust investors. Front-end charges have inched upwards. Now at least the investor knows his costs.

Customer Agreements

The SIB's original rules required firms to sign a customer agreement with private customers.[65] The purpose of this contract was to disclose to the customer his rights and duties and to outline the customer-firm relationship. Gower was against the concept of customer agreements on the grounds that investors wouldn't read them and firms would use them to evade their responsibilities.

The SIB initially required the customer agreement to contain investment objectives, restrictions on investments, warnings about illiquid investments, disclosures of situations where the firm or client could cancel the agreement, discussion of instances when the firm could refuse the client's instructions, arrangements for accountings to the client, information on how the securities and funds are to be held, and whether the client's securities could be hypothecated.[66]

In reaction to, if not in protest of, the SIB rule book, firms distributed detailed, incomprehensible customer agreement letters, used them to create waivers of liability, or treated them as a joke. One firm distributed a twenty-

---

65. SIB RULES, *supra* note 5 at Ch. III, rules 4.01–4.18. There was an exception for execution-only investors. For business or expert investors, a "terms of business" letter was sent which described the terms and services to be provided and described the client's status.

66. *Id.* at rule 4.04. The agreements had to be signed by customers by the end of 1988, or the firm's relationship to a customer could only be on an execution-only basis. The content of the customer agreement letters remain only for private customers investing in derivative products.

nine page letter to its clients, most of which was designed to protect the firm by including disclaimers and exemption clauses.[67] Even worse than criticism is scorn. Another firm, Capel Cure Myers, joked in a cover communication that if the customer could not understand the agreement, neither could they. It apologized in advance to its 8,000 clients "for any brain damage caused."[68]

Many long-time clients resented having to sign such a document and to disclose what they thought was personal information. Others refused to sign because they didn't understand the implications of the agreement and felt, correctly in many cases, that the brokers were attempting to absolve themselves from any liability. For clearing banks with millions of customers, the regulations were quite burdensome.[69]

In November 1988 the SIB backtracked and published a simplified three-page standard customer agreement that prohibited exculpatory clauses and was written in plain English. Today, when a firm provides investment services to a private customer, it must send a customer agreement that merely sets out in adequate detail the basis on which these services are provided. If a firm provides investment services to private customers involving options, futures, or other derivative products, the investor must sign a "two-way customer agreement."[70] Such an agreement must be entered with all kinds of customers where the firm is managing an account on a discretionary basis.[71] Firms are unable to use the customer agreement or any other communication to exclude liability under the act or regulatory system or to restrict duties of care, skill, and diligence.[72]

---

67. Wolman, *Walker Says No to Major Changes to Investor Rules*, FIN. TIMES, July 6, 1988 at 1.

68. *British Investors' Bill of Rights*, ECONOMIST, Apr. 30, 1988 at 80.

69. Some large American pension funds draft their own management contracts and require their external investment advisors to sign them. They were informed by U.K. advisors that the documents did not comply with British regulations for customer agreement letters and had to be changed.

70. CORE CONDUCT OF BUSINESS RULES, *supra* note 48, rule 14. An agreement signed by a customer is termed a "two-way customer agreement" and contrasts with a letter from the firm detailing its services. There is an exception to signing a two-way agreement if the customer is ordinarily resident outside the United Kingdom and the firm reasonably believes that he does not wish an agreement to be used.

71. *Id.* Firms must set out in adequate detail the basis on which the services are to be provided and, where relevant, the extent of the discretion to be exercised by the firm. There is no longer any obligation for firms to enter into standardized customer agreements with non-private clients where they are providing investment services on a non-discretionary basis, or with private customers where services are provided on a nondiscretionary basis other than in respect to derivative transactions.

72. CORE CONDUCT OF BUSINESS RULES, *supra* note 48, rule 15.

The Costs of the Investor Protection Framework

One benefit of a practitioner-based regulatory system over a governmental agency approach, it was thought, was that the former would be less expensive and paid for by the regulated, instead of burdening the public fisc.[73] The new system has proven more expensive than expected—few things in life or politics are not. Regulatory frameworks are not exempt from this axiom. Because the expenses of a self-regulating system are borne by the industry, the costs have been quite burdensome to many firms which, though not on the fringe ethically, have been marginal economically.

Before its formal designation, the SIB incurred substantial launching costs.[74] The Bank of England provided a loan at the Bank's base rate to meet the start-up costs. The SIB repaid the loan, together with interest due, in equal annual installments over a five-year period ending March 31, 1992.[75] Some assumed that once the system was put in place, the SIB's costs would decline, the SROs would take over day-to-day monitoring, and the designated agency would have a more passive role. However, this has not been the case.

Costs overruns have been caused by unexpectedly large enforcement expenditures. The SIB only has a small in-house legal staff and must retain outside counsel and accountants when it engages in investigatory and enforcement activities. The SROs and their members are of differing financial

---

73. Sections 112 and 113 of the Act provide that an applicant for recognition or authorization shall pay an application fee. Those who receive recognition or authorization shall pay periodical fees to defray the costs of the system. The SIB's funds came from application fees levied upon potentially recognized bodies and from firms that directly applied for authorization. The amount of the application fee was based upon the size of the firm as defined by categories in the financial resource rules and the number of employees. Several criteria are used to set the periodical fees. SIB RULES, *supra* note 5 at Ch. VIII.

74. The SIB ran a deficit of £1,437,152 in its first nine months, ending March 31, 1986, SECURITIES AND INVESTMENTS BOARD, SIB's APPROACH TO ITS REGULATORY RESPONSIBILITIES, § 33 (Feb. 1987). £4,778,000 in 1987–88, and £1,382,000 in the year ending March 31, 1988. SIB ANNUAL REPORT 1987/88, *supra* note 286 at 72 (1988). In 1989 the SIB had a surplus of £4,573,000 which was reduced in 1990 to £164,000, SECURITIES AND INVESTMENTS BOARD, REPORT OF THE SECURITIES AND INVESTMENTS BOARD FOR 1990/91, 81 (1991) [hereinafter 1990/91 SIB REPORT].

75. In the year ending March 31, 1991, the SIB spent £16,614,000 on administrative expenses. Its income consisted of £15,914,000 in fees from applications, periodical fees, and levies on SROs or other recognized bodies, £90,000 in interest expenses, £345,000 from the sale of rule books and publications, and £429,000 from sales of extracts of the central register. It reduced its accumulated deficit to £961,000. 1990/91 SIB REPORT, *supra* note 74 at 84–89.

strengths with LAUTRO and SFA being the strongest, then IMRO, and FIMBRA the weakest. Everyone in the financial services sector has complained about the financial burden of the regulatory system. Part of the expense is due to direct costs of membership in the various recognized bodies. The greater outlay, however, is for the indirect regulatory expenses of adhering to rules imposed by the SIB or the SROs.

It is extremely difficult to obtain hard data on the total costs of the new system. Estimates of compliance expenditures in the first year ranged from £100 million to £1 billion.[76] Direct annual costs of the SIB, the SROs, and the recognized professional bodies have been estimated at £50 million per year.[77] These costs have occurred in a difficult economic climate for financial services firms.[78] When considering the approach to securities legislation, the implementation costs and ongoing expenses were not sufficiently considered.

The total expenses of the system are far higher than the costs of running the SIB and the various self-regulating bodies. Less visible expenses are the compliance costs to the firms: establishing the compliance systems, seeking professional counsel to educate the firm members and to provide ongoing advice, and hiring and training compliance officers. Employees of financial services firms had to master new and more complicated ways of conducting business. Firms and their employees had to learn new rules, keep better records, segregate client monies, and maintain and report on the complicated capital adequacy requirements. Additional computer capacity had to be installed. Ultimately, many of these expenses would be passed on to the consumer. The biggest gainers are attorneys and accountants, the grease of any regulatory system.

The assumption that a self-regulatory system would be less expensive than a statutory system may not be valid. Duplication within the regulatory framework and the need of firms to join several regulatory organizations enhanced the cost inefficiencies. Expenditures were less noticeable in the rising, highly profitable market situation prior to the October 1987 market break. In the current environment, where profits are highly variable if extant, a firm's cost burden is much more apparent.

The financial implications of the new system to firms were staggering. A major clearing bank has compliance costs of £1 million per year and a com-

---

76. LOMAX, *supra* note 46 at 198; Marin, *First Big Bang, now Big Brother*, INSTITUTIONAL INVESTOR, May 1988 at 58 [hereinafter *First Big Bang*].

77. Waters, *Regulation compliance costs take a hiding*, FIN. TIMES, Apr. 3, 1989 at 9, col. 4.

78. For a summary of the economic conditions of the financial services sector, *see* 1990/91 SIB REPORT, *supra* note 74 at 10–16.

pliance staff of thirty-five.[79] Pressures on smaller firms may force out all but the most efficient.[80] The compliance burden makes firm entry more difficult. Thus, competitiveness may be decreased. Not all firms' added expenditures are due to the new regulatory system. Some costs such as more advanced computer capacity would have been introduced anyway, albeit at a slower pace. Computerization has led to increased efficiency in firm trading because trades are more transparent and failures may be reduced. Internal management systems have improved because of the recordkeeping requirements. An immeasurable benefit is confidence in the system by the public.

However, these are difficult times financially. The regulatory system has raised costs, but the opportunity to increase revenues is more limited and variable since the 1987 market break. Transparency and disclosure of costs to the public has made it more difficult to boost profits in the old *sub rosa* way. The capital adequacy requirements place a particularly heavy burden on smaller firms. Almost no one, especially at the SIB, projected the costs of this system, and very little, save abolishing the whole framework or cutting down enforcement, will significantly reduce them. Ultimately the public will pay.

The City's Reaction to the Rules

The publication of The Securities Association's rule book was the event that galvanized the City against the new framework. The president of the Securities Association, Stanislas Yassukovitch, a prominent figure in The City, condemned the regulatory system as "the worst form of compromise. I think it would have been better either to have left the markets to regulate themselves or to establish a body like the SEC."[81]

---

79. Confidential interview; *see First Big Bang, supra* note 76 for confirmation. Commercial Union, a large insurance company, spent £2.2 million in start-up costs and has an annual expenditure of £800,000. Of the initial start-up costs £1.7 million was spent in its life insurance division, of which £700,000 went into installation of two computer systems. The first met the product disclosure requirements of the act, for instance, sending cancellation notices to new clients. The second was for systems management. £600,000 were spent on printing, of which 30% to 40% would have been spent anyway. The remaining £400,000 went for personnel costs and SRO dues. Waters, *Regulation compliance costs take a hiding*, FIN. TIMES, Apr. 3, 1989 at 9, col. 4.

80. The fee structure can impose an intolerable burden on smaller firms. Coley and Harper, one of the most active traders on the Baltic and Baltic International Financial Futures Exchange (Biffex), withdrew from Biffex because of the combination of fees, which totaled £95,000 to AFBD and to clearing houses, plus additional costs for a staff member to deal with compliance and to upgrade the computer system. Blackwell, *Regulation costs likely to 'obliterate' small broker*, FIN. TIMES, Apr. 14, 1990 at 16, col. 1; Campbell, *AFBD to seek more funds from members*, FIN. TIMES, Oct. 4, 1989 at 24, col. 4.

81. Wolman, *Merrill Lynch Man to Chair Securities Association*, FIN. TIMES, Nov. 24,

The reaction to the rule books became an attack upon Berrill. After months of conflict The Securities Association sought to remove Berrill when his term expired. The clearing banks had particular grievances against him and used their influence to force a change.[82] They could not forgive polarization; restrictions on cold calling, which prohibited bank officers from discussing investments unless approached; customer agreement letters, when they had millions of customers; and compliance costs, which because of their size and scope of operations were astronomical. The clearing banks felt the SIB's rules were geared for institutions that engaged in one line of business at the expense of the financial conglomerates.[83] Using the old-boy network, they complained informally to the Bank of England. In a speech to the House of Commons in November 1987, Robin Leigh-Pemberton, Governor of the Bank of England, said that contributions of professionals had been overshadowed in drawing up the rules. He called for more involvement by institutions to create a balance between protection of small investors and promotion of professional markets.[84]

After Mrs. Thatcher's reelection, the cabinet was reshuffled. One of her favorites, David Ivor Young, Lord Young of Graffham, replaced Paul Channon as Secretary of State for Trade and Industry. In a speech to the Conservative Party conference in Blackpool on October 8, 1987, Lord Young said: "I have a simple rule of thumb: my department should spend far more of its time finding ways to help industry trade, than it should do inventing and enforcing rules and regulations to stop industry trading."[85]

DTI's attitude toward the Financial Services Act, the SIB, and the rule book changed. Young quickly removed the forward-pricing of unit trusts

---

1987 at 1; Fidler, *American Englishman with the Diplomatic Touch*, FIN. TIMES, Nov. 24, 1987 at 13. An early proponent of the new regime, Stock Exchange Chairman Sir Nicholas Goodison, criticized the new system as far too expensive. Searjeant, *Exit Sir Kenneth*, THE TIMES (London), Feb. 27, 1988 at 1. John Morgan, chief executive of IMRO, who had been very clearheaded on issues such as Section 62, called the SIB "schoolmarmish" and said it had outlived its usefulness. He recommended that the SROs run the system. Nanbrough, *Head of IMRO attacks SIB*, THE TIMES (London) Feb. 27, 1988 at 25, col. 7. Even the SIB's deputy chairman, Sir Mark Weinberg, was unprepared for the system that emerged: "If we had known all of the difficulties, I dare say we might have come up with a different system, and it might have been somewhat simpler and less bureaucratic. But we needed to get to the end of the road to find that out." *First Big Bang, supra* note 76.

82. *Hush ... whisper who dares*, THE TIMES (London), Jan. 6, 1988 at 19, col. 6.

83. *Bank Objections to SIB proposals for FSB*, THE TIMES (London), June 24, 1986 at 21, col. 6.

84. John Jay, *Relief as Berrill is Dethroned*, THE SUNDAY TIMES (London), Feb. 28, 1988, at D, col. 1.

85. P. HENNESSEY, WHITEHALL 428 (1988). One of his first acts was to take senior DTI staff on a retreat. He returned to instruct his department to give a radical boost for business. On October 13, 1987, Young issued a press release stating his intention to create a larger market through privatization and deregulation. *Id.* at 433.

issue from the SIB. In consultation with Leigh-Pemberton, he decided not to reappoint Berrill when his term expired at the end of the following May. Berrill learned of this on February 26, 1988. He and the SIB's staff were shocked. Within days, the Secretary of State and the Governor of the Bank of England had selected and announced that David Walker would succeed Berrill as SIB chairman.[86] Walker, who was forty-eight years old, was a director of the Bank of England and had been responsible for City affairs. He also had played an important background role for the Bank in the events leading to the Big Bang.[87]

At the Bank of England, Walker was responsible for financial markets and institutions. Walker was an interventionist and involved himself in all of the problems in the City—restrictive practices on the Stock Exchange, the Big Bang, the Lloyd's scandals, and the collapse of the tin market.[88]

A reassuring selection for the City and the SIB staff, Walker had a visible role at the Bank and was considered a candidate to succeed Leigh-Pemberton. The new chairman had excellent links to the City establishment and was more personable and diplomatic than his predecessor. At the Bank he was called "Walker the Talker." To some he symbolized the Bank's growing role in securities regulation.[89]

With one appointment, the tone and texture of the SIB changed. Walker was intelligent, ameliorating, and sensitive. He understood the City, knew everyone, and appeared more sympathetic to its problems. In his first public statement after assuming the chairmanship, Walker announced that the SIB was considering a substantial simplification of its rule book and had established a feasibility study. He also hinted that Section 62 would be reconsidered.

Walker's appointment did not mean that the SIB had been captured by the City. He quickly indicated that polarization would stay, but that much simpler rules were required to ease the burden of compliance. Firms still needed to know precisely what they could and could not do. He also prom-

---

86. Actually, Walker was the third choice. Sir Nicholas Goodison and Sir Mark Weinberg had declined the position. Jay, *Relief as Berrill is Dethroned*, THE SUNDAY TIMES (London), Feb. 28, 1988 at D, col. 1.

87. Searjeant, *Bank Tightens Control over the City*, THE TIMES (London), Feb. 27, 1988 at 1, col. 3.

88. S. FAY, PORTRAIT OF AN OLD LADY: TURMOIL AT THE BANK OF ENGLAND 27 (1987).

89. *Id.* at 27. *First Big Bang, supra* note 76. A graduate of Queens College, Cambridge, Walker had joined the Treasury in 1961. He was private secretary to the Joint Permanent Secretary from 1964 to 1966 and seconded to the staff of the International Monetary Fund in Washington from 1970 to 1973. He became Assistant Secretary of the Treasury from 1973 to 1977 and joined the Bank of England in 1977 as Chief Advisor, then Chief of the Economic Intelligence Department. Walker had been an executive director of the Bank since 1982.

ised to reexamine the compensation scheme and the impact of disclosure on independent intermediaries.[90] The flood of protests over the complexity, prolixity, and cost of the new rules had prompted a shift in emphasis to a more simple, flexible approach. Within months of the implementation of a new system, the SIB retrenched to the rule-making approach originally suggested by Professor Gower: general principles.

The New Settlement

The Principles

The first tangible expression of the Walker regime was the publication in late November 1988 of a consultative document, *Conduct of Business Rules: A New Approach*, whose underlying purpose was to recast the 1987 rules and regulations into a more simple and user-friendly form. The object of the review of the total rule book was not to change the substance of the rules, but to make them clearer, to enhance their effectiveness, to present them in a more coherent and logical structure, and to plainly differentiate between transactions with professional investors and sales to the general public. The principled approach, or "new settlement" to use the SIB's phrase, was a reaction to criticism that the rule book was needlessly detailed and camouflaged the underlying purpose of the regulations.[91] The SIB hoped to simplify the regulatory regime, gain City support, and in some magical way, although it did not specify how, reduce its costs. The new SIB approach became effective in 1990 and was accompanied by amendments to the Financial Services Act to loosen the equivalence requirement of SRO rules and permit more flexibility by SROs.[92] It seeks to develop the appropriate balances between the SIB and the recognized bod-

---

90. Bell, *City Watchdog in drive to simplify rules*, THE TIMES (London), July 6, 1988 at 23, col. 2; Wolman, *Walker says no to major changes in investor rules*, FIN. TIMES, July 6, 1988 at 1.

91. Kingsford-Smith, "Recent Developments" Bulletin 2 (Dec. 1988) in FINANCIAL SERVICES LAW AND PRACTICE, *supra* note 22 at 1. Originally there were ninety-three principles which were extracted from the existing rules. The criticism of the bottoms-up approach was that the SIB was starting at the wrong end and the member of principles would only lead to increased litigation. After substantial criticism of its new principled approach, the SIB again switched field and decided to use a three-tiered or "top-down" approach. In August 1989 it published a new proposal that pruned the ninety-three principles to ten, which immediately became known as the "ten commandments."

92. This resulted in legislation, the Companies Act, 1989, Ch. 40, which gave statutory backing to the changes and were clearly differentiated between professional and private investors, requiring differing levels of protection.

ies, and in the protection of retail clients, between reliance or disclosure and the need for regulatory requirements.

Under the principled approach there are three tiers of rules: ten general principles, forty core rules, and underneath, more detailed rules of the SROs that actually bind investment firms in the conduct of their business. The principles are intended to be a universal statement of normative behavior and call for firms to observe high standards of integrity and fair dealing in their relations to customers.[93] They do not give rise to a cause of action

---

93. The principles came into effect on April 30, 1990. They are not exhaustive of the standards expected. Conformity with the principles does not absolve a failure to observe other requirements, while the observance of other rules does not necessarily amount to conformity with the principles. The principles are

1) *Integrity*, a firm should observe high standards of integrity and fair dealing;

2) *Skill, Care, and Diligence*, a firm should act with due skill, care and diligence;

3) *Market Practice*, a firm should observe high standards of market conduct. It should also, to the extent endorsed for the purpose of this principle, comply with any code or standard as in force from time to time and as it applies to the firm either according to its terms or by rulings made under it;

4) *Information about Customers*, a firm should seek from customers it advises or for whom it exercises discretion any information about their circumstances and investment objectives which might reasonably be expected to be relevant in enabling it to fulfill its responsibilities to them;

5) *Information for Customers*, a firm should take reasonable steps to give a customer it advises, in a comprehensible and timely way, any information needed to enable him to make a balanced and informed decision. A firm should similarly be ready to provide a customer with a full and fair account of the fulfillment of its responsibilities to him;

6) *Conflicts of Interest*, a firm should either avoid any conflict of interest arising or, where conflicts arise, should ensure fair treatment to all its customers by disclosure, internal rules of confidentiality, declining to act, or otherwise. A firm should not unfairly place its interests above those of its customers and, where a properly informed customer would reasonably expect that the firm would place his interests above its own, the firm should live up to that expectation;

7) *Customer Assets*, where a firm has control of or is otherwise responsible for assets belonging to a customer which it is required to safeguard, it should arrange proper protection for them, by way of segregation and identification of those assets or otherwise, in accordance with the responsibility it has accepted;

8) *Financial Resources*, a firm should ensure that it maintains adequate financial resources to meet its investment business commitments and to withstand the risks to which its business is subject;

9) *Internal Organisation*, a firm should organise and control its internal affairs in a responsible manner, keeping proper records, and where the firm employs staff or is responsible for the conduct of investment business by others, should have adequate arrangements to ensure that they are suitable, adequately trained and properly supervised and that it has well-defined compliance procedures; and

10) *Relations with Regulators*, a firm should deal with its regulator in an open

for damages under Section 62, but are used for discipline and intervention by recognized bodies against firms. Beneath the principles are the core conduct of business rules, which expand upon the exhortations in the principles and are binding and legally enforcing against the SROs[94] and through them bind authorized investment businesses and their employees. Violations are actionable under Section 62. Under the new approach, the greatest obligations are placed upon those conducting business with public customers. The obligation to others is to comply with a rule to the extent it is fair and reasonable to expect a firm to do so in the circumstances.

The Core Rules

The Core Conduct of Business Rules, which became effective in 1991, are mandatory statements of good business practices, some of which are not unfamiliar to American financial services firms.[95] Each of the SROs have third-tier conduct of business rules, as well as rules that ensure their member firms have adequate capital to conduct their business. Some SIB regulations apply across the financial services landscape to all investment businesses regardless of SRO membership or the nature of the business. These rules include client money regulations, which deal with how firms handle investors' money and seek to protect clients' funds from the claims of creditors in the event of a firm's insolvency and to prevent firms from using clients' funds to finance their business.[96]

Other SIB rules that directly affect authorized firms include rules on the cancellation rights of investors who enter a contract and have second

---

and cooperative manner and keep the regulator promptly informed of anything concerning the firm which might reasonably be expected to be disclosed to it.
SECURITIES AND INVESTMENTS BOARD, THE FINANCIAL SERVICES (CONDUCT OF BUSINESS) (AMENDMENT) RULES 1990.

94. They are binding on the SROs under FSA § 63A. For a detailed discussion of the Core Conduct of Business Rules, *see* Grieg et al., *The Core Conduct of Business Rules*, in 1 FINANCIAL SERVICES LAW AND PRACTICE, *supra* note 22 at 367–513.

95. *Compare* the rules on churning, which is the practice of excessive trading of a discretionary securities account by a broker for the purpose of generating commissions. Rule 15c1-7, 17 C.F.R. § 240.15C1-7 *with* SIB Core Conduct of Business Rule 26, Churning and Switching, SIB RULES, *supra* note 48 and American Stock Exchange Rule 422, 2 ASE GUIDE CCH ¶ 9942 and SFA Conduct of Business Rule 26, SECURITIES AND FUTURES AUTHORITY, BOARD NOTICE NO. 2, PART 1, CONSULTATIVE DOCUMENT ON NEW CONDUCT OF BUSINESS RULES (1991) [hereinafter, SFA NEW CONDUCT OF BUSINESS RULES].

96. *See* SECURITIES AND INVESTMENTS BOARD, FINANCIAL SERVICES (CLIENT MONEY) (INTERMEDIARIES) REGULATIONS (1991); SECURITIES AND INVESTMENTS BOARD, FINANCIAL SERVICES (CLIENT MONEY) (COMPREHENSIVE) REGULATIONS (1991).

thoughts, known in the United States as "cooling off" regulations;[97] rules on unsolicited calls;[98] and rules relating to "packaged products," unit trusts, life insurance policies, and investment trust savings schemes.[99] Of particular importance to the regulatory framework are the rules governing the amount of financial resources required of authorized firms.

Financial Supervision Rules

Like most SIB rules, the Financial Supervision Rules[100] have two primary purposes. One is to regulate firms directly authorized by the board. The other, more indirect purpose, is to set out in workable form, rules that can be compared to SRO rules to determine if the latter are "adequate" under requirements of the statute.[101] All authorized firms are expected to comply with the three principles and five core rules that relate to financial resources' requirements.

The three financial resource principles are that a firm should ensure that it maintains adequate financial resources to meet its business commitments and to withstand the risks to which its business is subject. Second, a firm must organize its internal affairs in a responsible manner, keeping proper records and having well-defined compliance procedures. A firm's employees or independent contractors working under firm aegis should be adequately trained and properly supervised. Third, firms must deal openly and cooperatively with regulators, keeping them promptly informed of matters which might reasonably be expected to be disclosed.[102]

The core rules, which together with the principles establish the overall obligations of firms, require that firms must have available at all times the amount and type of financial resources required by its SRO or regulator. A firm must ensure that it maintains adequate accounting records and must prepare and submit, in timely fashion, such reports as are required by its regulator. Firm records must demonstrate the firm's financial situation and its compliance with financial resources requirements. Firms must ensure that their internal controls and systems are adequate for the size, nature, and complexity of their activities. Additionally, firms must promptly notify

---

97. SECURITIES AND INVESTMENTS BOARD, FINANCIAL SERVICES (CANCELLATION) RULES (1991).

98. SECURITIES AND INVESTMENTS BOARD, UNSOLICITED CALLS RULES (1991).

99. *Id.*

100. SIB RULES, *supra* note 5, ch. II, *Financial Supervision* (1990), [hereinafter cited *Financial Supervision Rules*].

101. FSA, sched. 2.

102. *Financial Supervision Rules, supra* note 100 at 1.02.

regulators if they are in breach or are about to become so, and auditors must be appointed and dealt with in a spirit of cooperation.[103]

Of particular concern is that firms conduct investment businesses with adequate capital. This is an extremely complex area that has drawn much heat and where it is difficult to offer light. Basically, an investment business that trades in the securities markets needs three types of capital. First, base capital, which is set at three months' expenses or £5,000 to £10,000, depending on whether the three-month or the monetary figure is higher. This is a cushion of resources to cover certain unquantifiable or unforeseeable risk. It is calculated with reference to a firm's annual expenditures.[104] Second is counterparty risk capital, which covers the risks of breaches by parties with whom the firm deals.[105] Third is position risk capital, which covers the risk of loss to a firm because of changes in market prices that affect a firm's position in a type of security.[106] The type of capital requirements differs depending upon the riskiness of the firms' business.

Conduct of Business Rules

Most directly protecting the investor are the core conduct of business rules. These rules differentiate between protection provided for transactions with or on behalf of professional or institutional clients and a higher level of protection that is provided for retail customers, the public. Of the forty core conduct of business rules, only half, mostly dealing with market trading, apply to nonprivate clients.[107]

The first client distinction is between market counterparties and customers. Market counterparties are professional traders, market makers, firms, and others who trade as a principal or as an agent for an unidentified principal in the same type of investment business as the firm with which it is trading.[108] A customer is any person other than a market counterparty or a trust beneficiary.

There are two categories of customers. One is an ordinary business investor which, includes governments, local and public authorities, together with bodies corporate and trustees of trusts meeting predetermined size requirements. The second type of customer is the private customer, for whom

103. *Id.* at 1.03.
104. *Id.* at 4.08.
105. *Id.* at 5.09, sched. 4.
106. *Id.* at 5.10.
107. 1990/91 SIB REPORT, *supra* note 74 at 5.
108. SIB RULES, *supra* note 5, Ch. III, Financial Services Glossary 1991. SFA NEW CONDUCT OF BUSINESS RULES, *supra* note 95 at Part 2, § 3.1. CORE CONDUCT OF BUSINESS RULES, *supra* note 48.

the most protection is provided. The private customer is an individual who does not act in the course of carrying on an investment business or is a "small business investor."[109]

The core rules are divided into seven areas: independence, advertising and marketing, customer relations, dealing (trading) for customers, market integrity, administration, and general. The independence rules require a firm to take reasonable steps to ensure that its advice to a customer is unbiased by inducements or benefits from a third party or by material interests in the transaction giving rise to a conflict of interest.[110] The advertising and marketing rules require firms to make certain types of prescribed nonmisleading disclosures in advertising and in communications to private customers.[111]

---

109. *Id.* A small business investor is a company, partnership, or trustee of a trust which does not meet the size requirements enabling it to be treated as an "ordinary business investor," and is therefore entitled to less protection than a private customer. In additon, a private customer can agree in writing to be treated as a nonprivate customer, but only after receiving a written warning of the consequences, which includes the loss of some protections provided by the Conduct of Business Rules. CORE CONDUCT OF BUSINESS RULES, *supra* note 48, rule 39. However, the nonprivate customer does not lose the right to bring a civil action for damages under FSA § 62A because of a firm's breach of the more limited protections afforded for non-private customers. Core rule 39 allows a firm to treat a U.K. client as a non–private customer only if it can show that it believes on reasonable grounds that the customer has sufficient experience and understanding to waive the protections provided for private customers, has given a clear written warning to the customer of the protections under the regulatory system which he will lose; and the customer has given his written consent after a proper opportunity to consider that warning.

110. The independence rules are (1) inducements (prohibiting employees from accepting or soliciting inducements which would conflict with the duties owed to customers; (2) material interest (firms with a material interest in a transaction which give rise to a conflict of interest cannot give advise or engage in a discretionary transaction without ensuring fair treatment for the customer; (3) soft commission (provides that firms that receive benefits in kind provided by brokers to fund managers in return for a commitment to provide a certain amount of business must reasonably be expected to assist in the provision of investment services for customers, and that customers must be given adequate prior and periodic disclosure about such soft commissions; and (4) polarization (requiring firms which advise on life insurance policies or unit or investment trusts must do so as a member of a marketing group or as an independent intermediary.)

111. Rules 5–8 deal with advertising (basically firms must apply appropriate expertise when issuing or approving advertisements, and the burden is upon the firm to demonstrate that it believes on reasonable grounds that the advertisement is fair and not misleading). Rules 9 (fair and clear communications), 10 (customers' understanding), 11 (informtion about the firm), and 12 (information about packaged products) require that information disseminated to private customers be presented fairly and understandably so they can make an informed decision. Rule 13 (appointed representatives) requires firms to satisfy themselves that their appointed representatives, essentially sales people, are fit and proper to act in a particular capacity and that firms have adequate resources to monitor and enforce compliance with such standards.

The core customer relations conduct of business rules deal with the contractual basis between the firm and the customer, standards of advice on investment products, charges for investment services, and requirements for communications regarding a customer's transactions or account.[112] Dealing for customers rules are trading rules to ensure that the customer obtains the best execution possible under the circumstances.[113] Marketing integrity rules deal with the prohibitions against insider dealing, the limited permissibility of stabilization of securities prices, transactions with market makers off an exchange, and obligations to report trades.[114] Administrative

---

112. The customer relations rules deal with: (14) customer agreements (requiring a written contract to set out in adequate detail the basis on which services are provided, and where derivative transactions [futures and options for instance] and discretionary accounts are involved, the customer must sign the agreement; (15) customers' rights (firms can't seek to use the customer agreement or other communication to exclude liability or duty of care and diligence); (16) suitability (firms must know their customers and should not make personal recommendations that are unsuitable for the customer given the facts about the customer known to the firm); (17) standards of advice on packaged products (requirement of a higher standard of obligation for firms to know the market and give best advice for customers than in the case of ordinary broking transactions; (18) charges and other remuneration (firms' charges must not be unreasonable and their basis must be disclosed); and (19) confirmation and periodic informtion (customers must be sent in timely fashion details of transactions and periodic reports about their portfolios).

113. Dealing for customer rules are: (20) customer order priority (firms should deal with customers' orders and their own orders fairly and in turn. Under the prior rules, firms' orders went to the back of the line); (21) timely execution (execute trades as soon as reasonably practicable in the circumstances); (22) best execution (obtain the best price available in the relevant market for the customer); (23) timely allocations (trades must be fairly allocated among customers); (24) fair allocation (trades should be allocated fairly between customers and, where there is a shortfall, customers should given priority over house orders); (25) dealing ahead of publciations (a prohibition on front running, i.e. before recommending a security, a firm can't trade in that security for its own account until customers for whom the recommendation was intended had a reasonable opportunity to react to it); (26) churning and switching (firms can't trade with excessive frequency and switch products in a customer's portfolio beyond an amount that is reasonable under the circumstances); and (27) certain derivative transactions to be on an exchange (a new rule which prohibits off-exchange transactions for private customers except where their liability is limited to a single initial payment or where they are hedging currency risk).

114. Rule 28, insider dealing, creates a civil right of action under FSA § 62 against member firms who have been guilty of insider dealing. Under the statutory instrument promulgated pursuant to Section 62A, Financial Services Act, 1986 (Restriction of Right of Action Regulations), S.I. 1991, No. 489, such a right of action is specifically not limited to private customers. *See generally* Ch. 5, rule 29, stabilization (firm taking action to stabilize the price of securities must comply with the SIB's stabilization rules). Rule 30, off-exchange market makers (when firm sells to a private customer securities unquoted on an exchange and sells the security as a market maker, the customer must be given notice that he can resell his security for a specified period and price). Rule 31, reportable transactions (firms must report to their SROs all transactions effected off a recognized investment exchange).

rules deal with the responsibilities of firms to implement systems to ensure that they comply with the mandates of the investor protection requirements.[115] Finally, there are general rules that concern standards of reliance on the core conduct of business rules or guidance from an SRO, exceptions for classes of customers, and the application of the core rules.[116]

The Third Tier of Regulation

The third tier of firm regulation consists of the rules drafted by the SROs, which are complemented by guidance commentaries.[117]The third tier-rules are more flexible than the SIB core rules, reflecting the investment business of the particular SRO. There are differing standards of conduct for different types of investors depending upon their degree of skill and experience in investment transactions and the degree to which they rely on a firm for advice.

The SROs had the option of retaining their existing rule books, with which their members had become familiar, or drafting new ones. The SIB would phase out its rule book. The third-tier rules contain requirements that more specifically relate to the business context of the SROs' members than the core rules. The third-tier rules have differing standards of conduct

---

115. The administrative rules are: (32) safeguarding of customer investments (firms must provide safe custody facilities to a customer, segregate customer securities and investments, and register them in the customer's name); (33) scope of business (firms can carry on only the investment businesses that they are authorized to by their SRO); (34) compliance (firms must establish and maintain adequate compliance procedures and records to ensure that employees act in conformity with the requirements of the regulatory system); (35) complaints (requiring firms to have an effective and timely system of handling complaints from customers); (36) Chinese walls (requiring material information to be withheld in certain circumstances between different parts of a firm, for example keeping separate information developed in the investment banking division from other divisions such as trading); and (37) cessation of business (firms withdrawing from a particular area of business must complete or transfer any outstanding business of private customers).

116. Rules of general application are: (38) reliance on others (persons act in conformity with the core rules to the extent the relevant SRO has issued formal guidance on complying with them, and in reliance on the standards in the guidance, the person reasonably believes he is acting in conformity with the rules); (39) classes of customer (conditions when private customers can elect to be treated as nonprivate customers); and (40), application of the core conduct of business rules (when and how the rules apply to businesses, advertisements, and sources of interpretation and application).

117. The guidance commentaries do not have the status of rules. Therefore, breach of a guidance provision will not, by itself, lead to disciplinary action of a firm by an SRO or subject the firm to civil liability under FSA § 62. However, there is a rebuttable presumption that a firm has breached a rule if it has not complied with the relevant guidance commentary. SFA NEW CONDUCT OF BUSINESS RULES, *supra* note 95 at Part 2, § 1.5.

for different types of investors depending upon their degree of skill and experience in investment transactions and their reliance on the firm for advice. Breach of third-tier rules are acts of misconduct subject to SRO disciplinary procedures and actionable under Section 62.[118]

The Principled Approach

The SIB adopted a new tack on the issue of equivalence and in dealing with recognized bodies. It did not require SROs to adopt its rules and used more flexible criteria to judge equivalence. The language of the SRO rule books has been simplified. The SROs now have more latitude to create their own rule books to minister to the needs of their members so long as they don't contravene the SIB's principles or core rules. The new rule books lesson the detail and are more pliant than their predecessors. Firms can seek rule interpretations from the SROs and in appropriate situations gain waiver of a rule. The danger of the new rule books is that as the SIB loosens its reins over the recognized bodies, the SROs will succumb to their trade association instincts to protect their members at the expense of the public.

Initially the SIB's new approach was met with less than ecstasy in the City. Some felt that this merely added another layer of rules to which firms could be held liable for breach. Behind the assumptions of rule book completeness was the belief that it would serve as a barrier to courts' expansive views of civil liability to plaintiffs. The principled approach would undermine this because they were rules and would add a subjective factor in regulators' and courts' judgment as to whether there was a breach. This would make the position of practitioners more uncertain.

The "principled" approach sharply redefines the investor protection framework and signifies a new role for the SIB. It may signify a philosophical change as well, tipping the balance toward true self-regulation and away from the statutory context. In attempting to gain the support of the City, the SIB utilized a typically British approach—a call to the past, the tradition of self-regulation. However, the past is gone, forever. Self-regulation in the absence of a firm, rule-based regulatory system no longer works and cannot work in the context of the modern financial markets.

The turn to principles and a simplification of the rules creates an impression of retreat from a firmer regulatory grip. The principles are hortatory

---

118. The third-tier rules are accompanied by guidance commentaries. The commentaries do not have the status of the rules. It is a rebuttable presumption that a firm has breached a rule if it has not complied with the relevant guidelines. SECURITIES AND FUTURES AUTHORITY, BOARD NOTICE NO. 2, PART 2, CONSULTATIVE DOCUMENT ON NEW CONDUCT OF BUSINESS RULES: GENERAL EXPLANATORY NOTES, § 1.5 (April 1991).

and ambiguous. They offer firms more latitude. Despite the criticism of the legalistic approach, the City adjusted to it. In introducing the new proposals, Walker, stated "Emphasizing fundamentals should indeed make the regulatory system more robust and contribute to still higher standards."[119] However, in the insurance area neither FIMBRA nor LAUTRO has shown great interest or initiative in increasing investor protection.

Will the necessary ambiguity of principles provide new leeway for managers to avoid the affirmative responsibilities of the existing rule book? The theory of the new principled approach according to David Walker is that now the senior people will become involved with the enforcement regime because the principles are few and readily understandable, and the system will work more efficiently.[120]

The SIB is concerned with the cost-effectiveness of its rules. Simplifying the rules may make compliance cheaper. The SIB and the SROs are also engaged in an effort to harmonize the different rule books so as to assist firms authorized by more than one recognized body. Where possible, rules will be similar across the financial services sector. In a difficult economic climate, firms still have incentives to cut corners. When the desire to uphold high principles of business behavior conflicts with harsh economic reality, which will yield? In loosening the grip over SROs, the SIB may be encouraging their trade association instincts. Without the oversight of the SIB, will the SROs and their members have sufficient initiative to engage in vigorous enforcement of their members?

Under the latest approach the SIB will be a more distant body from the industry. It will have a greater international focus. The principled approach may allow for more harmonization with Europe after 1992. However, the government and the Bank of England will be the primary international regulator. Whether the City will respond in the hoped for way under the new principles remains to be seen.

The Rule-making Process: What Went Wrong

The first months of the new regulatory system created conflicting pressures on the SIB and a need to achieve immediate results. The new system had to be implemented as soon as possible, and the financial services industry and the public needed to be educated quickly regarding the changes underway. In the process the SIB needed to gain acceptance and support from the financial services sector. In this it failed badly. The implementation pe-

---

119. Alexander, *The right way to regulate the market*, ECONOMIST, Sept. 23, 1989 at 24.
120. Waters, *The ten commandments of honest dealing*, FIN. TIMES, Aug. 9, 1989 at 8, col. 4.

riod offers a window on the wisdom of the regulatory approach. When the SIB exercised its rule-making authority, the burdens of the new framework on the industry began to be felt. Clearly the reaction to the SIB's rules demonstrated that consensus had not been reached. There was almost unanimous reaction by the financial services sector that the rules were arbitrarily imposed without adequate consultation of practitioners who knew the business. Instead of building support for the new regime, the implementation created outright resistance.

The SIB had a staggering task. It had to oversee the evolution of the SRO structural framework across the spectrum of financial services and introduce rules in widely differing areas, affecting markets whose participants ranged from the most untutored members of the public to professional market makers dealing in highly sophisticated and arcane financial instruments. The SIB was caught between Scylla and Charybdis. It had to achieve legitimacy from two contrasting sources with different interests and demands: government and the industry. The board also was faced with an excruciating time deadline. The system had to become fully operational less than two years after the statute's enactment.

Another problem was that the financial services constituencies were at differing levels of development and sophistication in their thinking. The DTI had shepherded the bill through Parliament. Its civil servants and the SIB staff had a singular vision of the new framework. Despite the length of the statute, the legislation was vaguely drafted with disturbing generality as to the actual structure of the self-regulatory system. The lack of existing structures forced the designated agency to spend much of its time during the initial months sorting out alignments, mediating disputes, and developing the SRO framework. Unfortunately, it was not until the end of the legislative process that the City awakened to the impact of the statute upon them. When the SIB's rules were published, the day of reckoning for the City became all too apparent. This meant that the debate proceeded at different levels between interest groups. The DTI and SIB were involved with the issues from an earlier point in time, so the City could protest only in a reactive way. This did not help build consensus.

Time pressures led to a rushed quality of rule making, for the rule books needed SIB and Office of Fair Trading approval before an SRO could obtain recognition. Implementation strains and the SIB's interpretation of equivalence made it inevitable that the rule-making process would herald a shift to a bureaucratic, rule-dominated system. It is paradoxical that the detailed, complex statute created the type of regime it sought to prevent—an inflexible, intrusive, arbitrary agency. The detailed approach of the SIB rule book meant that all rules would be lawyers' rules. Technical input became more important than practitioners' experience.

The implementation of the rule books were unnecessarily confrontational. In retrospect—and unfortunately the only analysis seems to have been in hindsight—the most suitable person to lead the implementation effort would have been a more diplomatic, personable individual with a career in the City. Instead of building consensus through dialogue, Sir Kenneth Berrill engendered antagonism through arbitrary policy choices. Polarization may have been a correct decision, but if its implications upon the whole insurance sector had been more thoughtfully considered, it might not have been introduced so soon. Polarization always would have been a controversial issue, but its timing seemed unnecessarily disruptive with inadequate contemplation of the indirect impact on tangential regulatory issues, and it has not been finally resolved.

The implementation deadline did not facilitate long-range forecasting or strategic planning. The decisions dealing with foreign banks seemed to be a series of ad hoc steps. Nor was there a realization of the impact of the system upon practitioners' costs. No one foresaw the complexity of the system or the reaction it would engender.

The first years of a new regulatory system are a time for education of the regulated, of the public, and of other constituencies affected by the legislation. Informing interested parties about the system serves to build support or at least acquiescence. These educational goals were never met; rather, they were undermined by the perception of arbitrary rule making. Firms had to turn to experts in order to achieve authorization.

Important in the early years of a regulatory system is consensus building, whereby the regulated industry and the public accept the regime as necessary. It takes time to build such support. More so than in the United States, in the United Kingdom the personal touch is important. The use of informal approaches to achieve policy acceptance contrasts with the American approach of holding public hearings, educating the public through the news media, and then reaching a consensus. There was an insufficient effort to achieve assent. The result was lack of support by the leading interest groups, which in turn led to a lack of respect, if not outright hostility, for the designated agency and the investor protection framework.

The Financial Services Act did not cause the Big Bang. Nevertheless, it oversaw the impact of those developments. The rule-making process influenced market structure. It became an impetus for technological change on a variety of fronts through increased computerization and transparency and the use of screen-based trading systems. Despite the criticism of the rules and of the legislation, one must note that they did not drive business away from London nor prevent the system from becoming operational. Given the ideological policies underlying the legislation in the eyes of the government, the rule making was a disaster. In contrast to Thatcherite policies elsewhere (where regulation was lessened) in financial services reregulation was the dominant force. Competition led to the survival of the biggest, not necessarily of the most fit. The complexity and cost factors favored larger economic conglomerates which ultimately limit competition. Government ambivalence to the financial services regime was demonstrated by the reversal of the DTI as well as by the increasing regulatory hegemony of the Bank of England in light of the single European market.

The new settlement requires firms to relearn the rules and change procedures that were difficult to master originally. After five years of ongoing rule making and alterations of course, it may make sense for the regulatory system to remain stable for a period of time.

However, only change seems constant. After implementing the new settlement, Sir David Walker chose not to seek reappointment for another term as SIB chairman. He was succeeded by Andrew Large, a banker, who was a former head of The Securities Association and in late 1991 had become chairman of London FOX after a scandal. Large is the first practitioner to head the SIB. Through the introduction of the principles Walker did calm the relations between the City and the SIB. However, he was unable to tilt the balance in favor of investor protection in his dealings with the insurance industry. Nor has the self-regulatory system provided sufficient protection for pensionholders.[121]

Further tinkering with the structure of the system continues. There is likely to be additional consolidation of the SROs. The roles of the oversight institutions—the DTI, Treasury, the Bank of England and the SIB—have become less clear, all of which creates future uncertainty. Given a rapidly changing marketplace, the continuing overlap of regulatory bodies, and the manifest weakness of IMRO and FIMBRA, more restructuring is in the offing.

---

121. Large had also been a member of the Council of the Stock Exchange and the Takeover Panel. *New Chairman Named for British Regulator*, N.Y. TIMES, Jan. 31, 1992 at D3, col. 5. Waters, *Reluctant regulator and his guarded successor*, FIN. TIMES, Jan. 25, 1992 at 8, col. 1.

FIVE

ENFORCEMENT, DUE PROCESS, AND ADJUDICATION

We have discussed the legislative and the rule-making functions of the SROs. In this chapter we focus upon their judicial and prosecutorial activities. Perhaps an ultimate measure of the success of the new system is whether investors are in fact protected. After all, that was a most important rationale for its introduction.[1] We will outline some of the SIB's information gathering, compliance, intervention, and investigation powers. We also will look at the due process protections for individuals and firms denied authorization or accused of wrongdoing. Then we will examine the weaknesses of the present system of enforcement and suggest changes to make it more effective.

Attendant to market deregulation was the introduction of a more stringent regulatory framework. One of the goals of the regulatory framework was to increase investor confidence in the financial services industry as "a clean place to do business."[2] To create such an environment and to encourage investor confidence, an enforcement scheme had to be implemented that broadened disclosure, improved business practices, and efficiently discovered and sanctioned securities law violators.

An effective securities regulatory framework should hold out the vision to the investor of fairness in the marketplace. This can be accomplished through increased disclosure so that informed decisions can be made on the basis of accurate information, through prevention of violations, by increased monitoring and reporting requirements, and through prompt, effective, and vigorous prosecution of securities law violations.

1. SECRETARY OF STATE FOR TRADE AND INDUSTRY, FINANCIAL SERVICES IN THE UNITED KINGDOM: A NEW FRAMEWORK FOR INVESTOR PROTECTION, 1985, CMND. SER. NO. 9432 at § 5.1 (hereinafter WHITE PAPER).
2. Id. at § 3.1(iii).

Despite the new regulatory framework, securities law enforcement in the United Kingdom could be improved significantly. The enforcement regime has not been able to thwart insider dealing or other fiduciary violations. It has been unable to create an aura of effectiveness. The barriers to effective enforcement include organizational problems; deficiencies in the enabling statute, particularly the insider trading act; weaknesses in the self-regulatory system; difficulties in changing attitudes toward certain kinds of behavior; deregulation itself, which has brought together contrasting cultures with differing standards of business behavior; and the globalization of securities markets, which has made enforcement of securities violations in one country more difficult without international cooperation.

Authorization and Enforcement

Securities regulation is a process of discrete stages that cumulatively should result in an effective system of enforcement. Financial services enforcement in the United Kingdom has three principal elements: 1) prevention, including the screening and elimination from the financial services industry of all obviously unsuitable firms and individuals; 2) information gathering, consisting of the creation of an effective monitoring and reporting system extending from within the firm itself to the self-regulating body to the SIB; and 3) deterrence, including prompt prosecution and sanctioning of violators. These components are designed to combat three of the greatest problems of the previous system of securities protection: deficiencies in evaluation at the entry level, breakdown of shared norms of behavior, and ineffective enforcement of violations.

The government designed the Financial Services Act to protect investors from securities law violations through both preventative measures and the vigorous prosecution of wrongdoers. Prevention is pursued primarily through regulatory control of "investment business" authorization. Under the new regulatory framework, no firm can engage in an investment business unless it is authorized to do so by the SIB or by an SRO after a review of its background, finances, and business plans.[3]

The definition of investments sets the boundary of the regulated activities and is interpreted quite broadly. The rationale for the system of authorization is that allowing only fit and proper persons to engage in investment business will be the most effective, cost-efficient way to prevent abuse. There are severe criminal and civil sanctions for operating an unauthorized

---

3. Financial Services Act, 1986, Ch. 60, § 3 [hereinafter, FSA].

investment business. Similar to the U.S. system, there are ongoing disclosure requirements by firms.

The protection of investors was the most important rationale for the system's introduction.[4] Several approaches can be used to ensure protection. The most important is preventive action. The authorization process is designed to create a filter so that firms with questionable capabilities, assets, or business practices are prevented from entering the financial services industry, thereby protecting the unsuspecting public. However, if authorization requirements were unreasonably high, entry would be excessively difficult. Competition within the industry would suffer and public transaction costs might increase. Thus, a balance must be reached with standards sufficiently high to protect the public, yet flexible enough to permit entry of new firms.

At the other end of the continuum, effective enforcement against those who have broken the rules provides an important deterrence against future violations. Enforcement efforts consist of early identification of violators, timely investigation, effective prosecution, and appropriate sanctions against those convicted.

Prosecution of commercial fraud is difficult and requires vast resources. In addition, enforcement by private bodies must be weighed against the danger of arbitrary action against the accused. The U. K.'s enforcement regime has been ineffective because of the lack of prosecutorial experience, the absence of full investigatory powers by certain enforcement agencies, overlapping and conflicting lines of authority, and a dearth of trained personnel.

The Financial Services Act provides the SIB and the recognized bodies with a full arsenal of information gathering, intervention, and investigatory powers and also provides elaborate rights of due process and appeal to the accused. Some of the enforcement powers are exercisable concurrently with the secretary of state. The recognized bodies' authority is based upon contract as opposed to statute.

The principal powers of intervention and enforcement are investigatory powers, civil and administrative actions, and criminal prosecution. The Financial Services Act creates several offenses for which the SIB is the prosecuting authority.[5] Perhaps the most important offense that the SIB has the right to prosecute is unauthorized engagement in an investment business.[6] Most criminal offenses under the act carry a maximum sentence of two years imprisonment and/or a £2,000 fine.

---

4. WHITE PAPER, *supra* note 1 at 1.

5. FSA § 201(4).

6. *Id.* § 4.

With regard to civil and administrative actions, the SIB can seek injunctions and restitution orders against individuals who have carried on business without authorization or have breached rules and regulations.[7] The restitution order is a device to restore monies or property to investors who have suffered losses as a result of prohibited transactions. The SIB can liquidate firms and obtain administrative orders to oversee businesses under the Insolvency Act of 1986.[8]

In addition to injunctions and restitution, the SIB and the SROs can intervene in the affairs of a firm authorized by them and impose restrictions when there has been a breach of the Financial Services Act or where there is a need to protect investors.[9] For example, the SIB can disqualify persons from being employed in an investment business if they are not "fit and proper," and it can issue public statements regarding a person's misconduct.[10] Broad oversight and investigative powers permit inquiry into the affairs of individuals or investment businesses.[11] The designated agency is also charged with oversight responsibilities of collective investment schemes.[12]

While the SIB has broad monitoring and investigative authority, the powers of the recognized bodies are limited by their contractual relationships with members. Members' acceptance of recognized bodies' disciplining and monitoring authority is the quid pro quo for their authorization. Because they lack subpoena powers, the recognized bodies coordinate their enforcement efforts with the SIB. Perhaps the most important enforcement tool is the requirement of periodic disclosure to the investor and to regulators. The British system creates an ongoing disclosure framework, analogous to the requirements of Section 12(g) corporations under the Securities and Exchange Act of 1934.[13] The Financial Services Act has given the SIB broad authority to mandate a continuous flow of information that provides an early warning system for regulators and creates an important paper trail if investigations are necessary.

---

7. *See id.* § 72.
8. *Id.* §§ 72–74.
9. *See id.* § 65.
10. *Id.* §§ 59–60.
11. *See id.* § 105.
12. *See id.* §§ 75–95.
13. 15 U.S.C.A. § 78l(g)(2) (1988). Section 13(a) requires corporations to file annual and quarterly reports and other information that the Securities and Exchange Commission requires. 15 U.S.C.A. § 78M(a) (1988).

Enforcement Powers

Hierarchy of Enforcement Powers

The effectiveness of the regulatory scheme rests upon the nature and scope of the enforcement tools. The Financial Services Act creates a hierarchal and overlapping enforcement system to monitor firms and individuals, investigate reported problems, and prosecute violators.

The enforcement process commences with the individual firm, which must establish compliance procedures to ensure that the firm and its employees adhere to the SRO's rules. When the firm is authorized by an SRO, it agrees to abide by the SRO's rules and to provide such information as the SRO demands. In fact, SROs are defined as bodies that regulate the conduct of any kind of investment business by enforcing binding rules upon their members or others subject to their control.[14]

The SROs have the most direct monitoring, compliance, and enforcement powers over their firms,[15] much as the stock exchanges or the National Association of Securities Dealers can discipline member firms in the United States. Authorized individuals and firms must agree to abide by the rules of their SROs. The SROs require that firms develop internal compliance systems.

The SROs have broad information gathering powers over their members, which is crucial to effective oversight. This aids them in early identification of problems. The statute provides that the SROs have the equivalent powers over their members as the SIB has over directly authorized firms.[16] Thus, SROs can require a firm to provide information or refrain from participating in certain activities. The SRO can fine, discipline, expel, or otherwise sanction its members.[17]

Because SROs lack the power of subpoena, they are unable to seek documents or information from third parties who are not members of the SRO or not engaged in an investment business themselves. In practice, this means

---

14. FSA § 8(1).

15. The SRO is responsible for the day-to-day enforcement of investment businesses. It is subject to the SIB's rules and criteria for recognition. Only after the SIB is satisfied that the SRO will be an effective regulator and can meet the criteria outlined in the statute will the SRO receive recognition. Among the criteria are that the SRO have an effective scope rule to preclude its members from carrying on an investment business of a kind with which the SRO is not concerned and that the SRO willingly agree to cooperate and share information with the SIB. FSA, *supra* note 2, schd. 2.

16. FSA, schd. 2, ¶ 3.

17. *Id.* (¶ 3 confers upon the SRO the same powers of enforcement as conferred upon the SIB in FSA ch. VI, part I).

that most SRO investigations will be in cooperation with the SIB, which can exercise its investigatory powers against third parties.[18] In the alternative, the SIB can delegate to the appropriate officials in the SRO the authority to conduct the investigation on the SIB's behalf.[19]

The SIB monitors firms that are directly authorized by the SIB and are not members of an SRO. The SIB is also responsible for recognizing and monitoring the performance of the SROs. Only after the SIB is satisfied that the SRO will effectively regulate its firms will it be recognized.

The SIB's investigatory and enforcement powers over individual firms and individuals are usually indirect, but it can intercede if the SRO is not aggressively fulfilling its responsibilities. An ineffective or recalcitrant SRO can be disciplined by the SIB. In conducting investigations, the SIB can seek information from the Bank of England or the DTI.[20]

The SIB's enforcement responsibilities end at the investigatory stage. It must turn over its efforts to the Serious Fraud Office (SFO)[21] and the DTI for prosecution. Historically, all investment businesses and other corporations were subject to the DTI, which retains broad powers of investigation into the affairs of corporations, their employees, and their dealings in securities.[22] All of the enforcement bodies remain subordinate to the DTI, a governmental agency overseen by the secretary of state for trade and industry, which has ultimate responsibility over the investor protection framework.

The secretary of state can prescribe any rule that the Financial Services Act mandates or authorizes.[23] However, he has transferred many of his powers under the statute to the SIB.[24] Among the powers transferred by the secretary of state is rule-making authority. Except for the few directly authorized firms, the SIB exercises largely secondary or coextensive compliance and enforcement powers, as discussed above. However, its indirect authority is vast through its rule-making powers, the heart of any regulatory system, and its supervision of the SROs.

The Financial Services Act requires the SIB to promulgate rules mandating high standards of integrity and fair dealing in the conduct of investment business.[25] It also must make such rules that are necessary relating to firms'

---

18. *Id.* § 105(2).

19. *Id.* § 106.

20. *Id.* schd. 13, ¶ 3, schd. 9, ¶ 13(1).

21. *See infra* p. 192 & note 217.

22. *See* J.H. FARRAR, COMPANY LAW 436–44 (1985) [hereinafter J. H. FARRAR].

23. FSA § 205. This rulemaking authority is subject to annulment by resolution of either house of Parliament.

24. *Id.* § 114 as amended by Companies Act, 1989, ch. 40, schd. 23, 12 (1989) (giving the Secretary of State the authority to transfer power).

25. *Id.* § 48. Schedule 8 requires that the SIB rules mandate disclosure of material facts

financial resources,[26] cancellation of investment agreements by investors,[27] and notification by investment businesses of various circumstances to their SRO or the SIB.[28] The SIB must also make provisions to meet the enabling statutes' objective of ensuring investor protection.[29] As a result, a complex network of norms, procedures, and regulations bind investment businesses.

Monitoring and Information Gathering

Monitoring and information gathering powers are important preventives to rules violations. They force firms to create procedures that will aid in compliance and provide, in some cases, incriminating paper trails. They enable regulators to identify problems early, act as a deterrent to wrongdoing, and assist in the ability to gather evidence. The SIB's statutory monitoring, information gathering, and investigatory powers have a spill-over effect on the SROs, which have similar rules or practices regulating their members.

Notification Requirements

Pursuant to Section 52(1) of the Financial Services Act, the SIB has promulgated notification regulations requiring directly authorized persons to disclose certain information upon the occurrence of specific events. The SIB also requires authorized persons to furnish certain financial and business information on a periodic basis.[30] The notification regulations apply to a broad range of information, including the nature of the investment business, the nature of any other business carried on in connection with the investment business, any proposal by an authorized person to alter the nature or extent of investment business carried on, the financial position of an au-

---

such as commissions, interests, and the capacity in which the firm deals with a client. In addition, the SIB must require firms to disclose sufficient information to ensure informed decisions by investors, provide for protection of customers' property, keep records, and provide for their inspection. *Id.* sched. 8.

26. *Id.* § 49.

27. *Id.* § 51.

28. *Id.* § 52.

29. These rules include: the promotion of high standards of integrity and fair dealing in the investment business; the subordination of authorized persons of their interests to those of their elements and to act fairly between clients; the disclosure of material interests and facts to the customer; the disclosure of the capacity in which and the terms on which the firm acts, enabling investors to make informed decisions; and the protection of investors' property. *Id.* sched. 8.

30. *Id.* § 52(2), (4). The notification regulations do not apply to firms authorized by an SRO or other recognized body; however, because of the equivalence requirement, the SROs have promulgated similar requirements. *See id.* § 52(3).

thorized person regarding the investment business or any other business conducted, and any property or money held by an authorized person on behalf of other persons.[31] In addition, the notification regulations require that annual reports must be filed by each firm.[32]

Power to Call for Information

Under Section 104(1), the SIB can require directly authorized and automatically authorized firms to provide such information as may be reasonably required for the exercise of its functions under the act.[33] The power to call for information is an informal and preliminary step to an investigation, analogous to a "request for cooperation" from the SEC. If the request is made, the information must be produced within a reasonable time and verified as the SIB specifies.[34] Failure to comply with a call for information can lead to statements of misconduct, injunctions or restitution orders, or an action for damages.[35] However, the SIB's powers are checked by statutory due process protections of individuals and firms. In addition, the SIB is required to follow principles of public or common law. Judicial review is available if the designated agency's actions are arbitrary or capricious.[36]

Monitoring the SROs and Other Recognized Bodies

The SIB has direct monitoring responsibilities over SROs and other recognized bodies. It has promulgated notification regulations requiring the recognized body to provide information at specified times or in respect of

---

31. *Id.* § 52(4)(a)-(f). The SIB's regulations are divided into three parts: the first applies to directly authorized firms under Section 25; the second, to insurance companies and registered friendly societies pursuant to Sections 22 and 23; and the third to European Community-based firms authorized under Section 31.

32. The SIB's Financial Services (Appointment of Auditors) Rules of 1987 (revised, 1988) require directly authorized firms to appoint an auditor before they engage in an investment business. *See id.* § 107(1) (the auditor must be retained until he has prepared the firm's financial statement for its second financial year). *See* SECURITIES AND INVESTMENTS BOARD, FINANCIAL SERVICES RULES AND REGULATIONS, ch. 2, pt. 10, § 10.02(4) (as amended 1988) [hereinafter SIB RULES]. The auditor must be given access to any information he feels is necessary to carry out his responsibilities. If there is good reason to do so, the SIB can direct a firm to submit to a second audit. FSA, *supra* note 1 at § 108. Knowingly furnishing an auditor misleading information is a criminal offense. *Id.* § 111.

33. *Id.* § 104(1) (discussing automatic authorization).

34. *Id.* § 104(3).

35. *Id.* §§ 60–62, 104(4).

36. Morse & Walsh, *Monitoring, Enforcement and Challenge of Decisions,* in 1 FINANCIAL SERVICES LAW AND PRACTICE 356–57 (A. WHITTAKER, ed., 1989) [hereinafter Morse & Walsh].

such periods specified in the regulations.[37] If a recognized organization breaches, revokes, or adds to its rules, it must inform the SIB of such action within seven days.[38] Violation of the notification requirements is not a criminal offense, but the SIB could revoke recognition, seek a compliance order in court,[39] or, after consultation, direct the alteration of the rule or alter the rule itself so as to protect the investor.[40]

Pursuant to Section 14,[41] the SIB promulgated the Financial Services (Notification by Recognized Self-Regulating Organizations) Regulations of 1987,[42] which require the SROs to notify the designated agency upon the occurrence of specified events. These events are appointment or cessation of appointment of the management team of an SRO; constitutional changes; imposition of fees and charges; delegation of monitoring of compliance functions; dismissals of officers or employees for misconduct or their resignation while under investigation for misconduct; or insolvency. In addition, SROs must provide periodic information such as annual reports, auditors reports, and quarterly financial results.[43] SROs are also required to submit information to the SIB about their member firms.[44] SROs must compile and report statistics relating to the firms' adherence to SRO rules for each quarter of the preceding financial year.[45] The SIB may require any recognized body to furnish it with such information as is reasonably necessary for the exercise of the SIB's functions under the act.[46]

---

37. *See* FSA § 14. Information must be given in the specified form and verified in a specified manner. *Id.* § 14(4).

38. *Id.* § 14(6).

39. *Id.* § 12.

40. *Id.* § 3.

41. *Id.* § 14.

42. SIB RULES, *supra* note 32 (Notifications by Recognized Self-regulating Organizations) (1987).

43. *Id.* at Rule 2. There are also notification regulations for other recognized bodies. *See infra* Part III.

44. This information includes membership; refusal, withdrawal or suspension of membership; investigation into the activities of a member; the investigation's findings; any action taken pursuant to such finding; intervention against a member; disciplinary action against a member; information from an auditor communicated to the SRO pursuant to the financial services (appointment of auditors) rules; insolvency of member firms; and any evidence that a person or member firm has committed an offense.

45. The information includes the number of firms in breach of financial adequacy regulations; the names of any members in breach on more than one occasion during the year; other submissions, such as firms unable to comply with the SRO's rules; the number of its members subject to inspection; and complaints received presented on a quarterly basis and distinguished between those about the SRO's performance and those about SRO members' activities. The resolution of the complaints also must be submitted.

46. FSA § 104(2).

Investigative Powers

The Financial Services Act provides the SIB and the recognized bodies with investigatory powers. Prior to enactment of the Financial Services Act, the Companies Act of 1985 had granted the DTI the exclusive power to seek information from investment businesses.[47] Under Section 104 of the Financial Services Act, these powers, as well as additional investigative powers, were granted concurrently to the DTI and the SIB. However, Section 105 limits this capability by providing that the power to investigate member firms under the control of recognized bodies resides with these bodies unless they ask the SIB to participate or they fail to pursue a satisfactory investigation.

The SIB's investigatory powers are relevant to the regulation of unauthorized firms that might engage in investment business; authorized firms directly regulated by the SIB; interim authorized firms; or situations where the affairs of the authorized firm (that is, a member of an SRO or recognized professional body) present special problems that lead the SRO or recognized body to seek the SIB's statutory assistance.[48] The purpose of investigation is to gather information for a subsequent civil or criminal action.

In most cases involving member firms, the locus of investigatory responsibility lies with the recognized body, while the SIB remains in a backup position. However, the SIB's power to subpoena "connected persons,"[49] such as the investigated party's banker, auditor, or solicitor, is an important investigative power upon which the recognized bodies frequently rely. Because of their inability to investigate third parties themselves, SROs seek the assistance of the SIB. It is important to note, however, that the SIB's investigative powers with respect to connected persons is limited by specific legal, professional, and bank privacy privileges.[50]

Under its specific investigatory powers, the SIB can require a person under investigation to appear before it, to produce specified documents, and to answer questions.[51] Failure to comply with an investigatory request can lead to severe consequences: namely, a criminal conviction.[52] Additionally, when the SIB has reasonable cause to believe certain specified violations of

47. It also has investigatory powers under the Police and Criminal Evidence Act of 1984 and the Banking Act of 1979.
48. Securities and Investments Board, Report of the Securities and Investments Board For 1988/1989 19 (1989), [hereinafter SIB Annual Report 1988/89].
49. FSA § 105(a).
50. *Id.* § 105(6)(7).
51. *Id.* § 105(3).
52. *Id.* § 105(10).

the Financial Services Act or other related criminal offenses—such as insider dealing—have occurred, it may obtain a warrant to search for documents.[53] This power must be exercised concurrently with the DTI. It is usually used only after a party has refused to comply with a request to produce documents.[54] Although the SIB's power to conduct searches is broad, it is limited by the requirement that there be a "good reason" for the investigation and that the desired documents be "specified."[55] Given the procedures for obtaining warrants and the demands on the SIB's stretched resources, it seems unlikely that the investigative power will be abused or overused.

One way in which the SIB can expand its investigative power is to appoint an outside party to conduct an investigation. Under Section 105, if the SIB has good cause to investigate someone, it can assign all of its powers to a third party, provided that the scope of the investigation is limited to a specifically named individual.[56] By appointing compliance officers in firms or SRO board members as outside investigators the enforcement efforts of the firms and the SRO's can be greatly enhanced.

In its first two years, the SIB investigated forty firms. Fifteen were authorized and ten were unauthorized. Out of those forty instances where Section 105 powers were invoked, twenty-one required further action.[57] Many investigations resulted in follow-up action by an SRO, winding up actions by the SIB,[58] an SIB injunction or restitution action,[59] action by the DTI, or criminal prosecution.

The SIB's most significant exercise of investigatory powers concerns inquiries of unauthorized investment activities. From April 29, 1988 to March 1990, the SIB undertook 330 investigations of unauthorized investment business of which fifty-seven required further action.[60]

The effectiveness of the SIB's enforcement has sharply contrasted with the maladministration of the DTI. In several highly publicized actions since the enactment of the Financial Services Act, the SIB moved swiftly to suspend the authorization of several companies involved in questionable sell-

---

53. *Id.* § 199(2).

54. A. WEDGWOOD, G. PELL, L. LEIGH, & C. RYAN, A GUIDE TO THE FINANCIAL SERVICES ACT 109 (1986) [hereinafter A. WEDGWOOD, G. PELL].

55. FSA § 105(1)(4).

56. *Id.* § 106. Additionally, the SIB has broad power to investigate and subpoena unit trusts, other collective investment schemes, and their managers. In matters involving collective investments, the SIB appoints an inspector who issues a report that may be published. *Id.* § 94.

57. SIB ANNUAL REPORT 1988/89, *supra* note 48 at 20–21.

58. FSA § 72.

59. *Id.*

60. SIB ANNUAL REPORT 1988/89, *supra* note 48 at 21.

ing activities to unsophisticated investors. Prior to the creation of the SIB, suspected violators customarily ignored the DTI's warnings. Sluggish investigations by the DTI resulted in large losses by investors. All too frequently, the DTI produced reports long after the financial scandals had unraveled. By the time action was taken, the funds had disappeared. The SIB's powers have enabled it to act much more swiftly than enforcement agencies operating prior to the enactment of the Financial Services Act.

The DTI has been burdened by a patchwork of responsibilities, bureaucratic sluggishness, a severe shortage of investigative staff, a lack of investigative tradition and initiative, and a poor reputation within the government and without.[61] In contrast, the SIB, with a narrower focus, has been able to intervene quickly and effectively in tandem with the SROs. The notification requirements and the monitoring system provide an effective early warning system, allowing the SIB to act early and preemptively. In the financial services sector, an SIB request for an injunction often means that a firm will collapse financially shortly thereafter, whereas an ongoing investigation by the DTI allows the violating firm to conduct its business as usual until the probe is completed.

Enforcement in Practice

Typical of the difference between the SIB and the DTI were their respective actions in 1988 in connection with DPR, a futures and options broker that used high-pressure tactics (e.g., repeatedly calling potential investors) to sell high-risk futures and options with higher commission charges. In order to create the appropriate atmosphere to encourage unsophisticated investors to part with their savings, during the telephone call the firm played a recording of a frenetic trading room. DPR was a classic "boiler room" operation. Commissions were five times those of reputable firms.[62] Accounts were churned, and financial statements were difficult to obtain.

Although the DTI investigated the scam, its response was too late, too slow, and too limited. According to evidence accumulated by *The Times*, the DTI had received a stream of complaints about DPR's questionable business tactics for nearly a year before it acted. The department also had received warnings from legitimate futures firms.[63]

In contrast, the SIB moved quickly and effectively once it became aware of the case. DPR had applied to the Association of Futures Brokers and

---

61. *See* J. H. FARRAR, *supra* note 22 at 436–44.
62. Lever, *Investors Count Cost of Dealing with DPR*, THE TIMES (London), July 13, 1988 at 29, col. 1.
63. *A Nasty Trade Pattern*, THE TIMES (London), July 13, 1988 at 17, col. 1.

Dealers (AFBD) for authorization. While waiting for final authorization, it was approved on an interim basis. The AFBD had received several letters complaining of high-pressure sales techniques.[64] It turned those complaints over to the SIB, and in July 1988 the SIB rejected DPR's application. The SIB then moved to put DPR out of business. On Monday it suspended DPR pursuant to Section 28[65] on grounds that it was not a fit and proper person to carry on the investment business in which it was engaged. Then SIB sought an injunction under Section 61.[66] On Wednesday of the same

---

64. Hargreaves and Tucker, *DPR Case Takes Shine Off Futures*, FIN. TIMES, July 14, 1990 at 4, col. 1.

65. FSA Section 28 states in part:

Section 28 Withdrawal and suspension of authorization 28(1) [Power of Secretary of State] The Secretary of State may at any time withdraw or suspend any authorization granted by him if it appears to him—

(a) that the holder of the authorization is not a fit and proper person to carry on the investment business which he is carrying on or proposing to carry one; or

(b) without prejudice to paragraph (a) above, that the holder of the authorization has contravened any provision of this Act or any rules or regulations made under it or, in purported compliance with any such provision, has furnished the Secretary of State with false, inaccurate or misleading information or has contravened any prohibition or requirement imposed under this Act. FSA, *supra* note 2 at § 28.

The Secretary of State has delegated the power of withdrawal and suspension to the S.I.B. *Id.* at § 114.

66. FSA Section 61 states in part:

61(1) [Power of Court on application by Secretary of State] If on the application of the Secretary of State the court is satisfied

(a) that there is a reasonable likelihood that any person will contravene any provision of:

   (i) rules or regulations made under this Chapter;

   (ii) sections 47, 56, 57, or 59 above;

   (iii) any requirements imposed by an order under section 58(3) above; or

   (iv) the rules of a recognized self-regulating organization, recognized professional body, recognized investment exchange or recognized clearing house to which that person is subject and which regulate the carrying on by him of investment business or any condition imposed under section 50 above;

(b) that any person has contravened any such provision or condition and that there is a reasonable likelihood that the contravention will continue or be repeated; or

(c) that any person has contravened any such provision or condition and that there are steps that could be taken for remedying the contravention, the court may grant an injunction restraining the contravention or, in Scotland, an interdict prohibiting the contravention or, as the case may be, make an order requiring that person and any other person who appears to the court to have been knowingly concerned in the contravention to take such steps as the court may direct to remedy it. *Id.* § 61.

week, the SIB petitioned the High Court and received a winding up order pursuant to Section 72.[67] At that time, DPR was still solvent. Because DPR had only received interim approval from the AFBD, it was subject directly to the SIB's enforcement powers. The SIB commenced an investigation to determine whether there was fraud or criminal conduct. Its report was forwarded to the SFO to commence criminal prosecution.

The principals of DPR eventually were acquitted of criminal charges of "dishonest trading," a result that may reflect more on the SFO's prosecutorial skills than on DPR's blamelessness.[68] After the principals were acquitted, the AFBD still refused to authorize them to conduct a futures business and the SIB continued to seek restitution of £1.7 million pursuant to sections 61(3) and 61(4) of the Financial Services Act.[69]

Another case demonstrates even more vividly the DTI's deficiencies and the SIB's capacity to act swiftly. This case involved Barlow Clowes (BC), a fund management group that had received £ 180 million from investors. BC was founded by Elizabeth Barlow and a high-living Manchester resident, Peter Clowes, in 1973. Barlow had fled the country in 1981 just before the collapse of a brokerage firm with which she was involved. Clowes had been closely associated with Bernard Cornfield, a participant in the Investors Overseas Services scandal of the 1960s. BC had subsidiaries and connected companies in places such as Gibraltar and Geneva. Nearly 18,000 investors, many of them retired persons, invested in Barlow Clowes companies.

Originally, BC promised high yields through "bond-washing," a process of converting income from gilts (government securities) into equities, which offered tax advantages. "Bond-washing" was outlawed in 1985, except by small investors, but BC continued to promise extremely high yields. In addition, it used high interest rates to entice investors to deposit their funds in Gibraltar rather than London. For example, in December 1987, BC granted a 4.2 percent return to investors in London and a 10.7 percent re-

---

67. FSA Section 72 states in part:

72(1) [Power of court to wind up] On a petition presented by the Secretary of State by virtue of this section, the court having jurisdiction under the Insolvency Act 1986 may wind up an authorized person or appointed representative to whom this subsection applies if—

(a) the person is unable to pay his debts within the meaning of section 123 or, as the case may be, section 221 of that Act; or

(b) the court is of the opinion that it is just and equitable that the person should be wound up.

68. *See* Tucker, *Four Cleared of Dishonest Trading,* THE TIMES, July 13, 1990 at 18, col. 1.

69. *See* Bennett, *Regulators May Act to Recover Pounds 1.7 m. From DPR,* THE TIMES (London), July 14, 1990 at 40, col. 1.

turn on funds invested via Gibraltar. Most of the money went offshore where it was loaned to other Clowes companies.[70] In the 1980's, nearly £ 130 million were shifted to Gibraltar, and £ 7 to £ 14 million pounds to Geneva.[71] There were also accounts in Jersey, the Channel Islands, the Isle of Man, and elsewhere.[72]

Warnings about BC activities flowed into the DTI for several years before it finally acted. As early as 1984, the National Association of Securities Dealers and Investment Managers (NASDIM), an SRO,[73] had alleged that BC had been illegally trading securities for over a year without obtaining a securities license or joining NASDIM.

Even local authorities and other government offices had become suspicious of BC's activities. One year before the firm collapsed, the Regional Crime Squad in Manchester commenced an investigation of BC after receiving information about lavish spending by its employees and the shipment of cash abroad on chartered airplanes. The Regional Crime Squad placed the file containing the product of the investigation in its "difficult tray." No further action was taken.[74] The Inland Revenue Department had also been tipped off about conspicuous expenditures by BC officials and had conducted a preliminary investigation. In 1984, the Stock Exchange began to deliver warnings to the government and the Bank of England, and in 1987 the Exchange refused to grant membership to BC.[75] In neither case was any substantive action taken.

Despite these warnings and investigations, the DTI issued a securities license to BC on October 28, 1985. This license was renewed even though the statutorily required auditors' reports had not been filed.[76] Not until November 1987 did the department commence an investigation.

---

70. Lever, *DTI Breached Rules Over New Clowes License*, THE TIMES (London), July 22, 1988 at 21, col. 2; Lever, *Jet-set Lifestyle of Peter Clowes*, THE TIMES (London), June 16, 1988 at 23, col. 2; Lever, *Barlow Clowes Victims Vent Anger on DTI*, THE TIMES (London), June 24, 1988 at 1, col. 5.

71. Lever, *Barlow Firm Is Closed in Gibraltar*, THE TIMES (London), June 8, 1988 at 25, col. 8.

72. Lever, *Interest Free Loans Made to Clowes Firms*, THE TIMES (London), June 10, 1988 at 25, col. 2

73. NASDIM alleged that Barlow Clowes had been traded illegally for over one year without obtaining a securities license or joining NASDIM. Under the Prevention of Frauds (Investments) Act this was a criminal offense.

74. Lever, *Police Knew a Year Ago of Clowes Danger Signs*, THE TIMES (London), June 25, 1988 at 1, col. 7.

75. Lever, *City Shunned Barlow Clowes*, THE TIMES (London), June 30, 1988 at 1, col. 2.

76. Lever, *DTI Accused over Clowes Deals*, THE TIMES (London), June 10, 1988 at 11, col. 1.

Initially the DTI defended its inaction by arguing that BC was a partnership rather than a corporation and therefore it was not subject to the enforcement and investigative powers granted to the DTI in the Companies Act. However, this argument was plainly incorrect because the DTI had required BC to incorporate before it received its license. Not surprisingly, the DTI was roundly criticized in the City and beyond for proffering this flimsy justification. Moreover, under the Prevention of Frauds (Investments) statute, the DTI and the director of public prosecutions were empowered to prosecute any securities firm that was neither licensed nor exempt, regardless of its incorporation status.[77] Privately, the department conceded that it could not investigate each applicant because of understaffing and that licensing had become a process of registration, rather than review and approval.

Concurrent with the DTI, the SIB commenced its own investigation in November 1987 by appointing investigators to examine the affairs of one corporation in the BC group, Barlow Clowes Gild Managers Limited. By April 1988 the investigators' report had been completed. The SIB uncovered evidence of falsified client records and accounting figures and of lending to corporations controlled by Clowes which had nothing to do with financial services.[78] Within days of the investigators report, the SIB had successfully petitioned for a winding up order. The investors were the big losers in this scam. While the perpetrators have been caught in a mire of civil and criminal legal proceedings, the fraud was uncovered too late for the investors' money to be saved. Unfortunately, the investors were not covered by the industry-wide compensation scheme because BC had only received interim authorization under the new Financial Services Act regulatory scheme.

In the aftermath of this debacle, the government commissioned two studies of its enforcement efforts in the case. One of these concluded that there had been significant maladministration by the DTI and that if matters had been handled properly, the operations of BC would have been brought to a halt before the money was lost. The report recommended government compensation to investors.[79] Although the government did not accept the report

---

77. Lever, *DTI Under Fire Over Clowes*, THE TIMES (London), June 11, 1988 at 25, col. 2.

78. Lever and Fletcher, *Papers Were Shredded at Clowes HQ*, THE TIMES (London), June 11, 1988 at 1, col. 1.

79. *See Five Areas Where DTI was at Fault*, THE TIMES (London), Dec. 20, 1989 at 26, col. 1 (discusses the independent investigation of DTI and the Barlow Clowes affair conducted by Sir Anthony Barrowclough, Parliamentary Ombudsman); *Incompetent and Evasive*, FIN. TIMES, Dec. 20, 1989 at 16; *The End of the Affair*, THE TIMES (London), Dec. 20, 1989 at 15, col. 1.

or admit legal liability, it offered £150 million in compensation to the eighteen thousand defrauded investors.[80]

More than any other case, BC illustrates the weaknesses in the DTI's enforcement capabilities and the need for improved coordination among enforcement agencies. Unfortunately, Barlow Clowes is not merely a legacy of the old system. Under the Financial Services Act, the DTI still retains enforcement responsibilities, and as revealed by BC, a passive bureaucratic approach pervades the organization. Barlow Clowes also demonstrates the difficulties associated with investigating and prosecuting against sophisticated transnational commercial crime and highlights the need for coordination among enforcement agencies. The BC affair was just the kind of financial fraud for which the Financial Services Act was designed, but failed, to prevent. However, a silver lining to the BC cloud may be found in the good publicity received by the SIB. In contrast to the DTI's procrastination and maladministration, the SIB acted quickly and effectively once it became involved. The key to the different responses of the two agencies is that the investor protection model of the Financial Services Act is grounded in prevention, whereas the DTI's enforcement approach is reactive.

The greatest strength of self-regulatory enforcement is not so much its speed and effectiveness of prosecution, nor the deterrent effect of its sanctions, but rather, it lies in the ability to avert wrongdoing. The authorization process, whereby the firm must demonstrate its fitness to enter the financial services industry, weeds out fringe operators because its shifts the burden of proof from the regulator to the firm.

Thus, DPR and other questionable firms were caught by the SIB in the authorization net. The SIB could act quickly when abusive practices were brought to its attention. In contrast, the scope of the DTI's responsibilities, the lack of an investigatory tradition, its institutional culture, and the need for approval of investigative action from several bureaucratic layers made it much less effective in conducting any probe.

Over the past few years the SIB has caught a number of questionable firms in its net in the process of authorization. This denial of the entry of fringe operations into the financial services sector is just as critical a means of prevention as is the effect of strict enforcement against investment businesses guilty of wrongdoing.

---

80. Ashworth & Narbrough, *150m for Clowes Investors*, THE TIMES (London), Dec. 20, 1989 at 23, col. 2. Investors who lost less than £50,000, the vast majority of whom were retired persons, received 90% of their losses plus interest. Those who invested more received a lesser percentage according to a sliding scale. Clowes was sentenced to ten years in prison.

Compliance and Control Powers

Disqualification of Firms and Individuals

The SIB has the power to disqualify firms and individuals from the investment business. Central to the investor protection system is the requirement that no person can carry on an investment business unless authorized to do so or exempt from such authorization.[81] The justification for the system of authorization is that allowing only fit and proper persons to engage in investment business will be the most effective and cost-efficient way to prevent investor abuse. The SIB's power to disqualify firms and individuals allows it to control who is authorized to engage in investment businesses. The SIB can exercise its power both at the initial authorization stage, by a refusal to provide authorization, and later upon violation of certain provisions of the Financial Services Act, by issuing a disqualification directive. There are severe criminal and civil sanctions for operating an unauthorized investment business.[82]

Authorization of Investment Business   While authorization may be obtained in different ways, the most important is through membership in an SRO recognized by the SIB.[83] To obtain authorization, an applicant must submit to a recognized body of the SIB a profile of the applicant's business and its board of directors and senior management, its financial condition and history including any disciplinary proceedings or convictions, compliance arrangements within the firm enabling the applicant to abide by SRO rules, and a business plan that includes a profile of its proposed customer base.

The authorization process filtered out many marginal financial services businesses. Over six thousand firms commenced but did not complete the authorization process after regulators requested additional information or initially rejected them.[84] Many failed to gain authorization initially because they hadn't completed the application forms properly. Few appealed their initial rejection.[85] The authorization process did not, however, notify

---

81. FSA § 13.

82. Criminal sanctions include up to two years in jail. Civil sanctions include agreements being unenforceable and voidable at a court's discretion and the SIB right to seek injunctive and restitution orders. *Id.* §§ 4–6.

83. *Id.* § 15. See *supra* ch 3.

84. Riley, *A Birthday for Security Rules*, FIN. TIMES, May 2, 1989 at 19, col. 1.

85. *See* Waters, *Firms Fail to Gain Authorization*, FIN. TIMES, Aug. 26, 1988 at 16, col. 2. See *supra* chapter 3, p. 79.

the SROs that complaints had been lodged against certain firms and that individuals previously convicted of improper conduct were attempting to return to the industry.[86]

The SIB can withdraw or suspend an authorization if a person is not fit or proper to carry on an investment business, or if an authorized person or firm has contravened the Financial Services Act or any regulations pursuant to it, or has furnished false, inaccurate, or misleading information in purported compliance with any provision.[87] In such situations, the SIB must provide written notice of its intentions along with a statement of the reasons, dates, and notification of the right to have the matter referred to the Financial Services Tribunal (FST or tribunal).[88]

SIB Disqualification Actions Against Individuals   Most of the SIB's enforcement powers relate to firms, and individuals connected with those firms have residual liability.[89] However, for violations of the conduct of business provisions, the SIB can pursue individuals directly. If it appears that an individual is not a fit and proper person to be employed in an investment business, Section 59 permits the SIB to make a disqualification direction. The individual named is then prohibited, without the SIB's consent, from employment in the financial services sector.

The purpose of the disqualification directive is to prevent dishonest participants in one kind of investment business from moving to another sector after disqualification by concealing his former misdeeds or identity. A register of authorized persons lists individuals against whom a disqualification direction is in force.[90] Such information is not open to public inspection unless the member of the public satisfies the secretary of state that he has good reason for seeking the information.[91] The SIB will release names of those on the disqualification list to prospective employers upon receipt of a job applicant's national health number that matches a number on the list. There are, however, due process protections for such individuals. They must receive advance warning, the reasons for the action, and notification that the case may be referred to the FST.[92]

---

86. The flood of applications was so great at the beginning that some firms received interim authorization while their applications were pending. Some firms were conducting investment business in this period that would not gain final authorization.

87. FSA § 28.

88. *Id.* §§ 29, 31. Persons authorized in another EEC state have automatic authorization under § 31. However, their authorization may be suspended, withdrawn, and terminated in similar fashion except that the home supervisor will be contacted.

89. *Id.* § 202.

90. *Id.* § 102(1)(e).

91. *Id.* § 103(2)-(3).

92. In making a disqualification direction the SIB has broad discretion as to length of

Public Statements as to Misconduct

Another of the SIB's compliance and control powers is derived from Section 60. Under that section, the SIB can issue a public statement that a directly authorized firm or individual (as opposed to the firm's employees) has been guilty of violating the conduct of business or financial resource rules. The firm involved must be notified in advance and will receive all of the rights that accompany a disqualification direction. This is a very drastic penalty, as it may affect the firm in both its relations with the public and its reputation in the marketplace.

Remedies for Impermissible Transactions

Injunctions   One of the most effective and efficient enforcement remedies is the injunction. It is preventive in that it can forestall future conduct or repetition of a breach of the rules. It can be used to protect investors before they are hurt. It allows the enforcement agency to move quickly—a rarity when the judicial process is involved. In addition, injunctive relief may be more cost efficient than other kinds of enforcement because it can be narrowly tailored to provide only the minimum necessary relief, and it may obviate the need for a full trial.[93]

Injunctions may be used to force investment business to comply with the authorization requirement or with other regulations such as the ban on cold calling,[94] the restrictions on advertising,[95] the ban on the employment of prohibited persons,[96] or a violation of the conduct of business rules.[97] One advantage of the injunction is that the prosecuting party need only meet the civil rather than the criminal burden of proof. A court must grant the injunction if there is a reasonable likelihood that a person will contravene a provision of the statute, or that a person has already contravened it and there is reasonable likelihood that the contravention will be repeated. Failure to obey an injunction places the defendant in contempt of court, which can result in a criminal conviction.[98] It is also important to note that

---

time, conditions, and scope, and it may vary such directives once issued. The employer must take reasonable care not to employ a disqualified person or he may be subject to civil enforcement proceedings or a private action for damages. *Id.* §§ 59(6), 62(1)(d).

93. *See generally* Note, *Developments in the Law: Injunctions*, 78 HARV. L. REV. 994, 996 (1965) ("The expanding role of the injunction is partly due to the attractiveness of so flexible a remedy in a modern society with expanding regulation of complex economic and social affairs."

94. FSA § 56.

95. *Id.* § 57.

96. *Id.* § 59.

97. *Id.* § 61(1).

98. *Id.* § 6.

all sections relating to injunctions provide for other ancillary sanctions where appropriate. These include criminal penalties, unenforceability of contracts entered into by the sanctioned party, restitution, or damages.

Procedurally, the SIB can apply to a court to obtain an injunction or restitution order against a firm or individual who violates or is likely to violate provisions of the statute.[99] An injunction also may be obtained if there is a reasonable likelihood that a person will contravene the rules of one of the SROs of which the person is a member. However, the SIB cannot seek an injunction against an SRO member unless it appears that the SRO itself is unable or unwilling to take appropriate steps itself to restrain the individual.[100]

Restitution Orders   In certain cases, including some situations in which the issuance of an injunction would be proper, a court may grant a restitution order upon application of the SIB.[101] Such orders will be granted if: 1) the court is satisfied that a person has been conducting an investment business while unauthorized or has contravened other applicable statutory rules and regulations,[102] and 2) profits have accrued to that person, or one or more investors have suffered loss as a result of the contravention. The court may order the person concerned to pay into court the profits accrued or recover and pay into court a sum equivalent to the investors' losses or other adverse effects.[103]

It is uncertain whether a restitution order would apply to an investor who suffered a loss as a result of advice, as opposed to one who entered into a transaction and as a result incurred a loss or adverse effect or generated a profit for the investment business. The statute uses the word "transactions."[104] A court can also appoint a receiver to recover the profits, money, or property involved.[105] The use of a restitution order does not affect the right of the investor to bring an action for damages. Restitution orders are a form of ancillary relief, that give courts added flexibility in enjoining and minimizing the impact of violations of the Financial Services Act[106]

---

99. *Cf.* Securities Act of 1933 §§ 20(b), 21, 15 U.S.C.A. §§ 77(t)(b), 78(u)(d) (1988) (regarding the SEC's use of injunctive powers).

100. FSA § 61(2).

101. *Id.* §§ 6, 61.

102. *See id.* §§ 47–56.

103. *Id.* §§ 6(4), 61(4).

104. Morse and Walsh, *supra* note 36 at ¶¶ 27–28.

105. FSA, *supra* note 2, § 61(4).

106. Compare the SEC's development of ancillary remedies, which is based on the general equitable powers of federal courts rather than based on statute. Farrand, *Ancillary Remedies in Federal Securities Law: A Study in Federal Remedies*, 67 Minn. L. Rev. 865 (1983).

Voiding of Contracts   At common law, when a statute made a particular activity unlawful unless licensed, contracts entered into by the unlicensed individual were illegal and void. In the case of *Cope v. Rowlands*,[107] the plaintiff was not a licensed broker as required by the City of London. The defense to an action on a contract entered into by the broker and the defendant was that the plaintiff broker was not duly licensed, authorized, and empowered to act, therefore the contract could not be enforced. The court held that when a contract which the plaintiff sought to enforce was forbidden, either expressly or implied, by the common or statutory law, the court would not lend assistance to give the contract effect.[108] In recent years, such decisions have become less favored as courts have sought to avoid the forfeiture and penalty implications of illegality by upholding contracts on the basis of public policy or statutory interpretation.[109]

The Financial Services Act, however, specifically provides for the unenforceability of contracts in several settings. Contracts entered into by individuals who are carrying on an investment business are voidable when the individuals are neither authorized to conduct such investment business nor exempt from authorization.[110] The injured party can recover monetary damages or property paid or transferred by him under the agreement, together with any compensation for loss sustained as a result of having parted with the money. Parties may have agreed upon remedies; that is, liquidated damages.

The party seeking to enforce the contract may have a defense to an unenforceability claim if that party took all reasonable precautions and exercised due diligence as to authorization. The court could enforce the agreement if the person reasonably believed, upon entering into it, that he did not contravene Section 3 or did not know that the agreement was made as a result of an action by a person in default.[111] In such cases, the court would

---

107. 150 Eng. Rep. 707 (1836).

108. *Id.* at 710.

109. *See* Phoenix General Ins. Co. v. Administratia Asigurarilor de Stat, 1 Q.B. 216, 2 All E.R. 152 (1988). In Phoenix General the plaintiffs were not authorized to sell a particular class of reinsurance contract. The defen-dants, reinsurers, argued that the contracts were unenforceable thereby depriving the insured of any recovery. Plaintiffs successfully argued that the illegality did not affect the whole of the transaction with the insured. Where a statute merely prohibited one body from entering into a contract without authority and imposed a penalty upon him if he did sell, it did not follow that the contract itself was impliedly prohibited so as to render it illegal and void. whether or not the statute had that effect depended upon considerations of public policy and the mischief which the statute was designed to prevent, its language, scope and purposes, the consequences for the innocent party, and other relevant considerations. *But see* Davies, *Unauthorized Insurer Is Not Liable for Claims*, FIN. TIMES, June 21, 1989 at 14, col. 1.

110. FSA § 5.

111. *See id.* § 5(3).

consider whether it was inequitable for the agreement to be enforced or for money or property transferred to be retained. When an agreement is unenforceable, the investor must return any money or property received.[112]

Other situations where investment agreements may be held unenforceable include those made pursuant to an unsolicited call or in violation of the cold calling regulations.[113] Such contracts are unenforceable against the person on whom the call was made. That individual is entitled to restitution of money or property paid together with compensation for any loss sustained.[114] Agreements voidable under this section may be upheld if a court is satisfied that the person on whom the call was made was uninfluenced, or materially uninfluenced, by anything said during the call, or that the agreement entered into followed discussions other than the one during the call, and the person on whom the call was made was aware of the nature of the agreement and any risks involved in entering it.[115]

An agreement involving an unsolicited call would also be upheld if the call was not made by a person who would benefit as the result of such an agreement, for instance, someone benefiting only through a commission. The purpose of this section is to give the courts flexibility and to prevent an individual from using grounds of unenforceability to repudiate an agreement because some time later he changed his mind.[116]

Unenforceability also applies to contraventions of the restrictions on advertising.[117] After use of an advertisement, the advertiser is not entitled to enforce any agreement relating to that advertisement. Where an advertisement invites persons to exercise rights conferred by an investment (preemptive rights), the court may prevent enforcement of any obligation arising out of the exercise of such rights. The court may enforce agreements made after contraventions of advertising restrictions in the same circumstances that unsolicited call agreements can be enforced.[118]

Contracts that are subject to unenforceability are voidable rather than void in their making.[119] The injured party can have restitution of any funds

---

112. *See id.* § 5(4).
113. *Id.* § 56(2).
114. *Id.* § 56(2)(b).
115. *Id.* § 56(4).
116. There is a fourteen-day to twenty-eight-day cancellation period for certain kinds of agreements such as life insurance policies. SIB, FINANCIAL SERVICES TRIBUNAL (CONDUCT OF INVESTIGATION) RULES, 1988, at ch. V [hereinafter SIB CONDUCT OF INVESTIGATION RULES].
117. FSA § 57.
118. Another situation to which the unenforceability doctrine applies is an insurance contract promoted in contravention of provisions restricting unauthorized insurance companies from selling insurance. *See id.* §§ 131–132.
119. *Id.* § 5(6).

or property paid or, if the property has been transferred to a third party, the value of the property transferred. In addition, with the permission of the court, the injured party is entitled to recovery of expenses for loss sustained as a result of parting with the property or money as a reliance measure of recovery. Unless the innocent party waives the unenforceability of the contract, he is not entitled to benefits under the agreement and must return any property received under it.

The unenforceability provisions allow courts to shape a just and equitable response to violations of the statute. Ironically, there has been an absence of concern about these sanctions by the financial services industry in contrast to virtual paranoia over liabilities resulting from private actions for damages under Section 62. It has been suggested that the meek reaction to unenforceability reflects recognition of the flexibility of the courts' powers.[120]

Private Actions for Damages   In addition to direct enforcement actions available to the SIB, the Financial Services Act provides for a private cause of action by individuals who suffer loss as a result of violations of the Financial Services Act or a contravention by a member of an SRO or other organized body of the rules of the organization to which it is a member.[121] Violators of the conduct of business rules or the SIB's enforcement powers are subject to civil suit.[122] The grant of a private right of action was the most controversial single provision in the statute.[123] Under the 1989 Companies Act amendments, the right to bring suit under the statute has been limited to investing members of the public in the United Kingdom, a most nonlitigious group.[124]

Under the American system, the use of the private right of action by investors complements governmental enforcement of securities laws.[125] While American securities laws provide some express remedies,[126] courts have

---

120. Morse and Walsh, *supra* note 36 at ¶ 23.

121. FSA § 62.

122. In addition to being available for violations of the conduct of business rules, private actions apply to breaches of restrictions on business or dealing with assets (§ 71(1)); violations of certain authorized unit trust provisions (§§ 91(4), 95); failure to furnish information as requested by the SIB (§§ 104(4), 178(5)); violation of certain provisions relating to the insurance business (§ 130(7)), banking business (§ 185(6)), and violation of the Rules of Friendly Societies (sched. 11(22)(4)); contraventions of prospectus rules, a false or misleading prospectus (§ 171(6); or breach of a DTI notice limiting a foreign power to conduct investment business in the U.K. (§ 185(6)).

123. Practitioners feared that compliant courts would make it an expansive remedy similar to the SEC's rule 10b-5. *See* Morse and Walsh, *supra* note 36 at ¶ 23.

124. Companies Act, ch. 40, § 193, 1989 (adding § 62A to the Financial Services Act).

125. *See* J.I. Case v. Borak, 377 U.S. 426 (1964).

126. *E.g.*, Securities Act, 1933, §§ 11(a), 12(1), 12(2), 15 U.S.C.A. §§ 77k, 77l(1), (2)

found that Congress intended to give private parties implied rights of action for violations of many sections of the securities laws.[127] Because of the ambiguities in the legislative history of the American securities acts, the issue of whether private plaintiffs have a right of action for violation of a particular section of the securities acts has been a subject of ongoing judicial interpretation.[128] The lower courts were particularly responsive to the expansion of private rights of action, and this has had a multiplier effect upon the overall enforcement effort.

Though rights of action for damages are more explicit in the Financial Services Act, it is doubtful that private litigation will play nearly as important a role in the English system. The limitations on contingent fees for attorneys,[129] the weight of interest groups against the private right of action, and the absence of a plaintiff's bar make its use uncertain.

Powers of Intervention

The SIB has the power to enforce the provisions of the Financial Services Act by intervening in the business activity of a firm.[130] While a regulatory body should act as quickly as possible when an investment firm has violated the rules, it may be preferable for the body to use the minimum enforcement power necessary to correct the wrong and protect innocent people. A re-

---

(1988) (misleading registration materials, failure to comply with prospectus requirements, material misstatements by sellers of securities); or Securities Exchange Act of 1934, §§ 9(3), 16(b), 18(a), 15 U.S.C.A. §§ 78(i), 78p(b), 78r(a) (1988) (manipulation of exchange listed securities, disgorgement of insider profits, material misstatements and omissions in SEC filings).

127. The most important being an implied right of action for violations of rule 10b-5 and §§ 10(b) and 14(a) of the Securities Exchange Act of 1934. Herman and MacLean v. Huddleston, 495 U.S. 375 (1983) (reaffirming implied of action under § 10B and rule 10b-5); J.I. Case v. Borak, 377 U.S. at 438.

128. In *Huddleston*, 459 U.S. 375, the Supreme Court upheld a private plaintiff's right of action. However, the standard of proof is now a preponderance of the evidence standard. *See* Blue Chip Stamps v. Manor Drugs, 421 U.S. 723 (1975); *see generally* HAZEN, THE LAW OF SECURITIES REGULATION § 13.1 (2d ed., 1990).

129. In 1989, the British government proposed reform of the legal profession that would permit contingent fees. Attorneys would be able to charge at a higher rate than normal, but the maximum amount by which a lawyer's fee could be increased would be limited by the Lord Chancellor. LORD HIGH CHANCELLOR, LEGAL SERVICES: A FRAMEWORK FOR THE FUTURE 41 (1989). This reform will not open the litigation floodgates, however, as the losing party will still be required to pay the reasonable costs of his successful opponent, which is a deterrent to plaintiff. This will lead lawyers to conduct a more rigorous assessment of the profits and chances for success than in the United States. In addition, class actions would not be brought, discouraging strike or frivolous suits. LORD CHANCELLOR'S DEPT., CONTINGENCY FEES 6–7 (1989).

130. FSA §§ 64–71.

vocation of authorization would destroy the firm's ongoing business value and result in its liquidation. The SIB is authorized to intervene against directly authorized or automatically authorized businesses when it is desirable for the protection of investors, when the firm involved is unfit to carry on investment business of a particular kind or to the extent proposed, or when the authorized person has committed a breach of the statute or regulations or has furnished false or misleading information in purported compliance with the statute.[131]

Essentially, intervention permits the SIB or its appointed representative to intercede and run an investment business. The SIB can assume the normal powers of a board of directors. The intervention powers are analogous to American state corporate statutes, such as that of Delaware, which permit the appointment of a custodian as an alternative to dissolution.[132] However, the Delaware statute requires application to the Court of Chancery before such powers are granted, whereas under the Financial Services Act the SIB can exercise such power merely if it appears to be desirable for the protection of investors.[133] Intervention is a remedy that can be used without resorting to the courts, and it will not destroy a business as would revocation of authorization.

The power of intervention is unavailable against a member firm of an SRO or other recognized body, except that the SIB can require the transfer of investors' assets to an approved trustee if requested by the recognized body.[134] Section 65 allows prohibition of an authorized person from entering into certain transactions except in specified circumstances or to a prescribed extent. The SIB also can limit the solicitation of business to certain persons or can restrict the conduct of business.

A second type of intervention power available to the SIB is a restriction on dealing with assets, by which the SIB may prohibit an authorized person or appointed representative from disposing of or otherwise dealing with any assets or specified assets, including those located outside of the United Kingdom.[135] The SIB also has the power to vest in a trustee the assets belonging to an authorized person, an appointed representative, or investors.[136] Finally, the SIB may intervene by requiring an authorized person or appointed representative to maintain within the United Kingdom assets of such value "as appears to the Secretary of State to be desirable with a view to insuring that the authorized person or, as the case may be, appointed

---

131. *Id.* § 64.
132. DEL. CODE ANN. tit. 8, § 226(a) (1969).
133. FSA § 64(1)(a).
134. *Id.* § 64(4).
135. *Id.* § 66.
136. *Id.* § 67(1).

representative, will be able to meet his liabilities in respect of investment business."[137]

Before these intervention powers are implemented, the SIB has to provide written notice and give particulars of the firm's right to referral of the matter to the Financial Services Tribunal. Breaching a prohibition or requirement imposed under the intervention powers can lead to public statements as to misconduct, injunctions, restitution orders, and sanctions for damages.[138] From 1988 to 1990, the SIB used its intervention powers seventeen times. In ten of these instances, the SIB intervened to restrict an authorized business or firm from entering into a particular kind of investment business.[139]

Winding Up

When fraud is uncovered, there are usually insufficient assets to pay the accumulated debts. The SIB can petition a court having jurisdiction under the Insolvency Act of 1986[140] to liquidate an authorized person or firm if that person or firm is unable to pay his debts, or if the court is of the opinion that a liquidation would be just and equitable.[141] This section would apply to a firm authorized and regulated by a recognized body, if that body gives consent.

The liquidating power enables the SIB to use the Insolvency Act procedure without having to rely on a creditor's petition. Using the inability to pay debts as a ground for liquidation prevents further harm to creditors or investors. An authorized person who defaults on an obligation to pay any sum due and payable under any investment agreement is deemed to be unable to pay his debts.[142] A just and equitable ground for a winding up order is also available where the authorized person's main business has disappeared or the company was formed for a fraudulent purpose.[143]

Under Section 74, the SIB may present a petition under Section 9 of the Insolvency Act for the appointment of an administrator when a directly or automatically authorized person or member of a recognized body of the company is unable to pay their debts.[144]

---

137. *Id.* § 68.
138. *See id.* § 71.
139. SIB ANNUAL REPORT 1989/90, *supra* note 48 at 23.
140. FSA § 72.
141. *Id.* § 72.
142. *Id.* § 72(3).
143. Morse and Walsh, *supra* note 36, ¶¶ 268–71.
144. This procedure is somewhat analogous to a Chapter XI proceeding under the Federal Bankruptcy Act. Bankruptcy Act of 1978, 11 U.S.C. §§ 1101–12.

Compliance and Control Powers
Over Recognized Bodies

The SROs, professional bodies, investment exchanges, and clearing-houses must be "recognized" by the SIB. Recognition is granted if the organization meets requirements for recognition as outlined in the statute.[145] The "recognized body" is responsible for ongoing supervision of member persons and firms.

The effectiveness of a self-regulatory system depends on the enthusiasm of the private regulatory bodies in overseeing the activities of their members and enforcing compliance with the rules. Members of an industry can better regulate themselves because they can use their expertise.[146] Practitioners are more familiar with regulatory problems, may be more able to solve them, and the solutions may be more likely to receive the support of the regulated.[147]

Despite these advantages to practitioner-based regulation, there are countervailing pressures that may turn self-regulatory bodies into self-protecting industry trade associations. SROs have public responsibilities without a governmental agency's accountability to the public. All too often, self-regulation becomes self-protection. SROs may emphasize their trade association functions and attempt to restrict competition. The first criticism of self-regulatory enforcement is a lack of zeal. In this context, the SIB's supervision and ability to sanction recognized self-regulatory bodies becomes critical in ensuring that enforcement and regulatory intensity will exist at the SRO level.[148]

The SIB has three sanctions against recognized bodies: revocation of recognition, application to a court for a compliance order, and alteration of the recognized body's rules. Revocation of recognition is the SIB's equiva-

---

145. FSA §§ 9–10, 16, 17, 36–39, scheds. 2–4. The requirements for recognition include the members of the body to be recognized have to be fit and proper persons; the organization has to have fair and reasonable rules for admission, expulsion, and discipline; have safeguards for investors; have adequate arrangements for monitoring and enforcement of compliance with its rules; have members of the public on its governing body; have the capacity to investigate complaints; and promote high standards in the carrying on of investment business by its members. *Id.* sched. 2.

146. SECURITIES AND EXCHANGE COMMISSION, REPORT OF SPECIAL STUDY OF SECURITIES MARKETS, H.R. DOC. NO. 95, 88th Cong., 1st Sess., pt. 4 at 722 (1963) [hereinafter SPECIAL STUDY].

147. Karmel, *Securities Industry Self-Regulation—Tested by the Crash*, 45 WASH. & LEE L. REV. 1297, 1306 (1988).

148. *See* Miller, *Self-Regulation of the Securities Markets: A Critical Examination*, 42 WASH. & LEE L. REV. 853 (1985) (providing a critical view of the U.S. experience with self-regulation) *See also* Chapter 2, pp. 51–57.

lent of capital punishment. Theoretically, it may be used if any of the requirements for recognition are violated, if the recognized organization has failed to comply with any obligations to which it is subject under the act, or if continued recognition of the organization is undesirable with regard to the existence of one or more other recognized organizations.[149] This last factor, undesirability of continuing recognition, is the only conceivable situation where recognition might actually be revoked. For example, if an SRO or other recognized body merged, dissolved, or had its functions assumed by an existing recognized body with the approval of the SIB, its recognition might be revoked.[150]

A less drastic sanction is the compliance order, whereby the SIB can apply to the High Court or the Court of Session if an SRO has failed to comply with any obligations under the act or has violated a requirement for recognition.[151] The court may order the recognized body to take such steps as it directs to cure the breach or violation. If the rules of a recognized body, such as its conduct of business rules,[152] do not satisfy required investor protection safeguards, the SIB can direct the organization to alter the rules or it may alter the SRO's rules itself in such manner as is necessary.[153] Before making such direction, the SIB normally must consult with the organization. The SRO has the right to apply to the High Court or Court of Session to have the alteration set aside.

The Limits of Administrative Power

The Financial Services Act gives the SIB, and in turn the recognized bodies, expansive powers to take investigatory and enforcement actions against individuals and firms. As noted above, the effectiveness of enforcement depends on the scope of these powers. However, the fairness of the investor protection system should also be considered.

Generally, fairness is a function of the limits that are placed upon the exercise of power. These limits fall into two categories. The first are the statutorily defined boundaries to enforcement powers. The second are the procedural limitations which provide protection to persons subject to enforcement actions. These procedural limitations are the subject of the next section.

---

149. FSA § 11(1).
150. *See* Conclusions *infra* pp. 225–30.
151. FSA § 12.
152. *Id* at sched. 2(3)(1).
153. *Id.* § 13. The rule amendment capability is enforceable by mandamus in England or specific performance in Scotland.

SROs have a number of conflicting responsibilities. They are expected to set standards and discipline their members so that investors will be protected. Private SROs serve public purposes and, in fact, assume public and governmental responsibilities. Their power to set standards and to mandate how business is conducted, to discipline, restrict entry, and to expel is in reality a delegation of state power to private bodies. This power can provide the opportunity for abuses of authority.[154] Penalties to violators of rules may be draconian or inadequate. In addition, standard forms of governmental or judicial accountability may be absent.

Due Process Requirements

Self-regulatory systems often have been criticized for the lack of fairness in their procedures. Private organizations may act arbitrarily against non-members or those seeking entry. To protect against this, there are requirements throughout the Financial Services Act that the self-regulating bodies act with fairness and afford due process.

The requirement of due process means that when an individual's rights or interests are affected by administrative action, certain minimal procedures must be granted. At the least, the fact finder must be impartial. No party should have a decision rendered against him unless he has been given proper notice of the claim against him and a reasonable opportunity to be heard. In English law the phrase used is that interests affected by administrative actions are protected under principles of "natural justice."[155] Nor can an administrative body exceed the powers granted to it.[156] To counteract the dangers of abuse of authority against investment businesses or those seeking entry into the financial services industry, fairness and due process blanket the statute. The Financial Services Act requires both the SIB and recognized bodies to have reasonable rules and an independent procedure for appeals relating to the admission, expulsion, and discipline of members.[157]

---

154. *See generally* Lowenfels, *A Lack of Fair Procedures in the Administrative Process: Disciplinary Proceedings at the Stock Exchanges and the NASD*, 64 CORNELL L. REV. 375 (1979); Poser, *Reply to Lowenfels*, 64 CORNELL L. REV. 402 (1979).

155. Regina v. Panel on Takeovers and Mergers, *ex parte* Datafin, 1 All E.R. 564 (C.A. 1987).

156. Morse and Walsh, *supra* note 36 at ¶¶ 1313–15.

157. FSA sched. (2)2. "The rules and practices of the [self-regulating] organization relating to (a) the admission and expulsion of members; and (b) the discipline it exercises over its members, must be fair and reasonable and include adequate provision for appeals." Schedules 3, 4(5) applies such standards to recognized professional bodies.

The concern that there be adequate due process, that individuals, firms, and recognized bodies are protected is reflected throughout the self-regulatory system. This is somewhat of a break from the past, for the English approach traditionally has been to devise methods of regulation that operate along less formalized lines than in other countries, with less emphasis on statutory protections than are found in the American system. The elements of due process in the self-regulatory system established under the Financial Services Act include proper notice of the claim against the charged, a reasonable opportunity to be heard, an impartial fact finder, an absence of arbitrary decision making, and a right of appeal.

A distinction between English and American administrative law requirements is that the investor protection framework does not explicitly give those charged the right of representation by an attorney, though in practice this nearly always occurs.[158] The Financial Services Act provides avenues of appeal for most actions against a member by a recognized body. In addition, common law developments have limited the arbitrariness of private agency action.

Perhaps the most important enforcement power of a recognized body or the SIB is its control of entry into the regulated area both in terms of authorization and disqualification. If a firm seeks direct authorization and the SIB proposes to refuse such application or to withdraw or suspend an authorization granted, it must give the applicant or authorized person written notice of the intention to do so, giving the reasons for which it proposes to act.[159] In the case of a proposed withdrawal or suspension, the notice shall state the date on which it is proposed that the withdrawal or suspension should take effect, and in the case of a proposed suspension, its proposed duration.[160] If the reasons stated in the notice include comments about another person and are prejudicial to that person, his office, or employment, a copy of that notice will be sent to the other person.[161] Where the SIB intends to terminate or suspend authorization, notice must be given of intention to do so, stating the reasons for which it proposes to act and notice of the right to have the matter referred to the Financial Services Tribunal (FST).[162]

Intervention powers generally require the SIB to give the person or applicant written notice of the intention to take action, stating the reasons for

---

158. *See* Morse and Walsh, *supra* note 36 at ¶¶ 1401–03.

159. FSA § 29(1).

160. *Id.* § 29(2).

161. *Id.* at 60.

162. *See id.* § 96(3)-(4). Schedule 6 concerns the terms of office of tribunal members, their expenses, tribunal staff, procedures, appeals, and supervision by the council of tribunals. The secretary of state has made rules on the Tribunal's procedure. The SIB CONDUCT OF INVESTIGATION RULES, *supra* note 116, came into force on March 24, 1988.

which the SIB proposes to act and giving particulars of the right to require the matter to be referred to the FST. In seeking traditional civil remedies, such as an injunction or restitution order, application is made to a regular court and full due process procedures would apply there.

The recognized bodies have equivalent due process provisions. Each has built into its procedures an adjudicative panel plus an appeals tribunal.[163] To protect the public from arbitrariness and self-interested decisions, each recognized body must include on its board a number of persons independent of the organization and its members so as to achieve a proper balance between the interests of the membership, the interests of the organization, and the interests of the public. Board members, however, have a limited role in the day-to-day application of the rules.[164]

If the recognized body has failed to comply with the statutory obligations, or if another SRO is regulating the same business, the SIB can revoke recognition.[165] The notice provided by the SIB must inform the recognized organization that it is required to bring such notice or revocation to the attention of the members of the SRO or recognized body and to publish it in such a way as to bring it to the attention of other persons affected. The notice provided by the SIB to the recognized body must state the reasons for which the SIB proposes to act and give the particulars of the rights of the recognized body.[166] The recognized body then has three months to make written or oral representations to the SIB or to a person appointed to hear the representations to determine whether to revoke the recognition order. There is no appeal, however, to the Financial Services Tribunal.

The Financial Services Tribunal

The FST, established under the Financial Services Act, has the responsibility of investigating cases referred to it and reporting on these matters to the SIB.[167] Unlike the rest of the self-regulating system, the tribunal is an independent body paid for by public funds. Its powers are not transferrable to the SIB.[168]

---

163. "Any party to proceedings before the Financial Services Tribunal who is dissatisfied may bring an appeal on a point of law to the High Court or require the Financial Services Tribunal to state and sign a case for the opinion of the High Court." Tribunals and Inquiries Act of 1971, § 13, *as amended by* FSA § 96(b), sched. 6, ¶ 6.

164. Board members of the SIB and SROs are representatives of the industry who work full time for a financial services firm or public members unaffiliated with the financial services industry, FSA, sched. 2, ¶ 5(1)(b).

165. *Id.* § 11.

166. SIB CONDUCT OF INVESTIGATION RULES, *supra* note 116, rule 4.

167. FSA § 98.

168. *Id.* §§ 27, 33, 60, 64, 79, 91.

Members of the FST are drawn from a panel of not less than ten. The panel consists of persons with legal qualifications who are appointed by the lord chancellor after consultation with the lord advocate, as well as individuals appointed by the secretary of state, who appear to him to be qualified by experience or otherwise to deal with the types of cases that may be referred to the FST.[169]

When a case is referred to the FST, the secretary of state nominates three persons from the panel to serve as members, one of whom serves as chair. The chair must have legal qualifications, and one of the other members of the panel should have practical experience.[170]

When an individual receives a notice about a matter relating to the SIB's enforcement and disciplinary powers, he can require the SIB to refer the matter to the tribunal.[171] So that charges will not linger, the statute of limitations is twenty-eight days from the service date of the notice. There is also an expedited process requiring the SIB to transmit information more quickly.[172] Strict time limits require prompt reports of FST deliberations.[173]

When referral has been required by a person on whom notice is served, the FST must investigate the case and make a report to the SIB stating what would, in its opinion, be the appropriate decision in the matter and the reasons for that decision.[174] Where the matter referred deals with the refusal of an application for authorization, the FST may report that the appropriate decision would be to grant or to refuse the application, or in the case of an application for the rescission of a prohibition or requirement of authorization, to vary the prohibition or requirement in a specified manner.[175]

Where a matter referred to the FST is anything other than the refusal of authorization, the tribunal may report that the appropriate decision should be: (1) to take or not take the action taken or proposed by the SIB; (2) to take any other action that the SIB could take under the provision in question; or (3) to take any action within the power of the SIB under the Financial Services's provisions, such as withdrawal or suspension of direct authorization, termination or suspension of a Europerson's application, publication of a statement as to a person's misconduct, or any of the SIB's powers of intervention.[176] There are detailed evidentiary rules for testimony

---

169. *Id.* § 96(2).
170. *See supra* note 163.
171. FSA § 97.
172. SIB CONDUCT OF INVESTIGATION RULES, *supra* note 116, rule 4.
173. *See id.* rule 16(1).
174. F.S.A. § 98(1).
175. *Id.* § 98(2).
176. *Id.* § 98(3)-(4).

before the tribunal.[177] Any party to a proceeding before the FST may appeal on a point of law to the High Court.[178] However, FST decisions are normally final. The SIB has the power to publish the FST report if it sees fit.

Each of the SROs has analogous procedural arrangements to hear appeals of refusals for authorization or for disciplinary matters and to provide appellate review of that decision.[179] The SIB itself does not hear appeals of such SRO decisions. A person refused admission or expelled from an SRO may apply for direct authorization or attempt to gain standing before a regular court. However, the FST does not hear complaints of investors.

Access to Judicial Review

After consideration by the FST, there may be review by a regular court under narrowly defined circumstances. The Financial Services Act vests certain powers in the secretary of state who can then delegate those powers to a designated body, which can recognize self-regulating bodies to carry out some of the purposes of the legislation.[180] In exercising its authority to make rules and regulations, the SIB, as with more traditional administrative agencies, must follow the principles of public law and is subject to judicial review.[181] The SIB cannot exceed the powers granted to it by the statute, exercise its rules in an unfair or arbitrary way, fail to follow its rules, excessively misinterpret the law (so as to increase its authority beyond its jurisdiction), or fail to provide a fair hearing.[182]

The first legal decision involving the SIB's investigatory and enforcement powers occurred in March 1989 in the case of *Securities and Investments Board v. Pantell*.[183] Pantell, a Swiss company, mailed from abroad advertisements of its services to individuals in the United Kingdom. The advertisements offered investment advice, stressed the impartiality of that advice, and recommended shares in a U.S. company, Euramco, characterized as

---

177. Evidence may be taken orally or in writing. There is a right to counsel at Tribunal hearings. All participants have the right to receive transcripts of all oral evidence. All parties have an opportunity of inspecting the evidence and taking copies. The Financial Services Tribunal has subpoena powers. Evidence is given on oath. SIB CONDUCT OF INVESTIGATION RULES, *supra* note 116.

178. FSA, schedule 6(6).

179. *E.g.* FINANCIAL INTERMEDIARIES, MANAGERS AND BROKERS REGULATORY ASSOCIATION RULES, Rule 19 (1989) [hereinafter FIMBRA RULES].

180. FSA §§ 101, 114, 116.

181. Morse and Walsh, *supra* note 36 at ¶ 1423.

182. *Id.* ¶¶ 1311–1430.

183. 3 W.L.R. 698 (Ch. 1989).

"the share of 1988." The shares were said to be publicly owned and traded. In fact, Euramco was neither listed nor traded on any stock exchange. One of Pantell's directors was the president of the touted company.[184] Furthermore, it would have been illegal for a U.S. dealer to trade in Euramco's shares, which had been issued in Europe.[185]

Following the conversation with the Swiss public prosecutor, the SIB sought approval from the SIB board to institute a statutory investigation into the affairs of Pantell and any account it had with Barclays Bank. SIB staff were appointed to investigate on the same day board approval was received.[186] The SIB sought to freeze all of Pantel's funds. The legal issue before the court was whether, by sending circular advertisements from outside the United Kingdom to persons within, Pantell was carrying on an investment business within the United Kingdom. If so, Pantell was liable for violating several sections of the Financial Services Act [187] Another issue was whether the SIB had standing to seek an injunction restraining the distribution of assets even though it had no private right of action. In other words, the SIB itself had no beneficial interest in the money obtained from U.K. investors.

The court found that the designated agency had the right to obtain an order from the court either under Section 6 or 61, because Pantell had been carrying on an investment business in contravention of the authorization section,[188] and the SIB had the right to require Pantell to pay a sum of money to the SIB or otherwise to secure Pantell's profits. Sums paid in or otherwise secured would then be available for distribution to the hapless investors.[189] The court concluded that Section 61 conferred on the SIB powers similar to Section 6 to curb unauthorized advertisements. Parliament, by giving the secretary of state and delegating to the SIB a statutory cause of action, invested it with the necessary standing to apply for injunctive relief.[190] *Pantell* demonstrated that the SIB could act quickly and effectively

---

184. *Id.* at 699.

185. The SIB had been in contact with Swiss authorities about Pantell since December 1988. On Tuesday, March 7, the public prosecutor in Lugano informed the SIB that it had commenced action to close down Pantell on grounds of violations of Swiss banking law, the law of fiduciary firms, swindling, breaches of banking and saving laws, and the obligations of fiduciaries. Seized records indicated that Pantell largely had conducted business with U.K. investors. The company had sent checks from British investors to a Barclays Bank branch in London, which had instructions to transfer funds received into an account of a connected corporation in Guernsey. *Id.* at 700.

186. *Id.*

187. *Id.* at 701.

188. F.S.A. § 3.

189. *Pantell*, 3 W.L.R. at 702–703.

190. *Id.* at 703.

and that courts would define the designated agency's authority and the definition of "investment business" expansively. This was in contrast to the response of courts to the DTI's and the SFO's efforts to expand the crime of insider dealing.

In recent years, English courts have taken an expansive view as to what activities of private bodies will be subject to judicial review. This doctrine first saw light in the financial services area in *Regina v. Panel on Takeovers & Mergers ex parte Datafin*.[191] The Panel on Takeovers and Mergers, a self-regulatory unincorporated association, administers the City Code on Takeovers and Mergers, a code of conduct to be observed in tender offers of listed public companies.[192] The panel has no direct statutory, common law, or contractual powers over the City, but has been supported by certain statutory powers and the consensus of the City establishment. In the course of a takeover, Datafin, a tender offeror, unsuccessfully complained to the panel that other contestants for the target company had acted in concert in violation of the City Code. Datafin then sought judicial review of the panel's decision, which the lower court denied.

The Court of Appeal, however, concluded that if the responsibility imposed on a private body was a public duty, and the body was exercising public functions, a court had jurisdiction to entertain an application for judicial review of that body's decisions. Given the importance of the matters regulated by the City Code and the consequences of noncompliance, the panel was performing such a public duty and its actions were thus subject to review. However, the court would meet the need for speed in the context of a takeover and grant review only in those cases where there had been a breach of natural justice. Courts would defer to the panels' interpretation of its rules and only intervene sparingly in panel decisions.

In a later case, Guinness, as offeror, made a successful tender offer.[193] The panel decided Guinness had infringed the City Code and decided not to adjourn its ruling on the violation pending completion of a DTI inquiry. Guinness sought judicial review of the refusal to adjourn the ruling. The High Court said that although the panel had been lacking in consideration in refusing a limited adjournment, it was not a breach of natural justice. The court denied the application.

Datafin and *Guinness* suggest that while private self-regulating bodies are subject to review, courts will not allow themselves to be used, as is the American custom, as one more arrow in the quiver of tender offer tactics.

191. 1 All E.R. 564 (C.A. 1987).
192. *See id.* at 564.
193. Regina v. Panel on Takeovers and Mergers, *ex parte* Guinness, 1 All E.R. 509 (C.A. 1988).

The courts will not be a tool of delay in the takeover process. In accord with *Datafin*, a court has held that an SRO also has public duties and is subject to judicial review.[194] One can surmise that courts will be no more favorable to applications for review from recognized appeals tribunals than from the panel.[195]

Only recently have the SRO appeals tribunals started hearing cases. There are some aspects of SRO procedures that may attract a court's interest. The SROs have a more informal approach to the rules of evidence, and there is no right to counsel. In a wide departure from normal due process procedures, FIMBRA rules provide that its appeals tribunal is entitled to act on confidential information and documents without disclosing them or their source to parties.[196] This violates the cardinal principle of confrontation with one's accusers. IMRO provides that in appeals relating to authorization, confidential information need not be shown to the applicant, but the applicant must be given sufficient information to rebut the confidential information.[197] On the other hand, a criticism by staff of the Securities and Futures Authority's appeal tribunal has been that its procedures have become too legalistic and formal.[198] One can predict that this trend will continue as part of the overall legalization of financial services procedures.

Prosecution of Securities Fraud and Insider Trading

Several factors led to the introduction of the new investor protection framework, but perhaps the most important was the inability of the existing self-regulatory bodies and the DTI to deal with fraud, insider dealing, and market manipulation.[199] While the Financial Services Act created new institutions to regulate those entering the financial services industry and devices to ensure ongoing monitoring of investment activity, it left virtually

---

194. Bank of Scotland v. IMRO, 1989 Sess. Cas. 700, sec. 200 of the Companies Act, 1989, ch. 40, *amending* FSA § 188 grants jurisdiction for proceedings arising out of any act or omission of a recognized or the SIB in the discharge of its function to the High Court or the Court of Session.

195. Morse and Walsh, *supra* note 36 at ¶¶ 1427–30.

196. FIMBRA RULES, *supra* note 179, rule 9.5.5.

197. INVESTMENT MANAGEMENT REGULATORY ORGANIZATION RULES 1989, ch. VII, rule 1.4(2) [hereinafter IMRO RULES].

198. Confidential interview.

199. These were primarily the London Stock Exchange, Lloyd's of London, and the Takeover Panel. *See* Chapter 1.

untouched the mechanisms of prosecution. The framework was grafted upon an existing, ineffective system.

Perhaps unfairly, the investor protection system is judged only by the effectiveness of the prosecution of securities violators. Yet, effective prosecution and enforcement are not only important deterrents to crime, they set the tone for investor confidence in the financial markets and the image of the whole investor protection framework. The following sections outline the enforcement scheme with respect to fraud, insider dealing, and market manipulation.

Securities Fraud

The inability of British authorities to successfully uncover and prosecute commercial and securities fraud has long been notorious. The prosecutorial structure has been altered and reorganized under the new framework of investor protection with little apparent result. Criticism of the effectiveness of enforcement remains widespread. The lack of success of the British authorities in prosecuting financial fraud undermined parliamentary and public confidence in the old self-regulatory system. The government established a Fraud Trials Committee, which was known as the Roskill Committee,[200] to examine the difficulties in prosecuting commercial fraud and to offer recommendations for reform. The committee concluded that the public no longer believed that the legal system was capable of successfully prosecuting serious frauds and added that the public perception was correct. The committee's report stated that at every stage, during investigation, preparation, commitment, pretrial review, and trial, the arrangements offered an open invitation for abuse and delay, and that the largest and most cleverly executed crimes escaped unpunished.[201] It suggested fundamental changes in the law, in prosecutorial procedures, and in attitudes towards commercial crimes.

---

200. The official title of the committee is the Fraud Trials Committee. It was named the Roskill Committee for its chair, Lord Roskill.

201. FRAUD TRIALS (ROSKILL) COMMITTEE REPORT 1 (1986) [hereinafter ROSKILL REPORT]. The continued poor record of success of the SFO (its conviction rate is only 66%) and particularly the failure to obtain convictions against some of the *Guinness* defendants has again raised the call for reform of commercial fraud prosecutions. Though the jury is the target, it cannot be blamed for prosecutorial failure. *See* Mason, *SFO raises threshold on fraud cases*, FIN. TIMES, May 22, 1992 at 8, col. 1; Rice, *Case against the jury*, FIN. TIMES, Feb. 12, 1992 at 11, col. 1; Blom-Cooper, *How to avoid trial by ordeal*, FIN. TIMES, Feb. 24, 1992 at 28, col. 1; Hughes & Smith, *UK fraud reform call as Guinness trial collapses*, FIN. TIMES, Feb. 12, 1992 at 1, col. 3.

Many reasons exist for these enforcement problems, not the least of which are the difficulties inherent in the prosecution of securities fraud. First, such schemes are usually sophisticated, complex, difficult to unravel, international, and are often discovered only after the fact, when the money—and occasionally the perpetrators—have long disappeared. Investigation of fraud is labor intensive, time consuming, and burdensome on the understaffed and underfunded investigatory bodies, who may face the formidable task of examining thousands of documents in different venues.

Second, English law enforcement is plagued by a number of overlapping, competing organizations, lacking coordination or shared purpose. Third, there is neither an enforcement tradition nor the widespread expertise necessary to prosecute commercial fraud. A fourth, more amorphous reason, is attitudinal. In the words of Professor Michael Levi, a researcher of commercial fraud, "There is no political mileage in being a high-profile fraud buster in this country, the tradition of discretion and caution is too deeply ingrained."[202]

"Criminal prosecution is the sharp end of the system of control of financial institutions, the ultimate sanction for the serious wrongdoer."[203] Though it may be small satisfaction to defrauded investors, incarcerating perpetrators of financial misdeeds serves an important deterrence to future violators. The certainty of enforcement and prison for white-collar criminals is an effective deterrence.

One cause of ineffective enforcement is that several separate bodies are concerned with the pursuit of fraud. Some investigate, others prosecute, and the Inland Revenue Department combines both functions. This has hindered expeditious and economical disposal of criminal fraud proceedings.[204] Fraud complaints come from several sources. Information may be passed from one of the self-regulating bodies. The DTI may receive complaints from the public as might the Director of Public Prosecutions (DPP). Normally, commercial fraud cases are referred to the Crown Prosecution Service, headed by the DPP.[205] Insider trading and other financial frauds are prosecuted by the DPP, who is a public official, answerable to the attorney general. The DPP must institute criminal proceedings in any case in which the importance or difficulty of the issues makes it appear appropriate to the DPP that he should institute the action.[206] However, that office has failed to mount aggressive and successful prosecutions.

---

202. Wolman, *Police Gain Partners in Fight Against Fraud*, FIN. TIMES, July 20, 1987, 32 at col. 1.
203. M. CLARKE, REGULATING THE CITY 162 (1986) (hereinafter Clarke).
204. *See* ROSKILL REPORT, *supra* note 201, § 2.1.
205. Prosecution of Offenses Act, 1985, ch. 23, pt. I.
206. *Id.* § 3(2)(b).

In 1981 the DPP, the DTI, and the Metropolitan Police established the Fraud Investigation Group (FIG).[207] The FIG's function was to coordinate inquiries in major fraud cases at any early stage so as to increase the levels of cooperation between the police, the DTI, and the DPP. Despite the attempt to create a specialized group to handle major fraud cases, the police retained their independence, and the Inland Revenue and Customs and Excise Departments remained outside the FIG's jurisdiction.[208] Although one of the objectives of the FIG was to harness the various statutory powers available to the police, the DPP, and the DTI, most of the relevant powers remained the exclusive preserve of the individual agencies. Because of a dearth of experienced prosecutors, the absence of statutory mandates for cooperation, and the need for the expertise of other organizations such as Inland Revenue and customs, the FIG was unsuccessful.[209]

The most serious fraud offenses are investigated by the police and are handled by a special group of officers in fraud squads. Each of the forty-three police forces in England and Wales has its own fraud squad, whose members are not specially trained. Metropolitan Police officers are posted to the fraud squad for three-year terms. The borough of the City of London, the home of the financial district, has its own police force. Officers join for a longer period, perhaps seven or eight years. The lack of any proper career structure within fraud squads and the qualifications of their members leave something to be desired. For instance, police investigations need expert accountancy advice which is largely obtainable through the retention of private sector accountants, an expensive undertaking.[210]

Through its role as supervisor of the regulatory system for corporations and insurance companies, the DTI has many responsibilities relating to the control of fraud and the policing of corporate requirements.[211] It forwards evidence of fraud to the DPP. It can inspect companies, appoint inspectors with broad powers of investigation of a company's affairs, require the production of books and records, and report on inspectors' investigations. It has its own investigation staff, some of whom have police, accounting, or legal training. In the companies investigation branch, thirty-five members deal with investigations under Section 447 of the Companies Act of 1985. Under that section, if the DTI thinks there is reason to do so, it can require a corporation to produce its books or records for examination. Inquiries under this section are not publicly announced. Failure to comply with a DTI

---

207. In July 1984 the Fraud Investigation Group was placed on a permanent basis.

208. ROSKILL REPORT, *supra* note 201, § 2.25.

209. M. CLARKE, *supra* note 203 at 166–67 (noting that the FIG was at best "a modest start").

210. ROSKILL REPORT, *supra* note 201, § 2.73.

211. Companies Act 1985, ch. 6, §§ 431–34.

request is a criminal offense. The department can disclose to the police and the DPP information intended to show commission of a criminal offense. It has primary responsibility to prosecute insider dealing.

The DTI has fifty lawyers who are responsible for companies investigations. In the Legal Department there are four lawyers who provide advice to the company's investigations branch and deal with related prosecutions. An additional twelve lawyers and twenty-four investigating officers handle cases referred to them by the insolvency branch.[212] When an investigation into a corporation's affairs indicates criminal violations, it handled by the DTI. More serious cases are referred to the DPP or to the SFO.

As mentioned previously, the DTI has been ineffective. The House of Commons Select Committee on Trade and Industry found that the average time for completing a basic fact-finding (Section 447) inquiry was 105 days. The delays were attributed to difficulty in arranging interviews, overseas banks, and the unavailability of inspectors who are often barristers and have responsibilities in court.[213] The Select Committee Report concluded: "Rarely can a government department's discharge of its responsibilities have been held in such low esteem among others involved."[214]

The Roskill Committee was particularly critical of the manner in which cases were investigated, prepared, and tried. It recommended a unified body charged with the investigation and prosecution of major fraud with a staff comprised of lawyers and accountants together with police officers acting under the control of one operational head.[215] The government followed some of the Roskill Committee recommendations in establishing the SFO.[216] The Serious Fraud Office, which commenced activity in January 1987, is a seventy- person team of lawyers, accountants, and support staff with extensive investigative and subpoena powers. However, the government did not bring the police under the SFO umbrella; they remain independent. Thus, the SFO can not direct them or force coordinate action.

While the DTI had power to obtain information on insider trading, neither the police nor the Crown Prosecution Service had the specific authority

212. ROSKILL REPORT, *supra* note 201, § 2.16.

213. *Reforms in DTI's Methods Urged*, THE TIMES (London), May 24, 1990, 28, col. 1 [hereinafter *Reforms Urged*]. To ease the problem of delays, the Companies Act, 1989, ch. 40, has given more flexibility to appoint investigators who will not publish a report (§ 55), to discontinue an inspection (§ 57) and to cooperate more fully with overseas regulators (§§ 82–83).

214. *Reforms Urged*, *supra* note 213 at 28, col. 8.

215. *See* ROSKILL REPORT, *supra* note 201, § 2.48.

216. Criminal Justice Act 1987, ch. 52, § 1(3) [hereinafter Criminal Justice Act]; *see generally* Wood, *Serious Fraud Office: Regulatory and Enforcement Changes in the United Kingdom*, INTERNATIONAL SECURITIES MARKETS 219 (A. Beller, ed. 1988) [hereinafter Wood].

to force witnesses to disclose information.[217] The SFO has that power, if in the course of investigating a suspected offense it appears that the office has good reason to believe there has been a complex fraud.[218] The SFO can investigate any offense that appears to involve serious or complex fraud and may take over an investigation where such fraud appears to exist. If there is such good reason, the director of the SFO may require persons to appear before him and to produce documents relating to the investigation.[219] However, the SFO's powers are more limited than those of DTI inspectors investigating companies for insider dealings. The evidence that a suspect gives to the SFO under compulsion cannot be used against him in a criminal investigation, unless he gives contradictory evidence in court.[220]

While the SFO is a step toward coordinated enforcement, it has already come under criticism for the slowness of its investigations and the lack of success in its prosecutions. It has had difficulty obtaining evidence from abroad and has been criticized for closing courtroom hearings to the public.[221] Also, the office has appeared to limit its reach. In December 1988, an assistant director stated that normally the SFO would not use its powers to investigate insider dealing because that is a regulatory offense, rather than a serious or complex fraud.[222] The creation of the SFO is a half step on the road to efficient financial services enforcement. The ineffectiveness of insider dealing prosecutions demonstrates how much more is needed.

Insider Dealing

To the public, insider trading is perhaps the most notorious financial activity, for it casts doubt over the integrity of the financial markets. This section traces the development of insider dealing as a wrong, the statutory attempts to deal with it, the inability to stop such activity, and the failure of successful prosecution of inside traders. It analyzes the causes of the failures of enforcement and concludes with recommendations for reform.

Insider trading is the use of material, nonpublic, price-sensitive information of an issuer or another corporation in the purchase or sale of securities, when the individual knows that the information has been wrongfully

---

217. Wood, *supra* note 216 at 233–34.

218. Criminal Justice Act, *supra* note 216, §§ 1(3), 2.

219. *See id.* § 2, which includes criminal penalties for failure to comply or knowingly making false statements or destroying documents.

220. Wolman, *supra* note 202.

221. Tendler, *Problems Gaining Evidence Abroad Slows SFO's Work*, THE TIMES (London), July 14, 1989 at 28, col. 1.

222. Wolman, *UK Treads Carefully over Insider Trading*, FIN. TIMES, Feb. 7, 1989 at 28, col. 4.

obtained. In the United States there has been a common law and later a statutory prohibition against the use of certain types of nonpublic information by individuals affiliated with a corporation, typically directors, officers, or large shareholders.[223] Widespread norms have developed that such behavior is unethical. Recent litigation has been over the breadth of the net that prohibits insider trading.[224]

In the United Kingdom, in contrast, insider dealing did not become illegal until 1980. Particularly in the context of takeovers, within a relatively closed investment community, such dealing was considered a customary way of doing business in the City, a sort of fringe benefit.[225] Insider trading was tolerated because it helped to maintain an "orderly market," that is, one in which professionals did not lose money.[226] Because of single capacity and functional regulation of financial services, conflicts of interest within firms, which resulted in insider dealing, were less likely to arise. Even today, while there may be greater agreement that insider trading is morally wrong, many do not feel it should be prohibited.

Insider dealing violations are particularly difficult to detect. To obtain a successful conviction the necessary connection must be made between the investor and the possession of inside information. An investigator must learn what the dealer knew, when he knew it, and how he found it out. Usually there are two witnesses, the source and the inside dealer. Unless one of them confesses, the proof of the violation must be gleaned from patterns of trading. Although the computerization of trading provides tracks, much insider dealing is based upon circumstantial evidence.[227]

Insider dealing can be conducted quite subtly. An investment banker or broker might tip off a fund manager obliquely, "I wouldn't sell X," and be rewarded later with commissions after "X" has been taken over by "Y" at a substantial premium.[228] Despite the institution of internal controls by firms and added enforcement powers required by the Financial Services Act insider dealing among financial services firms is believed to be widespread. According to a poll of institutional fund managers in February 1989, when

---

223. Strong v. Repide, 213 U.S. 419 (1909); Securities Exchange Act of 1934 §§ 10(b), 16(b), 15 U.S.C.A., §§ 78j(b), 78p(b) (West Supp. 1991); SEC Rule 10b-5, 17 C.F.R. (1990), § 240.10b-5 (1990).

224. Carpenter v. United States, 484 U.S. 19 (1987); Dirks v. Securities and Exchange Commission, 463 U.S. 646 (1983).

225. Lohr, *The Case for an SEC in Britain*, N.Y. TIMES, Nov. 23, 1986, F9, col. 1.

226. *Paper Walls*, THE TIMES (London), Aug. 16, 1978 at 11, col. 1.

227. *See* H.R. REP. NO. 910, 100th Cong., 2d Sess. 15, *reprinted in* 1988 U.S. CODE CONG. & ADMIN. NEWS 6043, 6052 (discussing need for Insider Trading and Securities Fraud Enforcement Act of 1988).

228. Brewerton, *The Fat Old Grouse Gets Away with It Again*, THE TIMES (London), Aug. 17, 1988 at 21, col. 6

asked, "How effective would you say are the present arrangements for monitoring insider dealings?," over one-half responded that they believed them to be ineffective.[229]

Restraints on Insider Trading Before 1980

Prior to 1980, while there was no statutory prohibition against insider trading, there were requirements that directors observe fiduciary responsibilities and disclose and report their interests in the securities of their company, and in some circumstances, interests in other companies.[230] More importantly, the rules of the Stock Exchange required listed companies to have internal regulations governing the transactions of directors. The Stock Exchange's code for dealing with securities in which a firm has an interest or information is a minimum standard, yet it exceeds the scope of the statutory Insider Dealing Act.[231]

The Panel on Takeovers and Mergers required extensive disclosure of dealing and had rules relating to the use of confidential price-sensitive information in the context of a tender offer. The code, however, did not have the force of law. The panel would censure a violator, would refer the matter to the DTI, or would get the City establishment to exert pressure, in ways such as by drying up sources of capital.[232] Other self-regulatory bodies, such as the Council of the Law Society, the Institute of Directors, and the Society of Investment Analysts, had guidelines or policies against insider dealing.[233]

In 1974 the Stock Exchange developed surveillance facilities designed to identify insider transactions. It established a surveillance team in 1981 and in November 1984 set up an Insider Dealing Group. Originally its stock watch program relied upon a stream of market prices from jobbers on the trading floor. Suspicious price movements were spotted by eye and would be referred to an investigation's manager. If the movements seemed other than a normal fluctuation, a committee of the Council of the Stock Exchange would conduct a preliminary investigation.[234] The preliminary in-

---

229. Beresford and Blackhurst, *Insider Dealers Stay One Step Ahead*, THE SUNDAY TIMES (London), Feb. 26, 1989 at D1, col. 2.

230. Companies Act, 1967, ch. 81, §§ 27–29, *amended by* Companies Act, 1985, ch. 6, §§ 235, 324–328, sched. 13, pts. I, IV.

231. COUNCIL OF THE STOCK EXCHANGE, ADMISSION OF SECURITIES TO LISTING §§ 5.39, 5.41–48 (2d ed. 1985).

232. *See* M. CLARKE, *supra* note 203 at 109–14.

233. B. RIDER, INSIDER TRADING 113–14, 122–26 (1983) [hereinafter RIDER].

234. *Id.* at 127, 148–51; *Insider Trading in London*, ECONOMIST, Feb. 7, 1987 at 74. Today the Exchange has a surveillance database that contains a computer record of every

vestigation was an in-house inquiry in which evidence was taken from the firm. Most such investigations were settled informally. In the words of a senior official of the Securities Association, "club rules were utilized, which were very effective among members." This meant that a telephone call might unglue the transaction and lead to internal sanctioning by the firm. Regulation of insider dealing was suggested by the Jenkins Committee as far back as 1962,[235] but did not become law until 1980.

The Company Securities (Insider Dealing) Act, 1985

In contrast to the United States and other jurisdictions, insider trading in the United Kingdom is only a criminal offense: there are no civil remedies. The prohibition applies only to transactions listed on a recognized investment exchange.[236] The statute prohibits insiders from dealing, counseling, or procuring anyone else to deal, or communicating any information to any person, if he knows or has reasonable cause to believe that another person will make use of that information to deal on a recognized stock exchange in securities of his company or any other company with which he is connected and holds unpublished price-sensitive information.[237] Also prohibited from such trading are individuals who receive such information (tippees), crown servants and other public officials (employees of the SIB or SROs), and individuals involved in takeovers.[238]

An insider is one who, within the preceding six months, knowingly has been connected with or has been a director of that company or a related company, or is an officer or employee, or has occupied a position with the

---

transaction since the Big Bang. When material information is announced and unusual prices or rumors occur, the historical market background is compared to the stock's movements. Between 600 and 900 suspicious trading situations are flagged each month for initial inquiry. International Stock Exchange, *Insider Dealing and Investor Confidence*, QUALITY MKTS. Q, 25, 26 (Summer 1990) [hereinafter, *Insider Dealing and Investor Confidence*].

235. Report of the Company Law Committee, 1962 Cmnd. 1749, ¶ 89. During the 1970s, the subject dominated discussions of company law reform, securities regulation, and the adequacy of City self-regulation. *See generally* B. RIDER, *supra* note 233, ch. 6. Unsuccessful attempts were made to introduce such legislation in 1973 and 1978. Finally, in 1980 it became unlawful.

236. *See* Bornstein and Dugger, *International Regulation of Insider Trading 2*, COLUMBIA BUS. L. REV. 375, 388–89 (1987). For a discussion of the insider trading legislation, *see* B. HANNIGAN, INSIDER DEALING (1988); J.H. FARRAR, *supra* note 22, 344–58; A. WEDGEWOOD, G. PELL, *supra* note 54 at 97–121.

237. Company Securities (Insider Dealing) Act 1985, ch. 8, §§ 1–2 [hereinafter Insider Dealing Act].

238. *Id.* §§ 1(3),(4) (1980); (2), FSA § 173(2); Insider Dealing Act, *supra* note 237, § 1(5) (1980).

company involving a professional or business relationship.[239] The insider must be in possession of unpublished price-sensitive material, which he holds by reason of his connection with the company.[240] Also, it must be reasonable to expect a person so connected, and in that position by virtue of which he is connected, not to disclose that information except for the proper performance of the functions attaching to that position.[241] Additionally, he must know that the information is unpublished price-sensitive information in relation to those securities.[242]

"Unpublished price-sensitive information," or in American jargon "material non-public information,"[243] is information that relates to specific matters of concern to the company and that is not generally known to those persons who are accustomed to or would be likely to deal in those securities, but that if it were generally known to them would be likely to affect materially the price of those securities.[244] Whether information is price-sensitive is a question of fact for a court.

When an insider knowingly comes in possession of nonpublic price-sensitive information, he may not deal on a recognized stock exchange in those shares.[245] Nor may he deal in the shares of another corporation, if he fills the insider criterion in relation to that other company, and the information relates to a transaction between the two companies, such as a takeover bid.[246] The insider cannot pass the information to someone else to trade or to any person whom the tipper has reasonable cause to believe will make use of the information for purposes of dealing, counseling, procuring any person to deal on an exchange.[247]

Persons, such as tippees, who trade on inside information received from insiders may also be guilty of an offense under the Insider Dealing Act. A tippee is an individual who is in possession of unpublished price-sensitive information, that he knowingly obtained (directly or indirectly) from another individual, the insider, and who the tippee knows or has reasonable cause to believe held the information by virtue of being so connected. The tippee must know or have reasonable cause to believe that because of the

---

239. Insider Dealing Act, *supra* note 237, §§ 1, 9.

240. *See id.* § 1(1)(a).

241. *See id.* § 1(1)(b).

242. *See id.* § 1(1)(c).

243. The definition of material is found in TSC v. Northway, 426 U.S. 438, 449 (1976).

244. Insider Dealing Act, *supra* note 237, § 10.

245. *See id.* § 1(1)(c).

246. *See id.* § 1(2)(5). This prohibition would not relate to a transaction involving a third party. *Cf.* Moss v. Stanley, Inc., 719 F.2d 5 (2d Cir. 1983), *cert. denied*, 465 U.S. 1025 (1984).

247. Insider Dealing Act, *supra* note 237, §§ 7–8.

tipper's connection and position, it would be reasonable to expect him not to disclose that information.[248] Tippees are prohibited from trading.

There are some exceptions to the insider trading prohibitions. They include individuals who deal as liquidators, receivers, trustees in bankruptcy, and individuals stabilizing the price of international bond issues for a specified period. In addition, an individual who commences a trade before receiving the price-sensitive information may complete the transaction.[249] The act does not prohibit an individual, by reason of his possession of information, from doing any particular thing other than with a view to making a profit or avoiding a loss for himself or some other person by use of that information.[250] This clause, together with the scienter requirements, creates a sufficient safety net for directors who want to trade in their company's shares or someone who wants to pay off a pressing debt.[251]

Violation of any of the provisions of the Insider Dealing Act is a criminal offense, punishable by as much as two-years imprisonment and/or an unspecified fine.[252] No transaction is void or voidable by reason of violation of the act.[253] English law is less responsive to implied rights of action and to expanded fiduciary responsibilities of directors to shareholders. Several cases have involved corporate opportunities in which damages to the company have not been granted because provable injury to the corporation was lacking.[254] Professor Barry Rider, an expert on insider trading has written: "Given the clear intention of Parliament not to provide an express civil remedy in such cases, and the almost insoluble questions of causation and determination of damages that would arise in other than direct personal transactions, it is submitted that it would be most unlikely that a court would be prepared to find such a cause of action."[255] Still, the SIB might use injunctive or restitutionary actions under Section 61 for breach of the conduct of business rules. However, this section would apply only to an insider trading transaction by an authorized individual or firm and might exempt an outside director who is not in the financial services sector save for his board service.

---

248. *Id.* § 1(3).
249. *Id.* §§ 3(1)(b)(c), 3(2), 6.
250. *See id.* § 3(1)(a).
251. J.H. FARRAR, *supra* note 22 at 354.
252. Insider Dealing Act, *supra* note 237, § 8.
253. *See id.* § 8(3).
254. J. H. FARRAR, *supra* note 22 at 356.
255. B. RIDER & D. CHAIKEN, GUIDE TO THE FINANCIAL SERVICES ACT 1986 121 (1987).

The Financial Services Act and Insider Dealing

The Financial Services Act was only incidentally concerned with insider trading. Several sections were technical amendments to the 1985 Insider Dealing Act,[256] made to take account of changes in trading wrought by the Big Bang. For example, employees of the SIB and recognized bodies were forbidden to trade on the basis of material nonpublic information.[257]

Sections 177 and 178 furnish increased powers to investigate suspected inside trading. The Insider Dealing Act had no provision for the investigation of suspicious price movements. Thus, it had been difficult to obtain sufficient evidence to prove beyond a reasonable doubt that an individual traded while in possession of nonpublic price-sensitive information and did so with prior knowledge.[258] Section 177 gives the secretary of state for trade and industry the authority to appoint inspectors to investigate suspected insider dealing. The inspectors are to report to the DTI the results of their inquiry.[259]

Any person who is knowledgeable about or is a suspect in any contravention under the Insider Dealing Act may be required by the inspectors to produce documents in their possession or under their control relating to the company in question whose securities may have been improperly traded, to appear before the inspectors, and to otherwise provide assistance connection with the investigation.[260] Statements by a person in compliance with the request from an inspector can be used in evidence against him. Inspectors may examine under oath any person who may give information concerning insider dealing and shall make such interim and final reports that they think are necessary. The final report is submitted to the Secretary of State, who then decides whether to bring criminal proceedings.

Section 178 provides penalties for failure to cooperate with Section 177 investigations. If a person refuses to comply with a request or refuses to answer any question put to him by an inspector, the inspectors then certify such to a court, which will then inquire into the case. After a hearing, if the court is satisfied that there was noncooperation without a reasonable ex-

---

256. Insider Dealing Act, *supra* note 237 at ch. 8.

257. Section 2 of the Insider Dealing Act prohibits crown servants, that is civil servants, from using "price sensitive" information. FSA § 173 replaces the word "crown servant" with that of public servant, which has a broader meaning. As the SIB and the recognized bodies are private organizations, their employees are not crown servants. Other technical changes related to the changes in the method of trading. FSA, § 174.

258. A. WHITTAKER & G. MORSE, THE FINANCIAL SERVICES ACT 1986: A GUIDE TO THE NEW LAW 191 (1987).

259. FSA § 177(1).

260. Id. § 177(3).

cuse, it may punish the individual for contempt.[261] In the alternative, the court may direct that the secretary of state exercise his powers, which include cancellation of authorization to carry on investment business, disqualification from becoming authorized, and prohibitions from entering into transactions of specified kinds or with specified persons.[262]

Section 178(6) attempts to close a previous loophole in the investigation of insider trading cases.[263] Often a suspect refused to furnish information or cooperate on the grounds that at the time he was not aware of the identity of other persons involved or was subject to the law of another jurisdiction prohibiting such disclosure. The requirements under the Core Conduct of Business Rules of the SIB and the SROs that require a firm to "know their customer"[264] will undermine this traditional excuse. The penalties against an individual who fails to cooperate with the Section 177 investigation can be used by the recognized bodies against one of its members but are subject to a reservation that they are to be exercised concurrently with the DTI.[265] The Financial Services Act insider dealing sections allow the DTI to more easily investigate suspected wrongful trading and appoint the SIB to head the investigation.

The Stock Exchange's surveillance department examines approximately six to nine hundred situations per month for suspicious price movements. Roughly twenty are passed on to the surveillance department's Insider Dealing Group. After this review, approximately ten cases per week are referred to a second group for additional investigation.[266] Thereafter, the matter may be referred to the DTI for investigation with the aim of eventual criminal prosecution. Despite these additional investigative powers, insider dealing continued after the enactment of the Financial Services Act, and a

---

261. Id. § 178(3).

262. Id. § 178(2).

263. Id. § 178(6) (interpretation of reasonable excuse in § 178(2) states: A person shall not be treated for the purposes of subsection (20 above as having a reasonable excuse for refusing to comply with a request or answer a question in a case where the contravention or suspected contravention being investigated relates to dealing by him on the instruction or for the account of another person, by reason that at the time of the refusal—

(a) he did not know the identity of that other person; or

(b) he was subject to the law of country or territory outside the United Kingdom which prohibited him from disclosing information relating to the dealing without the consent of that other person, if he might have obtained that consent or obtained exemption from the law.)

264. SIB RULES, *supra* note 32 at ch. III, Core Conduct of Business Rules, rule 16, Suitability; SECURITY & FUTURES AUTHORITY, CONDUCT OF BUSINESS RULES, RULE 16, Suitability (1991).

265. FSA § 178(10).

266. Unsworth, *Insider Dealing Sleuths at SE*, THE TIMES (London), Aug. 20, 1988 at 23, col. 2.

series of notorious scandals tarnished the effectiveness of the enforcement framework and particularly the DTI.

Violations of the Insider Dealing Act in the Late 1980s

Insider trading activities have occurred with depressing regularity since the Big Bang. Many of these cases have arisen because of breaches in a firm's "Chinese Wall." A Chinese wall is a prohibition against the passing of confidential information from one department of a financial services institution to another.[267] Firms are expected to erect barriers between sources of material nonpublic price-sensitive information and securities brokers. Unfortunately, these barriers, like the original Chinese wall, are often breached.

Prior to the Big Bang, securities firms were separate from merchant banks, which were separate from clearing banks. The breakdown in functional barriers now meant that under the roof of a single firm would be individuals knowledgeable about proposed takeovers, departments with inside information about the corporate health of a particular client, and brokers acting as market makers and as agents for clients selling shares of companies.

The SIB's rules and those of the SROs require firms to have internal policies against trading where there is a conflict of interest, as well as a firm policy on its responsibilities where the firm has an interest in a particular security. The firm must also have compliance procedures to monitor such trading by employees.[268] Breaches of a Chinese wall are difficult to monitor. Unlike the earlier insider trading cases, those involving Chinese Wall breaches have been individuals at old-line firms. Often the trading was not conducted for personal enrichments, but for the firm's benefit.

Before the Big Bang, L.C.B. Gower had pointed out that the "lack of effective and successful enforcement up to now [of the Insider Dealing Act] has been disturbing."[269] To improve enforcement, the Financial Services Act introduced several amendments to the Insider Dealing Act of 1980. If it appears to the secretary of state that there are circumstances suggesting insider trading, he may appoint one or more competent inspectors to carry out such investigations as are necessary to establish whether any such con-

---

267. A SUPPLEMENT TO THE OXFORD ENGLISH DICTIONARY 503 (2d ed. 1972). Its name derives from the great wall built between China and Mongolia in the third-century B.C.

268. SIB RULES, *supra* note 32, ch. III, Core Conduct of Business Rules, rule 2, material interest; SFA RULES, *supra* note 264 at rule 2; FIMBRA RULES, *supra* note 179, rule 4.19, 4.24.

269. L. C. B. GOWER, REVIEW OF INVESTOR PROTECTION: REPORT PART II § 6.22 (1985).

travention occurred and to report the results of their investigations to him.[270] This is a nondelegable responsibility.

The Insider Dealing sections of the Financial Services Act were scheduled to be implemented in 1987. However, several flagrant insider trading incidents occurred in the latter part of 1986 which altered the permissive attitude in the City toward such transactions. The secretary of state implemented the insider trading provisions one-year early. These new insider trading schemes did not involve a misguided, low-level employee attempting to make a one-time killing; rather they were sophisticated conspiracies by experienced individuals.

Because of the computerization and technological developments nurtured by the Big Bang, for the first time the stock market tape was transparent so that all trading could be traced. Theoretically, it should have been more difficult to engage in insider dealing because the price, volume, and time of all equities transactions were reported to the Stock Exchange within minutes of the transaction. Prior to the Big Bang, trades were reported the following day, but without the time of the transaction.[271] Paradoxically, even with this new capacity to detect improper dealing, ever greater scandals occurred.

One of the ripples of the U.S. insider trading scandal involving the arbitrager, Ivan Boesky, was that he earned $50 million from insider trading activities conducted through a British investment trust, Cambrian and General Securities, of which he was chairman. The U.S. Securities and Exchange Commission (SEC) discovered the U.K. activities and transmitted information to the DTI under terms of a memorandum of understanding (MOU) signed by both governments in September 1986 to share information involving securities and commodities violations.[272] No one doubts that if the SEC had not transmitted information about Boesky's U.K. securities activities, the DTI would never have discovered them.

The SEC's investigation of Boesky raised questions about his role in the bitter battle between Guinness, the beverage and distillery company, and Argyll Group, in which each sought to take over Distillers Company, a leading maker of Scotch whiskey (Johnny Walker, Dewars, and Gordon's Gin). In April 1986, Guinness was the victor with a $3.8 million cash and stock bid. Based on information passed by the SEC, the DTI commenced an in-

---

270. FSA § 177.

271. Kohut, *U.K. Reforms Ensure Probity—Stock Exchange Chief*, REUTERS MONEY REP., Jan 27, 1987.

272. Memorandum of Understanding on Exchange of Information Between the SEC, CFTC, and the United Kingdom Department of Trade and Industry in Matters Relating to Securities and Futures, [1986–1987 Transfer Binder] Fed. Sec. L. Rep. (CCH), ¶ 84,027 (Sept. 23, 1986) [hereinafter MOU].

vestigation in December 1986 pursuant to Sections 432 and 422 of the Companies Act.[273] The DTI believed that a number of supposedly independent investors acted in concert to inflate the value of Guinness shares and purchased Distillers stock to pledge it to Guinness.[274]

Boesky first approached Argyll and offered to buy Distillers shares and warehouse them, that is, hold them for Argyll. Argyll declined. Apparently Guinness was more cooperative, because Boesky purchased Distillers shares shortly before the takeover. These shares were ultimately sold to Guinness. Additionally, Guinness invested $100 million in a fund run by Boesky.[275] Guinness purchased its own shares in order to drive up the price, thereby making the purchase of Distillers less expensive.

The Guinness affair sent shock waves throughout the City and the government. Former Conservative Prime Minister Edward Heath denounced what he called, "an orgy of insider dealing." Roy Hattersley, Labor Party spokesman, accused the government of being too friendly with "sleazy financiers."[276] Guinness demonstrated the ability of insider dealers to use nominee accounts to disguise themselves and the difficulty of discovering breaches of the insider trading statute.

In November 1986, Geoffrey Collier, the head of stockbroking at Morgan Grenfell, one of Britain's oldest and most patrician merchant banks, resigned after breaching his firm's insider trading rules by dealing in the shares of an engineering company subject to a takeover bid by one of the bank's clients.[277] While Collier only earned $22,000 from his insider dealing, next to nothing compared to Boesky, the fact that he was at the heart of the City establishment created a widespread belief that his actions were but the tip of a corrupt iceberg and that the Big Bang had nurtured a freewheeling, unregulated, dishonest environment.[278] The Stock Exchange referred the matter to the-DTI, and Collier later received a one-year suspended sentence, a $25 thousand fine and had to pay court costs of an additional £7 thousand.[279] These cases focused attention on insider trading, yet new scandals appeared with distressing frequency. Even the DTI became more active in investigating allegations of insider dealing.

The government was scandalized by the alleged insider dealing of two civil servants who used price-sensitive information in the course of their

---

273. Section 432 relates to fraud, misfeasance or other misconduct, and nondisclosure of information to shareholders that they might reasonably expect. Companies Act, 1985, § 432.

274. *Is Boesky Good for Guinness?*, ECONOMIST, 91, Dec. 6, 1986 at 91.

275. *Two More Quit in Guinness Scandal*, N.Y. TIMES, Jan. 21, 1987 at D19, col. 1.

276. *Id.*

277. HANNIGAN, *supra* note 236 at 23–24.

278. Lohr, *supra* note 225.

279. *British Insider Fined $40,000*, N.Y. TIMES, July 2, 1987 at D7, col. 6.

duties monitoring takeover bids for the Office of Fair Trading and the Monopolies Commission.[280] That public officials were involved was particularly shocking. In this period the government had real concern that the new discoveries of insider trading would force the SIB to become a Securities and Exchange Commission. These incidents suggested that the liberalization of the market's structure provided new avenues for corruption. They demonstrated weakness in the financial services sector's ability to regulate itself.

In September 1987 two clerks employed by the respected financial newspaper, the *Financial Times*, traded on the basis of published information that was not yet distributed to the general public. The employees, who were statisticians for FINSTAT, the paper's electronic share service subsidiary, gained prior publication access to copies of the *Investor's Chronicle*, a weekly business magazine that recommended low-priced shares. The clerks purchased the touted shares in advance and sold them when the recommendations became public. Because the shares were thinly traded, it was easy to pick up the movement in share prices. The editor of the *Investor's Chronicle* noticed the share movements and informed the Stock Exchange, which traced the transactions. The employees were terminated because they violated a *Financial Times* internal policy. The newspaper, however, insisted that this was an insignificant incident, marked by amateurish tactics and small sums of money.[281]

Recently, the DTI has had difficulties in obtaining convictions. At the end of 1989, three major cases were dismissed by the courts. In one, the director of an offeror purchased shares in a target company while negotiating on behalf of the offeror for purchase of a stake in the target. At the time the target's market price was 54 pence. The acquirer was offering 90 and the director made several purchases commencing at 65. The information was price-sensitive. The defendant had knowledge of the negotiations and was a classic insider.

The defendant argued that the information was in the public domain. A prosecution witness, the chairman of the offeror, called to produce docu-

---

280. Joseph, *Probe Marks New Twist in British Insider Trading Scandal*, REUTERS, Dec. 21, 1986. The defendants were ultimately acquitted because the prosecution abandoned the case after the director general of fair trading claimed that it would not be in the public interest for OFT documents relating to takeovers to be discussed at trial. Hughes, *Campaign Against Insider Dealing Suffers Setback*, FIN. TIMES, Jan. 24, 1990 at 11, col. 4.

281. Lohr, *Financial Times Dismisses 2*, N.Y. TIMES, Sept. 15, 1987 at D5, col. 1. *Cf.* Carpenter v. United States, 484 U.S. 19 (1987) (U.S. Supreme Court divided 4–4 on whether a columnist's trading on information contained in his columns was an insider trading violation on the basis of misappropriation of an employer's information); Securities & Exchange Comm'n v. Texas Gulf Sulphur, 446 F.2d 130 (2d Cir. 1971) (information not publicly distributed until it appears on Dow Jones tape and investors have a chance to react to it).

ments, testified on cross-examination that he thought he could purchase the target's shares at the time because the offeror was not engaged in a tender offer but only a negotiated purchase, therefore the information was not price-sensitive. The judge directed a verdict for the defendant because of conflicting evidence.[282] In another case, the conviction of a managing director under Section 1(1) with a fine of £7,000 was reversed on appeal. By the beginning of 1990, of the sixteen people charged under the 1985 act, there were only five convictions, of which four pleaded guilty.[283]

In mid-1988, there were recurring breaches of Chinese walls by employees of City institutions. Two dealers at County NatWest Wood-Mac, the investment banking subsidiary of the U.K.'s second largest bank, National Westminster, were dismissed for dealing on inside information relating to a proposed sale of Intercontinental Hotels. County NatWest was the advisor to the owner of the hotel chain, Grand Metropolitan. The bank's corporate finance department informed the dealing room of the proposed sale, and two market makers purchased shares from other market makers. However, the individuals did not themselves benefit. The sales were for the benefit of the bank.[284]

In the same week, three brokers from different firms were discovered to have used inside information to purchase shares of a casino-hotel corporation, Pleasurama, in advance of a tender offer. The three firms, Samuel Monntague, Morgan Grenfell, and Lazard Brothers, were all members of the City's establishment. In each case the corporate finance departments leaked information to other departments. While dealing rooms routinely transcribed all telephone calls, the corporate finance departments did not. In each case the employees were dismissed. The insider dealing was uncovered only when those who sold to the insiders complained. If the transactions had involved market makers dealing with the public, it is possible that nobody would have known.[285]

In the third incident of the week of August 14, 1988, the Stock Exchange examined an apparent leak of information immediately before the government's announcement of a referral of a tender offer bid to the Monopolies

---

282. Hughes, *A Case of Frustration for the DTI*, FIN. TIMES, Nov. 28, 1989 at 10, col. 7.

283. Hughes, *Insider Dealing Conviction Overturned*, FIN. TIMES, Jan. 26, 1990 at 1, col. 1.

284. *Leading Bank Sacks Two for Insider Dealing*, THE TIMES (London), Aug. 12, 1988 at 1, col. 1.

285. *New Insider Shock hits City*, THE SUNDAY TIMES (London), Aug. 14, 1988 at D1, col. 1; *Insider Deals Prompt City Security Check*, THE TIMES (London), Aug. 15, 1988 at 19, col. 2; *SE Widens Net on Dealing in Pleasurama*, THE TIMES (London), Aug. 16, 1988 at 11, col. 1; *The Fat Old Grouse Gets Away with it Again*, THE TIMES (London), Aug. 17, 1988 at 21, col. 6.

Commission. Such a referral normally would cause a decline in share price. One minute before the public announcement, and four minutes after advisors to the companies involved in the takeover bid were informed of the referral, there were three trades prior to a sharp decline in the stock price.[286]

The next week, Kleinwort Benson dismissed one salesman and suspended another for personal stock transactions in violation of the firm's rules. The policy of most City institutions is that all employee share dealings must be carried out through the firm's own brokerage subsidiary or a company that it uses. This enables employee transactions to be monitored by the in-house compliance staff. In this case the brokers used outside brokers to trade in the shares of an over-the-counter company that was engaged in preliminary talks on an oil and gas investment deal, which would normally, when announced, cause the shares to rise.[287]

The Failure of Enforcement

The enforcement of the insider dealing statute has been ineffective. One problem has been the high burden of proof required for conviction under a criminal statute. As mentioned, egregious insider trading prior to the Financial Services Act was handled internally by the Stock Exchange. There was little due process for those charged and no required burden of proof. A second enforcement difficulty has been that insider trading investigations, even with transparent trading, requires substantial resources. Major insider trading is conducted by organized rings operating offshore using nominees and dummy corporations.[288] International cooperation and coordination are required for successful investigations.

A third problem has been the ineffectiveness of the DTI's Investigation Branch.[289] Under the Companies Acts, the DTI can appoint investigators to examine under oath and to inspect the books and records and affairs of corporations. Insider trading enforcement requires specialized experience, yet when the Insider Dealing Act was first enacted in 1980, the government declined to include special investigatory powers that had been introduced in an earlier bill. The government's view was that because special investigatory powers were not required for murder cases, they should not be needed for cases of insider dealing.[290]

---

286. Jay, *Insiders in Early Bale-out*, THE SUNDAY TIMES (London), Aug. 21, 1988 at D1, cols. 2–3.

287. Lever, *Kleinwort Salesman Sacked for Breach of Share Rules*, THE TIMES (London), Aug. 24, 1988 at 23, col. 6.

288. Wolman, *Insider Dealing Rings Operate Offshore Links*, FIN. TIMES, Mar. 4, 1986 at 1, col. 1.

289. *See generally* B. RIDER, *supra* note 233 at 283–325.

290. *Id.* at 116–17.

The Enforcement Record   The DTI's dismal record of insider trading investigations and prosecutions demonstrates the weakness of its statutory power and organizational commitment to enforcement. From 1980 to March 1986, the Stock Exchange conducted 284 investigations of insider trading and referred 93 cases to the DTI, which prosecuted only 5, resulting in 3 convictions.[291] Of those 284 investigations, 50 involved offshore companies.[292] The number of prosecutions increased only slightly toward the end of 1986. Over one hundred cases had been brought to the DTI's attention, resulting in a cumulative total of nine prosecutions by the end of the year. The Labor Party noted that during the same period, 138,918 social service claimants were prosecuted for fraud.[293] The comparison was not complete, for insider dealing more often than not involved complex, sophisticated, international commercial fraud. At one point in 1986, the DTI asked the Stock Exchange to be more selective when referring suspected cases of insider trading to the department.[294] The request for a more judicious referral policy reflected the department's lack of priority for these cases.

In 1989 the Stock Exchange Insider Dealing Group sent an average of one case of suspected insider trading every other week to the DTI. In these cases, it took an average of eleven months for the DTI to complete its basic fact finding. In February 1989, it had thirty-nine cases in its docket: four awaiting trial, fifteen being investigated by DTI inspectors, two on special inquiries, and eighteen awaiting a decision on whether to appoint investigators.[295] By 1990 the DTI's ten-year scorecard totaled twenty-six prosecutions and eleven convictions.[296] None of those convicted has been sentenced to prison. Those convicted are fined, but not always to the full extent of their profits.

The early cases brought forward for prosecution involved the occasional insider dealer, often a lower-echelon employee, such as a secretary, who had made a one-time prohibited trade. The defendants were unsophisticated and were caught because of naivete or stupidity. They did not try to hid

---

291. Lever, *Exchange Told Not to Act on Hunches of Inside Dealing*, THE TIMES (London), Mar. 5, 1986 at 17, col. 4.

292. Wolman, *supra* note 288.

293. *City Scandals: Lovely for Labour*, ECONOMIST, Dec. 6, 1986 at 66–67.

294. Lever, *supra* note 291.

295. *Reforms Urged, supra* note 213, at 28, col. 1; Beresford and Blackhurst, *Insider Dealers Stay One Step Ahead*, THE SUNDAY TIMES, Feb. 26, 1989, at D1, col. 2. The Government has been unsuccessful in obtaining convictions when it prosecutes inside traders. Hughes, *Third Case Fails on Share Dealing*, FIN. TIMES, Nov. 23, 1989 at 10, col. 5.

296. Rice, *Insider Dealing: Legal Failings Lead to Pressure for Reform*, FIN. TIMES, Feb. 7, 1990 at 8, col. 1.

their purchases or profits. The sums involved were small—£1,000 to £10,000 profits—as were the fines. Invariably, the perpetrators were fired or resigned from their positions.[297] The cases were tried in provincial courts and officially unreported.[298] In the most publicized of the early cases, Maurice Naeger, a director of W. H. Smith, the U.K.'s largest news distributor, traded on advance information of a takeover bid. His profit was £4,200, his fine £1,300. Because he was scheduled to retire as director, he was not otherwise punished.[299]

The investor protection system's reporting requirements and the increased computerization of securities trading enabled the Stock Exchange to monitor suspected insider dealing. However, the gains in detection were not matched by improvements in prosecution. The DTI and the other enforcement bodies were burdened by statutory and organizational weaknesses, along with a lack of experience in prosecuting commercial fraud.

Organizational and Statutory Weakness   The Stock Exchange has been by far the most successful in uncovering suspected insider trading. Yet, its effectiveness was often nullified when the results of its surveillance were turned over to the DTI, which would then conduct an investigation and forward its results to the appropriate prosecutor. This was a rather circular approach.

The 1989 Companies Act empowered the DTI to delegate investigatory and prosecutorial powers to the Stock Exchange on a case-by-case basis for simple insider dealing violations.[300] The Exchange has been successful in its initial prosecutions.[301] It can act more swiftly than the DTI and seems to have more expertise. Granting the Exchange such powers is a step in the right direction, but more widespread delegation of investigatory and prosecutorial powers to investigate commercial fraud should be furnished to a separate agency, probably the SIB.

The main statutory weaknesses of the Insider Dealing Act are the lack of civil or administrative remedies and the amorphous definition of the crime.

---

297. J. H. Farrar, *supra* note 22, at 357.

298. *See* 2 Company Law 278 (1981) (*Bryce's* case); 3 Company Law 185 (1983) (*Dickensen's* case); 4 Company Law 117 (1983) (*Titheridge's* case).

299. The case is unreported but is discussed in Hannigan, *supra* note 236 at 79–80.

300. Companies Act 1989, ch. 40, § 209 (1989).

301. Hughes, *Convicted as SE Wins First Insider Dealing Case*, Fin. Times, Nov. 8, 1990, at 24, col. 2. Two brothers were convicted of selling shares in a corporation shortly before it warned of losses. They learned of the corporation's problems from the company's accountant. By selling their stock, the brothers saved approximately £5 thousand. They were fined a total of £1250 plus costs. Durman, *Two Pleaded Guilty to Insider Deals*, Independent, Nov. 8, 1990 at 26, col. 2. *Insider Dealing and Investor Confidence, supra* note 234 at 28.

There have been suggestions of lowering or shifting the burden of proof in insider trading prosecutions.[302] However, the creation of civil and administrative remedies might serve the same purpose. A civil remedy would also quicken many investigations and result in the disgorgement of gains. Administrative remedies may already exist in the ability of recognized bodies to discipline members engaged in insider trading for violations of the conduct of business rules,[303] or similar rules of the appropriate recognized body.

Because of a drafting error in the Financial Services Act, the scope of insider dealing investigations had to be restricted. Section 177, which gives the DTI the power to appoint outside inspectors with the right to question witnesses under oath, could only be used prospectively for contraventions of the Insider Dealing Act of 1985, which consolidated the prior insider dealing statutes. This act became effective in the second half of 1985, and investigators examining share dealings that predated that statue could not use Section 177.[304]

When the DTI receives evidence of insider dealing violations, it can: (1) appoint inspectors under Section 177 of the Financial Services Act; (2) prosecute without appointing inspectors; (3) authorize the Stock Exchange to prosecute; or (4) take no additional action, but inform other regulators. From 1980 until 1989, it often took the last course of action. Insider dealing

---

302. The Select Committee Report castigated DTI's procrastination and general role in presenting insider dealing cases. The Committee recommended that the burden of proof in insider dealing cases shift to the defendant once a prima facie case had been made. To expedite the resolution of insider trading matters, the Report recommended that penalties be more flexible than under the Company Securities (Insider Dealing) Act. It suggested a system of plea bargaining whereby an individual who was investigated, and confronted with a statement of facts, could, if he did not dispute them, pay a fine. The report suggested introducing sanctions which would have a lower standard of proof and that DTI expedite the appointment of investigations and completion of investigations. *Reforms Urged, supra* note 213 at 28, col. 1. The Core Conduct of Business Rules adopted in 1991 create a private right of action against member firms that have been guilty of insider dealing. SFA RULES, *supra* note 264, rule 28. Under a statutory instrument made under FSA § 62A such a private right of action is specifically not limited to private customers. Financial Services Act 1986 (Restriction of Right of Action) Regulations 1991, S.I. 1958, No. 489. The government has recommended that the SFO gain the option of bringing civil or criminal proceedings against those accused of financial fraud. This would lower the burden of proof needed to obtain a conviction.

303. FSA at § 48.

304. Lever, *DTI Error Limits Scope for Insider Inquires*, THE TIMES (London), Aug. 1, 1988, at 19, col. 2. In R v. Secretary of State for Trade and Industry, *ex parte* (1988), the court held that § 105 of the powers could not be exercised in relation to any information relating to business that occurred prior to the effective date of the FSA. *See* Barister, *Investigation Powers are not Retrospective*, FIN. TIMES, Dec. 2, 1988 at 21, col. 3.

investigations are but a small part of the DTI's responsibilities. Under the Companies Act it is responsible for enforcing the corporate law statutes and can undertake fact-finding inquiries of company law violations.[305] Inspectors appointed, particularly for company law violations,[306] were usually accountants or Queens Counsel[307] with full-time outside practices. More recently, the DTI has appointed its own staff, officials of the SIB or of a recognized body.[308]

The DTI sometimes took up to six months to appoint an inspector for insider dealing cases. By the time it checked the inspector's references and the inspector familiarized himself with the case, the trail had grown cold, the perpetrators had fled the jurisdiction, and the gathering of evidence for a successful criminal prosecution was made more difficult. The DTI's choice of inspectors probably delayed the investigation further. Because of their ongoing practices, inspectors' investigatorial activities for the DTI might not be their greatest priority.[309]

The DTI's problems in investigating and prosecuting insider dealing violations were caused by insufficient staff, the broad responsibilities of the department, and a lack of investigatory zeal throughout the organization. Overlaying these problems, the department was never able to build up a reservoir of experienced inspectors or a DTI staff with cumulative experience in the investigation of insider dealing. Nor has the agency been able to make good public use of its reports when issued. It has allowed inspectors to criticize named individuals, but only in moderate terms.[310] Some reports did not attribute blame for wrongdoing. Others were unpublished for fear of hampering a criminal investigation or because of concern about defaming the parties mentioned. Publicity about investigation results is not only a deterrence to fraud, it may be good public relations.

Judicial Barriers to Enforcement—Process, Inexperience, and Conservatism It has been surprisingly difficult to obtain convictions under the Insider Dealing Act when there have been prosecutions.[311] In part, this is due

---

305. Companies Act, 1985, ch. 6, §§ 431, 442, 447 (1985). Difficulties of DTI's patrol of corporate law violations led to Parliament granting the department more flexible powers of inspection and investigation. Companies Act, 1989, ch. 40, §§ 55, 57, 82–83.

306. *Id.* § 423.

307. Queens Counsel are experienced barristers who can be appointed to represent the government in certain matters.

308. B. Rider, *supra* note 233 at 117.

309. The House of Commons Committee recommended that inspectors appointed by the DTI devote 75% of their time to the inquiry. *Extracts, supra* note 213 at 28, col. 6.

310. Extracts, *supra* note 213, at 28, col. 6.

311. *See supra* notes 292–293.

to the statute's failure to define specifically the nature of the offense. Each violation, at least in the early cases, seemed particularly factually oriented. Second, in the absence of a civil remedy, the prosecution must meet the criminal burden of proof beyond a reasonable doubt. It has been difficult to convince courts that such evidence produced meets that standard. Nor have defendants been willing to plea bargain, for several reasons. The first is that there is not yet broad agreement that insider dealing is really wrong and should therefore be punished by a criminal conviction. Second, the highly publicized failures to achieve successful prosecutions encourage a spirited defense.

This attitude carries over to the judiciary. When there have been convictions, the penalties have been less than the profits made or losses avoided by the trades, making the punishment more a cost of doing business to the defendant than a deterrent to others.[312]

A problem in securing insider dealing convictions has been that cases have been brought in the Crown Courts, lower courts unfamiliar with the complex cases of commercial fraud. In the United States, violations of the federal securities laws must be tried in federal district court.[313] Most of the insider dealing cases have been tried in the Southern District of New York, which has developed substantial experience in these complex cases. In the United Kingdom, however, the lack of cumulative experience in the investigation, prosecution, and adjudication of commercial crimes remains a hindrance to effective enforcement. The Roskill Report recommended that a special Fraud Trials Tribunal be created to handle complex cases of commercial fraud. This would ease judicial insecurities over dealing with these types of cases.

The discharge of the defendants in the second and third *Guinness* cases was in part due to the failure of the judge to control the tempo of the trial and the inability of the prosecutor to make timely objections as the trial dragged on until one of the defendants, representing himself, was near men-

---

312. In the United States, the traditional remedy for civil or administrative actions was disgorgement of profits. In 1984, Congress increased the penalties for violating the 1934 Securities Exchange Act or its rules. The Insider Trading Sanctions Act of 1984, 15 U.S.C.A. 78u(d)(2)(A), provides for trebling the profits gained or losses avoided by the defendant. Criminal penalties were increased from $10,000 to $100,000 thousand. In 1988, the Insider Trading and Securities Fraud Enforcement Act made employers and controlling persons liable for the acts of their employees if the controlling person knew or acted in reckless disregard of the fact that the controlled person was likely to engage in illegal insider dealing and failed to take adequate precautions to prevent the prohibited conduct from taking place. 15 U.S.C.A. § 78U-1(b)(1) (West Supp. 1990). For controlling persons, the treble damages penalty was not to exceed the greater of one million dollars or three times the profits gained or losses avoided. 15 U.S.C.A. § 78T-1(a) (West Supp. 1990).

313. *See e.g*, Securities Exchange Act of 1934, § 27, 15 U.S.C.A. § 78aa (West Supp. 1990); Securities Act of 1933, § 22(a), 15 U.S.C.A. § 77u(a) (West Supp. 1990).

tal collapse.[314] More experienced prosecutors and courts seasoned in the complexities of commercial crime would avoid these pitfalls.

Another cause for the lukewarm judicial reception of the insider trading cases, which is much more difficult to document, is the innate conservatism of the judiciary. This conservatism is exhibited by members of local courts dealing with a vague criminal statute involving a totally new crime. These judges may be reluctant to interpret this new crime expansively without direction from higher courts, particularly when asked to force a journalist to divulge sources and waive a privilege. The rigidity of the statutory remedies also may have contributed to the strict interpretation of the statute. Civil or administrative options, if available, can weed out some of the closer cases.

Lower courts that are unfamiliar with the statute have not favorably responded to its nuances. In the first case interpreting the Insider Dealing Act, the issue was whether someone who traded upon nonpublic price-sensitive information received from another was a tippee, in violation of the statute, when the source volunteered the information, as opposed to the receiver "obtaining" it through his own efforts. Did the word "obtained" in Section 1(3) of the Insider Dealing Act include information freely offered? A businessman, Brian Fisher, was informed by a merchant bank with a relationship to a company involved in a takeover that a takeover bid had been agreed upon and that the information was confidential. Fisher then purchased six thousand of the company's shares on the stock exchange, sold them after the information became public, and made a profit of £3,000. The lower court acquitted the defendant, but the Court of Appeal reversed, and the House of Lords affirmed the reversal. Whether the information was solicited or received did not increase or decrease the undesirability of making use of it. The appellate decision reinforced the statute.

What is disturbing about judicial interpretations of the insider dealing statute is the lower courts' restrictive view of its enforcement powers. Another Crown Court decision, fortunately also reversed, involved a journalist, Geoffrey Warner, who refused to assist an insider dealing inquiry on grounds of a journalist's privilege.[315] The journalist published articles in which he accurately forecasted the result of inquiries into two takeover bids conducted by the Monopolies and Mergers Commission and the Office of Fair Trading.[316] It was highly probable that the information had been leaked

---

314. Hughes, *Case unravels as judge finds Seelig too ill for trial*, FIN. TIMES, Feb. 12, 1992 at 6, col. 1; Rice & Waters, *Fraud office drops charges in third Guinness case*, FIN. TIMES, Feb. 8, 1992 at 1, col. 3.

315. *In re* an Inquiry Under the Company Securities (Insider Dealing) Act, 1985, 2 W.L.R. 33 (C.A. 1988).

316. *Id.* at 38–39.

by official sources within those offices. The information also was given to individuals who used it for insider dealing.

The secretary of state appointed inspectors to investigate the suspected leaks, which were violations of the Insider Dealing statute.[317] The journalist, who knew that the information was price-sensitive, declined the inspectors' request to give evidence on grounds of a journalist's privilege not to disclose his sources.[318] Following the refusal, the inspectors referred the matter to the High Court to determine whether Warner violated the Contempt of Court Act.[319]

The High Court ruled that the inspectors had not proven that the need for Warner's testimony to prevent a crime outweighed the public interest in protecting his source.[320] If this decision had been affirmed, investigations of insider dealing and multilateral cooperation would have been hindered. However, the Court of Appeal reversed[321] and the House of Lords affirmed the reversal.[322] Nevertheless, unless the lower courts become more responsive to investigations, insider trading enforcement will be hindered.

Deregulation   Deregulation integrated functionally segmented sectors of the financial services industry to enable British financial services firms to compete in global capital markets. Two important political goals of the Big Bang were to increase competition, which in turn would lower the transaction costs of trading securities, and to attract the small investor to the securities markets.[323] "Peoples capitalism" required a belief by the small investor in the fairness of the marketplace, that they would not be discriminated against or taken advantage of because of the size of their holdings or their unequal access to information. The markets' legitimacy and integrity

---

317. FSA § 177(3).

318. *In re* Inquiry 2 W.L.R. at 39 (1988).

319. *Id.* at 40. This referral was pursuant to FSA § 178, the relevant parts provide:

(1) if any person—(a) refuses to comply with any request under subsection (3) of section 177 above; or (b) refuses to answer any questions put to him by the inspectors appointed under that section with respect to any matter relevant for establishing whether or not any suspected contravention has occurred, the inspectors may certify that fact in writing to the court and the court may inquire into the case.

(2) If, after hearing any witness who may be produced against or on behalf of the alleged offender and any statement which may be offered in defense, the court is satisfied that he did without reasonable excuse refuse to comply with such a request or answer any such question, the court may—punish him in like manner as if he had been guilty of contempt of the court; . . .

320. *In re* Inquiry 2 W.L.R. at 45–46 (1988).

321. *Id.* at 57.

322. *Id.* at 71.

323. J. PLENDER & P. WALLACE, THE SQUARE MILE 18–20, 219–22 (1985).

would be enhanced by improving business practices, by increasing disclosure to equalize information disparities, and by creating greater transparency in trading to aid enforcement.

The Big Bang mandated new standards of behavior backed by criminal penalties for their violation. However, it is one thing to legislate a change in morality, it is quite another to change the business culture to create new norms and patterns of behavior. As noted earlier, because of the computerization and technological developments nurtured by the Big Bang, for the first time the stock market tape was transparent so that all trading could be quickly traced.[324] Yet even with a new capacity to detect improper dealing, notorious scandals continued to occur.

One may attribute the persistence of insider dealing to the widespread belief that it is really a victimless crime. Other types of securities violations such as market manipulation, clearly recognized as illegal in the United States,[325] are considered merely venial wrongs and assumed to be widespread. Market manipulation is a violation of the Financial Services Act[326] However, it did not become illegal until 1986 and is considered by stockbrokers to be acceptable trading practice between professionals who should be able to protect themselves.[327]

In November 1990 the Stock Exchange investigated suspected "bear raids" on approximately one dozen companies.[328] Despite the widespread perception that "bear raids" exist, there has been only one prosecution and the penalty was modest: a £1,150 fine and five-year prohibition of serving as a board member.[329]

Undoubtedly insider trading and breaches of Chinese walls occur regularly. It is insufficient for firms merely to have policies requiring Chinese walls or rules against the misuse of material nonpublic information. They must also have the means and the desire to enforce such strictures. In the United States, doubts about the effectiveness of firms' Chinese walls led to

---

324. Prior to the Big Bang, trades were reported the following day, but without the time of the transaction. Kohut, *U.K. Reforms Ensure Probity—Stock Exchange Chief*, REUTERS MONEY REP., NEXIS Jan. 27, 1987.

325. Securities Exchange Act of 1934, §§ 9, 10(b), 15 U.S.C.A. §§ 78i, 78j(b) (West Supp. 1990).

326. *Id.* § 47(2).

327. Hudson, *London Exchange Probes 'Suspicious Dealings' in Stocks That May Have Been Bear Raid Targets*, WALL ST. J., Nov. 7, 1990 at C12, col. 2.

328. *Id.* A "bear raid" occurs when a speculator spreads false and malicious rumors about a company in the expectation that the firm's stock will fall. Typically, the speculator sells borrowed stock, known as selling short, in the hope that the stock price will fall. After the market reacts to the false information by pushing down the stock's price, the manipulator purchases the stock to replace the borrowed shares and earns a profit.

329. *Id.*

an amendment of the Securities Exchange Act to expand exposure to civil liability for insider trading beyond the violators themselves, to securities firms and other controlling persons who knowingly or recklessly fail to take the appropriate measures to prevent insider trading by their employees.[330]

Insider dealing cut to the heart of the viability of the self-regulatory system and the integrity of the marketplace. Because of the government's Personal Equity Plan to encourage more shareholders and the publicity surrounding the Big Bang and the Financial Services Act, the City itself became more transparent to the public than ever before. Insider dealing destroys the investing public's faith that the market presents a level playing field. If the market is rigged, the public will shun investment in securities. The insider dealing scandals were shocking because of the notoriety of those involved. These individuals were at the heart of the City or civil servants thought to be above reproach. The whole structure of regulation trembled. Even some Tories concluded that a statutory commission would be needed.[331]

Insider dealing becomes the moral measure of the new framework's effectiveness. The admitted difficulties of prosecution for insider trading violations means that such improper transactions will decline only when there is a consensus that it is wrong, when there is a fear that engaging in such activity will be discovered, and when prosecution is effective and timely. Given the present enforcement system, it is uncertain that such a goal can be reached.

Multilateral Cooperation

Because of the transnational nature of securities fraud and the need to procure evidence from foreign nations and regulators, there has been a movement, spearheaded by the U.S. Securities and Exchange Commission, to foster cooperation between regulators through memoranda of understanding (MOU). These memoranda grant a regulatory authority, such as the DTI, access to a foreign regulator's information about an investor or suspect or to information the foreign regulator could obtain through "best efforts." Traditionally, foreign regulators have been less than cooperative with one another. The DTI once refused an SEC request for a telephone number![332] In September 1986, the United Kingdom and the United States signed such an MOU.[333]

---

330. Insider Trading and Securities Fraud Enforcement Act, 15 U.S.C.A. § 78u-1(b)(1) (West Supp. 1990).

331. *See* Stovall, *Economic Spotlight—London Scandals*, REUTERS, Jan. 21, 1987.

332. Note, *The British-U.S. Memorandum of Understanding of 1986: Implications After Warner*, 11 FORDHAM INT'L. L. J. 110, 111, n. 5 (1987).

333. MOU, *supra* note 272.

The MOU provides that requests for information must relate to the prevention of insider dealing, fraudulent securities dealing, or market manipulation.[334] Information requested may be refused when it is held by the DTI in a nonsecurities capacity or on grounds of "public interest."[335] This MOU formalizes previously existing unofficial contracts between the SEC's Division of Enforcement and the Stock Exchange's surveillance department. Because requests for cooperation may be fought by those named, the courts must provide ancillary support for cooperation to be implemented. However, such support may not always be forthcoming. At this point in time, the United Kingdom has been the beneficiary of the U.S.'s efforts for multilateral cooperation.

Perhaps of greatest concern to British regulators has been the insider dealing standards of the European Community. Despite criticism of the U.K.'s statute and the lack of enforcement, the Insider Dealing Act is the most advanced in Europe. Common insider dealing standards within the Community would be an effective means to improved enforcement. The government's fear has been that the EC directive would be less practical and effective than the United Kingdom's. A draft proposal on insider trading had a broader definition of such dealing and regulated practices than the United Kingdom's.[336] In June 1989, the ambassador to the EC agreed on a directive against insider trading. They met British concerns by narrowing the definition to trading on the basis of sensitive, nonpublic information with which traders are closely associated. Some countries, such as Germany, were concerned with the definition of tippee, which has not been prohibited under German law.[337] In 1992, insider dealing will be illegal throughout the EC.[338]

Important for multilateral cooperation is that the directive calls for exchange of information.[339] Penalties will continue to vary between countries. Insider trading is a new offense in several EC countries.[340] As the British experience demonstrates, it is a long journey from the passage of a statute to effective cooperation in law enforcement. The linkages between United

---

334. *Id.* at ¶ 88, 244–45.

335. *See* Note, *supra* note 332, at 110; *see* also Bornstein and Dugger, *supra* note 236 at 413–17 (1987) (analyzing the U.S.-U.K. MOU).

336. *See* 30 O. J. EUR. COMM. (No. C 153) 8 (1987).

337. Binyon, *EC breakthrough over 1992*, THE TIMES (London), June 19, 1989 at 27, col. 1.

338. It will be a criminal offense for the first time in West Germany, Italy, Belgium, and Ireland.

339. Draft directive Art. 8.

340. *See* Note, *Securities—Insider Trading—The Effects of the New EEC Draft Insider Trading Directive*, 18 GA. J. INT'L. & COMP. L. 119 (1988).

States and United Kingdom financial markets and the efforts of the SEC will assist multilateral cooperation between the two countries. The effectiveness of the EC's efforts against insider dealing must await an agreement by the financial communities about what practices are impermissible.

The Viability of Self-regulation

Self-regulation is the fundamental principle underlying the investor protection framework. It recalls the traditional English approach to securities regulation and offers a guide for the successful implementation of the current system.[341] If self-regulatory principles no longer apply, the SIB will become an SEC and the self-regulating bodies will have a reduced role.[342]

The success of the principle of self-regulation can be seen in the history of the U.K.'s Panel on Takeovers and Chargers. The limits of the concept and its viability as a regulatory tool in the future is presented in the Blue Arrow affair, where the norms of behavior broke down.

The Panel on Takeovers and Mergers: A Case Study

The United Kingdom is unique in its regulation of mergers and takeovers, for there are no statutes that guide the procedures when a takeover situation comes into play. The most successful and effective self-regulatory agency is the Panel on Takeovers and Mergers, which supervises the City Code on Takeovers and Mergers, a set of rules designed to establish fair play in the market.

Once, the Takeover Panel was the prototype of effective self-regulation. However, times have changed. Deregulation, international competition, and the participation of individuals and firms who did not share the norms that underlay self-regulatory principles have placed the panel's future into doubt. The United Kingdom has responded by giving the panel statutory backing and forcing it to adopt more legalistic procedures. Doubts remain as to whether the panel can be an effective self-regulating body in the future, a question that reflects upon the whole framework of investor protection.

The origins of the panel and the code date to the postwar period when the number of companies with such attributes as underutilized assets and insufficient management made them easy targets for corporate raiders. There was a perceived need to achieve an orderly market where shareholders received a fair deal, yet the market itself was allowed to work. In 1959,

---

341. *See* Chapter 1, *supra* p. 3.
342. *See* Chapter 2, *supra* p. 7.

a working party of City institutions was convened by the Bank of England. This group laid down rules of fair play, Notes on Amalgamation of British Businesses, which were inadequate to control inappropriate practices.

Another working party was created in 1968, and this one resulted in the first City Code and the Panel on Takeovers and Mergers, the latter a full-time body to supervise the principles in the code.[343] The panel is not a regulatory body with formal statutory authority. In 1969, the panel arranged with the Bank of England and the DTI a guarantee that the DTI would use the sanctions available to it if the Panel so requested.

The City Code on Takeovers and Mergers contains ten general principles and thirty-eight rules supplemented and explained by practice notes. The principal concern of the code is the protection of shareholders. In addition, since 1981, the code includes Rules Governing Substantial Acquisitions of Shares to prevent "dawn raids," the speedy, organized acquisition of shares in a target company.[344]

The panel's effectiveness harked back to the original concept of self-regulation of the City, a shared sense of values and behavior.[345] Anyone who desired to engage in mergers and takeovers had to abide by the City rules or face banishment from the resources of the City establishment. All offerors had to go through a few City institutions that handled the paper work and issued the necessary documents. These institutions, merchant banks, are few in number and accepted the principles of the code. In addition, they are watched by the Bank of England. Section 14 of the Prevention of Fraud (Investments) Act[346] virtually obligated all tender offers to be conducted through licensed dealers, members of the Stock Exchange, or exempted dealers. All of these bodies adhered to the principles of the code. This tightly knit group made it impossible for outsiders to conduct a takeover without using responsible local intermediaries.

Sanctions available to the panel did not have legal backing, but had the power of moral persuasion, and the bidders realized that the voluntary self-regulated code of principles was backed by access to city financial resources. Failure to follow the code meant that one could not use the facilities of the securities markets, that one might be shunned by other companies, and that needed capital could not be obtained.[347] The work of the

---

343. *See generally* DeMott, *Current Issue in Tender Offer Regulation: Lessons from the British*, 58 N.Y.U. L. REV. 945 (1983); M. V. BLANK & A. L. GREYSTOKE, WEINBERG AND BANK ON TAKEOVERS AND MERGERS (4th ed. 1979).

344. L.C.B GOWER, GOWER'S PRINCIPLES OF MODERN COMPANY LAW 697–98 (4th ed. 1979 & Supp. 1988).

345. H. MCRAE & F. CAIRNCROSS, Capital City, 153–54 (rev. ed. 1985).

346. FSA § 14.

347. M. CLARKE, *supra* note 203 at 109–12.

panel was conducted informally and behind closed doors. It would review documents in advance and worked via telephone rather than through formal published opinions.

While the effectiveness of the panel has been criticized from time to time, it has survived for twenty years and has reviewed approximately five thousand takeovers.[348] The Panel on Takeovers and Mergers has often been cited as a successful SRO. In its original conception, the panel was very much a City institution, exemplary of how self-regulation should work. Its sanctions were based upon censure and persuasion. Its decisions were swifter than any statutory body and were without appeal. In contrast to the SIB, which has had so much trouble recruiting in the City, the director general of the panel and two-thirds of its fifteen-person staff are seconded from City institutions, the Bank of England, or Whitehall.[349] However, the original concept of the panel as a purely self-regulatory body based upon the consensus of City institutions is a thing of the past.

The globalization of securities markets and mergers and takeovers has made the private future of the panel uncertain. The legalization of the tender offer process has resulted from legal appeals of panel decisions.[350] While the panel has been supported by the courts, it has been forced to become more formal in its rules and proceedings, and to seek indirect support under the Financial Services Act. Pressures on the panel have led to a formalization of its procedures, particularly in light of the Guinness affair and the Datafin case,[351] which held that the panel was a public law body whose decisions could be scrutinized by the courts and reversed if they violated natural justice. The judgments of the panel are now published and resemble judicial opinions in style and length. Since the Guinness affair, when most of the parties seemed to play loosely with the rules of the City code, the panel has been under pressure to resist the logical step of placing it under the aegis of the SIB.

With the internationalization of mergers, and particularly through the use of American tender offer techniques, such as the tactic of running into court, the panel has been criticized for its inability to deal with breaches of the code and its insufficiency in this new climate.[352] In the past, the panel's greatest threat was to bar violators from access to British capital. This is not much of a penalty to foreign firms with other resources.[353]

348. Brown, *Watchdog Learns to Bite*, THE TIMES (London), Jun. 30, 1988 at 21, col. 1.
349. *Id.*
350. *Ex parte* Datafin, 1 All E.R. 564 (C.A. 1987); *ex parte* Guinness, 1 All E.R. 509 (C.A. 1988).
351. *Ex parte* Datafin, 1 All E.R. 564 (C.A. 1987).
352. *Guinness*, Panel Beating, ECONOMIST, Jan. 31, 1987 at 72.
353. *See* M. CLARKE, *supra* note 203 at 111.

In light of Guinness, the DTI and the Bank of England commissioned a study of the Panel's operations in January 1987. The study concluded that the panel's role has changed from that of essentially an arbitrator to one of an investigator and enforcer. This has necessitated closer relationships with the SIB and the DTI, and the formalization of its role within the new investor protection framework. The panel has maintained a delicate balance of being outside the framework, yet has been able to use the sanctioning powers of the SIB and recognized bodies. Stricter takeover rules have been promulgated: offerors have to declare their interest and trading activities at much lower thresholds, rules require greater disclosure from investor groups acting in concert, and nominee companies have to disclose their owners.[354]

The SIB issued a rule that called for "cold shouldering" of those listed by the panel, and for firms to assist panel investigations by providing information.[355] The SIB has encouraged the recognized bodies to adopt similar rules.[356] As the panel has no statutory power, nor even the contract-based authority of the recognized bodies vis-à-vis its members, it can neither subpoena documents nor force attendance at hearings. However, individuals who are members of a recognized body are now subject to panel discipline.

When a person has been named by the panel, or a firm has reason to believe that an individual has not complied with U.K. practice and standards in takeovers, the firm may not act on behalf of such a person in connection with a takeover and must comply with any request for information from the panel. The government also made an order granting the panel the right to privileged information pursuant to Section 180 and the DTI's investigative powers.[357]

The panel will be under increasing stress in the future. Though it has maintained its independence, it has moved towards the statutory model. Its ability to continue effectively is intertwined with the success of the recognized bodies and the SIB. Looming in its future is the EC's approach to changes in corporate control within the single European market.

The Limits of Self-regulatory Enforcement: The Blue Arrow Affair

Self-regulation is based upon the belief that most individuals and firms strive to uphold the norms of business practice. These standards are set by

---

354. Lohr, *Tough British Takeover Rules*, N.Y. TIMES, Feb. 2, 1987 at D3, col. 1.

355. SIB CONDUCT OF BUSINESS RULES, *supra* note 32, ch. III, rule 2.12.

356. SFA Rules, *supra* note 264, Rule 41—Support of Takeover Panel's Functions.

357. Dickson, *Takeover Panel Given Greater Powers Following City Scandals*, FIN. TIMES, May 12, 1987 at 1, col. 3.

the leading firms—the establishment. Enforcement problems are expected to be directed at those firms on the fringe. Self-regulation is also grounded in the belief that the spirit of the law is more important than its letter. But what if firms at the center ignore the standards? That brings into question the whole basis of regulation.

In July 1989 the DTI charged that National Westminster Bank,[358] the U.K.'s second largest in size of assets, through its merchant banking subsidiary, misled the Bank of England, the International Stock Exchange, and the public in the course of an underwriting of stock of the Blue Arrow Corporation. The history of the Blue Arrow affair challenges the theory of self-regulation and suggests that the Big Bang has created institutions of unmanageable size.

Blue Arrow involved deliberate evasion of the disclosure requirements of the Companies Acts, misleading the public and supervisors as to the nature of placement arrangements, rigging of the market and manipulating the price of shares, lying to the Bank of England about legal advice received, failure by a major bank to supervise its employees or to get to the truth of a subsidiary's misdeeds, and failure of compliance officers to concern themselves closely enough with the facts or the spirit of the rules. The scandal resulted in the destruction of careers over a score of individuals of varying degrees of guilt, and overall, a severe gouging of the concept of City self-regulation.

The Blue Arrow affair began in the summer of 1987 when Blue Arrow Corporation commenced a bid for Manpower, the U.S.'s largest employment agency. In the run-up to the tender offer, Blue Arrow began to purchase Manpower shares. Stealth is an important though sometimes impermissible tactic for an offeror in a takeover. Under the International Stock Exchange's rules,[359] Blue Arrow was required to disclose these purchases if they were worth more than 5 percent of its capital. Such disclosure, however, would have disrupted Blue Arrow's takeover ambitions. County NatWest (CNW), the investment banking subsidiary of National Westminster Bank (NatWest), was the advisor and underwriter of a new stock issue for Blue Arrow that would raise capital to purchase Manpower.[360]

---

358. National Westminster (NatWest) has $178.5 billion in assets, making it larger than any U.S. bank holding corporation except Citicorp. Natwest is the leading bank in market capitalization. Greenhouse, *NatWest's Chairman Resigns*, N.Y. TIMES, July 26, 1989 at D1, col. 6.

359. COUNCIL OF THE STOCK EXCHANGE, ADMISSION OF SECURITIES TO LISTING (Looseleaf), § 6.08 (2d ed. 1985).

360. The advice of County NatWest's compliance office was "Won't disclose. Announce in two weeks. Worse case = rapped on knuckles. No chance of shares being delisted." The corporation unsuccessfully sought a waiver from the Exchange. Then, it launched an £837

There was inadequate interest in the new issue. Only 38 percent of the new shares were taken up. The leading underwriters, CNW, Phillips & Drew, a subsidiary of UBS, a Swiss bank, and Dillon Reed, decided to purchase an additional 10 percent themselves, which saved the issue. Although the deadline for purchases had expired, Lloyd's Bank, the registrars, allowed the extra purchases. This enabled the underwriters to announce that nearly half of the shares had been sold. Then the lead underwriters attempted to sell the remainder of the issue. Only 71 percent of the total issue could be placed.

On September 28, 1987, CNW issued a press release stating that all of the shares had been sold on the market at a price above their issue price. It then parked its remaining Blue Arrow shares, placing just under 5 percent of each (because 5 percent would have required disclosure) in its corporate advisory department. Another block was placed with County NatWest Securities, and a third with Phillips & Drew under a profit and loss sharing arrangement.

Officials in CNW rationalized that because the shares were acquired in the course of a market-making business, the share parking did not have to be disclosed pursuant to Section 209 of the Companies Act. Section 209 allows market makers' holdings to be exempt from a group's disclosure requirements if they are held in the normal course of business.[361] This was a very tenuous legal argument, for Blue Arrow stock had been parked in order to disguise the failure of the underwriting issue. The Bank of England had been informed in August of the amount of shares underwritten by CNW. On September 30, 1987, the Bank was misled when a CNW representative stated that CNW had taken "double and treble" legal advice as to the bank's legal position.

To maintain Blue Arrow's share price, on 1 October several officials of CNW purchased between five hundred and one thousand shares each. This was permissible under CNW internal procedures. However, the executives were in possession of the price-sensitive, nonpublic information that Blue Arrow was about to appoint a new chief executive. CNW officials had second thoughts and told the executives to unwind the purchases. Thereafter,

---

million pound bid for Manpower through a new stock issue. The tender offer and rights issue was particularly important to CNW and its parents, because it would demonstrate that CNW was a major player in merchant banking. NatWest provided an £837 million bridge loan. Dept. Trade & Industry, County NatWest Rpt. (1989) *excerpted in Damning Chronicle of the Failure of a Huge City Deal,* FIN. TIMES, July, 21, 1989, at 10, col. 1; Fleet, *The Path of Blue Arrow Affair Targets Post Big Bang Banking,* THE TIMES (London), July 22, 1988, at 19, col. 5; *County Natwest: Anatomy of a Cover-up,* ECONOMIST 78, (Jan. 28, 1969).

361. Companies Act, 1985, ch. 6, § 209.

CNW purchased options to hedge its large holding. The market was unaware that so much Blue Arrow stock was held by CNW, a fact which, if known, would have depressed the price of the options and the stock.

On October 2, Phillips & Drew placed a tombstone advertisement in the *Financial Times* announcing that it had successfully placed shares not taken up by existing shareholders at a premium. At best, this was a misleading statement because CNW and Phillips & Drew had retained seventy-seven thousand shares because they couldn't sell them. The whole affair might have remained undetected, if not for the market break of October 19, 1987, which halved the price of Blue Arrow shares and left CNW with a potential £ 80 million pound loss. Such a loss could not be concealed.

In December, the NatWest board was informed of the entire sequence of events, because CNW was seeking an £80 million pound injection of capital from its parent. In that month, CNW made a public announcement of its holdings in Blue Arrow, but did not disclose its Blue Arrow stock held by agreement with Phillips & Drew. On February 23, 1988, CNW's chairman and chief executive resigned, as CNW reported a loss of £116. Three days later, NatWest launched an internal inquiry that was transmitted to the Bank of England, which then reported the problems to the DTI.

The DTI inquiry, published in July 1989, concluded that the market had been misled, that provisions of the Companies Acts had not been complied with, and that there had been no justification for what had happened. The report blamed the corporate finance departments of Phillips & Drew, CNW, and NatWest because in conducting the internal inquiry the bank never asked the proper questions. The report criticized three executive directors at NatWest for their part in the muddled internal investigation. None had the experience to examine critically what CNW executives told them, and they accepted too readily what they were told. The DTI report was passed on to the Bank of England and the SFO.[362]

The Bank of England wanted a proper response from NatWest, which it very shortly received. The Bank was furious that it had been misled. It responded by sending letters questioning whether some of the individuals involved were fit and proper persons to be involved in banking. That ended a number of City careers. The Bank has the power to blacklist individuals it feels are not "fit and proper."[363]

---

362. Department of Trade and Industry, County NatWest Limited/County NatWest Securities Limited (1989). For an account of the Blue Arrow affair and summaries of the report, *see* FIN. TIMES, July 21, 1989 at 10, col. 1. A series of articles in the ECONOMIST first brought the Blue Arrow affair to light. *See With a Little Help from NatWest's Friends,* ECONOMIST, Jan. 7, 1989 at 65; *County NatWest: Anatomy of a Cover-up,* ECONOMIST, Jan. 28, 1989, at 78; *The Tarnishing of NatWest,* ECONOMIST, Jan. 28, 1989 at 14.

363. *Top Charterhouse Man Goes in Blue Arrow Affair,* THE TIMES (London), Aug. 3, 1989 at 21, col. 2.

In the aftermath of the Blue Arrow affair, the chairman and three directors of National Westminster's board resigned, as did several of the principle players involved in the deception. The chairman of NatWest, Lord Boardman, stepped down a few months before his retirement and was replaced by Lord Alexander, the forceful head of the Takeover Panel and the first NatWest head without a banking background. Although the directors were not involved in the Blue Arrow scheme, they had not inquired with sufficient diligence when the scheme was uncovered within the bank, and their conduct had fallen below what was expected of responsible executives.

The Bank of England forced the resignation of Jonathan Cohen as vice-chairman of Charterhouse Bank. Cohen, who had been chief executive of CNW during the Blue Arrow underwriting, and had been cleared of wrong-doing by the DTI inspectors. The Securities Association brought disciplinary action against twenty-four individuals named in the DTI report and others. Such action could have led to a finding that the individuals involved were not fit and proper, and to the discipline of the firms that those named are now associated with, and of CNW and Phillips & Drew.[364] Prior to such a determination, most of the principals resigned or were forced out of their positions.

The SFO brought criminal indictments against CNW, Phillips & Drew, and eleven individuals, some of whom had been exonerated in the DTI report. NatWest and Phillips & Drew later offered compensation to investors who had purchased shares after the announcement of the "successful" placement and before October 26, 1987 when the shares sank to their lowest price. Most purchasers had been institutions. Four of the Blue Arrow Defendants were convicted and received suspended sentences after a trial lasting over one year. The total cost of the Blue Arrow affair for all parties is estimated to be £35 million and still increasing. After the verdicts the DTI reopened its inquiry to investigate the roles of NatWest senior management in the affair.[365]

The scope of the deception explains the rapidity of the response by the Bank of England and The Securities Association. Clearly, self-regulation did not work. Unknown is whether the Blue Arrow affair reflects normal business practice in the City or it was atypical, an example of financial con-

---

364. Feltham, *TSA Considers Action Against 24 in County NatWest Affair*, FIN. TIMES, July 22, 1989, at 17, col. 2. UBS Phillips & Drew was ordered by TSA to introduce broad changes in the way it ran its Compliance Department. Waters, *Changes Demanded at UBS Phillips & Drew*, FIN. TIMES, Nov. 15, 1989 at 20, col. 5.

365. Bennett & Narbrough, *NatWest Offer of 30m Over Blue Arrow*, THE TIMES (London), Feb. 15, 1990 at 25, col. 2. Mason, *Blue Arrow jury convicts four*, FIN. TIMES, Feb. 16, 1992 at 1. Mason, *Record saga ends with shrugs and resigned smiles*, FIN. TIMES, Feb. 16, 1992 at 5. *DTI reopens inquiry into Blue Arrow*, FIN. TIMES, Mar. 13, 1992 at 6.

glomeration gone awry. Was Blue Arrow a demonstration of the size and complexity of an institution exceeding the ability of managers to control it? The board of directors may not be focused sufficiently to monitor the activities of a diffuse financial empire. Before Blue Arrow, NatWest had the reputation as Britain's best managed bank.[366] If compliance and monitoring procedures were inadequate there, what were they like at other firms? Self-regulation requires effective compliance procedures even in times of a bear market. Bryan Gould, then Labor Party spokesman for trade and industry, said that the Bank of England was too close to the people it regulated and too slow and soft in acting. "The raised eyebrow is no longer enough to deal with the old boys and the fly boys."[367]

Gould is incorrect. While there was delay in uncovering the wrongdoing, and the self-regulatory concept has been questioned because NatWest seemed more concerned with dampening a spreading fire than with getting to the truth, the public denunciation of NatWest was unparalleled. Formerly, if a DTI report had been commissioned, it would have taken years to complete. Disciplinary action would have been meted out quietly, and only those in the City establishment would have known about it. " ... [A]ny dirty linen would have been quietly bleached. Not now ... the dirty linen ... was hung up for all to see."[368]

The impact of Blue Arrow goes beyond the careers of those destroyed or even the reputation of National Westminster Bank. It reaches to the very heart of the concept of self-regulation. Given the relatively blasé attitude toward stretching and ignoring the rules, one is left with the feeling that such practices uncovered in Blue Arrow are widespread. If evasion of the rules of the Companies Acts and the Stock Exchange are a matter of course, the new regime is based upon a very flawed premise. The inefficiency of internal controls, the willingness of compliance officers to turn the other way when large amounts of money are involved, and the ineffectiveness of internal investigations are all profoundly disturbing. The after-the-fact purge of the participants by the Bank of England and The Securities Association cannot hide the fact that something is seriously awry. Blue Arrow undermines some of the rationale behind the mergers of banks and other financial services businesses.

Blue Arrow also revealed differences between the securities and banking businesses and how securities subsidiaries can pose new risks to their banking parents. Whereas traditional banking has an orderliness and predictability in earnings and risk, this is absent in the securities business, which

366. Riley, *The High Price of Banking Error*, FIN. TIMES, July 27, 1989 at 20, col. 3.
367. *Labour Attacks City Self-regulation*, FIN. TIMES, Jul. 27, 1989 at 8, col. 5.
368. *The City After County*, ECONOMIST, July 29, 1989 at 17.

may not be understood by banking regulators. The difference in experience and approach to securities risk and the separation of securities from banking regulation is in sharp contrast to conventional European regulation where banks have long been engaged in the securities business.[369]

One of the fundamental beliefs of self-regulation is that the spirit as well as the letter of the rules must be followed. In Blue Arrow, the only concern was whether the action taken was legal, or if not, whether a technical legal argument could be made in favor of it. For all brokers, the willingness to cut corners in the face of financial loss is tempting in the difficult times of the post-October 1987 environment. If other firms facing losses engage in similar practices, the future of the self-regulatory concept looks bleak indeed.[370]

However, the Blue Arrow affair, repeated insider dealing scandals, and increased investigation of market manipulation may indicate not that fraud is increasing, but that detection is better. While the framework of investor protection has introduced new rules to reflect new financial patterns, they have been grafted onto norms of behavior that no longer exist, and perhaps cannot, given the new financial realities.

Integrated financial services firms require more capital to conduct business, and there are substantial costs to comply with the self-regulatory system. It is at the firm level where effective self-regulatory monitoring and enforcement must commence. In a period of contracting business when even well-run firms have difficulty turning a profit, the pressures to cut corners are irresistible.[371] It may well be that the norms upon which self-regulation is grounded reflect a financial environment that no longer exists. Can we expect the modern firm, bound by a complex system of rules, to go beyond the letter of the law or to live up to the aspirations of self-regulatory principles?

Conclusions

Compared to the English structure of enforcement, the American approach is centralized, yet flexible, unified, and efficient. The success of the

---

369. Lascelles, *Order in the Marketplace*, FIN. TIMES, Sept. 25, 1989 at 35, col. 3.

370. *The Market Was Misled*, FIN. TIMES, July 21, 1989 at 20, col. 1; Fleet, *The Path of Blue Arrow Affair Targets Post Big Bang Banking*, THE TIMES (London), July 22, 1989 at 19, col. 3; Waters, *Eleven Face Charges in UK over Blue Arrow Affair*, FIN. TIMES, Nov. 10, 1989 at 1, col. 8.

371. The market break in October 1987 ended a five-year bull market in securities in the United Kingdom, the consequences of which were felt years later. In 1989 brokers commissions ran at an annual rate of £650 million, but estimated costs for equity operations were £1 billion. This led to firms withdrawing from certain markets and to widespread layoffs. *See Shrinking to Fit*, ECONOMIST, Nov. 25, 1989 at 86.

SEC's enforcement efforts is due to its centralized enforcement structure combined with substantial in-house capabilities, flexible remedies that increase prosecutorial choice, and good coordination with criminal agencies. Additionally, the SEC has a reputation for vigorous and effective investigation and prosecution that has embellished its reputation among the public and contributed to the creation of an esprit de corps within. This in turn has made recruitment easier. The system of continuous disclosure and review by the SEC and the investment community deters material omissions and misstatements in corporate documents. The Commission's accordion-like powers, which range from a request for information to referral to the Department of Justice for criminal prosecution, make it an extremely effective enforcement agency. With a staff of 2,420 and a budget of $225.8 million in 1992, it is one of the smallest administrative agencies. Each year it returns more to the U.S. Treasury through its fees and fines than it receives in appreciations.[372]

Many of the SEC's enforcement remedies are similar to those available under the Financial Services Act and other legislation. The difference is that the SEC's enforcement efforts are much more coordinated. SEC enforcement of the securities laws has waxed and waned over its history. There has been a recent movement to increase SEC powers.[373] As enforcement problems have become more complex and international, the SEC has been at the forefront of law enforcement, setting a standard that other nations are just starting to follow and encouraging multilateral cooperation.[374] English enforcement of securities violations is not of the same caliber.

More important than its statutory powers has been the SEC's enforcement tradition, its reputation for effectiveness, and the enthusiasm, even prosecutorial zeal, of its attorneys. Unlike the ramshackle British structure, enforcement efforts are centralized and coordinated. Locating investigation and enforcement completely within the SEC is a more effective way to conduct investigations. Within the Division of Enforcement is a mix of career employees and young attorneys. Those who do not remain for the du-

---

372. *Breedon Asks for $24 Million Budget Increase, 11 Percent over 1992,* 24 SEC. REG. & L. REP. (BNA) 375 (Mar. 20, 1992). In 1992 the SEC estimates it will collect $311 million in fees equivalent to 138% of the agency's funding. Personnel figures are as of April 3, 1992 and obtained by telephone from the Personnel Office, Securities and Exchange Commission, April 15, 1992.

373. The Securities Enforcement and Penny Stock Reform Act of 1990, Pub. L. 101–424, 104 Stat. 931 (codified in scattered sections of 15 U.S.C.) permits the SEC to bypass the federal courts and use the administrative process to levy monetary penalties against SEC-regulated persons (up to $100 thousand) and entities (up to $500 thousand) if securities laws are violated. Individuals who violate those laws may be suspended. *See* Ruder, *Securities and Exchange Commission Enforcement Practices,* 85 N.W.U.L. REV. 607 (1991).

374. *See generally* Bornstein & Dugger, *supra* note 236.

ration of their professional careers work for the SEC for three to four years and then may move to a law firm with a large securities practice. Although the "revolving door" between industry and government service has been criticized, it does imbue attorneys for the regulated with the norms and expectations of the SEC, which assists compliance and self-regulation when these lawyers work in the industry.

Another strength is the continuous disclosure system required of corporations, which creates an ongoing informal dialogue with the SEC. For instance, under the proxy rules, a corporation must file its proposed proxy statement with the SEC. The corporation has the right to distribute the information to its shareholders ten days after it has been filed with the SEC.[375] In fact, the corporation will wait for the SEC to approve. Such informality has been a hallmark of SEC procedures. It is a powerful, yet flexible tool of enforcement.

In contrast to the American experience, British securities enforcement has been marked by overlapping authority and a lack of coordination.[376] Ironically, when U. K. securities enforcement was the preserve of the Stock Exchange, informal regulation was the norm. In the words of a senior official at The Securities Association: "club rules were utilized which were very effective among members." Thus, if a member firm could not meet the Stock Exchange's capital requirements, there would be informal inquiries—a telephone call—and the firm would have time to get back in line. There was no public notice, and enforcement was flexible and quick. Will the new SIB rules offer sufficient flexibility for lower-level enforcement? A literal reading of the rules suggests that such flexibility may no longer be available to enforcers. For many years the Takeover Panel operated informally. At this point, the English system seems to have lost its informality, but has yet to replace it with something more efficient. So long as securities enforcement is spread over many competing agencies with their own often different priorities, prosecution of financial misdealing in the United Kingdom will not approach the SEC's effectiveness.

Effective enforcement is the bedrock of an investor protection framework. The investigatory and prosecutorial structure has not eliminated in-

---

375. Securities Exchange Act, rule 14a-5, 17 C.F.R. § 240.14a-5.

376. In 1991 officials of the London Futures and Options Exchange (FOX), a recognized investment exchange, attempted to shore up an ailing property-futures market and trading in other commodities by creating false trades to give the impression of increased volume. Even after evidence of the scandal came out, the SIB was unable to conduct the investigation because under the FSA although the SIB could authorize FOX, it did not have the power to conduct the investigation it. Bray, *Scandal Spotlights U.K. Exchange's Ills*, WALL ST. J, Oct. 22, 1991 at A13D, col. 1; Waters, *London Fox probe widens*, FIN. TIMES Oct. 10, 1991 at 22, col.2. The SFA became the disciplining body as most of those responsible for the market fixing were members of that SRO.

sider dealing nor has it created an aura of effectiveness. Deregulation of industry boundaries partly contributed to enforcement problems because multifunctional securities firms created informational problems which "Chinese walls" in practice do not resolve adequately.[377]

The failure to obtain convictions of alleged commercial and securities violators publicly demonstrates the greatest weakness in the new system: the muddled organizational structure of overlapping and competing agencies. Despite the lack of prosecutorial success, the capacity to uncover fraud and improper conduct has improved because of the increased reporting requirements and the transparency of the markets. The extensive monitoring and reporting requirements are designed to prevent fraud. They create more-effective early warning systems. To its great credit, the SIB has reacted swiftly and effectively to instances of wrongdoing.

The two greatest deficiencies in the U.K.'s enforcement regime are the number of bodies that must become involved to prosecute a violation and the lack of a trained staff to investigate and prosecute. The SROs do not have subpoena powers over third parties who are not members of their organizations. The DTI has shown itself to be completely overwhelmed by its enforcement responsibilities. As long as the police are separated from the SFO, and that office is unsure of the scope of its jurisdiction, it will remain just another layer in the enforcement bureaucracy.

Enforcement efforts will never improve until the duplication and overlap between enforcement bodies is replaced by a unification of the governmental investigatory and prosecutorial units and improved coordination develops between self-regulatory and governmental bodies.

Given the lack of resources for the prosecution of commercial crime, and the length of time and intensive usage of personnel required to build a case, the most cost-efficient approach to enforcement may be the best. That approach calls for centralization in one locus of *all* criminal functions from police investigations to prosecution.

Investigation and enforcement must become more professionalized and must turn away from the *ad hoc* appointment of investigators who lose invaluable time while undergoing recruitment, reference checks, and briefings on the details of a particular case. The SIB-SRO system lacks a reservoir of enforcement expertise. The system has not recruited individuals with prosecutorial mentality or experience.

There is a desperate need for a full-time cadre of mostly career employees to investigate and prosecute securities fraud. Professionalism creates a cumulative expertise which in itself leads to efficient and effective enforce-

---

377. *See* N. POSER, INTERNATIONAL SECURITIES REGULATION: LONDON'S BIG BANG AND THE WORLD SECURITIES MARKET § 3.5 (1990) (discussing conflicts of interest).

ment. Intra-SRO or RIE enforcement arms should also have career personnel. An enforcement tradition takes time. The use of career people and centralization of enforcement functions will also breed an esprit and zeal which has been the hallmark of American efforts.

The most sensible future role for the SIB may be as the government's compliance, investigative, and enforcement arm or as a separate, independent governmental agency. Enforcement should be apolitical. The SIB has acted swiftly and vigorously in the exercise of its investigatory powers. It should be solely responsible for the investigation and prosecution of commercial fraud and compliance with reporting requirements. It would still oversee the enforcement efforts of SROs and other authorized bodies who would refer matters to it for prosecution.

To fulfill these new responsibilities the SIB would have a staff of investigators, attorneys, and accountants that would handle cases of commercial fraud from start to finish. It should be awarded full subpoena powers. All enforcement duties should be removed from the DTI, including company law compliance.[378] Special courts should be created to handle sophisticated commercial fraud. This would allow judges involved in such cases to develop the expertise needed.

As an enforcement agency, the SIB should develop its own cadre of experts and should operate similar to the U.S. Department of Justice's white-collar crime units. A mixture of career and short-term employees should be developed. Agency esprit would follow which would nurture a prosecutional tradition. These recommendations require further legislative action, but the real hurdles would be the political minefields laid down by existing enforcement agencies ranging from the police to the DTI. Effective enforcement requires a whole new beginning.

The Insider Dealing Act should be amended to provide for civil remedies, a common recommendation, and also to define the nature of the wrong. A civil remedy would allow for more flexible, expeditious enforcement requiring a lower burden of proof. More specific definitions of the crime will deter some improper dealing and will stop the threats now facing the statute every time it is challenged in court. The jurisdiction of insider dealing cases should be moved to the High Court, which has greater experience in dealing with the sophisticated concepts involved.

Perhaps the most difficult task will be for SROs and other recognized bodies to change the business culture so as to develop new norms and pat-

---

378. In contrast to this suggestion, the Labor Party has proposed beefing up the scope of DTI authority and has hinted that the self-regulatory system would be changed to an SEC model. *Cf.* Atkins, *Labour Sets Out Plans to Curb Insider Deals*; *City Regulation*, FIN. TIMES, Dec. 14, 1990 at 8, col. 2.

terns of behavior that reflect the mandates of the investor protection system. Creating a new value system takes time. The decline in social and professional standards and sanctions predated and were a cause of the introduction of the investor protection system. One must doubt that the current framework will rise to the enforcement tasks of the future. Given its sources, the SIB necessarily will continue to expend undue energy overseeing a complicated system rather than rooting out abuses.

The internationalization of financial services and the growth of commercial fraud can be expected to continue. Unless the enforcement approach is changed, the next boom cycle in the financial markets will demonstrate the system's fatal weaknesses.

SIX

THE STRUCTURE OF
THE MARKETPLACE AFTER
THE BIG BANG

The Big Bang wrought a revolution. Yet like most upheavals, its course could be neither predicted nor controlled. In this chapter we examine the securities marketplace after the Big Bang. Perhaps the most permanent changes were technological as the Stock Exchange introduced a computerized marketplace. We first outline some market information and settlement developments. Then we look at the problems of trading after the Big Bang and the impact of the market break of 1987 on the securities industry and particularly on the Stock Exchange. Finally, we examine the challenge of 1992, the single internal market of the EC, on London's financial markets.

Technological Developments

Even more important than the deregulation of fixed commissions which led to the Big Bang have been technological developments that changed the nature of securities trading and settlement procedures and called into question the necessity of a central investment exchange. The Stock Exchange undertook to create a fully automated electronic marketplace for trading and settlement of international and domestic stocks, gilts, and bonds. Its purpose was to reduce trading costs to enable London to compete with other financial centers. The implementation of a completely computerized trading system, however, has been hindered by interest groups' public disputes over trading rules and approaches to settlement, skepticism over the cost and design of the systems, questions as to whether the Exchange should be the provider of the new services, and difficult market conditions including reduced trading volume, overcapacity, and decreased profitability.

The Stock Exchange Automated Quotations System

Unlike the New York and American Stock Exchanges which utilize an order-driven auction market, the Stock Exchange adopted an electronic, screen-based trading system: the Stock Exchange Automated Quotations System (SEAQ). SEAQ, which commenced operation on October 27, 1986, is similar to the National Association of Securities Dealers Automated Quotation (NASDAQ) system. By publishing price quotations over a system of electronically connected screens, SEAQ allows competing market makers to offer prices to agency brokers, other market makers, and investors.[1] Over ten thousand screens are located in subscribers' offices.[2]

The Exchange chose a screen-based system to accommodate eventual twenty-four-hour trading, promote greater price visibility and liquidity, and provide a structure around which the market could develop and expand.[3] Unlike an order-driven market, customers' orders are not transmitted to a central trading floor. A broker who has been instructed to buy or sell on behalf of a client accesses the current stock market price by typing the stock symbol on his desktop computer keyboard. Initially, screen-based trading was not expected to eliminate the Exchange's trading floor. Market makers were to have the choice of face-to-face trading or office trading by telephone onto the trading floor of the Exchange. Six months after the introduction of SEAQ, the Exchange announced it would close its floor to securities trading for lack of use.

The broker's screen displays the stock's previous closing price and updated prices quoted by market makers. A market maker is a member firm that holds itself out to the rest of the market and is willing to provide a firm price to buy or sell a particular stock. Market makers receive certain privileges such as exemption from the stamp tax on bargains and the ability to borrow stock. Market makers input price information via direct links to SEAQ from their firm's trading room. A broker dealing on his SEAQ screen selects the market maker who quotes the best price for his client's stock. He then telephones or faxes that firm and confirms the screen price. If the broker is satisfied with the best price, he executes the trade. The rationale of SEAQ complements the philosophy of free competition that furthered the

1. Barings and Schroders, *Blessed are the Middling Rich*, ECONOMIST, Nov. 26, 1988 at 90.

2. INTERNATIONAL STOCK EXCHANGE, 1987 Annual Report 12 (1987) [hereinafter 1987 ISE REPORT].

3. Poser, *Big Bang and the Financial Services Act as Seen Through American Eyes*, 14 BROOKLYN J. INT'L LAW, 317, 324 (1988).

Big Bang. Market makers compete with one another, and investors receive the lowest prices in a central marketplace because prices, volume of trading, and records of trades are transparent on the computer screens.[4]

SEAQ International

London has long been a center for trading in international securities, that is, shares issued by firms incorporated in a country other than that of the exchange on which they are traded. Over two-thirds of all shares traded outside their domiciles and 95 percent of international stock transactions within the EC occur in London. Nearly 50 percent of the value of turnover on the ISE in 1990 was from trades of foreign equities.[5] Introduced in 1985, SEAQ International provides an electronic display of international equity quotations from competing market makers. Trades are made by telephone. SEAQ International does not provide screen trade confirmation or a link to cross-border settlement systems.

Trading averaged £1.2 billion per day in 1990. The average transaction size was £150,000.[6] SEAQ International traded £147 billion of foreign se-

---

4. SEAQ operates at three levels. Level one displays the desk bid/offer price for most frequently traded stocks without the names of market makers. Level two provides more detailed information to all market users. It displays, in order of the best price, all market makers quoting prices for that stock, and whether he is offering to buy or sell. Level two also displays a stock's six previous trades and cumulative daily totals. Level three is available to registered market makers and gives them access to SEAQ, enabling them to insert bid and offer prices into the system. THOMAS, THE BIG BANG 107 (1986) [hereinafter THOMAS].

Stocks are grouped by liquidity. Originally, securities were grouped into four categories—alpha, beta, gamma, and delta—based upon frequency of trading. On January 14, 1991 this system of classifying stocks was replaced with one based upon normal market size (NMS), which is based on the value of customer turnover in the stock over the previous twelve months and is expressed as a number of shares. Each security is assigned to one of twelve NMS bands which range from 500 to 200,000 shares. International Stock Exchange, *Quality of Markets Update*, QUALITY MKTS. Q. REV. (Autumn 1990)at 8. Because a security's NMS is directly related to its liquidity in terms of the amount of customer turnover, NMS determines whether stocks have immediate, delayed, or no publication on SEAQ.

5. The value of turnover, rather than the number of shares traded, is used as the basis of comparison both within markets and between markets. In the first quarter of 1991 the percentage of domestic turnover increased. Figures for SEAQ International are from Worthington, *Global equity turnover: market comparisons*, 31 BANK ENG. Q. May 1991 at 241–249 [hereinafter *Global equity turnover*]. London is the most important center for international trading surpassing the combined volume of New York and Tokyo where cross border trades amount to 10% to 20% of volume. Waters, *A tune-up for City Trades*, FIN. TIMES, April 9, 1992 at 14, ed. 3.

6. ISE, *Market Quality Update*, QUALITY MKTS. Q. REV. Summer 1990 at 13. The larg-

curities in 1990, up from £85 billion in 1989 and £40 billion in 1988.[7] Over 750 "blue chip" stocks from twelve leading industrial nations are listed. Usually, these stocks are the major equities in their respective domestic markets. Slightly over 300 have firm quotes on the SEAQ screens that are provided by competing market makers. The other stocks have indicative price quotes.[8]

SEAQ International services an institutional market. Trades valued over £100,000 are common. The normal quotation on the SEAQ screen is equivalent to a trade valued between £50,000 and £100,000. Because of the typical size of the average transaction and the depth of the international equity market, stocks with firm quotes have relatively narrow "touches"—the difference in price between a market maker's offer to buy and sell the equity.[9] Transaction costs are kept lower on SEAQ International than on some domestic exchanges because of savings on commissions, turnover taxes, and stamp duties. Though European exchanges have introduced "little bangs," thus far there has been no impact on London's preeminence.

The SEAQ International service is distributed globally by several commercial vendors including ISE's TOPIC. Quotes are presented from competing market makers. Indicative quotes of the less actively traded stocks are displayed under the name of the market maker registered in that stock.[10] Settlement arrangements are determined by both parties at the time of the transaction. Trades are matched and confirmed by the Exchange's SEQUAL. The normal practice is to settle according to the procedures in the security's domestic market. Settlement is arranged by one of two European clearers, Euroclear or CEDEL.

---

est group of foreign stocks traded in 1990 was Japanese, accounting for 25% of turnover, followed by German shares, which accounted for approximately 23% of foreign equity turnover. American shares account for approximately 5%. *Global equity turnover, supra* note 5 at 247.

7. *Global equity turnover, supra* note 5 at 247. The figures are exaggerated as accurate data on foreign equity trading in London only became available in February 1990 with the full introduction of SEQUAL, the Stock Exchange's trade reporting and confirmation system for stocks quoted on SEAQ International. Since 1990, exchange members have been required to report all foreign equity trades in London whether the equities are quoted on SEAQ or not. Approximately 50% of trading of non-U.K. stocks is done via SEAQ International.

8. There are approximately 55 market makers on SEAQ International, representing the large global financial services firms, nearly 90% of which are non-U.K. owned. The average number of market makers per stock with a firm quote is 9.4. *The Evolution of the UK Equity Market: Assessment of the Recent Rule Changes*, QUALITY MKTS. Q. REV. Spring 1989 at 19, 24.

9. *Id.* at 26.

10. Where relevant, essential dealing information on particular settlement considerations, stamp duty, and registration is displayed on the screen.

In 1992 the Exchange will attempt to enhance SEAQ International so as to consolidate its preeminence in international trading volume. Domestic and international stocks will be traded together rather than separately.[11] Non-ISE member firms will be permitted to trade in securities listed on SEAQ International. This step would attempt a *fait accompli* in creating a European wholesale securities market. Doubtless other European exchanges will react to this effort. SEAQ International also will attempt to update its technology to include trade reporting and confirmation arrangements. Currently it is little more than an electronic bulletin board.

SEAQ International has been the clearest success of the Big Bang. Favorable economic conditions; the growing sophistication and increasing institutional nature of investors, which encouraged international portfolio diversification; the deregulation of capital flows; and technological innovation have eased cross-border trading.[12]

SEAQ Automatic Execution Facility

The SEAQ Automatic Execution Facility (SAEF) allows automatic execution of transactions in the most liquid stocks. Introduced in February 1989 after an eighteen-month delay and £4 million cost, SAEF currently handles orders up to one thousand shares from broker dealers direct to market makers. SAEF is operated by the Stock Exchange and permits buyers and sellers to trade directly off the screen in approximately two hundred companies. SAEF will be expanded to handle orders up to five thousand shares in the future and could handle up to fifty thousand transactions per day.[13] When a transaction is completed, SAEF reports the details of the

---

11. This would also resolve differences in transparency between the domestic and international markets. Details of large transactions of domestic securities had to be published within 90 minutes of the trade; smaller ones were published immediately. On SEAQ International, trades do not have to be published until the next day. Waters, *Making sure SEAQ stays at the centre of cross-border share trading*, FIN. TIMES, Nov. 8, 1991 at 29 [hereinafter *Making sure*]. The two standards of transparency have been changed. *See infra* p. 267.

12. *Global equity turnover, supra* note 5 at 247.

13. Bunker, *Electronic Stockmarket Takes a Leap Nearer*, FIN. TIMES, Feb. 13, 1989 at 8, col. 4 [hereinafter Bunker]. The Exchange hopes that SAEF will lower combined settlement costs by approximately £5 per trade. THOMAS, *supra* note 4 at 165. Market makers are required to subscribe to SAEF, but few firms apart from market makers have joined. Fleet, *Exchange Under Pressure as It Puts the Market in SAEF Hands*, THE TIMES (London) Feb. 11, 1989 at 19, col. 6. On its first day of operation SAEF executed only 140 trades compared to 30,000 for the market as a whole. Waters, *Stock Exchange Dealing Changes Come into Effect*, FIN. TIMES, Feb. 14, 1989 at 7, col. 1. The broker/dealer who subscribes to SAEF can key in an order. SAEF transmits the instructions to the Exchange's SEAQ screen-based price quotation system which identifies the market maker displaying the most

trade to the Stock Exchange, which then enters it into the overnight checking process and TALISMAN (Transfer Accounting Lodgement for Investors/Stock Management for Principals), the Exchange's settlement system. SAEF allows brokers to purchase or sell small blocks of shares for market makers automatically. If a market maker's price moves out of line with other market makers, it can protect itself by setting up stock positions or upper thresholds that establish the number of shares it will trade through SAEF. Once the order is complete, SAEF automatically transmits the details directly to the Exchange's overnight clearing process and TALISMAN settlement system.[14]

SAEF directly competes with two Exchange member firms, Kleinwort Benson Securities and Barclays De Zoete Wedd, which operate their own electronic trading systems, BEST and TRADE. Both were on-line prior to SAEF, and both guarantee to meet the best price available in the marketplace. Both quote more stocks than SAEF, currently handle trades up to five thousand shares, and are capable of trading fifty thousand share blocks. Kleinwort's BEST gives a broker the best price showing on SEAQ even if BEST is not itself showing that price.[15] TRADE is planning to publish research concerning its system and distribute it to its subscribers. By contrast, SAEF is a single-function system designed to execute a specific transaction at a specific price and then record it.[16] BEST and TRADE bypass the exchange and fragment its centrality as the place where all prices and transactions are visible to all traders. SAEF leaves the Stock Exchange open to charges that it has exploited its regulatory powers to enhance its commercial interests and compete with private enterprise .

---

competitive price. If the system finds several market makers all quoting the best price, SAEF will automatically rotate its order execution among them. The originator of the order receives immediate confirmation of the trade which is reported simultaneously to the market makers and to the Exchange for checking and settlement.

14. SAEF has not drawn the support expected. There are relatively few subscribers, and in a 1989 survey of Exchange members, approximately half felt that no further resources should be put into the product. Brokers can get the same or better prices from market makers over the telephone. SAEF reflects the conflicting roles of the new Stock Exchange.

15. An SAEF trade costs up to 75 pence per transaction, whereas the same trade on BEST or TRADE would be free of charge to subscribers. The private services allow interfacing between a broker/dealer and the systems database by giving a complete ninety-day history showing all transactions the broker has conducted with the system for a given client.

16. Barings and Schroders, *Blessed are the Middling Rich*, ECONOMIST, Nov. 26, 1989 at 90; Bunker, *Electronic stockmarket takes a leap nearer*, FIN. TIMES, Feb. 13, 1989 at 8, col. 1.

Teletexed Output of Price Information by Computer

Teletexed Output of Price Information by Computer (TOPIC) is the Exchange's private videotext service. It offers a wide range of financial information to a network of terminals including prices and volumes of shares of leading American securities, which are provided by NASDAQ. In the first year after the Big Bang, TOPIC handled seven million queries per day, compared to two million before the Big Bang.[17] Not only is the Exchange's role as a central marketplace under attack by duplicative screen systems, but its information services contend with commercial competitors who believe that these Exchange functions are incompatible with its regulatory duties and claim that the Exchange has abused its regulatory responsibilities to favor its commercial information business. Other information service organizations such as Reuters and Extel desire access to publish similar information.[18] These private competitors have claimed that the Exchange's regulatory responsibilities give it an unfair advantage over them. The Office of Fair Trading (OFT) has examined these charges.

The Exchange's commercial activities provide a means for dealing with increasing costs. Two-thirds of the Exchange's income in 1988 and 1989 came from providing settlement and information services. However, there is a conflict of interest between its regulatory responsibilities as a recognized investment exchange, which allows for prior access to price-sensitive information, and its position as a commercial purveyor of information similar to wholly commercial competitors.

In August 1989, the Exchange reacted to an OFT inquiry by allowing competitors such as Reuters to join TOPIC, thereby giving them access to information. This does not remove TOPIC's competitive advantage, as the Exchange still controls the timing of information dissemination. The Exchange's current plan is to separate the regulatory aspects of collecting company information, which is necessary to maintain an orderly stock market, from commercial news supplied to TOPIC subscribers. The Exchange intends to protect its regulatory news service from outside competition by fixing costs at a wholesale level.

---

17. Fleet, *Unhappy Returns for the City's Big Bang*, THE TIMES (London), Oct. 27, 1987 at 27, col. 7.

18. Waters, *Farewell to the City's Discrete Gentlemen*, FIN. TIMES, June 22, 1989 at 13, col. 4. Reuters, the international news and information firm, launched its own U.K. share information service, U.K. Equity Focus, which competes directly with TOPIC. Waters, *Bid for a share in a heated market*, FIN. TIMES, Oct. 14, 1991 at 10.

Clearing and Settlement Systems

Securities trading in the post-Big Bang era has been burdened by antiquated clearing and settlement systems. Clearing involves the management and administration of information and funds prior to settlement taking place. Settlement is the process which transfers ownership of securities from the seller to the buyer.[19] Settlement currently consists of the exchange of shares for consideration, registration of the shares in the new owner's name, and the physical transfer of the share certificates from the seller to the purchaser.

The root of the settlement problem has been the physical delivery of share certificates. Planning for the future centers upon abolishing the use of share certificates, a process known as "dematerialization." However, paperless settlement has been the holy grail of the 1980s and 1990s. The contours of the debate over the settlement system have been marred by political infighting between differing interest groups and by a failure to coordinate technical policy with cost-benefit considerations.

The Existing Clearing and Settlement System

When an investor sells his shares, he must send his share certificates plus a completed form to his broker. The broker then sends the shares and the form to the ISE Central Checking System, the main trade confirmation system for transactions in U.K. equities, gilts, and fixed-interest stocks. The checking system first validates the transaction's details entered by the two parties and "matches" the inputs. If the details agree, the transaction is confirmed and proceeds to the existing settlement system, TALISMAN.[20] TALISMAN then transfers certificates and information to the issuer's registrar who makes a journal entry recording the transfer. The purchaser must then send a form to his broker, who forwards it to the issuer's registrar. The company registrar then issues share certificates in the new buyer's name. Most basic transactions require three pieces of paper to six different locations.[21]

---

19. ISE, DICTIONARY OF FINANCIAL TERMS (n.d.). The terms are often interchanged, but some transactions, such as traded options, are cleared but not settled.

20. Essentially, TALISMAN matches buy and sell orders, or bargains. It provides bargain checking, transfer, and account clearing services to member firms for English and Irish securities and some Australian and South African equities. International Stock Exchange, *Equities Settlement Review*, QUALITY MKTS. Q. REV., Summer 1988 at 18–19; INTERNATIONAL STOCK EXCHANGE, 1989 ANNUAL REPORT, 1 (1989) [hereinafter 1989 ISE REPORT]. The system in 1987 handled an average of 40,000 bargains per day and has been upgraded periodically. Currently, it has a capacity of 60,000.

21. *London's Certificated Lunacy*, ECONOMIST, Mar. 11, 1988 at 75.

By contrast, settlement in the United States is partially dematerialized. While share certificates still exist they are usually held with a broker or in a "street name" by a nominee and remain there following a sale. In the United Kingdom there is fortnightly settlement, whereby share trades carried out within a given two-week period are settled all in one day. Settlement is normally due on account day, the sixth business day after the end of a two-week dealing period.[22] In contrast, the United States features five-day rolling settlement, whereby the settlement period is five business days after the trade.[23]

An immediate byproduct of the Big Bang was back-office problems caused by higher trading volume. In 1986 the average number of individual transactions in U.K. equities per day was under 20,000. For 1987 there were nearly 50,000 transactions per day, peaking with an average of 60,000 in July 1987. On October 21 and 22, 1987, over one hundred thousand transactions took place each day.[24] The increase in trading after the Big Bang led to a dramatic increase in unsettled bargains. An unsettled bargain is one where the seller has failed to deliver the physical stock by the settlement date. The bargain is unsettled until the securities are delivered. Unsettled trades after the Big Bang increased fourfold.[25] This backlog placed additional financial stress on firms.[26]

The decrease in turnover after the 1987 market break ended the settlement backlog, but the fundamental problems remain. If a customer fails to deliver the stock in time, a firm's ability to repay the stock may be affected. It may have sold stock not yet received on the basis of a previous purchase transaction. As a result, the firm will have to "borrow" stock from a money broker for a fee. This borrowed stock will have to be repaid. If the customer defaults, the broker will have to purchase the stock in the market and might

---

22. On account day, sellers of stock must have delivered their certificates and transfer documents. Settlement frequently occurs on the last date allowable or not at all.

23. The Group of Thirty, a think tank of former economic and financial policy makers, has recommended that by 1992, national securities settlement systems be subject to a common international standard with a target of settlement three days after a trade (T + 3). Waters, *Fundamental Questions*, FIN. TIMES, Nov. 12, 1991 at IV.

24. The average fell to 26,700 bargains in 1988. International Stock Exchange, *Equities Settlement Review*, QUALITY MKTS. Q. REV. Summer 1988 at 17, 19 [hereinafter *Equities Settlement Review*]. Volume improved in 1989. In the fourth quarter of 1990, volume averaged 29,342 contracts per day, but volume for the year was below 1989's.

25. Lohr, *London's Huge Back-Office Burden*, N.Y. TIMES, Aug. 17, 1987 at D1, col. 3. Nearly £10 billion of unsettled bargains occurred during the 1987 bull market. *London's share markets: outlook unsettled*, ECONOMIST, May 4, 1991 at 78.

26. One positive side effect of the inefficiencies of the settlement system was the increase in business of money brokers who lend stock to market makers because of late delivery or settlement.

have to pay a higher price.[27] Thus, inefficiencies in the settlement system increase transaction costs. The shorter the period between execution and settlement, the lower the risk of losses for the market maker due to price changes if it has to go into the market to obtain stock.[28] There seems to have been little foresight that settlement problems would increase. In the prelude to the Big Bang, firms emphasized hiring sales and trading people rather than upgrading the back office.

Aggravating the settlement problems were new patterns of trading: an increase in short-term "in and out" transactions, in contrast to the past where investors held onto their equities for a longer period. Additionally, the privatization of nationalized industries created millions of new small shareholders.[29]

Dematerialization should lessen the settlement backlog in periods of high volume and reduce transaction costs by ending the labor-intensive, back room paper shuffle. It will lower the number of bargains incomplete at the settlement date and lessen the need to borrow shares. Sometime in the halcyon dematerialized future, brokers will access price quotations from their desktop SEAQ screens and execute a trade with a market maker. The order will be electronically matched by SEQUEL, or the broker will execute orders directly from the screen through SAEF. Locked trades will be settled by TALISMAN, and confirmed transactions will be processed electronically. Unfortunately, the political interests of the present have hindered the introduction of such a system.[30]

---

27. *Equities Settlement Review, supra* note 24 at 19–20.

28. Clearing and settlement outlays are estimated to be £340 million yearly and account for nearly one-half of the total annual losses of securities houses dealing in British equities. *London's Certificated Lunacy*, ECONOMIST, Mar. 11, 1989 at 75.

29. At the same time, there was an increase in velocity of share transactions to 62%, whereas in 1984 the velocity was 35%. Velocity is the frequency in one year with which a share is traded. Velocity is measured by turnover divided by market valuation; i.e., number shares traded divided by total shares outstanding. In 1984 a share changed hands on the average of once every three years. After the Big Bang, it traded once every two years. *Market Quality Update*, QUALITY MKTS. Q. REV. Summer 1987 at 8. When the New York Stock Exchange deregulated fixed commissions in 1975, it took eight years for velocity to double. *Id.* at 10.

30. The Stock Exchange has introduced partial electronic settlement through SEPON and the Institutional Net Settlement (INS) service. SEPON is a central Stock Exchange electronic settlement system for market makers and is based upon a nominee system for shares. The INS service enables institutions to clear all payments for U.K. equities to and from member firms with a single net transfer of funds via the Exchange. The service was initiated in August 1988. 1989 ISE REPORT, *supra* note 20 at 22.

Transfer and Automatic Registration of Uncertified Stock

Planning for the paperless, electronic settlement system, Transfer and Automatic Registration of Uncertified Stock (TAURUS) commenced in 1983 and has undergone several versions, revisions, and postponements. TAURUS will phase out the use of share certificates. Settlement will occur through a computerized accounting system that will involve a central registry accessible by a computer. Ownership transfers from seller to buyer will be posted by the broker firm's operations staff by directly keying in the information through their terminal.[31] TAURUS was resisted at various times by share registrars, bank custodians, and smaller firms each of whom feared that the new system would either take away their lucrative business or be too expensive to implement. Listed companies feared that it would be difficult for them to identify their shareholders. The securities industry believed the banks' control of payment systems would give an advantage over independent brokers who will require bank guarantees to back purchases made through TAURUS.[32] Smaller firms that offered full services to private clients feared their clients' transactions would become more complicated and they would be unable to bear the additional costs of investing in TAURUS.[33]

There was also concern that intermediation would increase by permitting investment managers to trade among themselves and plug into TAURUS or bypass the Exchange completely.[34] Throughout the 1980s the internal politics of the Stock Exchange and its own inefficiencies led to a variety of committees, plans, and delays.[35] The first phase of TAURUS was scheduled for

---

31. Wolman, *TAURUS is a sign of troubled times to come*, FIN. TIMES, Feb. 6 1989 at 6, col. 4.

32. Waters, *Fundamental questions*, FIN. TIMES, Nov. 12, 1991 at IV, col. 1.

33. *See* Dobie, *Inside the City: Death of the traditional broker*, INDEPENDENT, May 20, 1991 at 21. Instead of share certificates there will be share statements and personal identity numbers. Five-day settlement will make bank-owned firms more attractive to private clients as they will more readily offer banking services for their clients.

34. Banks and large brokerage houses have their own financial messaging system, SWIFT, through which trade details are communicated. The largest institutional funds are developing their own international confirmation system. Confirmation is the link between the agreement of a transaction and settlement. This link could also be used for settlement purposes, thereby serving to bypass the Exchange completely. *See* Cohen, *Institutional investors flex their settlement muscles*, FIN. TIMES, Oct. 10, 1991 at 31.

35. Some observers felt a separate organization to develop settlement procedures would have introduced a new system much quicker and that the Stock Exchange was satisfied with the existing settlement system because it was a profit center. *London Stock Exchange, Unsettled Taurus*, ECONOMIST, Oct 26, 1991 at 98.

start-up on October 27, 1989, the third anniversary of the Big Bang, but the date has been deferred time and again. Though the government promised in 1990 to eliminate the stamp duty of 0.5 percent on share dealing, the largest transaction cost to institutional investors, after TAURUS was operative, it delayed in introducing the necessary legal reforms to allow paperless shares. Many participants have spent large sums building TAURUS systems.

After years of false starts, procrastination, rising costs, interest group conflicts, and technological and legal difficulties, TAURUS is now scheduled to commence in April 1993 at the earliest. The system will be phased in. The first step will be the elimination of share certificates and their replacement by electronically generated account statements. At first only the most actively traded securities will be dematerialized; that is, without paper share certificates. Less liquid securities will be added over the following two years. Initially, clearing and settlement will be the same but dematerialized. During this time, TAURUS will function along with TALISMAN, the existing settlement system, and INS (Institutional Net Settlement), which allows institutional investors to settle on a net basis with the Exchange rather than with each other. The second step will be the linkage of payment and stock clearing systems so that payment and share transfer occur at the same time.

TAURUS will be run by the Stock Exchange.[36] Participants in TAURUS, termed "TAURUS Account Controllers" (TACs) will include brokers, banks, institutional investors, custodians, and share registrars. They will be connected electronically to the Stock Exchange's computers and to each other. They will maintain accounts on the Exchange's computers which will show totals held by each participant and be available for book entry block transfers to other participating institutions. Instead of holding investors' share certificates, the account controllers will hold the investor's account statement.[37]

---

36. The ISE will issue a rule book for the system's users and will authorize the TAURUS Account Controllers (TACs), the organizations that will maintain the electronic record of share ownership. Existing custodians of shares, predominantly banks, will have the option of recording share ownership held in special TAURUS accounts or becoming commercial TACs and holding the accounts themselves. Brokerage houses and large fund managers may become TACs. Currently, 86% of all securities are held by three custodial banks, Lloyd's, National Westminster, and Barclays. The Stock Exchange will be accountable to the DTI. For a description of how TAURUS will work, *see* Heath, *TAURUS: Solution to Settlement*, FIN. TIMES, Nov. 7, 1991 at 7, col. 1.

37. Investors can choose who maintains their accounts: an account controller paid by the corporation or a commercial account controller, a broker, or a fund paid by the investor. Most private shareholders will stay with the corporation's account controllers. Waters, *The implications of paperless dealing*, FIN. TIMES, July 1, 1991 at 11.

TAURUS will differ from other certificateless systems by allowing direct access to the settlement facility instead of going through a custodian. Legal ownership of stock will be recorded in each company's register of shareholders. Beneficial entitlement will be recorded by TACs and duplicated in the control records of the Exchange. A concern of listed companies is that TAURUS will encourage the use of nominee names so that the corporation will not know the true owners of its stock.[38]

Though the Companies Act of 1989 provided the legal basis for the TAURUS system by removing the need for share certificates to be used to transfer title to stock,[39] the regulations to implement the provisions of the act were not laid before Parliament by the DTI until December 1991. Before a corporation's shares will be demateralized, three quarters of the shareholders must approve the change. Then shareholders will select who will hold their account record: the corporation's custodian or the brokerage firm. When 60 percent of the trading volume is paperless, rolling settlement will be T + 10, or ten days after the trading date. That will probably not occur until six months after TAURUS commences. T + 3 will be possible when 90 percent of trading volume is paperless, an estimated twelve to fifteen months after the start-up date. The estimated savings from using TAURUS over ten years is £230 million. The start-up costs have risen to £65 million.[40]

There will be no central registry or record of individual shareholders, although TACs' records will be duplicated in control records maintained by the Stock Exchange. Investors will be protected from fraud through TAURUS by a £100 million compensation plan that will pay up to £500,000 to private investors for losses. The compensation plan will be funded through a levy on members, insurance, and guaranteed financing. There will be a complaints commissioner and an appeal to the Financial Services Tribunal.

As difficult as agreement has been on a U.K. settlement system, the 1990s will bring efforts to harmonize international settlement. Currently each country's clearing and settlement system differs. Because international

---

38. This would enable corporate raiders to build up blocks of stock without detection. Under the system, shares will be held in two types of accounts, designated and pooled accounts. Shares in designated accounts will have the names of holders in the company registers, though they might be nominees. In the pooled accounts, the names will be given to the corporations only once per month. *Id.*

39. Companies Act, 1989 Ch. 40, § 207.

40. Rudnick, *Why* TAURUS *is a sign of hope for the custodians*, THE TIMES (London), Dec. 13, 1991 at 35, col. 1. *London Stock Exchange, Unsettled TAURUS*, ECONOMIST, Oct. 26, 1991 at 98. TAURUS will be paid for by an ad valorem charge on assets for the clients of account holders.

business is a small percentage of the trading on exchanges other than London, it has yet to come to the forefront of their concern. The current expense of settlement, estimated at £20 to £50 per bargain, makes resolution of the settlement issues crucial. But for all its difficulty and delay in implementation, TAURUS is but a giant first step.

The Marketplace: From the Big Bang to the Big Break

The Big Bang initiated a new era. In one giant step, English stockbroking moved from a sheltered backwater to the cutting edge of an electronically linked global financial services network. At first impression, the deregulation of the markets seemed a triumph of Thatcherism. In twelve months the securities industry had fundamentally transformed itself. An English industry, now competitive, was poised to retain its preeminent role in international finance.

The Markets After the Big Bang

The atmosphere immediately following the Big Bang was euphoric. Trading volume surged. SEAQ, the new computerized trading system, worked. Though a settlement backlog was troubling, it was expected to be a short-term problem until TAURUS came on-line. The weekly value of securities traded rose to £7.4 billion from £4.5 billion during the months immediately prior. The traded options market handled 50,000 contracts daily, 180 percent more than before October 1986. Monthly growth there exceeded nine percent. In the third quarter of 1986, 20,000 equity bargains were transacted daily. In the first nine months of 1987 the average was just under 59,000. The value of such turnover was £1.1 billion per day compared to £600 million in 1986.[41] As much business in common stocks was transacted in one month as was conducted in one year prior to 1983. Trading in non-British securities ran 70 percent higher. Nearly £25 billion in capital was raised through new issues brought to market including £9 billion from three privatizations compared to £12 billion the previous year.[42]

Stock prices reached historic peaks. However, they had been rising over a five-year bull market, increasing 262 percent in that period. From October

---

41. ISE, *Big Bang One Year On—Highlights and Achievements*, QUALITY MKTS. Q. REV. Autumn 1987 at 5, 9.

42. Goodison, *Big Bang anniversary: a year of revolution and growth*, THE TIMES (London), Oct. 27, 1987 AT 25, COL. 2; 1987 ISE REPORT, *supra* note 2 at 78.

1974 to September 1987, stock prices had risen 1,446 percent, the second-best performing market in the world during that period.[43] The market had risen because of positive economic news: an improvement in the economy, a growth of market liquidity assisted by the expansion of the institutional market, and the influx of foreign funds. Real GNP improved, interest rates and inflation had declined, and sterling stabilized. Relative to other markets, equities were inexpensive.[44] Still, the Big Bang provided a qualitative and quantitative impetus to longer-run trends.

As expected after the Big Bang, commission charges to institutions fell by almost 40 percent from pre-October 1986 levels. Private investors, however, often were charged the old rate and more. This assisted some smaller firms, as private investors shifted their accounts because they received better service. The decrease in commission rates eroded some firms' profits. Whereas the larger brokerage houses increased their market share,[45] many smaller firms that only executed trades and did not have a large number of private clients had difficulty. Market makers had problems too because many competed in the most widely traded stocks, thereby lowering spreads between bid price and offer price and making it difficult to earn reasonable returns. Some firms traded for their own account, a more profitable but riskier venture that tied up their capital.[46]

The gilts markets became even more competitive as American banks sought to capture a market share and lowered spreads between offers and bids to 0.03 percent on a £50 million transaction. In October 1986 there were 27 market makers in the United Kingdom with a turnover of £530 billion, compared to the American treasury bond market, which was twenty times larger with a turnover of $10 thousand billion per year with only 38 primary dealers. The international equities market was stronger, and commissions there were much higher. Trading in foreign shares was 70 percent higher than the previous years, and turnover reached £500 million per day.[47]

The increased volume and the success of the computerized trading system hid several sins. Future difficulties, which would become clear to all after the market break, were augured in the statistics of market trading. There was increased competition in trading, which was centered in larger firms. Competition in common stocks was focused among fewer market makers.

---

43. REPORT OF PRESIDENTIAL TASK FORCE ON MARKET MECHANISMS, I-5, 1988 [hereinafter PRESIDENTIAL REPORT].

44. *Id.* at I-5–6

45. Warburg by 30%

46. *Has Big Bang Knocked City Profits Flat?* ECONOMIST, Jan. 24, 1987 at 69.

47. *Id.*; Goodison, *Big Bang Anniversary: A Year of Revolution and Growth*, THE TIMES (London), Oct. 27, 1987 at 25, col. 2.

The top ten market makers accounted for 80 percent of all equity trading. The more liquid the stock, that is, the more frequently traded, the narrower was the difference between the best bid and offer prices advertised by market makers.[48] This was bound to cause problems for nonmarket-making brokerage houses.

Expansion had been focused on the front office rather than the back. A settlement backlog was not only due to volume. The productivity of British workers in the back rooms was inferior to their American counterparts, and the amount of computerization in clearing and settlement was low.[49] Even before the 1987 market break, it was clear that firms had overexpanded in preparation for the Big Bang and that trading could not generate sufficient profits. In September 1987, Shearson Lehman announced staff cutbacks. Others, too, began to scale back their operations. After the market break came wholesale retrenchment by firms who one year previously had expanded regardless of the expenditure. The ability to gain market share and the possibilities of growth in the U.K. market had been overestimated. Costs had been underestimated. Still, the first year following market deregulation seemed a great success. On October 19, 1987, one week shy of the Big Bang's first anniversary, came the market break that so altered the financial services landscape.

The October 1987 Market Break

From Monday, October 19 to Friday, October 23, 1987 the U.K. Financial Times/Stock Exchange (FT/SE) 100 Index, comparable to the Dow Jones Industrials, fell 22 percent in value. The crash not only ended a five-year bull market in common stocks, it shattered many of the assumptions underlying the Big Bang and revealed that the new regulatory system, a heavy expense in good times, was an albatross of fixed costs in a period of economic difficulty.

In London, as in most other major markets, stock prices had peaked in July and started eroding. Economic indicators caused the slippage. They included an unexpected deterioration in the balance of payments, an in-

---

48. From the spread between the offer and bid prices comes the market makers' profit. The number of bargains, not including transactions between market makers, transacted by investors directly with a market maker rather than through a broker declined, but the average value of each market maker's transaction with investors increased by one-third. Measured by value, direct transactions between investors and market makers accounted for half of all business. *Nice Market, Sorry About the Backlog*, ECONOMIST, Aug. 29, 1987 at 71.

49. Sterngold, *Shearson Is Expected to Lay Off 150 in London*, N.Y. TIMES, Sept. 14, 1987 at D6, col. 3.

crease in interest rates, and undersubscription of public offerings. Despite these developments the market rallied in September. On October 5, the FT/SE index price-to-earnings ratios reached a historic multiple of 19.2 with a yield of 2.9 percent.[50] No one was prepared for the enormity of the market break.

The New York markets had declined sharply during the week prior to the crash, particularly on Friday, October 16, which was abnormally quiet in London because of severe weather conditions. The London market fell 249.6 points on Monday, 10.1 percent of its value. This record was eclipsed on Tuesday by a 250.7-point decline. More than 2,000 stocks declined, while only 75 rose. Volume of 798 million shares was 250 percent greater than the previous year and 31 percent over the previous week. Although stocks in New York and Tokyo recovered somewhat over the next ten days, prices continued to decline in London, so that by the end of two weeks the comparative change in price of the stock indices declined 28.9 percent in London, declined 18.6 percent in New York, and 13.5 percent in Tokyo.[51] During the week of October 19, the volume of share transactions reached unprecedented levels. Intramarket turnover, transactions between market makers, which normally accounted for half of the total turnover, dropped to 40 percent. The spread between offer and bid tripled.

While the markets remained formally open throughout the week of October 19, SEAQ screens were overwhelmed. On Wednesday, October 20 the ISE was forced to stop computing the FT/SE 100 Index for approximately three hours, during which trading was halted on options and futures on the index.[52] During much of the week of October 19, the Exchange declared "fast markets." This meant that prices on SEAQ screens were indicative only and had to be confirmed prior to dealing with market makers.

During the week of the break, the market in international equities was swamped with sell orders. Volume soared as did average daily customer value and bargain size.[53] On October 19, SEAQ International screens became indicative only. Brokers could not get the "best price" if they could get any price at all. As most trading went to telephone, it often became impossible to reach market makers at all. There has been some controversy over the unanswered telephones.[54]

---

50. PRESIDENTIAL REPORT, *supra* note 43 at I-6–7.

51. This section is based on International Stock Exchange, *Survey of Markets*, QUALITY MKTS. Q. REV. Winter 1987/88, pp. 9–16 [hereinafter *Survey of Markets* 1987/88]. *See also* Staff of the SEC, STUDY at 11/8–11/9 1988 [hereinafter SEC Report].

52. SEC Report, *supra* note 61 at 11–9 n. 30

53. *Survey of Markets*, 1987/88, *supra* note 51 at 27–29.

54. *The Trials and Tribulations of Trading*, ECONOMIST, Nov. 14, 1987 at 83–84. There was controversy over the unanswered telephones. *See* Waters, *Market-Makers Not Ignoring*

By the end of 1987 the London equity market had fallen 26.3 percent from the level of October 14 compared to a 17.8 percent decline in New York and a 19.1 percent decline in Tokyo. The high proportion of overseas investors in the U.K. market, the reluctance of U.K. institutional investors to reenter the market after the crash, and the paucity of stock repurchase programs by corporations may have encouraged price volatility during the week.[55]

The New Financial Era

The market break signaled the beginning of a new, more disciplined, leaner era. Trading patterns changed, and volume and velocity declined. Daily turnover in domestic stocks declined almost one-half from £1.3 billion daily in September 1987. International trading declined by 20 percent. Spreads between offers to purchase and sell increased except for the most liquid stocks, where there was intensive competition and spreads were so narrow that profit making was difficult regardless of the market share. The market-making system was capital intensive, extremely competitive, and very unprofitable. The number of market makers declined, and some firms withdrew from market-making activities. Too many firms were fighting for shares in sluggish or shrinking markets. Retrenchment, reduced salaries, and layoffs became the norm.[56] Firms were frustrated by unfulfilled ambition, overcapacity, and unprofitable operations. They began paying the price for poor strategic planning and inexperience in many of the new markets into which they had rushed.

Fewer new issues came into the market. A scheduled offering for British Petroleum went forward. Underwriters were threatened with a £500 million pound loss, but the Bank of England guaranteed a floor at which it would buy up excess shares. Free competition had its limits. The government's privatization program was temporarily postponed. For the small investor, many of whom entered the market through the government's privatization program, the market crash brought a harsh reality: stock prices declined as well as increased.[57]

Phones, Says SE, FIN. TIMES, Oct. 23, 1987 at 2, col. 4. The ISE maintained that the 40% increase in transactions caused an overload of the international market, but a more reasonable explanation is that sell orders were so imbalanced and buyers so scarce, market makers simply withdrew from trading. Market makers claimed that they did not honor posted quotes because they could not change them fast enough.

55. Unlike the United States, the use of derivative products and index arbitrage was less developed and considered less influential in affecting prices.

56. Fallon, *City Market-Making Made Difficult*, THE TIMES (London), Dec. 13, 1987 at 53, col. 1.

57. Previously, investors who were able to purchase original issues of newly privatized

The new environment highlighted the difficulties of pre-Big Bang firm consolidations. There were clashes of cultures, traditions, and functions, such as between brokers and bankers or combining research, banking, and market-making firms. In 1988, ISE members lost £600 million in equity trading, traded options, and foreign shares, and gilts losses continued through 1990.[58] One would have to look at the declining nationalized industries such as coal and steel to find losses of that magnitude. The liquidity in the equities market declined to an annual £185 billion worth of customer business from £310 billion. In two years, nearly one-third of the capital in the gilts market was erased. The process whereby investors diversified portfolios into foreign securities was reversed.[59] Prior to the crash, 50 percent of trading was between market makers. This declined to 40 percent, which meant that commissions paid by customers rose to 60 percent. The size of the average commission increased as well.[60]

In 1988, even leading firms such as James Capel and Kleinwort Benson reported losses. Morgan Grenfell, a successful corporate finance and merchant bank, closed its securities arm, which was able to capture only a 3 percent market share and lost £40 million.[61] Other firms improved efficiencies and attempted to increase market share until the marketplace accelerated again. There was growing disillusionment by U.S. firms over their London operations. They began withdrawing from especially unprofitable markets and pruned overhead or narrowed their focus. The bear market demonstrated the low risk tolerance of banks for securities firms. Some of the most ambitious banks had the largest layoffs and biggest losses at their securities subsidiaries.[62]

---

companies could sell their stock for an immediate, and until October 19, automatic gain. These first-time investors became the largest block of sellers. Lohr, *Long Honeymoon Ends for Investors in Britain*, N.Y. TIMES, Oct. 22, 1987 at D17, col. 1.

58. *Blitz on City Profits*, ECONOMIST, Dec. 24, 1988 at 84. In 1990, firms lost an estimated £350 million. SECURITIES AND INVESTMENTS BOARD, 1990/91 ANNUAL REPORT 13 (1991). In 1991, firms moved into the black.

59. The percentage of business by overseas clients fell from 19.9% in 1987 to 14.6%. Foreign clients trading international shares fell to 47.5% of all transactions, down from 55%. Trading in American depository receipts, though recovering slightly, did not reach pre-October 1987 levels. *Id.*

60. In 1988 the stock market index rose by only 2%, compared to 12.4% in the United States and 34% in Tokyo. Fuerbringer, *Foreign Stock Gains Outpaced U.S. in 1988*, N.Y. TIMES, Jan. 2, 1989 at 52, col. 1. While the volume increased in part of 1989, profits did not recover. In 1990, volume declined. In 1991, it rose.

61. *Morgan Grenfell Bows Out*, ECONOMIST, Dec. 10, 1988 at 84. After pulling out of gilts and securities, Morgan Grenfell increased its pretax profits by 50%.

62. No one did so poorly as the American banks. Chase Manhattan had purchased Laurie Millbank and Simon and Coates, second-level firms to begin with, that could not compete in the new marketplace. Even acquiring quality couldn't help some. Citicorp had the

Disaster wasn't the sole province of the American invasion. Phillips & Drew, the old-line English firm that was at one time a leading research house, had been purchased by the Union Bank of Switzerland in 1986. UBS tried to expand Phillips & Drew's trading capacity to make it a leading market maker. In February 1989, UBS announced it had lost over £115 million on its London securities business since April 1987. Phillips & Drew had lost £66 million in the year ending March 1988 and an additional £30 million in the next nine months. It was doubly hit by a $48 million loss in the market crash, $21.5 million of it coming from the firm's share of the Blue Arrow rights issue.[63] The firm had grown too fast in response to the Big Bang and had neither the management nor technology to succeed. Other losses came from disastrous settlement problems, the overall unprofitability of gilts trading, and speculation for its own account in the precrash market. Its overhead costs increased in 1989 when it moved into huge new offices.[64]

There were some successes. Warburg and Barclays, who attempted an integrated securities approach, had purchased the best firms available and had a clear strategy.[65] Long-established relationships were not severed by

---

greatest aspirations and perhaps the worse results. In the prelude to the Big Bang, Citicorp had purchased two reputable old firms, Scrimgeour Kempt Gee and Vickers Da Costa, for £140 million and merged them. It then attempted to impose the Citicorp culture on two disparate firms, called Citicorp Scrimgeour Vickers (CSV). This affected Scrimgeour's institutional analysis and led to defections. In 1987, Citicorp injected a further £40 million into its securities subsidiaries. By 1988, with losses mounting, the bank pulled out of the gilts market and reduced its Far Eastern securities business, where Vickers Da Costa had its strength and reputation. In 1989, CSV reduced its market making to only a few key stocks and in the beginning of 1990, Citibank admitted failure and withdrew CSV from the securities business. *A Phoenix for Citicorp?* ECONOMIST, Feb. 4, 1989 at 76; Lascelles and Waters, *Insecurity dogs securities business*, FIN. TIMES, Jan. 4, 1990 at 8, col. 1.

One of the first American banks to purchase an English securities firm was Security Pacific which obtained a 29.9% share of Hoare Govett in 1982 and later acquired the whole company at an inflated price. In 1989 the bank sold its broking subsidiary to Hoare Govett's managers in a management buyout in which it would have a minority role. Brewerton, *Security Pacific Ready to Blaze The Trail Again*, THE TIMES (London), Oct. 31, 1989 at 33, col. 3. Unprofitability was not the sole reason for the sale. Under Federal Reserve regulation K, 12 C.F.R. Part 211 (1979), the overseas securities subsidiaries of American banks are prohibited from holding equity stakes of more than $15 million in a single company, which limits underwriting efforts. There is also a 20% limit in the outstanding equity that an overseas subsidiary can hold in one company. These strictures affected future possibilities of profitability.

63. *See* Chapter 5, pp. 219–225.

64. *Plunge from the Top*, THE TIMES (London), Feb. 19, 1989 at D3, col. 1; Philips and Drew, *No More Secrets*, ECONOMIST, Feb. 18, 1989 at 82; Lascalles, *UBS Announces 115 Million Pound Loss on Its London Securities Business*, FIN. TIMES, Feb. 14, 1989 at 1, col. 3.

65. The financial writer, John Plender, has remarked that success is relative. Warburg's

the Big Bang. Corporations desired a separation of broking and merchant banking.[66] Traditional merchant banks such as Kleinwort Benson and Hill Samuel survived the Big Bang and the big break quite well, at least in their traditional functions.

Independently owned firms such as the merchant banks Baring Brothers, Schroeders, and Casanove shunned the fashions of the merger movement and remained the same quality houses as before. The wisdom of their approach was revealed in their balance sheets as they did not have to expend capital to support money-losing operations. In 1991 the SIB questioned whether integrated firms, a by-product of the Big Bang, should be permitted.[67] While stock prices subsequently rebounded and in 1991 firms were profitable, the securities industry has never recovered from the crash.

The Markets

Equities

In 1991, Stock Exchange member firms had combined profits of £286,000,000 compared to a loss of £353,000,000 in 1990. However, the return on capital invested in the market was just over 10%, a lower figure than obtainable by investing in tax free gilts. Turnover increased by 14% and broking commissions rose by 19% to £1 billion over the previous year.[68]

Persistent problems remained. The trading system was expensive and costs were hard to control. Though the City complained most loudly about the costs of regulation, transactional and fixed costs, and the costs of trading remained high. Even well-run, lean firms had difficulty making money. Another problem was excess capacity, estimated at 30 percent, for the vol-

had problems in the United States and Japan, and for BZW revenues may not be worth the cost.

66. The corporate banker advises companies on stock market trends and fixes the price of a new share or tender offer. In the United States this would be done by an investment banker. Merchant bankers lend money, provide advice on takeovers, and offer general financial advice. *The Surprising Survival of the City's Old Guard*, ECONOMIST, Feb. 13, 1988 at 73.

67. For Lazard, *see Artful Dodgers*, ECONOMIST, Oct. 3, 1987 at 91; for Barings and Schroders, *see Blessed Are the Middling Rich*, ECONOMIST, Nov. 26, 1988 at 90; for Warburg, *see The Ghost of Warburg Yet-to-Come*, ECONOMIST, July 22, 1989 at 72; Waters, *UK Watchdog Casts Doubt on Future of Integrated Firms*, FIN. TIMES, Dec. 12, 1991 at 17, col. 2.

68. Waters, *UK brokers see return to profit in 1991*, FIN. TIMES, May 28, 1992 at 9, col. 1 *citing* STOCK EXCHANGE Q., Jan.-Mar. 1992.

ume of trading.[69] The new market-making structure was supposed to encourage competition, and it did with a vengeance. The underside of increased price competition was that the industry could not generate
sufficient income to cover costs.

Too many market makers remained. Though some firms withdrew from
market making and trading, the number remaining bore no relation to the
financial reality of the equities market.[70] Firms' strategies seemed to be to
hang on until competitors withdrew. At that point, surviving firms would
increase market share and achieve profitability in an oligopolistic future.

In the meantime, private investors waited on the sidelines. The securities
industry shrank as layoffs continued. The total City workforce has been estimated at 375,000. Total job losses in the City have been estimated at
40,000, with employment in the securities industry falling from 40,000 in
October 1987 to 35,000 at the end of 1989. Of the 5,000 jobs lost, 1,200
were estimated to be brokers.[71] Other markets faced difficulties as well.

Gilts

One of the most significant changes of the Big Bang was a restructured
gilts or governmental securities market. Central to the new gilts marketplace was an enlarged community of market makers, money brokers, and
the emergence of Interdealer Brokers (IDBs) who ensured that liquidity was
maintained within the market.[72] Prior to the Big Bang, gilts brokers had
only single capacity. Two jobbers were dominant, and twelve brokers collec-
tively controlled about 90 percent of the business by value with a restricted
client base. There were minimum commissions for all gilts with a maturity
over five years. Price spreads were relatively broad. Short gilts, securities
which expired within a short period of time, were similar to money market
instruments and were heavily traded by banks. Longer-dated gilts were investment vehicles and were traded by pension funds and insurance
companies.[73]

The essential change introduced in the new market was that in place of
the single-capacity structure the market-making function was undertaken
by dual-capacity gilt-edged market makers (GEMMs). Twenty-seven firms

---

69. Waters, *The City's Policemen Contemplate a Busier Beat*, FIN. TIMES, Jan. 9, 1990
at 7.

70. The number of market makers declined to 24 at the end of 1990 from 33 in 1986.

71. MacKay, *British Equities Firm Suit by ANZ*, N.Y. TIMES, Nov. 16, 1989 at 25, col.
8; Andres, *City Faces Further Reductions in Jobs*, N.Y. TIMES, Nov. 20, 1989 at 25, col. 2;
Shrinking to Fit, ECONOMIST, Nov. 25, 1989 at 86.

72. IDBs allow market makers to unwind positions anonymously with other market
makers by posting bids and offers for large amounts of stock on their dealing screens.

73. ISE, *The Gilt Market*, QUALITY MKTS. Q. REV. Summer 1987 at 16.

commenced operations as GEMMs. Many were foreign owned, having acquired existing brokers and jobbers in the prelude to the Big Bang. The new gilts market had five objectives: (1) liquidity in a continuous secondary market sufficient to ensure that investors could readily buy and sell and the government's funding aims could be achieved; (2) competition among market firms to maintain market efficiency and act as a safeguard for investor protection; (3) opportunities for international firms to participate in the market; (4) provision for regulatory and prudential supervision of market firms, including appropriate requirements of their capital adequacy; and (5) application of computer and information technology where this could improve functioning of the market.[74]

The increase in participants expanded the capitalization of the gilts market from £100 million prior to the Big Bang to £595 million. Immediately thereafter, three new Stock Exchange money brokers (SEMBs) joined the six existing SEMBs to provide a stock-lending and financing service for the GEMMs. Six IDBs began operations in gilts to provide anonymous dealing services for the GEMMs.[75]

Gilts prices are not transparent. Mid-prices of gilts issues are displayed on the Exchange's view data system, TOPIC. The IDBs set prices for the secondary market. Market makers display prices of new issues on SEAQ.[76] Daily turnover exploded after the Big Bang, rising to £6 billion per day from £1.5 billion.[77] Turnover increased and market liquidity expanded because of the development of market makers and IDBs.[78] Average turnover

---

74. *The gilts edged market since Big Bang,* 29 BANK ENG. Q. BULL. Feb. 1989 at 49 [hereinafter *The gilt-edged market since Big Bang*].

75. Market makers may acquire an unbalanced mix in their gilts portfolios which they desire to unwind. Anonymity in trading is needed to disguise to other market makers what position they are trying to correct. The obligation of the GEMMs is to make a market in the full list of gilt-edged securities across the maturity range. This obligation has been supervised by the Bank of England. The Stock Exchange regulates the marketplace itself. *Id.* at 50–51.

76. Prices of trades are published the following day in SEDOL. *Gilts, A sweat, but no bath,* ECONOMIST, Apr. 11, 1987 at 78. The IDBs do not themselves take positions but merely arrange trades. Legally, however, the IDB is a principal buying from one GEMM and selling to another. He earns his profit from a small commission, typically 1/128 percent of the transaction. ISE, *The Gilt Market* QUALITY MKTS. Q. REV. Summer 1987 at 17. The IDBs also provide an electronic notice board where market makers advertise their offerings. The wholesale market now trades off the exchange floor over a telephone network with direct lines to major clients. Computerization has caused much of the expense of entering the gilts market. A central gilts office provides computerized book-entry transfer facilities and assured-payments arrangements for market participants. *The gilt-edged market since Big Bang, supra* note 74 at 49.

77. 1987 ISE REPORT, *supra* note 2 at 9.

78. Goodison, *Big Bang anniversary: a year of revolution and growth,* THE TIMES (London), Oct. 27, 1987 at 25, col. 2.

by value of transactions rose from £1.25 billion per day before the Big Bang to just under £4 billion per day in 1990.[79]

With increased turnover, market makers were profitable but not at a rate at which they could recover an estimated £50 million spent to enter the gilts market.[80] As with the equities markets, institutional investors gained. Before the Big Bang they had to pay a 0.1 percent commission on all transactions. In the wholesale market, the vast majority of customer business is now done without commission because it is conducted with market makers. This has benefited large traders who have taken advantage of the lowered transaction costs and increased execution efficiency. Dealing spreads halved.[81] Customer turnover was 65 percent higher than in the previous year, and including business between market makers and IDBs, volume trebled.[82]

The five years following the Big Bang have been a bleak period for dealers. Between 1986 and 1989, GEMMs' combined trading losses totalled £200 million. In 1990, market makers had a combined profit of £40 million, but profit margins were quite slim.[83] In the 1986 to 1990 period the number of market makers declined to eighteen and IDBs to three.[84] As GEMMs withdrew from the gilts market, the capital committed to the market has declined from £600 million to £400 million.[85]

From 1988 to 1990 the British government switched from its traditional role of borrowing in the gilt-edged market to one of repurchasing and repaying outstanding debt, becoming a net buyer of gilts. This further shrank the market and hindered liquidity. In 1991 it began issuing gilts to fund public sector borrowing requirements and could sell an estimated £25 billion in 1992.[86] GEMMs diversified into developing market-making func-

---

79. *The gilt-edged market: developments in 1990* 31 BANK OF ENG. Q. BULL., Feb. 1991 at 50 [hereinafter *The gilt-edged market: developments*].

80. *The gilt market sweats it out*, ECONOMIST, Jan. 16, 1988 at 71.

81. Dealing spreads are measured in ticks. A tick is one thirty-second of a pound. Spreads are two to four ticks for short- and long-term gilts. *The gilt edged market since Big Bang, supra* note 74 at 51.

82. *The gilt market sweats it out*, ECONOMIST, Jan. 16, 1988 at 71.

83. *The gilt-edged market: developments, supra* note 79 at 50.

84. Merrill Lynch, for example, withdrew from the gilts market in August 1989 after incurring $55 million in losses over three years. Waters, *Merrill Lynch quits U.K. gilts after £35m in losses*, FIN. TIMES, Aug. 16, 1989 at 1, col. 7. The number of GEMMs may increase as foreign institutions become market makers. The impetus is sterling's entry to the European Exchange Rate Mechanism (ERM). London, *Overseas queue forms to join gilts*, FIN. TIMES, Oct. 23, 1991 at 9, col. 5. Membership in ERM reduces perceived currency risk for overseas investors because sterling is linked to other currencies. This should increase gilt-edged stock's attractiveness and demand.

85. *The gilt-edged market: developments, supra* note 79 at 50.

86. The government issued £6.8 billion worth of securities in the first six months of 1991. Webb & Montagon, *Losing its lustre*, FIN. TIMES, Nov. 27, 1991 at 14, col. 3.

tions in nonfixed interest sterling securities and European Currency Unit denominated instruments. Other GEMMs have sought to widen their client base, to develop derivative products based on gilts, or to integrate more closely their gilt-edged and money market activities.[87] Though profitability has been restored to the market as a whole and rising gilt sales are foreseen, competition remains intense. If large international banks become GEMMs, some of the smaller U.K. market makers may not survive.[88]

Additionally, the structure of the gilts market has come under criticism on grounds that it is primitive by international standards. Specifically, gilts traders have suggested the introduction of a set calendar for gilt issuance; an end to withholding taxes when interest is paid; the use of Eurobond clearing houses to hold gilts, which would improve liquidity; and the establishment of a repurchase (or bond-lending) market in gilts, which would add liquidity to the market and offer an additional return to gilts holders who lent out their securities for short periods.[89] The Bank has particularly resisted the latter suggestion for fear it would reduce its regulatory authority.

Options

An option carries the right, if exercised, of entitling the holder of the option to deal in a security at an agreed price up to a specified date in the future.[90] Two types of options contracts have been transacted on the ISE: traditional options and traded options.[91] Traded options, which have only been traded on the Stock Exchange since 1987, are risk management tools, available only for the most liquid securities.[92] There are significant differ-

---

87. *The gilt-edged market since Big Bang, supra* note 74 at 55.

88. In 1990 the combined share of the top six GEMMs was a little above 60% of the market. The bottom six firms have a 10% market share. *The gilt-edged market: developments, supra* note 79 at 51. The four largest GEMMs are Warburg Securities, UBS Phillips & Drew, Midland Montagu, and Barclays de Zoete Wedd.

89. Webb and Montagon, *Losing its lustre*, FIN. TIMES, Nov. 27, 1991 at 14, col.3.

90. There are three types of options: a call option, which entitles the giver to buy back the stock at the agreed price during the option period; a put option, which entitles the giver to sell the stock at an agreed price during the option period; and a put and call for double or put or call option, which enables the giver to either buy or sell the stock at the agreed price during the option period provided the total amount of stock exercised does not exceed the amount specified in the option contract. ISE, *The Traditional Options Market*, QUALITY MKTS. Q. REV. Summer 1988 at 30.

91. Traditional options date to the seventeenth century. A traditional option contract is an agreement between two parties to buy or sell an agreed quantity of a security at a predetermined price on or by a given date for a premium. ISE, *The Traditional Options Market*, QUALITY MKTS. Q. REV. Autumn 1987 at 17.

92. The traded option market operates differently from the underlying stock market in

ences between the traditional options and traded options markets concerning size and transferability, availability, exercise, contract period, clearing, and dividend entitlement.[93]

The traded options market is exponentially larger. By 1988, over nine million options contracts had been traded since its founding, and trading had returned to the precrash volume of over fifty thousand contracts per day.[94] The traditional options market is much quieter, with an average daily volume in 1988 of just over £1 million worth of the underlying securities.

However, the London Traded Options Market (LTOM) has not thrived as have options markets in other financial centers.[95] In 1989, options traders demanded more autonomy from ISE and a closer alliance with the London International Financial Futures Exchange (LIFFE), which has been much more innovative and technologically advanced than LTOM. The basic criticism was that the options market, if it was to be successful and to survive, must be controlled by options traders and practitioners rather than by the Stock Exchange Council, whose primary interest was in the underlying equity market. Still, LIFFE's growth has not been as great as hoped, though in 1990 the number of contracts traded increased by 43 percent over 1989's figures to 34 million.[96]

In April 1990, LIFFE and LTOM unexpectedly announced a merger, which became effective in 1992. The combination was spurred by derivative users groups and the Bank of England, which was concerned about London's position in the derivatives market. For the first time equity options will trade alongside of financial futures. Transaction costs of trading several products on one market will be less.

The LTOM moved to the LIFFE headquarters. The open outcry system of trading has been retained, though screen-based trading could be intro-

---

three ways: it is an open outcry market where prices and transactions are made on the trading floor; all transactions are visible to the participants; and price displays indicate the best bid and the best offer of the last transaction rather than for the upcoming transaction, i.e., prices represent "historic" prices only of the traded options. *Id.*

93. Traded options are normally for standard lots of 1,000 shares and are transferrable during the life of the contract. Traditional options are bilateral and nontransferable, but they are available for negotiable quantities. Traded options are on a limited range of highly liquid stocks, whereas traditional options are available on almost any listed U.K. equity. Traded options can be exercised on any business day up to the expiration date. Traditional options can be exercised on only one day, the declaration day, per account. Traded options are available for expiration dates of three-, six- or nine-month periods, whereas traditional options may not be extended beyond approximately three months.

94. 1989 ISE REPORT, *supra* note 20 at 11.

95. In 1990 a little more than eight million contracts were traded, down 14% from the nine million traded in 1989. 1990/91 SIB REPORT, *supra* note 58 at 13. In 1991, daily volume averaged 25,000 contracts.

96. *Id.*

duced in the future. The success of the new equity options market will depend on an increase in firms willing to be market makers in individual stock options,[97] the health of the underlying stock market, substantially increased traded option volume, and the need to attract retail business.[98] The combined exchange should make London the preeminent derivatives exchange in Europe.

The Euromarkets

In their first twenty-five years the Eurobond markets displayed extraordinary freedom from regulation, impressive innovation and entrepreneurial skill, lucrative financial rewards to underwriters, and seemingly unending growth. The Euromarkets were the last frontier of classic nineteenth-century free-market financial capitalism. In the second half of the 1980s, generally unfavorable market conditions ended that era. There was an overcapacity in a number of issues, a surfeit of underwriters, and a decline in profits.[99] A particular problem was the lack of liquidity in the secondary markets. As a result, some underwriters and market makers withdrew from the market. The few global firms that remain hope that their survival will lead to a new dawn of profitability. Because of the problems of the secondary market, Euromarkets have become more of a traditional exchange. The concept of caveat emptor has given way to transparency and disclosure, and U.K. regulators have sought to fit the London-based markets into the overall regulatory framework.

The technological revolution has created the possibility of a transparent market where prices are transmitted immediately. This has been resisted by Eurobond traders, for their eyes are upon the short term, the transaction they are currently engaged in, rather than the long-term integrity of the

---

97. Firms are more interested in trading equity index options based on the FT/SE 100 Index option than on the individual stock options. Corrigan, *Uncertain future for stock option trading*, FIN. TIMES, Dec. 17, 1991 at 22, col. 4.

98. In 1991, institutional business constituted 70% of LTOM trading, and retail 30%. The percentages are reversed on the CBOE in Chicago. On the European Options Exchange in Amsterdam, with much higher volume, retail participation constitutes 80% of trades. Corrigan, *Liffe merger improves outlook for equity options*, FIN. TIMES, Oct. 29, 1991 at 27, col. 1.

99. *Strains in the Euromarkets*, FIN. TIMES, Aug. 22, 1989 at 14, col. 1. New activity in the Eurobond market declined in 1990 by 5% over 1989. The volume of Eurocommercial paper and domestic bond transactions increased sharply in 1990. 1990/91 SIB REPORT, *supra* note 58 at 11. In 1991 a record $263.02 billion was raised, up 41% from 1990. However, for all but the largest firms, profits were slim. Power & Purushothaman, *Euromarket Issues Soar, But Profit Still Lags Behind*, WALL ST. J., Jan. 2, 1992 at R32, col. 1.

markets. The International Securities Authority (ISMA) has met resistance from firms to link TRAX trade matching and risk management systems.[100]

Perhaps the greatest innovation in the Euromarkets has been the introduction of electronic monitoring to detect insider trading and other securities violations. The SFA introduced COBRA (Capture of Bond Reports and Analysis), a computer system that tracks secondary Eurobond transactions and tradings in equities that take place off an exchange. In addition to tracing insider dealing, COBRA can uncover instances of front-running, where firms deal in advance of their clients, and artificial price supports.[101]

The primary markets have not been as affected by regulation as the secondary markets. The main problem in the primary markets has been the lack of disclosure. ISMA has deferred to the International Primary Markets Association, a trade group, to establish principles governing new issues. The Financial Services Act permits stabilization of the price of new issues,[102] but the question has arisen whether a firm must inform the market that an underwriting has been unsuccessful, that is, that the issue has not been sold out.[103]

Whither the Stock Exchange

The institution most affected by the Big Bang has been the Stock Exchange. In the words of its chairman, Andrew Hugh Smith, "The Big Bang

---

100. *See* Chapter 3.

101. The information comes from data produced IMSA Trax system and clearing systems. SFA will monitor only those transactions where one of the parties is authorized under the Financial Services Act. Firms are required to input the details of their transactions the day after they took place unless they had reported such information to a foreign exchange that has an agreement to share such information with SFA. Waters, *London Eurobond market to be electronically monitored*, FIN. TIMES, Sept. 1, 1989 at 18, col. 2.

102. FSA § 48(2)(i), sched. 8, para. 8.

103. The custom has been for underwriters to claim success or to say nothing. One justification has been that a Eurobond issue, unlike a domestic issue, is not placed in one day but over a period as long as one month. The question has arisen whether this failure to disclose the results of an underwriting is misleading under Section 47 of the Financial Services Act. In September 1989 the investment bankers, Baring Brothers, publicly announced that it had placed only 55% of an issue of Allied Lyons. It stated that it was making this announcement on advice of solicitors to avoid violating Section 47. Allied Lyons was a domestic U.K. debenture even though it was distributed on the Eurobond market. Cohen, *Launch brings thorny issue of disclosure*, FIN. TIMES, Sept. 18, 1989 at 22. *But cf.* FSA § 48(7), which seems to provide an exception. Whether disclosure is required of international or non-U.K. company issues is uncertain. Some of these issues are listed on foreign exchanges. Neither the SFA nor the DTI have taken a position on the issue, nor seem eager to do so, perhaps because the practice of inadequate disclosure is so grounded in customs of the marketplace. In addition, the investors are professionals who can protect themselves, and the Euromarkets easily can move to less restrictive regulatory climes.

was rather like throwing a rock into a lake—now we're seeing the ripples. There are many big issues still to be worked out, and we need to adapt to the many changes in the market."[104] The Exchange's fundamental problem has been to discern its proper role in an electronic age where a central trading floor, formerly the symbol and heart of London's equity market, has become as anachronistic as manually operated elevators. In some ways the Exchange resembles postwar Britain, a second-level player attempting to maintain first-level status in a new order. The Exchange no longer affords monopoly access to market makers, formerly jobbers. Publicly available prices, previously kept in the jobbers' book, undermine the securities markets' intermediaries: the brokers. The SFA has taken over the most important "public" roles of investor protection, and the admission of international members has weakened institutional loyalty to the Exchange. New derivative products have moved to their own exchanges. The ISE has an increasingly unjustifiable cost structure and faces outside competition for its services.[105]

The increased diversity and complexity of the marketplace has expanded exponentially the very notion of a trading market. This has forced the Exchange to reexamine itself in order to attain a proper fit in a new environment. One aspect of the ISE's quest for an appropriate role has been its expansion into commercial ventures such as TOPIC, the commercial information system that supplies the marketplace with price quotations and company news.[106]

Organizational Muddle

Since the Big Bang the Stock Exchange has been in transition. New projects and technology have coexisted with an antiquated organizational structure. The Exchange engages in several conflicting activities. Under the new regulatory framework it is the authority responsible for overseeing the listing requirements of companies.[107] It is also a recognized investment exchange under the Financial Services Act.[108] As such it develops rules for trading in securities, gilts, and options. Under the structure imposed by the Financial Services Act there has been an unnatural separation between the Exchange and its former enforcement and monitoring division, the SFA, the

---

104. *Stock exchange confirms chief's decision to resign*, N.Y. TIMES, June 22, 1989 at 29, col. 3.

105. Waters, *Making the stock market relevant to its members*, FIN. TIMES, Feb. 19, 1990 at 16, col. 3.

106. *See generally* Waters, *Finding a role for the exchange*, FIN. TIMES, Oct. 4, 1989 at 16, col. 3.

107. FSA, Part 4: Official Listing of Securities.

108. *Id.* at § 36, sched. 4.

recognized SRO that monitors securities firms dealing in equities and gilts. The two organizations share space and, at one time, staff. However, the SFA has become more important than the Exchange. The investing public turns to the SFA to make complaints. Its membership is broader than just equity traders, and it is the key liaison with the SIB and the DTI.

Organizational sclerosis as much as anything caused the inability to solve pressing problems, such as its expensive settlement and registration systems for share transactions.[109] The Exchange's decision-making process was likened to a gentlemen's club. Formal decision-making authority remained centered in the council. However, the council did not represent all of the interests serviced or affected by the Exchange. Nor were member firms' representatives on the council the best and most influential individuals from a particular firm, a factor that affected the council's and Exchange's reputation in the City and beyond.[110] Power lay not with the staff, as some believed, but in the 94 committees staffed by Exchange members on a part-time basis.

Not until 1991 did the Exchange reform its management structure by adopting a more corporate form of organization that represented the diverse constituencies of the exchange community. The council was replaced by a smaller board of 25, still a substantial size. For the first time, five senior executives of the Exchange staff serve as directors. The overhaul of the governing board brought senior figures from domestic and international securities firms, chairmen of public companies, and fund managers.[111]

More important than the structure of the governing board has been the massive reorganization of the Exchange's bureaucracy by chief executive Peter Rawlings. The Exchanges's staff and budget have been trimmed by one-quarter. Most of the committees were eliminated, and Exchange departments were reorganized into three discrete divisions based on function: primary issues, trading markets, and settlement.[112] The new corporate structure should allow senior management to focus upon strategic planning issues that need immediate attention.

The Exchange exists in an increasingly competitive marketplace. Its information and settlement systems, the most important sources of revenue, may not be part of its future. The difficult financial environment and the

---

109. Waters, *Farewell to the City's discrete gentlemen*, FIN. TIMES, June 22, 1989 at 13, col. 4.

110. *International Stock Exchange: Wakey, Wakey*, ECONOMIST, May 20, 1989 at 9.

111. The Council was made up of 30 mostly dispensable representatives of member firms and only two employees of the Exchange. The new board is much more substantial in reputation than the Council. Waters, *SE proposes 14 senior figures for its board*, FIN. TIMES, Sept. 3, 1991 at 8.

112. *London's Stock Exchange; Foundation work*, ECONOMIST, Aug. 17, 1991 at 74.

relatively low level of commission income compared to the Exchange's budget requires a program-by-program justification. If its services are not financially competitive, they should be assumed by more cost-efficient private bodies. There remain questions as to whether the Exchange can continue to conduct business in its current fashion and maintain its position as Europe's leading equity market.

A fundamental difficulty is the Stock Exchange's conflicting roles as a regulator, a trade association, a symbol of London's preeminence as a financial center, and a commercial enterprise in and of itself. It has not yet been able to resolve these problems.[113]

Back to the Future: Criticism of SEAQ

Ambush of the Market Makers

The Big Bang may have been the wave of the future, but many large securities firms desired to return to the more opaque uncompetitive past. As volume declined after the 1987 market break, the transparency of the securities markets began to blur, and centrifugal forces emerged.

The screen-based SEAQ system, which offers price quotations, became a focus of criticism. Smaller market makers took advantage of advertised bargains by larger market makers to lay off or pass on their own risks. That is, smaller market makers who could not place large blocks of stock with investors dumped their inventory on other market makers, taking advantage of the latter's quoted prices. This led market makers to immediately change their bid and offer quotations in response to the publication of a large trade on a SEAQ screen which increased quote and price volatility and dealing costs. It became increasingly difficult for market makers to profitably undertake large transactions.[114]

In large block transactions, market makers would deal only at a discount to the SEAQ price if the market maker was purchasing, or at a premium to the screen price if it was selling. This difference between the trading and screen price reflected the impact of instantaneous publication on the ability to resell or repurchase stock and led to wider price spreads for larger deals. The system was supposed to narrow spreads on larger bargains.[115]

---

113. Waters, *Farewell to the City's discrete gentlemen*, FIN. TIMES, June 2, 1989 at 13, col. 4.

114. ISE, *The Evaluation of the U.K. Equity Market, Assessment of the Recent Rule Changes*, QUALITY MKTS. Q. REV. Spring 1989 at 19, 20–23.

115. For example, an institutional investor wishes to sell a block of one million shares and the largest size quote on the SEAQ screen is 398 pence (P) to 402P for one hundred

Market makers began to defend themselves from being "hit" in two ways. First, they would lower the price at which they were willing to buy stock.[116] This would mean that the original market maker who had the one million share block could not make a profit on his transaction. Smaller investors would be faced with increased volatility in a company's share price. Market makers for large investors would have to quote wider prices for large block trades.

Unlimited trading among dealers away from the SEAQ screens distorted the market and placed the largest institutional traders at a disadvantage. A form of market-making arbitrage arose. By studying the SEAQ quotations, smaller market makers could discover who was short of shares and who was overloaded because of a large transaction with an institution. The small market maker would adjust its price, ensuring a loss for a firm that tried to sell its inventory of the issue. The market maker with the large block of stock would be "hit." This led to the charge that false markets were created, based not on customers' demands but on opportunistic trading by

---

thousand shares. A market maker purchasing a block of one million shares takes a significant position risk because other investors wishing to purchase such an amount will take some time to find. In the period the market maker seeks to resell such a large block, the price of the shares could fall. To protect himself, the market maker would insist on a discount on the transaction to purchase the one million shares, for example, bidding 395P per share for the block.

Thereafter, the market maker will attempt to resell the stock. It will be difficult to unload his position because of the size of the block unless a bargain price is quoted, such as 399P, compared to the best market price of 402P listed on the SEAQ screen. Liquidity is the market's capacity to take on business brought to it without causing undue price fluctuations. In an adequately liquid market the market maker could buy the one million shares at 398P and sell them at 402P while the difference between the offer and sale price, the touch, would remain the same. Thus, liquidity reduces volatility in quotations in normal market sizes.

However, in less liquid market conditions a market maker taking on a one million share block might have difficulty in finding investors to purchase that block even at a bargain or discounted price. Because other market makers were offering to purchase one hundred thousand shares at 398P the market maker would be tempted to "hit" ten of them at that price, thus reducing the size of the block of shares for which a buying investor had to be found.

If the other market makers allowed themselves to be "hit," they would find themselves with shares that no one would wish to purchase at that price. In a less liquid market, a market touch of 398P to 402P in one hundred thousand share lots does not imply that there are investors wishing to buy such a large block as one million shares at 402P. This example reflects the reality of the marketplace in the post-1987 environment. This example is from ISE, *The Evolution of the U.K. Equity Market, Assessment of the Recent Rule Changes* QUALITY MKTS. Q. REV. Spring 1989 at 19, 20–21. U.K. securities prices are quoted in pence, one-hundredth of a pound.

116. In the example, the market touch at which 100,000 shares could be purchased or sold would fall to 395–399P.

other market makers.[117] Firms used screen prices to set prices for transactions that did not go through the SEAQ system.[118]

The result was that some market makers, those who covered their own exposure by trading with larger firms, traded without risk. The reaction of larger market makers, such as Barclays De Zoete Wedd, and Phillips & Drew, was to lower the size of the trade and the price that they would guarantee to make on SEAQ screens. They reduced the maximum size of a trade in the most frequently traded stocks to five thousand shares. Only on such small bargains would they guarantee to make firm prices for the marketplace, including other market makers.

The London securities market never became a totally screen-based system. Larger transactions regularly were transacted wholly by telephone rather than through SEAQ.[119] Even smaller brokers developed telephone networks with their customers rather than go through SEAQ. With the decline in volume after the 1987 market break, however, pre-Big Bang tendencies emerged. Trading again began to move off the Exchange to other markets or to unofficial markets that arose between firms and institutions.[120] What occurred under another guise was a partial return to jobbing. When large-sized transactions moved away from the computer screens, market efficiency was reduced. Traders no longer knew the best price of trades. Others claimed that SEAQ exaggerated price movements because when one market maker lowered the price of a security others would not know the reason for the decrease and would therefore lower their own prices more than they would under an auction or order-driven market. In other words, screen trading promoted inefficient markets because the price did not reflect available information.

Whatever the advantages of SEAQ for larger transactions in actively traded stocks, it has not worked well for smaller, less-traded listed companies. The average spread between the cost of buying and selling shares of smaller companies, which was 3 percent of the share price in 1987, had widened to 10.24 percent at the end of 1990. For some companies the spread widened to 20 percent.[121] This proved a powerful deterrent to investors and to wider share ownership, for it meant that a share's price had to improve by over 10 percent for a trader to make a profit.

---

117. Lohr, *New rules for stocks in London*, N.Y. TIMES, Feb. 14, 1989, §D, at 1, col. 6

118. Cohen, *A debate intensified by fear*, FIN. TIMES, May 22, 1989 at 19, col. 1.

119. *London's stock exchange loses its grip*, ECONOMIST, Nov. 26, 1988 at 115.

120. Off-exchange refers to transactions conducted directly between two non-members of the ISE which are not reported or regulated by the Exchange. Some of Britain's largest insurance companies established an informal market trading among themselves. *London bids farewell to a transparent stock market*, ECONOMIST, Feb. 25, 1989 at 69.

121. Waters, *Stock market goes back to the future*, FIN. TIMES, July 2, 1991 at 17.

Many trades of smaller companies occur off-screen to avoid the market maker's spread.[122] Institutional investors, who tend to trade quickly, have shunned smaller companies. The increased spread in smaller companies' shares has been accompanied by a disturbing decrease in volume.[123] This decline has occurred even though smaller companies' share prices outperformed the market as a whole by 4 percent in 1991.[124] Many listed companies don't trade at all which, increases the reluctance of market makers who may be stuck with stock they cannot unload.[125] Thus, three markets have emerged: a growing market in international equities; an active trade in U.K. blue chips; and an illiquid market in underpriced, infrequently traded U.K. companies.

Rule Changes

As often happened when trouble brewed, the Stock Exchange appointed a committee to review the dealing system. This Special Committee on Market Development was chaired by Nigel Elwes of Warburg Securities, one of the largest market makers. The special committee (the Elwes Committee) presented proposals for interim rule changes that were approved by the Stock Exchange Council over the objection of some American firms. Commencing in February 1989, market makers were freed from the obligation to deal with other market makers at the prices and volumes shown on the SEAQ screens. The purpose was to encourage market makers to quote prices for larger transactions. In response, Barclays De Zoete Wedd, and Phillips & Drew raised their minimum quotation prices to 25,000 shares, but not to the former standard SEAQ-quoted bargain price of

---

122. A random sample of ten companies taken by the Exchange in October 1991, found between 12% and 70% of trading was matched by brokers, rather than passing through market makers. Waters, *Survival of the biggest*, FIN. TIMES, Dec. 11, 1991 at 17, col. 1 [hereinafter *Survival of the biggest*].

123. In the last quarter of 1987, £23 billion of middle- and lower-ranked stocks were traded. By the last quarter of 1990 this had fallen to £10.5 billion. *Id.* In 1987, before the market break, investors traded approximately £200 million of shares in smaller companies every day, a figure that fell to an average of £40 million in 1991. Liquidity problems of smaller companies is nothing new. Before the Big Bang many smaller companies did not enjoy the benefits of competitive jobbing because there was little interest or profit in trading such shares. *Monopoly on the Exchange*, FIN. TIMES, July 3, 1991 at 12, col. 1.

124. *Survival of the biggest, supra* note 122 at 17. This is the first time since 1988 that smaller companies outperformed the market, but it had no impact on the liquidity of those stocks involved.

125. In June 1991, of 2,100 companies' shares listed on the Exchange, 1,300 were not traded at all. *Five Years Since Big Bang*, ECONOMIST, Oct. 26, 1991 at 23. Small-stock trading volume fell to as few as 472 transactions per day from nearly 4,000 in 1987. Forman, *London Market Looks Back to the Future*, WALL ST. J., July 10, 1991 at C1, col. 2.

100,000 shares. At the end of 1990 the obligation of market makers to deal with each other was reestablished.

Other rule changes that came effective in March 1989 allowed publication of deals of over £100,000 the day after the transaction instead of within five minutes. This helped market makers in the most liquid stocks who would be able to transact such bargains and not inform the marketplace. The theory of the rule change was that a market maker who purchased a particularly large block of stock could unwind or sell it before rivals knew that such a large block of shares was overhanging the market and adjust their prices to take advantage of it. This rule, which affected only 140 stocks, accounted for 80 percent of the value of shares traded, but it effectively undermined the efficiency of the market.[126]

Not coincidentally, the firms that benefited from the rule change were the old jobbing firms. The Exchange's anticipated liquidity would increase and encourage larger trades because market makers would be willing to take on larger blocks of shares if they didn't have to publicize them to the market.[127] While the rule change did restore some order and accuracy to share quotations, it failed to bring more large deals to the SEAQ screens. The new rules did not affect deals involving 100,000 or more shares, which accounted for 75 percent of the dollar value of deals and 7 percent of the number of transactions. The second purpose of the rule change was to encourage tighter spreads on large transactions. There was a reduction in spreads, but fewer deals were done at prices within spreads.[128] The argument against these rule changes was that the rule book should not be changed just because market makers were losing money. Nor was it the Exchange's job to structure the market to ensure that market makers turned a profit.[129]

The efficient capital markets hypothesis (ECMH), which posits that stock prices reflect all available information and that the securities markets are efficient because prices rapidly adjust to the flow of new data, was turned on its head. The argument against immediate transparency was that it was damaging the marketplace and harmed long-term firm-investor relationships. Thus, the rules were changed to make the market more inefficient. The Office of Fair Trading reported to the DTI that the rules were uncompetitive.

---

126. This rule was amended in January 1991 so that deals will be published within ninety minutes, a change caused by the Office of Fair Trading finding that the rule was anticompetitive.

127. Waters, *SE rule change 'failed to draw in large deals,'* FIN. TIMES, May 26, 1989 at 10, col. 1.

128. ISE, *The Impact of the Rule Changes,* QUALITY MKTS. Q. REV. Summer 1989 at 23–29.

129. Pagano, *Merrill puts SE changes under fire,* N.Y. TIMES, Feb. 28, 1989 at 25, col. 2.

At another level the debate had a definite xenophobic quality: the old English stock-jobbing fraternity had banded together to protect British firms at the expense of foreign firms attempting to establish a market share. The large American houses and agency brokers, that is, firms that did not maintain and trade shares for their own account but only for clients, objected to the rules. The international firms that had overexpanded and suffered huge losses felt with justification that the rule changes were biased against them. The real issue was not so much transparency and centrality of the Exchange, but profitability. Merrill Lynch led the opposition accusing the Exchange of adopting rules to suit the old players of a London club, a move that would threaten the commitment of foreign firms in London and harm the smaller domestic firms.

The nature, source, and shrillness of the complaint were shocking. Rather than utilizing the British approach of behind-the-scenes suasion, particularly appropriate for a U.S. firm in a foreign setting, Merrill Lynch went public.[130] To some extent, complaints of American firms resulted from their frustration and inability to establish a profitable beachhead in London. The firm loyalty of institutional investors did not crumble as expected, and some established English firms maintained their customer lists and profitability.[131]

Futures and options traders feared that the delay in the publication of large transactions would allow for manipulation of the options and futures markets, which would be difficult to detect and could promote volatility through index arbitrage so criticized in the United States. For example, a firm that completed a large trade involving a basket of stocks whose prices were not reflected on SEAQ screens could purchase futures and options on the basis of those trades, information unavailable to others until the next day. This informational advantage would lead to increased volatility once the information became public.[132] The SIB's response was that the Exchange's rule changes had to be temporary and were justified in the short

---

130. Also significant was that Stanislaus Yassukovitch, then Merrill Lynch's London head, was Deputy Chairman of the Exchange and Chair of the Securities Association. There were private calls for Yassukovitch's resignation. Merrill Lynch was supported by other American houses, albeit nonpublicly. Salomon Brothers, Chase Manhattan, and Goldman Sachs, all of which had representatives on the Exchange's Council, voted against the rule amendments. Smaller British houses that received business from the larger English firms were too reticent to make a public complaint. Peston & Dobie, *Discontent at proposals for city reforms*, N.Y. TIMES, Mar. 1, 1989 at 22, col. 1.

131. Plender, *The Row over rules of the game*, FIN. TIMES, Mar. 20, 1989 at 24, col. 3.

132. Fidler, *Fears of manipulation seen in change to London SE rules*, FIN. TIMES, Mar. 10, 1989 at 18, col. 1.

term because of firms' difficult market conditions. Walker stressed the conflict between the need for liquidity and transparency.[133] On January 14, 1991 new rules relating to the publication of trades became effective. The publication time of trades correlates to the normal market size (NMS) of the stock. NMS relates to a stock's liquidity. All SEAQ equities with an NMS of 2,000 shares or more (approximately 900 stocks) have immediate trade publication on SEAQ for all trades up to three times their NMS. Larger trades would be published after a ninety-minute delay. On an electronic-based pricing system, this is an eternity.[134]

In April 1992 the Exchange altered its rules once again, reversing a move to greater transparency. Market makers were no longer required to publish trades within 90 minutes. The range of prices at which each stock trades is not disclosed until the next day. Instead, hourly indicators of trading volumes will be published. Similar rules apply to SEAQ International.[135]

Bifurcating the Market: Sole Traders

To bring liquidity to smaller listed companies, the Exchange announced in mid-1991 that it planned to change the market-making system for up to three-fourths of listed companies and replace it with an order-driven market similar to the American specialist approach. The 500 most actively traded stocks would still be traded by competing market makers, but the Exchange would grant exclusive franchises in one or more of 1700 securities to specialists termed "sole traders."[136] By granting sole traders a mo-

---

133. Plender, *Easier London SE rules 'temporary,'* FIN. TIMES, Mar. 6, 1989 at 20, col. 2.

134. No trade publication occurs on SEAQ for trades of securities with an NMS of 500 or 1,000 shares, approximately 1,200 stocks. Publication of trades of less-liquid securities appears the next day in the Daily Official List. All bargains up to 10% of each stock's NMS are eligible for execution through the Exchange's automatic execution facility, SAEF. ISE, *Market Update*, QUALITY MKTS. Q. REV. Winter 1991 at 8.

135. Waters, *LSE poised to alter rules on disclosure*, FIN. TIMES, Feb. 24, 1992 at 15, col. 8. Waters, *A tune-up for City trades*, FIN. TIMES, Apr. 9, 1992 at 14, col. 3.

136. The proposed sole-trader system differs from the old jobbing system because jobbers dealt in more than one stock and more than one jobber handled most securities. The Exchange believes that the sole trader would improve the price-setting mechanism and ensure a continuous market. Under the market-making system there has to be someone willing to buy or sell. The most illiquid shares would be listed through an electronic bulletin board. *See* Waters, *Stock market goes back to the future*, FIN. TIMES, July 2, 1991 at 17; Forman, *London Market Looks Back to the Future,* WALL ST. J., July 10, 1991 at C1, col. 2. The proposal also differs from the specialist system in that the specialist follows and stabilizes the market whereas the monopoly sole trader will set the market price. Also, an American investor can specify the price at which he wishes to sell or buy a security or place a market order.

nopoly, the plan creates obvious antitrust implications and undermines much of the rationale of the settlement between the Exchange and the Office of Fair Trading that led to the Big Bang and the market-making system that assumes an investor's best price comes from competition for business.

The plan will also join trading of the leading domestic equities with international securities traded on SEAQ International and will harmonize trade publication times. The plan confirms the belief of smaller companies and private investors that the Exchange's true concern is with international rather than domestic trading. The Exchange will be creating a wholesale market in international and major domestic securities which, because of the delay in trade publication, will offer less investor protection than a purported retail market of domestic illiquid stocks that will offer greater transparency.[137]

Attracting the Small Investor

One consequence of the endless unprofitability was a return to pre-Big Bang roots and to one of its most profitable, yet least sought after, constituencies: the small investor. While eleven million Britons own shares, much of the recent growth has come from investors who purchased and quickly resold shares in recently privatized companies. The percentage of share ownership statistic is deceptive because 60 percent of those shareholders own stock in but one company. Only 14 percent own shares in as many as four. The percentage of individual ownership of listed companies has declined in the 30 years since 1960, from 50 percent to 20 percent. However, private investors still contribute 47 percent of brokers' commission income.[138]

The Big Bang was a revolution for institutional investors. Transaction costs for small investors have made direct investment in shares unappealing. The ISE is hopeful that recent initiatives will attract private investors. If TAURUS is implemented, settlement costs for all transactions might fall. For the smaller investor, the proposed elimination of the stamp duty will be less important than reducing commission rates. There have arisen a few discount brokerages. The Exchange, like so much of the system of financial services regulation, does not have an agreed upon version of its future much

---

137. One must question whether the Stock Exchange's assumptions are empirically correct. One would think that smaller public investors would rather purchase shares of the leading companies than those of smaller corporations.

138. *See* ISE, *Market Structure Transaction Survey Results*, QUALITY MKTS. Q. REV. Winter 1990 at 18.

less an idea of how to encourage the small investor.[139] The decision to segment the market into one for institutional investors and another for private ones creates new problems, not the least of which is developing a linkage between the two.

The Stock Exchange is an organization that has lost its direction. Its very future has been called into question. Whether the Exchange will remain the spokesman for the City's trading firms or become just another of London's and Europe's stock exchanges is unclear. The challenge of a difficult financial environment and the approach of "1992" make it imperative for the Exchange to develop an agreed upon strategy.

1992: U.K. Financial Services in the Single European Market

In 1992 the European Economic Community (EEC) will devolve into a single internal market competitive in size, wealth, and efficiency with the United States and Japan. More than a date, 1992 represents an ongoing process, the first stage of which will be financial integration. Thereafter will come free flow of goods and people. An integrated market in financial services means an unhindered flow of capital, financial products, services, and intermediaries. In fact, the development of a true single market for most financial products is unlikely for many years.[140]

The origins of a unified internal market and financial services can be traced to Articles 59 and 67 of the Treaty of Rome which call for the evolution of barriers to the provision of services across member state borders and progressive abolition of restrictions on capital movements "to the extent necessary to insure the proper functioning of a common market."[141] The real impetus for cross-border financial services unification came from a 1985 White Paper on financial services prepared by Lord Cockfield, British commissioner to the Common Market,[142] and from the Single European

---

139. One argument against helping the small investors is that in the pre-Big Bang era they were subsidized by institutions. The rationale of the Big Bang was to promote competitive costs and prices. Perhaps small investors should invest only in a portfolio of unit trusts.

140. Harrington, *The single European market: survey of the U.K. financial services industry*, 29 BANK ENG. Q. BULL. August 1989 at 407. [hereinafter Bank of England Survey].

141. Treaty Establishing the European Economic Community, Mar. 25, 1957, 1973, Gr. Brit. T.S. No. 1 (Cmd. 5179-II), 298 U.N.T.S. 11 [hereinafter EEC Treaty].

142. The European Commission is the executive body of the EEC. Its composition consists of seventeen commissioners, two each from Britain, France, West Germany, Italy, and Spain, and one each from the remaining seven countries. Commissioners are appointed by the head of their national government.

Act,[143] which reaffirmed the process of economic union. The White Paper suggested a timetable for financial integration of capital flows, financial services, and financial services products.

Financial integration on a global scale already had occurred in the wholesale markets. In the early 1960s, foreign exchange, Eurolending, and Eurobonds, and from the 1980s, Euroequities[144] were part of a worldwide market principally located in London.[145] A goal of 1992 is to create similar linkages within the EC in the retail markets. The initial step was the removal of exchange controls to permit free capital flows. In 1988 this step was mandated to come into effect.[146] By the end of 1992, Spain and Ireland will remove exchange controls, and Greece and Portugal by 1995. London should profit from removal of capital controls as capital should flow into London.

The second stage in the integration process is the creation of a common market for financial products, services, and intermediaries. The third stage is a common currency. There are EC directives pertaining to banking, investment services, unit trusts, insurance, stock exchange listings, prospectus requirements, and mergers.[147]

Because the financial cultures of the members of the EC are so different, a major question has been whether integration of financial services requires harmonization, that is uniform standards, or merely reciprocity, which is recognition of each state's power to authorize institutions granting those states home-country control but allowing the institution to conduct business in all other states. The EC has adopted the reciprocity approach.[148]

Banking and the European Monetary Union

Banking traditionally has been conducted on a more multilateral basis than other financial services, and the movement toward harmonization of

---

143. Single European Act, O.J.L. 169/1 (1987), COMMON MKT. REP. (CCH), ¶ 21,000 *amending* EEC Treaty.

144. Euroequities are shares sold outside of the corporate issuer's home country.

145. *Europe's Capital markets: A Survey*, ECONOMIST, Dec. 16, 1989 at 6 [hereinafter Capital Market Survey. *See supra* chapter 1. For a good general overview *see* Eisenberg and Laudati, *Regulation of Financial Services In The European Community: Where Are They Going and Why Should We Care?* BUS. LAW. UPDATE 6 (May/June 1991).

146. The United Kingdom and Germany already had removed exchange controls. Council Directive. 88/361, 1988 O.J.L. 178/5, *amending* 85/566, 1986 O.J.L. 322/22.

147. Directives are the mechanism by which the EEC carries out policies. They are issued by the Council of Ministers pursuant to Article 54(3) of the EEC Treaty. National legislatures are obliged to give effect to them in their jurisdictions.

148. R. OWEN & M. DYNESS, THE TIMES GUIDE TO 1992 101 (1989) [hereinafter 1992].

banking practices has a longer history in the EC than in other financial services sectors.[149] In 1973 the council proposed a directive permitting financial institutions freedom to establish and provide services throughout the community in the absence of nationality restrictions, discriminatory capital requirements, and reciprocity requirements.[150]

In 1977 the council issued the first banking directive which coordinated regulations governing credit institutions on such matters as authorization, supervision, and criteria for directors.[151] However, in Article 3 the directive contained a provision permitting a member state to continue local laws that restricted banks from localities on the basis of local need for seven to twelve years. This allowed national banking authorities to protect inefficient local banks against competition.

In 1988 a second banking directive was approved. This directive permits banks to conduct banking business anywhere in the EC after obtaining a banking license from the home banking supervisors in member EC states. A bank can open branches throughout the EC without additional authorization from the host state in which the subsidiary will operate. The second banking directive provides for home-country supervision of banks and subsidiaries and cooperation between the home- and host-country banking authorities. Thus, if a French bank establishes a subsidiary in London, that subsidiary will be supervised by the French banking authority. If the subsidiary fails to comply with local requirements, the Bank of England will contact its French counterpart, which has a duty to correct the problem. If the home-country supervisor fails to act, then the host authority can act directly.

The banking legislation covers commercial and investment banks, savings banks, building societies, and other deposit and credit granting institutions. Banks will be able to carry out traditional banking activities such as deposit taking, lending, and financial leasing, and also securities trading and underwriting of new issues. These last two categories will cause conflict and competition with securities firms. Banks have commenced preparation for cross-border banking services by purchasing subsidiaries in other European markets, by cross-frontier alliances cemented by cross-shareholdings, or by pooling resources and allowing each other's customers access to branches.[152]

---

149. *See generally* Siegel, *Slouching toward integration: international banking before and after 1992*, 11 CARDOZO L. REV. 147, 155–159 (1989) [hereinafter Siegel]. Schneider, *The Harmonization of EC Banking Laws: The Euro-passport to Profitability and International Competitiveness of Financial Institutions*, 22 LAW & POL'Y INT'L BUS. 261 (1991).

150. Council Directive 73/183, 1973 O.J. Eur. Comm. (No. 1194) 1.

151. Council Directive 77/780, 1977 O.J. Eur. Comm. (No. L 322) 30.

152. Deutsch Bank purchased a leading U.K. merchant bank, Morgan Grenfell. The

Banking unification will evolve further through the European monetary system, which has created the European currency unit (ECU). The ECU is a monetary unit composed of a basket of weighted European currencies that are issued by the European Monetary Cooperation Fund in exchange for gold and silver dollar reserve deposits.[153] The next stage of the European monetary system is the European Monetary Union (EMU). The United Kingdom was reluctant to participate, but at the end of 1991 agreed to join.

The most far-reaching change in the financial markets will be U.K. membership in the EMU where, by the turn of the century, the United Kingdom and other members of the EC will cede control over their economic policies, establish the ECU as a common currency to replace their own, and create a European Central Bank to oversee monetary and fiscal policy. The Maastricht Treaty reached in December 1991 may be the most significant step toward economic and political union in the EC's history, for it will involve a surrender of national sovereignty over money supply, setting of interest rates, and budgetary policy.

The first phase of the EMU commenced July 1, 1990, when community nations sought to make joint economic policies to lower inflation rates and curb budget deficits. The second step, which commences in 1994, calls for the creation of the European Central Bank, termed the European Monetary Institute (EMI) in its transitional stage, which will coordinate economic policies. The board of the EMI will be composed of national central bank governors and a president appointed from outside that group. The transitional stage will last until the end of 1996.

The third stage will result in a common central bank that will set permanent exchange rates and bring sanctions against countries that continue to run excessive budget deficits. Thereafter, will be the creation of a single currency. The third stage will commence when a majority of countries who meet various debt or spending criteria elect to enter it or, if a majority of states does not decide to set the date for the beginning of the third stage by the end of 1997, it will commence on January 1, 1999.[154] The United King-

---

Bank of Scotland and Santander, a Spanish bank, established an alliance in 1988. Lloyd's Bank and Bayerische Vereinsbank of Germany allow each other's customers access to their branches. Barchard and Lapper, *Seeking a unified system*, FIN. TIMES, Dec. 18, 1991 at V, col. 1.

153. The EMS exchange-rate mechanism prevents bilateral exchange fluctuations of more than 2.25% in variance of a parity rate.

154. Before the end of 1996 an EC summit shall, by a simple majority of countries qualified by economic criteria, decide whether to launch EMU. If EMU fails to get the requisite majority by the end of 1997, the third stage will commence on January 1, 1999. There are also significant conditions and stages to the European Political Union. Excerpts of the EEC Treaty appear in *Mapping the Road to Monetary Union*, FIN. TIMES, Dec. 12, 1991 at 5, col.

dom gained an exemption or opt-out clause. It is not obliged to move to the third stage without a separate decision to do so by its government and Parliament.

The Investment Services Directive

Banking and monetary integration have proceeded because of a tradition of multinational contacts among regulators and the strength of multinational regulatory bodies such as the Bank for International Settlements. Both are lacking in the investment services area.[155] Related to the Second Banking Directive is the Investment Services Directive. Its key principle is that all firms authorized by any member state must be permitted by any other member state to conduct such activities either through a branch or through the provision of services from outside without additional authorization from the host state.[156] The host state, however, will be responsible for conduct of business rules. In addition, investment firms authorized to provide broking, dealing, or market-making services in their home states can enjoy a full range of trading privileges normally reserved to members of that member state's exchanges.[157]

The Investment Services Directive covers brokerage, dealing as a principal, market making, portfolio management, underwriting services, investment management advice, and safekeeping.[158] The directive, scheduled to be brought into effect by January 1, 1993, promulgates general principles for rules covering conduct of business in the financial services area. The rules should be of general application and no more restrictive than necessary to ensure investor protection, should permit advertising and marketing in accord with host-state provisions, and should not apply to business or professional investors.

The directive also establishes requirements for regulators. There are a number of regulatory issues. One is whether harmonization, that is, community-wide rules, is more desirable in this area than mutual recognition. Harmonization would benefit the United Kingdom because its regulatory

---

5. The Maastrict Treaty is also discussed extensively in the Fin. Times and N.Y. Times from December 7–12, 1991.

155. Sticking areas to bank unification are bank's reluctance to change their domestic clearing systems or cross-border currency transfers, a lucrative profit center. Barchard and Lapper, *Seeking a unified system*, Fin. Times, Dec. 18, 1991 at V, col. 1.

156. Proposal for a Council Directive on Investment Services, 189 O.J. C43/7.

157. One limitation is that stock exchanges do not have to accept branches of banks if they do not currently permit banks as members.

158. K. Woodley, European Community Regulation and the Conduct of Business in the City (1988).

system is more stringent than that of other member states. The principle of mutual recognition could place Britain at a competitive disadvantage as financial services firms may migrate to less-restrictive countries. Another issue is whether regulators should be civil servants or private or professional groups. This question, here raised in a community-wide context, is of course the same issue that surrounded the SIB.

The most important question is the amount of capital a firm must maintain to conduct its business. The Investment Services Directive is accompanied by a separate directive laying out minimum capital requirements. Capital adequacy refers to the level of resources a firm must maintain in order to conduct its activity so as to minimize its risk of bankruptcy. If financial services firms authorized in one state are to be able to conduct business in any member state, these firms must maintain agreed upon sufficient reserves to deal with the normal risks incurred in their respective businesses. As different kinds of firms enter the financial services market and engage in a wide variety of financial services, how one measures capital adequacy becomes crucial. The difficulty in reaching consensus over appropriate capital reserves reflects differences in the conduct of securities business and the role of banking institutions in EC member states, as well as a fear of competitive disadvantage with non-EC international financial centers.

It is desirable that the Investment Services Directive come into effect attendant to the Banking Services Directive so that securities firms are not at a disadvantage with banks who trade equities. A proposed Capital Adequacy Directive has attempted to lay down community-wide rules, but no consensus has been reached despite several draft amendments. The prime antagonists are the United Kingdom and Germany. In these countries, differing sectors of the financial services industry engage in securities trading. In the United Kingdom, independent firms whose primary business is as a broker dealer are the bulwark of the securities industry. In Germany, banks are the principal securities traders. EC banks' capital rules are governed by a Solvency Directive, part of the banking directive passed by the EC member states in December 1988.[159] The Solvency Directive considers credit risk in determining capital requirements. This approach is based largely upon standards developed by the Bank for International Settlements in Basle, Switzerland. German banks, the country's principal securities traders, are governed domestically by capital requirements appropriate to credit and deposit-taking institutions.

The theory of the U.K. approach to capital requirements for securities firms is that regulators monitor firms' exposure to risk and favor hedging

---

159. Proposal for a Council Directive on a Solvency Ratio for Credit Institutions, 1988 O.J. C135/4.

tactics to lower risk. This approach will offer better protection from default and will enhance competition by allowing more-efficient use of capital. Under U.K. rules, firms taking larger risks require greater capital than a bank would require for a normal risk.[160]

The United Kingdom desires a flexible system. Germany wants regulations similar to those covering its heavily capitalized banks, thus giving them advantage over all but the few U.K. securities firms that were affiliated with banks. The Germans wanted no distinctions between regulations governing banks and securities firms. Nonbanking firms would require large infusions of capital which would put them at a serious disadvantage. While higher capital requirements attempt to minimize system-wide risk and volatile global securities markets, they also have the effect of raising barriers to market entry. The Germans stress the need for prudential management in a volatile world market. The British fear is that business would be driven away not only from London but also from the other EC financial centers to New York and Tokyo.

The Capital Adequacy Directive is based on the principle that different sorts of capital requirements are needed for banks and for investment institutions because of the nature of the business and the difference in risks. For securities firms, the minimum level of capital was set much lower, capital was more broadly defined, and risk was taken into account.[161] A consensus was reached over capital adequacy levels in banking because of a strong international regulatory body such as the Bank for International Settlements. No such multinational securities body exists, making agreement in the investment services area more difficult. Progress towards common capital adequacy standards has been hindered by other disputes over investment services legislation, particularly issues of transparency of stock trading, how much should investment exchanges be regulated, whether banks should be allowed to be stock exchange members, and whether all trading must be conducted over an organized exchange.

Investment Exchanges and 1992

Investment exchanges seem the last refuge of rampant nationalism and protectionism in the EC. In other economic areas there is at least lip service to the convergence of policies and regulation. In the investment services

---

160. *See supra*, Chapter 4. Securities firms must have reserves between 10% and 25% of their exposure depending on the volatility and liquidity of the securities in the portfolio. Capital requirements are reduced for firms with diversified portfolios.

161. The Solvency Directive, which is an important part of EC banking legislation, considered only credit risk which was based on standards of the Bank for International Settlements, the international coordinating body for bank regulators.

area are deep divisions caused by differences in investment culture, in nature and breadth of trading, and in the technological approach of particular markets. Specific issues, though clothed in the language of policy, mask more basic national interests.

The single market ideal would establish common disclosure, listing, and trading requirements for stock exchanges throughout the EC. Today there are over forty investment exchanges in the community, and more are planned. Some are auction markets; others are order driven. Markets are fragmented and competing with differing rules on listing, trading, settlement, confirmation, and transparency.[162]

London desires to maintain its dominance in international equities and would like to colonize Europe with SEAQ International. Not surprisingly, the other major European exchanges, Frankfurt and Paris, have other ideas which favor them. The French have urged a linkage between the various European exchanges through adoption of a Eurolist of the largest most liquid listed companies that would be traded on all European exchanges. These companies would have to pay one listing fee and would satisfy reporting requirements by meeting the reporting requirements of the firm's domicile.[163] The Frankfurt Exchange, which offers fully automated trading, confirmation, and settlement through its IBIS system, desires central trading and settlement. In 1991, IBIS terminals arrived in London. Lurking behind the differing national approaches is the development of computerized information systems by Reuters and Extel and private, commercial settlement systems such as Euroclear, which is used for Eurobonds, that may obviate the need for trading on any organized exchange.

France, Italy, Spain, and Belgium desire all trading to be conducted on a regulated investment exchange to protect their smaller domestic exchanges from trading off of organized exchanges[164] The British, Germans, and Dutch desire open cross-border trading favored by institutional investors with minimal regulation. Such a European wholesale market would favor the Stock Exchange and German banks. The French and their allies desire

---

162. *See* Kellaway & Dickson, *Painful birth of single market*, Fin. Times, Dec. 19,1991 at 14, col.3; Hill, *Securities directive stalled by divisions*, Fin. Times, Dec. 17, 1991 at 2, col. 1; Waters, *Securities firms look across borders*, Fin. Times, Jan. 7, 1991 at 4, col. 1; Waters, *Stock Exchanges fail to bury the hatchet*, Fin. Times, May 22, 1990 at 26, col. 4; *Europe's share markets; Brussels babble*, Economist, June 1, 1991 at 76.

163. The Stock Exchange has argued that such a list would not provide the liquidity desired by institutional investors, who are more concerned with settlement. Given the Stock Exchange's settlement difficulties, this argument comes with a certain lack of grace. A small Eurolist is scheduled to commence in 1992.

164. Offmarket trading favors institutions with a large market share and excludes smaller traders.

more regulation and immediate transparency, which assists retail investors and protects their domestic exchanges, but is unattractive to the large institutional traders who favor SEAQ International.[165]

In 1991 the London and Frankfurt Exchanges opposed the continued development of Euroquote, a European-wide price dissemination and corporation news service that was to develop matching, confirmation, and settlement systems. Euroquote was a victim of Europolitics.[166] There have been some areas of agreement. The Mutual Recognition of Particulars Directive requires stock exchanges within the EEC to accept a company for listing if it has been listed on an exchange in another member state.[167] Some EC members only require a three-year trading history for a corporation before it may be listed on an exchange, whereas the ISE mandated a minimum of five years.[168]

The Recognition of Particulars Directive placed the ISE in a difficult position, for it had to sacrifice its junior markets and business from smaller firms at the expense of encouraging listings of multinational firms. As stan-

---

165. Another issue is whether banks, the engine of much German trading, should be permitted to become members of investment exchanges. This is favored by Germany whose banks dominate securities trading and where fund management divisions feed the securities divisions. In the United Kingdom, fund management and stock broking are kept separate. If banks have automatic access to exchanges, who needs brokerage firms? Kellaway, *Many rows on the way to market*, FIN. TIMES, Nov. 21, 1990 at 30, col. 5.

166. The ISE had favored Eurolist when it thought it would be limited to a price information network, but when the project was upgraded to include computerized trading, it became a competitor to SEAQ International.

167. Council Directive, No. 87/345, O.J. 1987 L185/81 and 90/211, O.J. 1990 L112/24 *amending* 80, 390, O.J. 1980 L100/1. This process commenced with a directive adopted in 1980 to harmonize rules allowing companies to do business in other member states. The directive required all stock exchanges to have minimum standards for listed companies. However, the ISE had much higher standards than this directive which would act as a barrier to listing of firms officially listed in another country. *See* Fitzsimmons, *EC Directives changes Securities markets*, FIN. TIMES, Feb. 15, 1990 at 26, col. 1.

168. In 1987 the Mutual Recognition of Particulars Directive required exchanges such as the ISE to recognize other state standards in allowing foreign listed securities on the exchange. Another directive requires minimum standards for prospectuses. Directive Coordinating the Requirements of the Prospectus to be Published when Transferable securities are offered to the Public, 89/298, O.J. 1989 L100/1. This meant that the ISE would be uncompetitive with foreign exchanges and would discriminate against U.K. firms. Foreign firms could be listed with a three-year history, whereas U.K. firms would need a five-year trading record. This brought the ISE in line with EC standards and made it more competitive with other exchanges, yet it undermined the viability of the unlisted securities and third markets which had three-year trading minimum requirements. Waters, *Market may be reshaped after community directive*, FIN. TIMES, Aug. 25, 1989 at 8, col. 4. In an effort to survive, the Unlisted Securities Market (USM) dropped its trading history requirement to two years. The third market merged with the USM.

dards become more lax and equivalent between exchanges, one of the rationales of ISE's self-regulation declines: that it provides higher standards than that of statutory regulation. As self-regulation yields to commercial necessity, it would seem to encourage the need for governmental supervision.

The areas of cooperation among investment exchanges are of less significance than the deep divisions. There is insufficient liquidity or demand for the services of competing exchanges. While the London Stock Exchange is favorably positioned, other nations have reacted by deregulating their exchanges and introducing more modern settlement procedures. The future will require cooperation between exchanges if for no other reason than technology and the predominance of large institutional investors.

UCITS Directive

As a result of the 1960s' equity funding scandal involving Investors Overseas Services, which was headed by Bernard Cornfield and which operated in a regulatory vacuum across Europe, states imposed legislation that prohibited cross-border sales of collective investments. After several years of negotiation, the Undertaking for Collective Investment in Transferrable Securities (UCITS) Directive was approved in 1985 and came into force in 1989.[169] A UCITS must be an open-ended unit trust or mutual fund with the sole object of investment in transferrable securities. It does not apply to closed-end funds, investment trusts, funds invested in over-the-counter shares, or in property or money market instruments. The sales of collective investments have been subject to restrictive national legislation and widely differing marketing practices in EC countries.[170]

The directive imposes tight controls on the investment of mutual funds. It permits leverage up to 10 percent of the value of a fund's assets. Funds must be provided in a detailed prospectus that must be made available to the public. Accounting on an annual or semiannual basis is required. A member state can place more severe requirements upon funds, but it can apply only to those funds run by domestic companies and not those offered by foreign competitors. On matters not covered by the UCITS Directive, such as marketing and advertising, member states can impose their own re-

---

169. Undertaking for Collective Investment in Transferable Securities (UCITS) Directive 1985, 85/711 O.J. 1985 L375/3 *amended* by 88/220, 1988 O.J. L100/31.

170. In France, 90% of the sales of unit trusts are through banks, whereas in the United Kingdom, independent financial advisors sell 35% to 45% and insurance companies 30% to 35%. In Belgium, they are sold through direct agents only. *See* Riley, *A 500 BN Market Opens Up*, FIN. TIMES, Oct. 2, 1989 at 19, col. 1.

strictions and all companies would have to comply with the conduct of business rules if they solicited customers within a member state. No fund could transact business within the EC unless it had been authorized by a member state.

Luxembourg has become the EC equivalent of an offshore center for UCITS, for it has established favorable regulatory and tax legislation.[171] The U.K.'s unit trust industry is mature and desirous of expanding throughout Europe. Other countries, such as Germany, retain quite restrictive legislation. The big challenge for U.K. unit trusts will be to develop distribution and marketing strategies. They will probably make an effort to expand into underdeveloped countries such as Spain and Greece as opposed to more mature areas such as Germany or France.

Insurance

An insurance directive that came in force in 1990[172] permits cross-frontier sales by larger companies, defined as those with a minimum turnover of £16 million or over 500 employees, and covers transfer risks such as marine and aviation, general liability, property, and fire. Most national governments derive substantial income from insurance taxes, and because the tax structure differs so much from one member state to another, the directive allows that taxes can still be collected by the state within which the risk is insured.[173] British insurers are well-equipped to become involved in writing nonlife policies on the continent. Life insurance will be much more difficult.

A proposed Life Insurance Directive focuses on situations where the insurer who is authorized elsewhere canvasses for customers in another member state. In that situation, the country into which the insurance company sells can require the insurer to seek host-country authorization, and the company would be required to meet any financial requirements or conduct of business rules of the host.

Where a prospective policyholder seeks life insurance in another member state without first being solicited, the supervisory rules of the home country

---

171. It has authorized over 600 unit trusts worth over $60 billion. Most of these funds are administered in other European countries but are attracted to the regulatory regime for authorization. *Id.*

172. Second Council Directive on the Coordination of Law, Regulations and Administrative Provisions Relating to Direct Insurance other than Assurance and Laying Down Provisions to Facilitate the Effective Exercise of Freedom to Provide Sources and Amending Directive 73/239, 88/357 O.J. 1988, L172/1.

173. 1992, *supra* 148 at 99. *See* Dolan, *Europe battles over rules on cross border insurance*, THE TIMES (London), Dec. 28, 1991 at 21, col. 1.

of the insurer apply. This allows unhindered access to the European market for those purchasing life insurance, but substantially less access for companies selling it. On this issue it will be a particularly difficult to obtain consensus. It should be some time before United Kingdom companies will be able to sell life insurance on the continent.

Mergers, Acquisitions, and Takeovers

The creation of the single European market creates a tension for manufacturing industries. It allows for cross-border economies of scale through consolidations, mergers, and liquidation of inefficient plants and businesses, but also could facilitate the combination of anticompetitive industrial groupings.[174] The balance between competition and economies of scale are kept in check through EEC competition policy. Article 85 of the Treaty of Rome gives the European Commission the authority to monitor business activities that have the objective or effect of distortion of competition within the Common Market. Article 86 provides that any abuse of the dominant position within the Common Market is prohibited. These powers under the treaty were long interpreted as post-merger authority whereby the commission could implement recessionary remedies rather than enjoining a proposed merger.

With the exception of the United Kingdom, EC member states have regulated antitrust problems through detailed and restrictive takeover statutes. One of the goals of the 1992 process is to remove some of these more constraining barriers. The depth of the problem in mergers and acquisitions is illustrated by the fact that in 1988 three-fourths of all European companies taken over were British. In half of the EC member states, there were virtually no takeovers. Of twenty-six hostile takeovers within the community, twenty-three were in the United Kingdom.[175]

A draft Directive on Mergers and Takeovers[176] issued in 1973 lay dormant until 1987 when Peter Sutherland, the recently appointed competition commissioner, indicated an intention to revive the stalled draft directive.[177] Another impetus for a comprehensive community merger and takeover policy came from a decision by the European Court of Justice in November 1987 which affirmed a decision by the European Commission allowing the

---

174. 1992, *supra* note 148 at 112.

175. Kellaway, *Brussels faces uphill struggle to remove takeover barriers*, FIN. TIMES, Nov. 27, 1989 at 5, col. 1 [hereinafter Kellaway]. The justifications for the paucity of merger and acquisition activity within the EC include the immature development of some financial markets, corporate attitudes, and close family or group control.

176. *See* 2 COMMON MKT. REP. (CCH), ¶ 2843.

177. 1992, *supra* note 148 at 114.

merger of two tobacco companies.[178] The decision was significant because it held that the European Commission had a legal obligation to investigate any merger or acquisition that could lead to the creation or consolidation of market domination. Heretofore, the commission had interpreted its Article 85 powers to be limited to price fixing. The court decision permitted Article 85 to be applied to anticompetitive mergers *before* the acquisition was completed. A new revised draft directive was issued for consideration in March 1988.

The U.K. government presented contradictory positions. It had long urged that member states lower takeover barriers to facilitate mergers and acquisitions. Yet, it alone resisted the call for a community-wide mergers policy because it feared the demise of its Takeover Panel which is flexible, private, and swift in contrast to the perception of the Brussels bureaucracy.[179] The United Kingdom was isolated on the issue of a community-wide mergers policy, although states had their own reservations about details.

In June 1988 the director general of the Confederation of British Industry, the English equivalent of the Business Roundtable or National Association of Manufacturers, issued a statement that squarely opposed the government's position. It stressed the need for EC merger controls and the crippling effect of the government's position on the DTI's campaign to prepare British executives for 1992. Thus, the British government became isolated from other EC states and was opposed by its own business community.[180] The government climbed down from its perch in January 1989. Thereafter, negotiations commenced in earnest over the final status of the merger legislation.

After sixteen years of consideration, the EC ministers agreed on a common merger policy on December 21, 1989. The policy is a compromise. Commencing September 21, 1990, individual governments may request approval from the Directorate General IV, the European Commission's Competition Division, to review proposed mergers and takeovers of firms with annual revenues over £3.75 billion. The threshold will be reviewed after five years. Proposed mergers under this threshold level (and other combinations where each company earns two-thirds of its revenues from one member state) must apply to that nation's state competition agency. The large multinational firms will no longer face multiple parallel investigations.[181] The legislation provides for specific timetables which the commis-

178. British American Tobacco Ltd. v. Commission, 142 S 156/84 [1987] 4487 COMMON MKT. REP. (CCH), ¶ 14,405. The case is analyzed by Korah & Lasok, *Philip Morris and its aftermath—merger control?* 25 COMMON MKT. L. REV. 333 (1988).

179. *See* Riley, *Directive attacked*, FIN. TIMES, Nov. 18, 1991 at 24, col. 1.

180. 1992, *supra* note 148 at 116–117.

181. Banks and insurance companies will be subject to the new rule. The bank threshold

sion must meet in reviewing an acquisition.[182] Mergers will be judged on competition grounds, as well as economic and technological impact. Member states can halt a proposed merger if it would affect national security, plurality of media ownership, or prudential rules for financial institutions.[183]

Along with the merger directive, several company law directives have been issued to improve the corporation's financial disclosure, to define the duties of management, and to protect the rights of shareholders. The Fifth Company Law Directive establishes one share one vote, duties of directors, rights of minority shareholders, and will promote the publication of information to enable analysis of the effect of proposed mergers in the marketplace.[184]

While the framework of the common merger policy is in place, substantial questions remain as to whether it will be effective. In 1989 the DTI commissioned Coopers and Lybrand to analyze EC rules to facilitate takeovers. The report concluded that such rules would be unenforceable because the EC lacked the resources to ensure its directives and procedures were obeyed.[185] Because of differences in corporate cultures and management goals, it will be more difficult to equalize attitudes to takeovers and to harmonize state legislation. Other criticisms include the complicated federalism of the takeover procedures, insufficient commission staff, and the commission's inability to negotiate with third-party states, which raises the spectre of fortress Europe closing off its markets to non-EC countries such as the United States and Japan.

The commission approval of the merger directive is but a midstep. When directives are adopted by the EC's Council of Ministers, member states must implement them within eighteen months through national legislation. Here is where delays occur. Even after implementing legislation has been

---

will be based on one-tenth of the bank's total assets. The insurance company threshold is one-tenth of its premiums.

182. Merger partners must notify the European Commission within one week of the announcement of the bid or proposed merger. The transaction is suspended for three weeks unless the Commission requests an extension. The Commission has one month from the notification date to commence an investigation. Four months after the investigation commences, it must deliver a verdict. Council Reg. No. 4064/89, O.J. 1989 L395/1 and O.J. 1990 L257/13.

183. Lee, *EC victory on merger controls*, FIN. TIMES, Jan. 24, 1990 at 7, col. 1.

184. Kellaway, *supra* note 175. The Thirteenth Company Law directive issued in February 1989 affects takeovers. Still to be determined is whether in all bids all outstanding shares must be purchased and whether there should be limitations of board powers while a bid is open. Other issues include the need to promote the rights of shareholders in such situations and requirements of shareholder approval of corporate self-purchases.

185. Young, *Merger rules in doubt*, N.Y. TIMES, Nov. 25, 1989 at 17, col. 2.

introduced, member states may procrastinate in enforcement or find ways to evade it. The EC can bring an enforcement proceeding in the European Court, but that process takes years.[186] One doubts whether the new legislation will actually increase the number of takeovers. The cultural problems are difficult. Continental management is less accountable to shareholders. Directors have different views of management responsibilities. Managers' first duty is to the firm, its employers, and its creditors rather than in maximizing value to the shareholders. The goals of European management have been to preserve good labor relations and to focus more on the long term, all of which counter the takeover environment. The company law and competition directives may not be able to change these attitudes.

London After 1992

The deregulation and restructuring of the marketplace rather than the new regulatory system have had the greatest effect on market developments. One is struck by how little control the regulatory system had over events during the market break. The London markets are more affected by international financial and technological developments than state-based regulatory systems. The investor protection framework's impact on market developments has largely been one of increased costs. However, with the development of a single European market, rigid-state based regulatory systems will increase transaction costs and encourage movement to more efficient centers. The need for an international regulatory perspective has been best comprehended by the banking sector. Market developments in the post-Big Bang period show the need for similar recognition in other areas of financial services.

Compared to the Continent, the United Kingdom's markets are already open, competitive, and experienced. Foreign firms are already located in London. The City's share of the world's international banking assets is 19 percent, compared to France's 7 percent and Germany's 4 percent.[187] It conducts more foreign exchange trading than any other center and still retains preeminence in Eurobonds and in other areas. If the City remains competitive in regulatory and transaction costs, it could become the gateway for Japanese and American financial services firms to enter the Common Market.

In securities trading, London has a large lead, but as other European financial centers deregulate and update their technology and gather experi-

---

186. *See Policing Europe's single market*, ECONOMIST, Jan. 20, 1990 at 69.
187. Capital markets Survey, *supra* note 145 at 29.

ence, they will become competitive.[188] Financial services firms fear that the U.K.'s regulatory environment might make London unattractive. There is also concern that the single market will lead to a fortress Europe against Japan and the United States. The regulatory hand is one of those qualitative variables that will affect U.K. firms and English investors. Greater regulatory pressure will increase the costs of doing business in London. For the private investor there is concern that shady firms will seek authorization in more lax or less-experienced member states to conduct business in the United Kingdom and fleece U.K. citizens.

The United Kingdom's complex regulatory scheme is very different from other European financial centers where supervision is state-based rather than privately based. The level of regulation compared to other European financial centers will be most important. As Europe opens up, London will undoubtedly lose some of its preeminence, but British firms remain optimistic about their opportunities.

The development of a true single market for financial products at the retail level is unlikely for several years. British firms expect an increase in competition from the internal market, but believe there will be great opportunities for U.K. financial institutions which, unlike their continental counterparts, have competitive and global experience.[189] Cultural differences in consumer tastes and marketing practices will make it difficult for community-wide products to develop.[190]

Despite the rhetoric of 1992, host-country regulators will still protect their own firms. Tax policies will affect the purchase of certain financial products as many of the member states provide tax advantages for purchase of a certain percentage of national securities in portfolios. Differential taxation levels create inefficiencies in the flow of capital. Capital will flow to the lowest level of taxation. This is starting to occur as Luxembourg and Ireland, two of the secondary EC countries, have structured their tax systems to distort capital flows by offering tax advantages that do not occur in other EC countries. Leading EC member states collect more tax at the source of the investment.[191] Thus far, attempts at harmonization of tax policy have not been successful. The success of the smaller countries and "offshore" nations such as Switzerland will provide the pressures to create uniform tax policies. Because of differences in marketing practices, national

---

188. Bank of England Survey, *supra* note 140 at 407.

189. Only in card-based products did the survey consider it possible to develop community-wide products. *Id.* at 408.

190. Riley, *A formidable task: Moves to unify the European financial services industry*, FIN. TIMES, Mar. 29, 1990 at 14, col. 1.

191. *Id.* Collecting income at its source makes it more difficult to evade and easier to collect from large financial intermediaries.

firms with distribution networks in place will have substantial advantages over firms attempting to establish them. Networks are unlikely to be acquired by nonmember state firms; because of the shortage in number their price will be too high to make economic sense.[192] Continental markets in the less financially developed countries will be the most fruitful for English penetration. Britain has advantages in international finance, corporate finance, merger and acquisition activity, and insurance. U.K. firms will have their biggest competition from the continental universal banks. It is the common wisdom that this increasing competition will benefit larger firms at the expense of smaller national institutions. The British experience in the aftermath of the Big Bang indicates that this may not necessarily be so. What is certain is that in the financial services sector, 1992 is part of a very long process in which the United Kingdom is in an excellent position to utilize existing competitive advantages.

---

192. Bank of England Survey, *supra* note 140 at 410.

SEVEN

THE FUTURE OF SELF-REGULATION OF BRITAIN'S FINANCIAL SERVICES: CONCLUSION

Several factors catalyzed the deregulation of the U.K.'s financial markets including rapid changes in technology that integrated the world's financial markets; domestic policy changes such as the relaxation of exchange controls and the privatization of nationalized industries; international portfolio diversification; and the growth of securitization. All challenged London's role as a financial center and British firms' abilities to compete in a global environment. Accompanying these economic challenges were several domestic scandals which demonstrated that the existing private regulatory systems such as the London Stock Exchange no longer were effective. Brought into question was the very integrity of the markets. Deregulation of financial services preserved London's role as a preeminent financial center and encouraged intense competition, which in turn fragmented markets, consolidated and reordered the financial services industry, and resulted in firms' withdrawal from some markets.

Attendant to market deregulation was the introduction of a new framework of investor protection, one of whose goals was to increase confidence by investors that the financial services industry was "a clean place to do business."[1] Increased trust was to be achieved through broadened disclosure to the unsophisticated investor and mandatory conduct of business rules that would set boundaries of behavior towards investors by firms. However, a changing economic climate led to overcapacity, ongoing un-

---

1. FINANCIAL SERVICES IN THE UNITED KINGDOM, 1985, Cmnd. 9432, 1985, 3.1 (iii).

profitability for firms, a withdrawal of the public from the securities markets, and renewed criticism of the regulatory framework. There has been widespread concern that the regulatory burden imposed by the new system has been greater than the benefits attained.

One measure of the effectiveness of the new regulatory system is whether its policy goals have been achieved, and if so, at what cost. In this chapter we will attempt to evaluate the transformation of Threadneedle Street and anticipate future developments.

Achievement of the Investor Protection Framework's Goals

Increasing Efficiency and Competition

Principal goals of the new legislation included promotion of efficiency, increased competition, and protection of investors with minimal governmental intervention. The results have been mixed. Requirement that transactions be transparent, that is, recorded by computer or other means, has improved efficiency in some areas such as the secondary market in Eurobonds where the number of failed trades has declined. Transparency also has assisted enforcement by allowing the government or SROs to monitor more easily compliance and trading trends, which should result in lower agency costs. The development of sophisticated computerized systems has promoted efficiency in trading, which in turn improves competition. No one could argue that governmental intervention, though indirect through the SIB, has been minimal.

The financial services revolution was expected to increase firm competition. Grounded in the belief that market forces provided the most cost-efficient means of ensuring competition, deregulation would enable financial services firms to meet the needs of investors, yet compete and succeed in the international capital markets. Easing of barriers to entry in London's securities markets and encouraging international firms to use the City as a financial center have been successful. Transaction costs for substantial investors in equities and gilts have declined, and competition has forced firms to become more efficient.

However, competition has many sides. The small investor's costs have increased. This has led to a multitiered market between institutional and public investors, one efficient and one less so. Competition threatens firms' survival by reducing profit margins. It has favored the larger firms, breeding not necessarily the survival of the fittest, but of the largest or most patient. This in turn raises the costs of market entry. Over time, free competition followed by survival of the strong will result in oligopoly and increased costs, a result that the government seems not to have contemplated. Smaller, more inefficient firms in the equities and gilts markets, in insurance, and building societies have disappeared. With the continued problem of over-capacity, smaller firms, even more-efficient ones, may not last.

One consequence of the Big Bang has been to set off smaller versions in other financial markets in part in preparation for 1992 and also to gain prominence in the single market. While London remains an attractive financial center, the weight of the system's rules and practices could make it less competitive to other deregulated financial centers[2] Thus, it is crucial for the Stock Exchange to resolve its settlement problems and to develop a coherent international strategy. On the other hand, a concerted effort to cut down insider dealing may contrast with the enforcement practices of other centers and reinforce London's attractiveness. In the 1990s, the government's belief that firms and investors are drawn to markets perceived to be honest will be played out.

Restoring Integrity to the Marketplace

Integrity of the marketplace is a multifaceted concept. If the City was perceived to be clouded by fraud and dubious practices, some trading would move elsewhere. Others would not invest. In fact, for institutional investors, the perceived integrity of the London markets has not been much of a problem. This may explain the continued presence of foreign firms in London. The public's perception of the markets' integrity is more difficult to discern.

An important political and economic goal was to attract the small investor to the securities markets. "People's capitalism" required a belief by the small investor in the fairness of the marketplace, that they would not be discriminated against or taken advantage of because of the size of their holdings or unequal access to information. The markets' legitimacy and integrity could be enhanced by improving business practices and by increasing disclosure that would equalize information disparities between the investor and the seller of the product.

The conduct of business provisions set boundaries to behavior and professionalized business practices. While business behavior has improved, at what cost? Undermining higher levels of integrity has been an economic cli-

---

2. For example, the requirement of customer agreements with clients requires firms to obtain counsel to prepare them and professional investors may need counsel to understand them. Other financial centers may not have such costs. *See* Martin, *Tell SIB, writing a rule book is tough*, FIN. TIMES, Oct. 31, 1990 at 16, col. 3.

mate which no amount of market rectitude can cure. The public's participation in the securities markets has been subverted by increased transaction costs to small investors at a time when competition has pared institutional commissions. In addition, many firms are disinclined to pursue the public investor. Instead, they concentrate on institutional clients. It is more difficult to find brokers willing to service the small infrequently traded account. Few firms are making much money from the securities markets, and certainly not from the small investor.

More damaging to perceptions of integrity has been the notoriety surrounding breaches of Chinese walls, insider dealing, and "bear raids" which artificially depress the price of stocks. These misdeeds seem to be an ongoing fact of life in the City. It is difficult to squelch the publicity surrounding such violations. While there may be no more fraud in the City than there ever was, it is more visible and may demonstrate to the private investor that the new system is no more safe than before. This is the downside of transparent markets. The attempts to punish insider dealing violations give small comfort.

Institutional Integrity: The Problem of Agency Capture

By definition, a self-regulatory system implies that it will be captured by those it supervises. Regulatory capture occurs when a regulatory agency comes to equate the public good with the interests of the industry it regulates.[3] The SROs and recognized exchanges have exhibited capture by their membership as they have fought the SIB and the government on behalf of their industry's interests. In contrast, the SIB has exhibited remarkable independence, often receiving the wrath of the industry. In fact, the major criticism of the self-regulatory framework has been the excessive zeal, not the laxness, with which regulation has been pursued. Critics of the SIB have commented that the United Kingdom has wound up with a Securities and Exchange Commission in all but name.

It has been suggested that when Sir Kenneth Berrill was replaced, the government rather than the designated agency proved itself susceptible to regulatory capture.[4] Responsiveness to the regulated is a positive aspect of a self-regulatory system. The SIB has been captured by the City neither through staffing nor attitude. The lack of practitioner-based experience,

---

3. Kay and Vickers, *Deregulatory Reform in Britain*, Econ. Policy, 285, 311 (Oct. 1988) [hereinafter Kay and Vickers].

4. Manger, *Discussion*, in Kay & Vickers, *supra* note 3 at 345.

however, has been a detriment. Despite a formal legal status as a private body, the SIB has operated as autonomously as a government agency. This promotes the perception of the regulatory system's integrity.

Disclosure

The purpose of a regulatory system based upon disclosure of financial information is to ensure the investor has the information needed to make an informed investment decision along with the belief that it is accurate. Disclosure protects the small investor, usually the least sophisticated and knowledgeable participant in the financial services sector. In the retail markets there are substantial informational asymmetries between purchasers and sellers. Perhaps the most important benefit to the public under the new system is improved disclosure.

Mandatory disclosure is an attempt to offset the bargaining advantages that sellers of securities or insurance have when they deal with unsophisticated consumers. Disclosure provides investors with a sound basis for making informed investment decisions. It also serves to deter insiders from engaging in unlawful or undesirable behavior.[5]

Overall, disclosure has helped smaller investors. Purchasers of financial products, particularly of life insurance and unit trusts, more surely know their costs and their potential liabilities. The investor's choice of selecting forward or historic pricing when purchasing unit trusts promotes flexibility. Disclosure of previously hidden costs and limitations on timing of trust portfolio valuations is a positive development. In the securities area too there is increased disclosure. Polarization of the life insurance industry and disclosure of independent intermediaries' commissions have been of mixed benefit. Increased disclosure is but a half step to full disclosure.

Throughout the financial services area the quantity of disclosure is obviously greater, but its quality is more problematic. Are holders of insurance policies helped by disclosure of costs that are provided after they've signed a contract? It is uncertain whether even simplified customer agreements that give the investor the ability to know his obligations and rights or buyer guides in the insurance area are actually of much assistance to the investor as opposed to the firm which can use such documents to limit liability. Does the public really read or understand the information provided by the seller? Has it been worth the cost which ultimately will be borne by the purchaser?

---

5. However, there is substantial dispute as to whether unsophisticated investors actually use or understand disclosed financial information and whether such disclosure is worth its cost.

Clearly, disclosure became an unnecessary burden on the wholesale markets where investors were sophisticated and did not need any of the mandated assistance underlying the investor protection framework. One of the most trenchant criticisms of the SIB has been its inability to differentiate between the wholesale and retail markets. In the former, where competition has tended to be cutthroat and profit margins slim, unnecessary disclosure increased transaction costs and became another grievance against the whole framework.

Enforcement

Effective enforcement is the bedrock of an investor protection framework. The investigatory and prosecutorial structure has not eliminated insider dealing nor created an aura of effectiveness. Deregulation of industry boundaries partly contributed to enforcement problems because multifunctional securities firms created informational problems that "Chinese walls," in practice, do not resolve adequately.[6]

The failure to obtain convictions of alleged commercial and securities violators publicly flaunts one of the new systems' greatest weaknesses: the muddled organizational structure of overlapping and competing agencies.[7] Despite the lack of prosecutorial success, the capacity to uncover fraud and improper conduct has improved because of the increased reporting requirements and the transparency of the markets. The extensive monitoring and reporting requirements are designed to prevent fraud. They create more effective early warning systems. Over six thousand firms did not achieve authorization, some of which would be unwilling or unable to meet the new standards of behavior. To its great credit, the SIB has reacted swiftly and effectively to instances of wrongdoing.

Preventive monitoring is a most important component of enforcement and commences at the firm level. In a self-regulatory system, the firm is the ultimate SRO. The creation of compliance departments and officers within firms should ensure better business practices. However, as the Blue Arrow affair demonstrated, the rush for profits impacts upon the quality of compliance. In the current difficult economic climate, the costs of compliance become an additional burden. Many in the City question whether the expense of the recordkeeping and compliance is worth the marginal returns in reducing fraud and dishonesty.

---

6. For a thorough discussion of conflicts of interest, *see* N. POSER, INTERNATIONAL CAPITAL MARKETS 3.5 (1990).

7. *See supra* Chapter 5.

A cost-effective complement to an enforcement regime is an efficacious complaint and ombudsman system which can be an effective alternative means of alternative dispute resolution. Such systems filter disputes away from the courts and regulators. Currently the complaint and ombudsman schemes replicate the overlapping prosecutorial framework. They are confusing to the public, and in some areas, such as in insurance and unit trusts, overlapping. Their complexity suggests they are more effective in deterring the disgruntled investor than resolving his complaint. This is an area where an industry-wide approach would make sense.

Enforcement efforts will never be effective until the duplication and overlap between enforcement bodies is replaced by a unification of the governmental investigatory and prosecutorial units and improved coordination develops between self-regulatory and governmental bodies. Given the lack of resources for the prosecution of commercial crime, and the length of time and intensive usage of personnel required to build a case, the most cost-efficient approach to enforcement may be the best. That approach calls for centralization in one locus of *all* functions from police investigations to prosecution.

If efficiency has any place within the investor protection framework, investigation and enforcement must become more professionalized and turn away from the ad hoc appointment of investigators who lose invaluable time while they are recruited, have references checked, and learn the details of a particular case. The SIB-SRO system lacks the reservoir of expertise within the enforcement bodies. Nor has there been recruitment of individuals with a prosecutorial mentality or experience. It seems that staff are relatively junior attorneys, civil servants, or individuals seconded by securities firms. An enforcement tradition takes time.

There is a desperate need for a full-time cadre of mostly career employees to investigate and prosecute securities fraud. Professionalism creates a cumulative expertise that in itself leads to efficient and effective enforcement. The use of professionals who can apply their expertise is the most efficient and effective method of enforcement. Intra-SRO or RIE enforcement arms also should have career personnel.

The most sensible future role for the SIB may be as the government's compliance, investigative, and enforcement arm or as a separate, independent governmental agency. Enforcement should be apolitical. The SIB has acted swiftly and vigorously in the exercise of its investigatory powers. It should be solely responsible for the investigation and prosecution of commercial fraud and for compliance with reporting requirements. It would still oversee the enforcement efforts of the SROs and other authorized bodies who would refer matters to it for prosecution.

To fulfill these new responsibilities, the SIB should have a staff of investigators, attorneys, and accountants and should handle cases of commercial fraud from start to finish. It should be awarded full subpoena powers. All enforcement duties should be taken from the DTI, including company law compliance. Special courts should be created to handle sophisticated commercial fraud. This would allow judges involved in such cases to develop the expertise needed. The Insider Dealing Act should be amended so that insider trading becomes a civil violation as well as criminal.

As an enforcement agency, the SIB should develop its own cadre of experts and should operate similar to the U.S. Department of Justice's white-collar crime units. Hopefully a mixture of career and short-term employees could be developed. Agency esprit would follow. These recommendations require further legislative action, but the real hurdles would be the political minefields laid down by existing enforcement agencies ranging from the police to the DTI. Effective enforcement requires a whole new beginning.

For most in the financial services business, one's word will continue to be one's bond. After all, most people in any profession live up to the aspirations and norms established by the professional community. The decline in social and professional standards and sanctions antedated and were a cause of the introduction of the investor protection system. One must doubt that the current framework will rise to the enforcement tasks of the future. Given its resources, the SIB necessarily will continue to expend undue energy overseeing a complicated system rather than rooting out abuses. The SROs will principally be accountable to their members. The forces of change and the corrupting influences upon the financial services industry still exist. The internationalization of financial services and the growth of commercial fraud will continue. Unless the enforcement approach is changed, the next boom cycle in the financial markets will demonstrate the system's fatal weaknesses.

The Burden of Regulation

The new system of investor protection promised to impose just enough regulation to ensure the integrity in the marketplace. Few in the City would agree that the legislation remotely approached this goal. If nothing else, the new system is one of rules. Support for the system has been undermined by the perception, if not the reality, that the regulatory burden is so heavy as to have the effect of direct regulation without the benefits. Perhaps nothing so demonstrated the City's hostility to the new system as the implementation of the rule books. The rule-making process should have served several conflicting purposes: building consensus, acclimating the City to the new order, educating investors and the industry, and promoting structural change. Instead, the complexity of the rule books became the focal point of criticism.

The rule books changed the financial community's attitude toward the new framework and the SIB, from which the latter never has recovered. The City felt that the rules had been sprung upon them, that it had inadequate input into the rule-making process, and that the rules were devised by inexperienced individuals with little understanding or experience in financial services. The introduction of the rule books illustrated the difficulties of achieving regulatory goals. However, structural change in regulation and enforcement did occur.

In the process, the SIB managed to clash with all of the City's vested interest groups. Insufficient attention was paid to building consensus or cultivating allies. As a result, the SIB failed to obtain interest group acquiescence on major policy issues. Given the rushed timetable in getting the system on-line, consensus may have been impossible. In contrast to the gradual implementation of the American framework of securities regulation, the SIB imposed its vision upon the SROs immediately through its weapon of authorization.

The SROs were in a rush to obtain authorization if not to capture regulatory turf. Thus, they copied the SIB's rule books and then fought back afterwards. The time pressures meant that rules and policy choices were rushed, leading to mistakes and the need to redesign the rule books. In other situations the SIB temporized. For example, the policies following the polarization decision concerning agents' disclosure were not well thought out. The SIB seemed to waffle and then to yield to the demands of the strongest interest group. The policy shifts on the rule books, which probably originated in the DTI, appeared as a sign of weakness, malleability, and indecision.

A fundamental error was the failure to differentiate sufficiently between the wholesale and retail markets and between professional and retail investors. The rush to implement the regulatory framework may have contributed to the failure to gauge the import of the rules on the wholesale markets or the firms. An extremely complex and expensive system was introduced to protect a relatively insignificant part of many financial services markets—the public investor. Investor protection does not mean all investors need be protected to the same extent with the same rules. Initially the rules seemed to apply with equal force to all. For professional investors this increased transaction costs and indicated that the SIB did not understand that professionals in the wholesale markets could protect themselves. The focus upon the public investor has masked the fact that they are a small factor in many markets.

While a supposed advantage of self-regulatory systems is ease of amendment and flexibility towards change, once a system is in place, it is extremely difficult to alter. For one thing, the costs of education and compliance must be repeated if the system is changed. Second, the many layers of review—SRO, SIB, and DTI—make the process of substantial amendment cumbersome.

The new settlement is not necessarily a step back to a more flexible, simpler system. It merely adds another layer to the rules. Firms will have to spend yet again on attorney's fees and incur additional compliance expenses. Clarification or simplification of the rule book merely reaffirms rule-making goals of creating predictability and certainty. The rules have professionalized business practices but at too great a cost. At this point one feels a general sense of regulatory malaise.

Costs of Deregulation and Investor Protection

The cost to maintain the new system of self-regulating bodies and recognized exchanges and the expense to firms of compliance requirements far exceeded estimates and became an ongoing burden. In the desire to build financial conglomerates and to obtain an international capability came improvident acquisitions of firms at inflated prices that in retrospect seem unwise. The expense of maintaining large capital-intensive operations made profitability uncertain in the best of times, and illusory otherwise. In some markets, too much capital chased too little profit. This has resulted in a painful retreat, an unbundling of acquisitions, a withdrawal from some markets, and scaled-down expectations.[8]

Underlying deregulation and investor protection has been the introduction of new technology and the the increased computerization of markets and recordkeeping. These changes would have occurred in any case, but at a more leisurely pace. The new framework with its increased monitoring and reporting requirements forced firms to computerize their operations more rapidly and extensively. This led to an increase in transaction costs at a time when commissions on large transactions were declining. The drop in share volume meant that there were fewer trades to cover the fixed costs of automation and compliance. Increased costs affected competition as it made market entry more expensive.

Because the Financial Services Act was implemented during a period of euphoric growth and prosperity in the securities markets, possibilities of alteration of the economic environment were inadequately considered, particularly as such change related to the burdens of compliance. How could

---

8. Perhaps the archetypal example is that of Security Pacific Bank of California which began the gold rush by purchasing Hoare Govatt in 1984, sold the firm to its employees a few years later, and in 1990 retreated completely from London. *See* Friedman, *Security Pacific sounds retreat*, FIN. TIMES, Dec. 12, 1990 at 17, col. 2. *See supra* Chapter 6.

the SIB not have considered the cyclical nature of the markets? Why didn't anybody hypothesize a market break could occur, or levels of trading would decline, that whole markets such as Eurobonds and gilts might become unprofitable, and that the new system would exacerbate economic difficulties in parlous times?

Because costs were levied upon firms, there were few ways to increase expenditures without hurting the members of the SROs. Costs could not always be passed on to investors who might trade elsewhere or not at all. The cost squeeze became particularly serious for some SROs such as FIMBRA, whose members, at best, had a precarious existence. Even relatively affluent regulators such as the SFA and the ISE were constrained by economic realities. The only way to keep costs under control without a slackening of investor protection is for regulators to become more efficient.

In implementing the investor protection framework, the SIB exhibited a lack of parsimony and circumspection. Parsimony is regulating only the minimal amount needed, creating no heavier burden than necessary. Circumspection is the ability to look at the consequences of policy choices, the regulatory side effects. The SIB exhibited a lack of parsimony by immediately exerting a heavy regulatory hand. Through the "equivalence" requirement and by rigorously supervising the approval of the SRO rule books, the SIB abandoned any attempt at parsimony. Once the heavy regulatory touch was felt, it was extremely difficult to withdraw from this approach. The shift to principles indicated vacillation or weakness rather than compromise and did not undo the earlier attitudes toward the regulator.

Because of the rush to implement the system, neither the DTI nor SIB exhibited circumspection. Neither body seemed to consider the consequences of its decisions nor the impact upon other sectors or forces in the economy. For example, the polarization decision had a severe impact on independent intermediaries. Many independent agents were retired people who sold insurance to supplement their pensions. The compliance costs made it economically unreasonable for such people to continue in business. Full-time independents rushed to tied agent status because the disclosure requirements were less onerous than for independents.

The SIB developed its complicated system seemingly with little regard to the impact of 1992. A nongovernmental agency, it attempted to negotiate with regulatory bodies who dealt only with comparable governmental counterparts or not with securities regulators at all. It entered into memoranda of understanding on enforcement issues that would be mooted by the single European market. Its disputes with the Bank of England over capital adequacy requirements and supervision of securities firms had a pyrrhic quality as the EC approach differs, and continental regulators preferred to deal with the Bank rather than a private body. The SIB is not alone in its inability to react to changes in the market or to foresee the impact of changes in the economic climate upon the regulatory burden. The SEC has been notably unsuccessful if not unwilling to oversee market structure. However, the SIB implemented its system as if it never considered the possibility that the five-year bull market might end or that regulatory costs would be affected by profits.

Securities Regulation: The Next Stage

A mixed system of self- and governmental regulation can be a viable approach to the supervision of the securities markets. The SIB believes that if the investor protection framework as currently structured is functioning properly, it should have a vestigial status in a manner similar to the traditional role played by the Bank of England in the banking sector. The existing currents are to push the SIB into the background and allow the SROs to do their business. This is not a formula for success.

The American experience suggests that view is naive if not reckless, for SROs will not live up to their responsibilities to the public without constant pressure or fear of greater regulation. If the SROs are permitted to go about their business, they will do just that—minister to the demands of their constituencies. In March 1992 the House of Commons Select Committee on Social Security criticized regulators and particularly IMRO for allowing Robert Maxwell to loot the pension funds under his control. The committee's report suggested that the way IMRO carried on its duties demonstrated "that this aspect of the system of self-regulation is—when the chips are down—little short of a tragic comedy . . . In other words, the system works where there is in fact little need for a regulatory system at all."[9]

Under the current system, the designated agency is a private body and the government, after authorization has been granted, only has the drastic remedy of revoking its SIB's authority or removing the governing board or taking similar action with the self-regulating bodies. This offers insufficient supervisory flexibility. If the self-regulatory approach is to be successful there must be a reorganization of the self-regulatory structure and a change in venue of the supervisory body.

Reorganizing the Self-regulatory Structure

The self-regulatory structure needs to be simplified. There are just too many SROs, RIEs, and other types of self-regulatory bodies. This has in-

---

9. Petre & Purnell, *MP's demand overhaul of pension law*, Daily Telegraph, Mar. 10, 1992 at 1; Timmins & Nisse, *MPs call for tough new pension laws*, Independent, Mar. 10, 1992 at 1.

creased the transaction costs for firms that conduct business in several markets.

Regulatory duplication adds to compliance expenses and requires the maintenance of overlapping bureaucracies. With the exception of the SFA there are too few experienced regulators. The merger of the Securities Association and the Association of Futures Brokers and Dealers should be a forerunner of extensive regulatory consolidation. IMRO and LAUTRO, and probably FIMBRA, the weakest SRO, should be combined into one SRO. This would be both cost-efficient and improve effectiveness.

The American approach to overlapping memberships by securities firms is a useful guide. Section 17d of the Securities Exchange Act of 1934 authorizes the SEC to allocate among SROs examining authority for broker-dealers who are members of more than one exchange. Many of the lesser stock exchanges have contracted their investigatory and monitoring authority to the National Association of Securities Dealers. The SROs might contract out authorization of individuals and firms to one experienced monitoring body, most likely the SFA.

The separation of the recognized investment exchanges from SROs is artificial. SFA, which was hived off from the market surveillance unit of the London Stock Exchange, not only has offices in the ISE building, but in the first few years had several officials who remained on ISE's payroll and retained Exchange responsibilities as well.

The prime responsibility of exchanges is to oversee rules to ensure fair trading in their particular markets. Consolidating the exchanges is more difficult. The size, if not the bureaucratic weaknesses of the ISE make merger with it an unsatisfactory option for smaller trading markets. Yet there are avenues of increased cooperation possible between various commodities and specialized exchanges, particularly as they relate to authorizing member firms. More important, in light of the market manipulation by London FOX, is the need for an aggressive overseer of the exchanges, a power that the SIB lacks.

Another sensible cut would be to separate the sale of retail products, such as insurance or securities sales, to a separate oversight body. This agency would supervise the sale of investment products to noninstitutional investors, who are most unsophisticated and for whom the informational asymmetries are the greatest. This suggests the reappearance in form, if not name, of the Marketing of Investments Board.

The Future of the Supervisory Body

The Labor Party has proposed that upon returning to power it would transform the SIB into a free-standing commission on the model of the

American SEC. Will that make self-regulation more workable? Probably not. The SIB has poisoned the well in regard to its relations with the SROs and the City under the present system. It has been accused of being a commission in all but name. Commission status might allow the SIB to withstand industry lobbying interests and to force SROs into molds that it may wish. However, when self-regulation works as it does in the United States, it is a cooperative enterprise. The shift in status if not stance of the SIB would not foster cooperation.

Transforming the SIB into a governmental agency would bring strictures of its own. The SIB's staff would become civil servants, which would formalize the antipathy felt by the City and end any possibility of support from City firms. Changing the SIB's status would mean that its funding would come from the public fisc. This would be welcomed by the City. For the SIB there would be a more restricted base to fulfill budgetary needs. It would be just one more supplicant in the annual budget and probably would not get the funding it would need.

Converting the SIB into a statutorily based commission would require major amendments to the Financial Services Act. It should be granted power to directly amend SRO rules, to involve itself in SRO disciplinary procedures, and to discipline SROs for laxity. Its investigative capabilities would have to be boosted, and the agency would probably increase substantially in size and budget.

Commission-type status will result in yet another major shift in administrative focus. One thing the current system does not need is another alteration in oversight philosophy. In summation, merely transplanting an American-style commission will not necessarily lead to a more efficient and effective regulatory system. A governmental agency means that all actions must be taken on the record with allowance of full due process. This would rigidify regulation and make it even more difficult to respond to changes in the economic environment. There is an existing body with the influence and power to make the self-regulatory concept work.

To energize the self-regulatory system, the Bank of England should assume the SIB's supervisory powers over the investor protection framework. The remaining role for the SIB, whose name as well as functions should be changed, would be to centralize investigation and enforcement of violations. The Bank can take advantage of the English propensity to handle matters behind closed doors in a more private way, an approach that can be effective in a self-regulatory system if the regulator is respected and feared if crossed. Despite the recent statutory underpinning that has formalized and enhanced its powers, the Bank still operates much in the old-fashioned way of a wink and nuance. When necessary it can act swiftly. Most importantly it has the broadest understanding of the economic environment, domestic and international.

As a central bank, the Bank of England is the logical contact point for other central banks and international financial bodies. There has been a reluctance of foreign governmental agencies to deal with the SIB. European banking regulators oversee securities activities and find it awkward to deal with a nongovernmental body. Even as a commission, the SIB would be duplicative. In the increasingly complex and international regulatory environment there is no need for domestic duplication among regulators. The Bank can better coordinate U.K. and multinational regulation, a development that is more advanced in the banking than the securities sector.

The Bank has a reservoir of experienced personnel who have garnered the respect of the City in a way that the SIB has not. While the SIB was supposed to work the way the Bank conducted business in the banking area, that never occurred. As an independent public body the Bank will be better able to combine the powers of suasion and legal authority which when exercised by the SIB gave the impression, often unfair, of action by fiat.

Politically, the statutory amendments transferring power to the Bank would be less disruptive than enhancing the SIB's status. Only the Bank of England could garner the support of the City to make the changes necessary to make self-regulation work. The changes discussed might come to pass when a very different post-Thatcher Tory philosophy emerges; with a Labor government, or if there is a financial breakdown or scandal that exposes the weaknesses of the present system.

The preceding recommendations offer the most promising formula for success. The Bank of England should be responsible for what it does best, oversight with a firm but subtle hand. The SIB will abandon many of the functions for which it was neither suited nor successful. It will, however, assume expanded responsibilities in the investigative area where it has accomplished much. Most importantly, this new framework would best enable the United Kingdom to deal with the challenges of 1992 and with the process of globalization that will continue when the world's financial markets commence their next upward cycle. Finally, it offers the only hope for success of the self-regulatory concept.

The transformation of Threadneedle Street has brought the U.K.'s financial services sector square into the twentieth century. Now is the time to restructure the existing arrangements so that they may be competitive and effective in the twenty-first.

Index